Psychological Evaluation of
Children's Human Figure Drawings

ELIZABETH MUNSTERBERG KOPPITZ, Ph.D.

Board of Cooperative Educational Services
Yorktown Heights, N.Y.

GRUNE & STRATTON
A Subsidiary of Harcourt Brace Jovanovich, Publishers
NEW YORK   SAN FRANCISCO   LONDON

Acknowledgments

THE STUDIES PRESENTED in this book are based on thousands of children's drawings which were collected over a ten year period in many different localities with the help and cooperation of a great many people, too numerous to mention here by name. My sincere thanks go to the many classroom teachers and school principals in the metropolitan area of Columbus and in Franklin County, Ohio, and in Broome County and Westchester County, New York, who gave generously of their time in order to obtain the large number of drawings of schoolchildren. My appreciation is also extended to the Juvenile Diagnostic Center and the Children's Mental Health Center in Columbus, Ohio, and the Board of Cooperative Educational Services in Yorktown Heights, New York, for offering me the opportunity to collect drawings of children with problems. I am further indebted to my friends and colleagues David D. Blyth, Margaret G. Lang, and Mary Wilson for their assistance in some of the studies presented here, and to Judie Linstra who helped in the preparation of the manuscript. But above all, I want to express my gratitude to my husband, Werner J. Koppitz, without whose continued help, support, and encouragement this book would never have been completed.

And finally, I want to say thanks to all the boys and girls whose drawings have given me so much pleasure and who taught me so much. This book is dedicated to them with the hope that it will be of value to psychologists working with children and thereby indirectly will be of help to the children themselves.

ELIZABETH M. KOPPITZ

Library of Congress Catalog Card Number 67-23057
International Standard Book Number 0-8089-0240-7

Grune & Stratton, Inc.
111 Fifth Avenue
New York, New York 10003

Printed in the United States of America

*For Marjorie
and all the other boys
and girls whose drawings gave
me so much pleasure and taught me so
much*

Table of Contents

List of Tables

Preface

THERE HAS NEVER BEEN any doubt in my mind that of all tests and techniques used by psychologists, who work with children, there is one that is more meaningful, more interesting, and more enjoyable than all others, and this technique is drawing, just drawing with pencil and paper. I know the value of drawing at first hand, having used it myself both as a child and as an adult to help me through periods of crises and inner turmoil. Drawing may involve "free drawing" of anything the child wants to depict, or the copying of designs, or the drawing of a specific topic at the request of the examiner, or the making of human figure drawings (HFDs). Even though I have watched hundreds and hundreds of children while they were drawing, I have never become bored and I keep on marvelling at the way boys and girls can express themselves and can reveal their attitudes through graphic images.

I love and enjoy all children's drawings, but especially HFDs. Like any person who is enamored by something, I consider the merits of drawings obvious and self-evident. But, as happens so often, these merits are not always as apparent to others. Some psychologists recognize only the values of certain limited aspects of drawings, while many clinicians fail to appreciate the merits of HFDs altogether. Some investigators even claim to have demonstrated by means of research studies that children's drawings are not clinically valid.

It is desirable and necessary that many more controlled investigations be conducted to determine the validity of children's HFDs. To date, such studies have been rather disappointing, and I find it sometimes difficult to accept when investigators conclude that drawings are not clinically meaningful just because their research findings are negative. After all, negative results in research studies may be caused *either* by a lack of validity of the HFDs, *or* by the manner in which the research was designed and executed and by the way in which the subjects were selected. The situation reminds me quite often of the aphorism of the 18th-century writer and wit Lichtenberg, who said that if a head and a book collided and there was a hollow ring, the sound need not always emanate from the book. In similar fashion, a lack of significant findings in a research study need not always emanate from the HFDs. The research results on children's drawings have been so far at best inconclusive. But to my knowledge, no one has ever made a comprehensive and systematic investigation of all the different aspects of HFDs and of their relationship to each other. Yet there is a real need for such an investigation. The work presented here is an attempt to fill this gap.

In this book, HFDs of children, age 5 to 12, are analyzed and scored both as a developmental test of mental maturity and as a projective test of children's interpersonal attitudes and concerns. Scoring systems for these two approaches to HFDs have been developed and have been standardized on the drawings of over 1800 public school children. In addition, a method for interpreting the content of HFDs is here described. Special chapters in this volume are devoted to the discussion of children's family portraits and to the use of HFDs in screening school beginners, in diagnosing brain injury, and in assessing a child's progress in therapy. It is also demonstrated how HFDs can be combined with other tests to increase their predictive power. And finally, ten case histories are presented to illustrate how the various aspects of HFDs can be integrated and applied in clinical practice. This book was written for clinicians and school psychologists. It is hoped that it will help to clarify the values as well as the limitations of HFDs of children, and that it will enable psychologists to use HFDs in a more comprehensive and meaningful way. It is further hoped that the studies reported here will stimulate more research in this area.

E. M. K.

1. Introduction

MOST CHILDREN love to draw and paint. If given the opportunity, they
will produce spontaneously pictures of animals, houses, cars, boats, planes,
flowers, and many other things. But most often, they will draw human
beings (Pikunas & Carberry, 1961). The interest in children's drawings
has a long and well-documented history in this country and in Europe.
Goodenough (1926) reports that, as early as 1885, an article appeared in
England by Ebenezer Cooke in which he described developmental stages
in children's drawings. Numerous other studies and papers by psychologists
and educators have followed since then. Several comprehensive reviews
of the literature on drawings and paintings by children have been published (Goodenough, 1926, 1928; Goodenough & Harris, 1950; Harris,
1963; Johnson & Gloye, 1958; Jones & Thomas, 1961); therefore, it is
not necessary at this time to discuss and reevaluate once more the many,
many articles, books and reports on the subject which have appeared
over the past 75 years or more.

Over the years, the emphasis in the literature has shifted from comparative investigations of graphic productions by children and primitive
people to clinical analyses of paintings and drawings of disturbed children,
to longitudinal studies of individual youngsters from their first scribbles
to mature drawings, and to the assessment of mental maturity by means
of human figure drawings. Studies have varied from descriptive observations to carefully controlled research and the use of statistical analysis.
Investigations have explored all manner of creative productions by children of all ages, ranging from infancy to adolescence. The works studied
have included fingerpaintings, watercolor paintings, and drawings made
with crayons, chalk or pencil, and they have represented objects or topics
specified by the investigator as well as "free" art productions. In the
present volume, the discussion will be limited to only pencil drawings of
human figures by children age 5 to 12.

Human figure drawings (hereafter HFDs) have become one of the
most widely used techniques of psychologists working with children. But
the purposes to which the drawings are put vary greatly. Two main approaches to the interpretation of HFDs exist today. The first of these
is employed mostly by clinicians who regard HFDs as a projective technique and who analyze the drawings for signs of unconscious needs,
conflicts, and personality traits. Representatives of the second school of
thought approach HFDs as a developmental test of mental maturity. Most
psychologists seem to adhere rather exclusively to one or the other
method of interpreting HFDs. This writer has been unwilling to accept
either method to the exclusion of the other. Years of clinical experience
and experimentation have convinced her that the HFD Test is one of the
most valuable techniques for evaluating children just because it can be
used both as a developmental test *and* as a projective method.

The foremost representative of the developmental approach to HFDs
was Goodenough whose book "Measurement of Intelligence by Drawings"

1

(1926) has become a classic. Goodenough's well-standardized and validated Draw-A-Man Test has become widely accepted and used, especially in schools and for research purposes. Some 35 years later, Harris (1963) went to great lengths to revise and extend the Draw-A-Man Test but found that Goodenough's work was so carefully designed and executed that relatively little could be added to improve it. Harris reports numerous studies which show a fairly high correlation between scores on the Draw-A-Man Test and IQ scores from intelligence tests. Harris makes a special point in stating that the Draw-A-Man Test measures mental maturity and is not a test of traits and personality dynamics. There is no doubt that those who are primarily interested in obtaining a Mental Age or IQ score from HFDs can use the Goodenough-Harris scoring method with a reasonable degree of confidence.

A different picture presents itself to clinicians interested in using HFDs as projective instruments. The foremost exponents of the projective approach towards HFDs are Machover (1949, 1953, 1960), Levy (1958), Hammer (1958), and Jolles (1952). These clinicians have studied HFDs of adults and teenagers extensively but have worked only to a limited extent with drawings of elementary school-age children. Machover's book "Personality Projection in the Drawing of the Human Figure" (1949) has become the most widely quoted book in the field and equals Goodenough's book in significance and influence. Though Machover's Draw-A-Person Test is largely based on her clinical experience with male adolescent and adult patients, she has extended her findings also to children (1953, 1960). Machover offers numerous hypotheses based on psychoanalytic theory regarding signs on HFDs, but she offers no scoring system and no controlled research data to support her claims.

To date, studies involving HFDs by children that were designed to test Machover's hypotheses have been at best inconclusive (Bennett, 1964; Bradfield, 1964; Brown & Tolor, 1957; Bruck & Bodwin, 1962; Butler & Marcuse, 1959; Craddick, 1963; Kates & Harrington, 1952; and McHugh, 1963, 1964, 1966). It is often difficult to assess and compare the findings of different studies since the variables are frequently ill-defined and different meanings are assigned to the same signs on HFDs. Most investigators of HFDs as a projective test ignore or minimize the developmental aspects of figure drawings while Harris in turn considers only developmental items and doubts the projective significance of signs on HFDs. Both Harris and Machover claim some of the same items on HFDs of children as indicators of mental maturity and of emotional conflict respectively. This is quite confusing, for can one item be interpreted in both ways?

In the writer's own experience, it is indeed possible for some items on HFDs to have both developmental and projective significance, but not necessarily for the same children nor at the same age level. For instance, an omission of the neck or feet on HFDs is not unusual for normal five year old boys; from a developmental point of view, one cannot or should not expect these items to be present at that age level. Their absence cannot therefore be considered to have clinical significance. But by age ten, one would normally expect children to draw figures with feet and a neck, so that the absence of these items would most likely indicate immaturity or emotional problems and becomes clinically significant. It appears therefore that a meaningful interpretation of HFDs of children presupposes a thorough knowledge of both developmental and emotional indicators on drawings at each age level and a clear differentiation between the two.

To the best of the writer's knowledge, no one has attempted so far to make a comprehensive study of HFDs of children, taking into account all aspects of such drawings and relating them to each other. The current body of information on HFDs consists mostly of unrelated, isolated studies. It is the purpose of this book to present a systematic investigation of HFDs of children age 5 to 12, as a developmental test *and* as a projective test. An attempt will be made to analyze HFDs objectively for developmental and emotional signs and symbols and to interpret them clinically for personality dynamics. In this volume, HFDs of normal public school pupils and of children with problems will be studied at successive age levels. And finally, controlled research studies and numerous case histories will be presented to support the hypotheses and suggestions put forth in these pages. The work presented here came about because of the writer's own need in her clinical work for an integrated, systematic way to interpret HFDs. None of the existing methods seemed to tap the full richness of HFDs. So the writer began to make her own explorations which proved to be quite helpful to herself and to some of her colleagues who then urged her to make the material available to other psychologists as well. This book was written for psychologists working with children in clinics, hospitals, schools, or in private practice. It is hoped that this volume will contribute to a fuller and more meaningful analysis and interpretation of HFDs in clinical practice and in research.

The kind of information and results an investigator obtains from his studies will depend to a large extent on the questions he sets out to answer. And the kind of questions he will ask will depend to a large extent on his theoretical orientation and on the purpose of his investigation. It is no chance that most analytically oriented psychologists report that HFDs reflect primarily a subject's unconscious needs and conflicts, his defense mechanisms, his psychosexual development, and his sexual identification, for these are the things analytically oriented clinicians are most interested in.

The present investigations follow somewhat different lines. The writer considers Harry Stack Sullivan's Interpersonal Relationship Theory as most useful for her work. Therefore, she is primarily interested in exploring a child's developmental stage and his interpersonal attitudes. In this volume, it is hypothesized that HFDs reflect primarily a child's level of development and his interpersonal relationships, that is, his attitudes toward himself and toward the significant others in his life. It is further maintained that HFDs may reval a child's attitudes toward life's stresses and strains and his way of meeting them; drawings may also reflect strong fears and anxieties which may concern the child, consciously or unconsciously, at that given moment. This means that the "body image" hypothesis, generally accepted for HFDs, is not necessarily considered valid by this writer. In the present studies, the HFD is not regarded as a portrait of the child's basic and enduring personality traits nor as an image of the child's actual appearance. Instead, it is believed that HFDs reflect the child's current stage of mental development and his attitudes and concerns of the given moment, all of which will change in time due to maturation and experience. The HFD's particular value is seen in its very sensitivity to change within the child, and these changes may be both developmental and/or emotional. The HFD is regarded here as a portrait of the inner child of the moment.

2. The HFD Test

THE HFD TEST, as defined here, requires that the child draw "a whole person" at the request of the examiner in his presence. The last point is important, for an HFD should always be the product of an interpersonal situation. The HFD represents a graphic form of communication between the child and the psychologist and as such differs from spontaneous drawings children may make when they are alone or with friends. The instructions given to the child are of significance and may influence the results obtained. Goodenough instructed her subjects to draw "a man;" Machover asks her patients to draw "a person" and then another person of the opposite sex; Harris requests the drawing of a man, a woman, and a self-portrait; while Hammer elicits both pencil and crayon drawings of a man and a woman. In the investigations reported here, the children were only asked to draw *one* whole person. It was left up to each youngster to determine the age and sex of the figure he chose to depict.

The studies presented here are based on the assumption that a child's HFD shows both a basic structure and a certain style which is peculiar to that particular child. As Kellogg (1959) observed, the structure of a young child's drawing is determined by his age and level of maturation, while the style of the drawing reflects his attitudes and those concerns which are most important to him at that time. If this hypothesis is correct, the drawing of *one* person should be sufficient for most cases. And if only one drawing is obtained, then it seems only reasonable to leave it up to the child to decide what kind of person he wants to draw.

The writer concurs with Machover that instructions to draw "a person" yield HFDs that are richer in projective material than are "self-portraits" drawn on request. Self-conscious prepubertal children and young adolescents are often reluctant to draw themselves, while young children have a tendency to focus on their clothing and trivial details of their appearance when trying to draw themselves. They often delight in copying the pattern of their dress and socks or may devote most of their energy and time to portraying new shoes or a baseball mitt which was a recent birthday gift, since such newly acquired items are of great importance to children. The nonspecific instruction to draw "a whole person" seems to lead the child to look into himself and into his own feelings when trying to capture the essence of "a person." The person a child knows best is himself; his picture of a person becomes therefore a portrait of his inner self, of his attitudes.

In clinical practice, there are of course occasions when it is helpful to compare several drawings of a single child. But for the screening of school beginners and for quick evaluations of children or for research purposes, it seems to be sufficient to obtain one HFD from each child. For most younger elementary school pupils, a second HFD, of the opposite sex, rarely adds sufficient additional information to justify the time and effort involved in obtaining it. Richey (1965) reported that same-sex HFDs of children tend to be superior in quality to opposite-sex HFDs. Since most children draw same-sex figures first, it follows that most first-drawn HFDs will be superior to later ones. Time is one of the most precious commodities a psychologist working in clinics and schools has to deal with. It is felt that the time saved by omitting a second HFD can be more fruitfully employed by administering another brief projective test like the Bender Gestalt Test (Koppitz, 1964) or a set of incomplete stories or incomplete sentences. If a second drawing seems essential, then a drawing of "your whole family" or a free drawing may actually be more revealing than a second HFD.

Another consideration prompted the writer to limit the HFD Test to a single drawing of a whole person. While it is true that most normal children love to draw people, it is also true that most children seen by clinical and school psychologists do not necessarily conform to the "normal" pattern of behavior. Many emotionally disturbed and/or neurologically impaired children are very self-conscious about their poor drawing ability and their inadequate HFDs. And, objectively regarded, their drawings are often quite poor compared with those of most other children of the same age level. Children seen in guidance clinics and by school psychologists have usually experienced so much failure in life that they are eager to avoid further defeat and embarrassment. Often, these youngsters volunteer enthusiastically to draw cars or planes or flowers, in fact anything but a person. If the HFD really presents an inner self-portrait, then it should come as no surprise that some children, especially those with problems, try unconsciously or even consciously to avoid revealing themselves and do not wish to come face to face with their own poor self-concept. Gentle persuasion on the part of the psychologist usually succeeds in getting even reluctant youngsters to draw one whole person, but many children resist drawing more than one person, and there is really no reason why they should be coerced into doing so.

Administration of HFD Test

The HFD Test can be administered either as a group test or as an individual test. Individual test administration is preferable, of course, since it enables the examiner to observe the child at work and permits him to ask clarifying questions about the figure if need be. It was also noted that most children produce richer and more revealing drawings in a one-to-one relationship with an accepting psychologist than in a group setting. But for research purposes or for the screening of school beginners and the like, group administration of the HFD Test is quite acceptable and more feasible.

When administering the HFD Test, the examiner should seat the child comfortably at an uncluttered table or desk and should present him with a blank sheet of paper size 8½" × 11" and a number 2 pencil with an eraser. The examiner then tells the child: *"On this piece of paper, I would like you to draw a WHOLE person. It can be any kind of a person you want to draw, just make sure that it is a whole person and not a stick figure or a cartoon figure."* The last part of the instructions was found necessary especially for group administration of the HFD Test.

Quite often, older and brighter children will draw stereotyped cartoon or stick figures as an easy way out, and thereby avoid the required task and the need to get personally involved. Cartoons and stick figures are quite useless when analyzing drawings as projective tests. For younger children who may not understand the meaning of "person," one can add: "You may draw a man or a woman or a boy or a girl, whichever you want to draw."

There is no time limit to the HFD Test. Most children will finish their drawing in less than 10 minutes, some will complete a HFD in just a minute or two. On rare occasions, the writer has sat for 30 minutes or more while a very perfectionistic and compulsive child worked on his figure drawing. A child is free to erase or to change his drawing if he so chooses. It is suggested that the examiner carefully observe the child's behavior while drawing and that he make notes of any unusual features. Special attention should be given to the sequence in which the figure is drawn, the child's attitude and spontaneous comments, the amount of time needed, and the amount of paper used. If a child is dissatisfied with his drawing, he is permitted to start over again on the back of the paper or on a second sheet upon request.

Some insecure children will search for models to copy in preference to drawing figures of their own invention. In group administration of the HFD Test, care should be taken to seat children as far apart as possible to minimize the likelihood of their copying from each other. When the HFD Test is administered individually, the child should be seated in such a way that he does not see a picture of a person on the wall or on a book or magazine cover which could serve as a model. There are occasions when children decide to draw an actual picture of the examiner when they are asked to make a HFD. Depending on the sensitivity of the child involved, this should be discouraged outright, or it should be accepted without much comment; but when the first drawing is completed, the child should be again asked to make "a picture of a whole person out of your own head." If a child draws a person without looking at the examiner but later declares that it is supposed to be the examiner, then the drawing is accepted quite matter-of-factly. The implications of drawing the psychologist are discussed more fully later on (page 76).

Interpretation of the HFD Test

An attempt will be made here to analyze HFDs according to several different dimensions. Methods for objective scoring and for clinical interpretations of HFDs will be described. The drawings will be scored for two different types of objective signs. One set of signs on HFDs is believed to be primarily related to children's age and level of maturation; these signs are called *Developmental Items*. The second set of signs is thought to be primarily related to children's attitudes and concerns; these signs are designated as *Emotional Indicators*. Detailed definitions and scoring manuals for both the Developmental Items and the Emotional Indicators are shown in the *Appendix*. The Developmental Items and the Emotional Indicators will be discussed in some detail, normative data and validation studies will be presented and their application will be illustrated in the following chapters.

The clinical interpretation of HFDs presented in this volume is largely based on the writer's own experience and intuition and on the findings of other clinicians. An effort will be made to integrate the various ways of interpretating figure drawings and to show how they can be combined with other tests. The practical use of the different methods of analyzing HFDs will be demonstrated in the screening of school beginners, in predicting school achievement, and in diagnosing, treating, and assessing the progress of psychiatric patients.

3. Developmental Items on HFDs

A DEVELOPMENTAL ITEM is here defined as an item that occurs only on relatively few HFDs of children of a younger age level and then increases in frequency of occurrence as the age of the children increases, until it gets to be a regular feature of many or most HFDs at a given age level. For some items, e.g., head, body, legs, this increase in occurrence takes place during the pre-school years so that practically all HFDs of school-age children reveal these particular signs. Other items, e.g., arms at shoulders, continue to increase in frequency of occurrence each year from age 5 to 12. This increase in occurrence may be gradual as with the drawing of elbows and profiles, or it may be quick as with two dimensions on arms and the neck (*Table 2*).

It is hypothesized that the presence of Developmental Items on a HFD is primarily related to the child's age and maturation and not to his artistic ability, to school learning, or to the instructions given or the drawing medium used.

The writer selected a list of items which were believed to be developmental in nature. The items were derived from the Goodenough-Harris scoring system and from the writer's own experience. Many of the finer details on drawings which are included in the Goodenough-Harris system were omitted from this list since the present investigation is limited to the HFDs of elementary school-age children. After extensive pre-testing and experimentation, it was decided that the following 30 signs on HFDs could meet the criteria set up for Developmental Items:

   1. Head
   2. Eyes
   3. Pupils
   4. Eyebrows or eyelashes
   5. Nose
   6. Nostrils
   7. Mouth
   8. Two lips
   9. Ear
  10. Hair or head *covered* by hat
  11. Neck
  12. Body
  13. Arms
  14. Arms two-dimensional
  15. Arms attached at shoulders
  16. Arms pointing downward
  17. Elbow
  18. Hands
  19. Fingers
  20. Correct number of fingers
  21. Legs

22. Legs two-dimensional
23. Knee
24. Feet
25. Feet two-dimensional
26. Profile
27. Good proportion
28. Clothing: one piece or none
29. Clothing: two or three pieces
30. Clothing: four or more pieces

Appendix A lists the 30 Developmental Items with detailed definitions and cites examples for each item. In the studies presented here, each HFD was checked for the presence of the 30 Developmental Items. Each such item present was scored as 1, while each item absent was scored as 0.

Reliability of scoring HFDs

The reliability of scoring HFDs for Developmental Items and for Emotional Indicators (page 35) was determined with the aid of another qualified psychologist.* The other psychologist and the writer scored independently of each other the HFDs of 10 randomly selected second-grade pupils and of 15 children referred to the school psychologist because of learning and behavior problems. The 25 protocols were checked for the presence of the 30 Developmental Items and the 30 Emotional Indicators. The two examiners checked a total of 467 different items for all drawings. Of these, 444 or 95 percent of the items scored were checked by both psychologists, whereas 23 items or 5 percent were scored by only one or the other of the investigators. The average number of items scored for each drawing was 19. On ten of the HFDs, there was a perfect agreement as to the scoring, while on 15 of the HFDs, the two examiners differed by one or two points only.

Normative study for Developmental Items on HFDs

A normative study was carried out by the writer in order to determine the frequency of occurrence of the 30 Developmental Items on HFDs of boys and girls at each age level from 5 through 12 years. The normative study is based on the HFDs of 1856 public school pupils representing 86 entire classes, kindergarten through sixth grade, in ten different elementary schools. Thirty-three percent of the children came from two schools located in residential sections of a Midwestern metropolis; 54 percent of the youngsters attended five schools situated in three small industrial towns in a Midwestern and an Eastern State; while the remaining 13 percent of the children were pupils from three schools in small villages or rural areas of the same states. One-third of the boys and girls came from low-income communities and included both colored and white children, one-third came from predominantly white, middle-income, communities, and the last third lived in high-income areas.

---

* The writer is indebted to Dr. Mary Wilson for her help with the reliability study.

The 86 classes used in the normative study included 19 kindergarten classes, 11 first grades, 12 each of the second, third, and fourth grades, and 10 each of the fifth and sixth grades. To avoid any bias in the selection of subjects, all children enrolled in each of the classes, who were present at the time of testing, were included in the normative population, provided they were between 5 years 0 month and 12 years 11 months old. Because of this, the N for each level differs slightly. *Table 1* shows the distribution of the normative population by age and sex. No specific information as to the mental ability of the subjects was available, but it may be assumed that they represent the full range of intellectual potential normally found in a cross section of public schools. To the best of the writer's knowledge, very few if any mentally retarded children and no children suffering from gross physical handicaps were included among the subjects.

Table 1.   **Distribution of Normative Population by Age and Sex**

Age	Boys	Girls	Total
5	128	128	256
6	131	133	264
7	134	125	259
8	138	130	268
9	134	134	268
10	109	108	217
11	105	112	217
12	52	55	107
Total	931	925	1856

Each classroom teacher administered the HFD Test to her class as a group following the instructions previously described (page 6). Only in the case of the kindergarten pupils were the HFDs obtained individually by the writer. Later, the writer checked all HFDs for the presence of the 30 Developmental Items. The results for the 30 Developmental Items are presented in terms of the percentage of children who revealed each item on their HFDs at each successive age level from 5 through 12 years. The percentages are divided into four frequency categories which include the *Expected* items, the *Common* items, the *Not Unusual* items, and the *Exceptional* items.

The first frequency category includes all items which are present on 86–100% of the HFDs at a given age level. These items are designated as the *Expected* items. Since these items are present on the HFDs of almost all normal children, they constitute the basic minimum of items one can expect on figure drawings of children of a given age. The absence rather than the presence of the Expected items is therefore considered significant. It is hypothesized that the omission of any Developmental Item which falls into the Expected category indicates either undue immaturity, retardation, or the presence of regression due to emotional problems.

The second category includes all scoring items that occur on 51–85% of the HFDs. These items are thought of as *Common*. They are present

Table 2. Percentage of Boys Showing Developmental Items on HFDs

5 years N 128		6 years N 131		7 years N 134		8 years N 138	
Expected		*Expected*		*Expected*		*Expected*	
Head	100	Head	100	Head	100	Head	100
Eyes	98	Eyes	99	Eyes	99	Eyes	99
Nose	87	Nose	91	Nose	90	Nose	94
Mouth	92	Mouth	97	Mouth	97	Mouth	95
Body	89	Body	97	Body	98	Body	99
Legs	97	Legs	98	Legs	99	Legs	97
Common		Arms	95	Arms	96	Arms	96
Arms	84	*Common*		Feet	87	Feet	86
Feet	73	Feet	80	Arms 2d.	86	Arms 2d.	96
Fingers	61	Fingers	60	*Common*		Legs 2d.	93
Hair	54	Hair	72	Legs 2d.	84	*Common*	
Not Unusual		Arms 2d.	62	Hair	76	Hair	78
Arms 2d.	48	Legs 2d.	70	Arm down	57	Arm down	71
Legs 2d.	37	*Not Unusual*		Neck	55	Neck	60
Arm down	21	Arm down	35	Fingers	76	Fingers	72
Neck	28	Neck	27	*Not Unusual*		Hands	55
Hands	33	Hands	42	Hands	50	*Not Unusual*	
Ear	25	Ear	33	Ear	42	Ear	40
Eyebrow	21	Eyebrow	28	Eyebrow	37	Eyebrow	37
Exceptional		Pupils	22	Pupils	38	Pupils	38
Pupils	11	Feet 2d.	22	Feet 2d.	43	Feet 2d.	50
Feet 2d.	8	5 Fingers	26	5 Fingers	38	5 Fingers	40
5 Fingers	13	*Exceptional*		Arm a.sh.	24	Arm a.sh.	40
Arm a.sh.	3	Arm a.sh.	14	Proport.	23	Proport.	26
Proport.	2	Proport.	5	*Exceptional*		Profile	25
Nostrils	2	Nostrils	5	Profile	15	*Exceptional*	
Profile	1	Profile	3	Nostrils	10	Nostrils	15
Elbow	1	Elbow	6	Elbow	4	Elbow	11
Two lips	2	Two lips	2	Two lips	6	Two lips	8
Knee	0	Knee	3	Knee	1	Knee	4

Clothing		*Clothing*		*Clothing*		*Clothing*	
0–1 item	90	0–1 item	70	0–1 item	46	0–1 item	37
Expected		Common		Not Unusual		Not Unusual	
2–3 items	9	2–3 items	25	2–3 items	31	2–3 items	37
Exceptional		Not Unusual		Not Unusual		Not Unusual	
4 items	1	4 items	5	4 items	23	4 items	26
Exceptional		Exceptional		Not Unusual		Not Unusual	

on more than half of the drawings at a given age level but not often enough to be considered absolutely essential. All scoring items found on 16–50% of the HFDs are included in the third frequency category and are labeled as *Not Unusual*. These items are present on less than half of all HFDs but they appear too often to be called rare or unusual. Neither the presence nor the absence of the *Common* items and the *Not Unusual* items is regarded as diagnostically important.

On the other hand, the fourth frequency category is believed to be quite

Table 2 (continued)

9 years N 134		10 years N 109		11 years N 105		12 years N 52	
Expected		*Expected*		*Expected*		*Expected*	
Head	100	Head	100	Head	100	Head	100
Eyes	100	Eyes	100	Eyes	99	Eyes	100
Nose	100	Nose	97	Nose	97	Nose	100
Mouth	99	Mouth	98	Mouth	97	Mouth	100
Body	100	Body	100	Body	99	Body	100
Legs	99	Legs	99	Legs	98	Legs	100
Arms	100	Arms	98	Arms	99	Arms	100
Feet	90	Feet	96	Feet	95	Feet	94
Arms 2d.	98	Arms 2d.	97	Arms 2d.	99	Arms 2d.	100
Legs 2d.	98	Legs 2d.	99	Legs 2d.	97	Legs 2d.	100
Common		Hair	89	Hair	88	Hair	90
Hair	81	Arm down	86	Arm down	93	Arm down	94
Arm down	78	Neck	89	Neck	93	Neck	98
Neck	81	*Common*		*Common*		Arm a.sh.	94
Fingers	81	Fingers	84	Fingers	83	*Common*	
Hands	70	Hands	58	Hands	69	Hands	56
Arm a.sh.	52	Arm a.sh.	54	Arm a.sh.	79	Fingers	77
Ear	59	Ear	59	Ear	67	Ear	65
Feet 2d.	69	Eyebrow	52	Eyebrow	54	Eyebrow	58
Pupils	56	Pupils	51	Pupils	57	Pupils	58
Not Unusual		Feet 2d.	72	Feet 2d.	74	Feet 2d.	75
5 Fingers	50	*Not Unusual*		5 Fingers	55	*Not Unusual*	
Eyebrow	42	5 Fingers	50	*Not Unusual*		5 Fingers	46
Proport.	31	Proport.	42	Proport.	38	Proport.	50
Profile	18	Profile	29	Profile	29	Profile	29
Exceptional		Nostrils	28	Nostrils	16	Nostrils	21
Nostrils	15	Elbow	23	Elbow	20	Elbow	35
Elbow	15	*Exceptional*		Two lips	17	Two lips	19
Two lips	8	Two lips	15	*Exceptional*		*Exceptional*	
Knee	10	Knee	10	Knee	11	Knee	15

Clothing		Clothing		Clothing		Clothing	
0–1 item	32	0–1 item	30	0–1 item	23	0–1 item	4
Not Unusual		Not Unusual		Not Unusual		Exceptional	
2–3 items	37	2–3 items	27	2–3 items	39	2–3 items	46
Not Unusual		Not Unusual		Not Unusual		Not Unusual	
4 items	31	4 items	43	4 items	38	4 items	50
Not Unusual		Not Unusual		Not Unusual		Not Unusual	

significant. This category includes all items shown on 15% or less of the HFDs. These items are called *Exceptional* and are considered unusual. It is hypothesized that Exceptional Developmental Items are only found on HFDs of children with above-average mental maturity.

Normative data for Developmental Items on HFDs of boys

Table 2 shows the normative data for the 30 Developmental Items on HFDs of boys. It can be seen that the frequency of occurrences of each item increases at succeeding age levels until the item is present on 90% or more of all the drawings. The number of Expected items increases steadily while the number of Exceptional items decreases from year to year until age 10; thereafter, no more significant developmental changes seem to occur on the HFDs. This finding is in agreement with Goodenough's results.

The following is a summary of the Developmental Items that fell into the Expected, Common, Not Unusual and Exceptional categories at each age level:

Five year old boys can be expected to include six basic items on their HFDs: head, eyes, nose, mouth, body and legs. The omission of any of these parts must be considered clinically significant. The presence of arms, feet, fingers, and hair is common, while two-dimensional arms and legs, arms pointing down, neck, hands, ears, and eyebrows are not unusual. At this age, there are ten Exceptional items: pupils, two-dimensional feet, correct number of fingers, arms at shoulder, good proportion, nostrils, profile, elbow, two lips, and knee. It is also the exception to find more than one piece of clothing on the HFDs of five year old boys. None or only one clothing item is to be expected.

Six year old boys can be expected to draw arms as well as the head, eyes, nose, mouth, body and legs. Common items on their HFDs include feet, fingers, hair, and two dimensions on arms and legs. Arms pointing down, neck, hands, ears, eyebrows, pupils, two dimensional feet, and the correct number of fingers are not unusual. The following items are exceptional: arms at shoulder, good proportion, nostrils, elbow, two lips, and knee. It is the exception to find four or more pieces of clothing on a HFD of a six year old boy. One or no piece of clothing is common, two or three clothing items are not unusual.

Seven year old boys include among the Expected items on their HFDs the head, eyes, nose, mouth, body, legs, arms, feet, and two dimensions on the arms. Common items are two dimensions on the legs, hair, arms down, neck, and fingers. It is not unusual to find hands, ears, eyebrows, pupils, two dimensions on feet, correct number of fingers, arms at shoulder, and good proportion. While profile drawings, nostrils, elbow, two lips, and knee remain exceptional. At this age level, it is not unusual to find anywhere from no clothing item to four or more pieces of clothing on HFDs.

Eight year old boys can be expected to show on their HFDs the head, eyes, nose, mouth, body, legs, arms, feet, and two dimensions on arms and legs. It is common at this age level for boys to draw hair, arms pointing down, neck, fingers, and hands. Two dimensions on feet, eyebrows, pupils, ears, correct number of fingers, arms at shoulder, good proportion, and profile are not unusual. Exceptional items include nostrils, elbow, two lips, and knee. It is not unusual to find no clothing at all or anywhere from one to four or more clothing items on drawings of eight year old boys.

Nine year old boys reveal the same ten Expected items on their HFDs as the eight year old boys: head, eyes, nose, mouth, body, legs, arms, feet, and two dimensions on arms and legs. Common items include: hair, arms down, neck, fingers, hands, ears, pupils, feet in two dimensions, and arms at shoulder. The correct number of fingers, eyebrows, good proportion, and profile drawings are not unusual. Four items are exceptional: nostrils, elbow, two lips, and knee. Any amount of clothing or lack of clothing may appear on HFDs of nine year old boys and should not be considered unusual.

Ten year old boys show on their HFDs 13 items that fall into the Expected category: head, eyes, nose, mouth, body, legs, arms, feet, two dimensions on arms and legs, hair, arms down, and neck. Common items include: fingers, hands, ears, pupils, feet in two dimensions, arms at shoulder, and eyebrows. The presence of the correct number of fingers, good proportion, profile, nostrils, and an elbow is not unusual. Only two items are exceptional: two lips and knee. It is not unusual to find no clothing or anywhere from one to four or more pieces of clothing on HFDs of ten year old boys.

Eleven year old boys can be expected to draw the same 13 items on their HFDs as ten year old boys: head, eyes, nose, mouth, body, legs, arms, feet, two dimensions on arms and legs, hair, arms pointing down, and neck. The Common items include: fingers, hands, ears, pupils, two dimensions on feet, arm at shoulders, eyebrows, and correct number of fingers. Not Unusual items are: good proportion, profile, nostrils, elbow, and two lips. Only the knee is exceptional. Once again, it is not unusual to find anywhere from zero to four or more pieces of clothing on the HFDs of boys at this age level.

Twelve year old boys do not differ markedly from ten and eleven year old boys on their HFDs. They can be expected to draw: the head, eyes, nose, mouth, body, legs, arms, feet, two dimensions on arms and legs, hair, arms at shoulders, arms pointing down, and neck. Common items include: fingers, hands, ears, pupils, two dimensions on feet, and eyebrows. Among the Not Unusual Items are: good proportion, correct number of fingers, profile, nostrils, elbow and two lips. The drawing of a knee remains exceptional. The drawing of less than two pieces of clothing on HFDs of twelve year old boys is exceptional and must be regarded as clinically significant.

Normative data for Developmental Items on HFDs of girls

Since boys and girls mature at a somewhat different rate and since some consistent differences were found on the HFDs of boys and girls, the normative data for the two sexes are presented here separately. *Table 3* shows the normative data for the 30 Developmental Items on HFDs of girls age 5 to 12. The Expected, Common, Not Unusual, and the Exceptional Items at each age level are listed below:

Five year old girls can be expected to draw at least seven items: the head, eyes, nose, mouth, body, legs and arms. The presentation of feet, hair, fingers, and two dimensions on arms is common. It is not unusual to find two dimensions on legs, and neck, hands, eyebrows, pupils, arms pointing down, ears and the correct number of fingers. Eight items are exceptional at this age level: feet two-dimensional, good proportions, nostrils, two lips, elbow, profile, arms at shoulders, and knee. It is common to find

Table 3.   Percentage of Girls Showing Developmental Items on HFDs

5 years N 128		6 years N 133		7 years N 125		8 years N 130	
Expected		*Expected*		*Expected*		*Expected*	
Head	100	Head	100	Head	100	Head	100
Eyes	100	Eyes	100	Eyes	100	Eyes	100
Nose	90	Nose	95	Nose	92	Nose	92
Mouth	91	Mouth	100	Mouth	100	Mouth	98
Body	91	Body	94	Body	100	Body	99
Legs	97	Legs	93	Legs	99	Legs	94
Arms	91	Arms	98	Arms	99	Arms	100
Common		Hair	91	Hair	94	Hair	97
Hair	85	Feet	89	Feet	94	Feet	90
Feet	75	*Common*		Arms 2d.	91	Arms 2d.	96
Arms 2d.	52	Arms 2d.	77	Legs 2d.	86	Legs 2d.	86
Fingers	59	Fingers	68	*Common*		*Common*	
Not Unusual		Legs 2d.	67	Fingers	71	Fingers	65
Legs 2d.	46	*Not Unusual*		Neck	62	Neck	76
Neck	25	Neck	37	Arm down	59	Arm down	73
Hands	39	Hands	44	Hands	57	Hands	59
Eyebrow	33	Eyebrow	48	Eyebrow	60	Eyebrow	70
Pupils	19	Pupils	34	Pupils	51	Pupils	59
Arm down	29	Arm down	38	*Not Unusual*		*Not Unusual*	
Ear	29	Ear	19	Ear	18	Ear	16
5 Fingers	18	5 Fingers	24	5 Fingers	38	5 Fingers	44
Exceptional		Feet 2d.	19	Feet 2d.	34	Feet 2d.	33
Feet 2d.	7	*Exceptional*		Arm a.sh.	27	Arm a.sh.	33
Proport.	2	Proport.	2	Proport.	17	Proport.	19
Nostrils	6	Nostrils	14	Nostrils	20	Nostrils	21
Two lips	4	Two lips	5	*Exceptional*		Two lips	17
Elbow	0	Elbow	7	Elbow	5	*Exceptional*	
Profile	1	Profile	7	Profile	11	Profile	8
Arm a.sh.	5	Arm a.sh.	11	Two lips	7	Elbow	5
Knee	2	Knee	2	Knee	1	Knee	3

Clothing		*Clothing*		*Clothing*		*Clothing*	
0–1 item	70	0–1 item	52	0–1 item	35	0–1 item	27
Common		Common		Not Unusual		Not Unusual	
2–3 items	27	2–3 items	40	2–3 items	42	2–3 items	46
Not Unusual		Not Unusual		Not Unusual		Not Unusual	
4 items	3	4 items	8	4 items	23	4 items	27
Exceptional		Exceptional		Not Unusual		Not Unusual	

only one or no piece of clothing on HFDs of five year old girls, however, two or three clothing items are not unusual. The presence of four or more pieces of clothing on a HFD is exceptional at this age level.

Six year old girls include among the Expected items the head, eyes, nose, mouth, body, legs, arms, feet, and hair. Only three items were found to be common: fingers, and two dimensions on arms and legs. Not Unusual items include: neck, hands, eyebrows, pupils, arms pointing down, ears, correct number of fingers, and two dimensions on feet. Seven items

Table 3 (continued)

9 years N 134		10 years N 108		11 years N 112		12 years N 55	
Expected		*Expected*		*Expected*		*Expected*	
Head	100	Head	100	Head	100	Head	100
Eyes	100	Eyes	100	Eyes	98	Eyes	100
Nose	93	Nose	95	Nose	97	Nose	98
Mouth	99	Mouth	99	Mouth	97	Mouth	98
Body	100	Body	100	Body	100	Body	100
Legs	99	Legs	95	Legs	96	Legs	96
Arms	100	Arms	100	Arms	100	Arms	100
Hair	99	Hair	98	Hair	96	Hair	96
Feet	99	Feet	94	Feet	96	Feet	95
Arms 2d.	99	Arms 2d.	99	Arms 2d.	100	Arms 2d.	100
Legs 2d.	92	Legs 2d.	92	Legs 2d.	96	Legs 2d.	96
Neck	93	Neck	94	Neck	96	Neck	100
Common		Arm down	94	Arm down	96	Arm down	100
Fingers	76	*Common*		*Common*		Arm a.sh.	93
Arm down	78	Arm a.sh.	71	Arm a.sh.	85	*Common*	
Hands	60	Hands	63	Hands	72	Hands	73
Eyebrow	79	Eyebrow	74	Eyebrow	84	Eyebrow	76
Pupils	74	Pupils	78	Pupils	67	Pupils	76
Feet 2d.	53	Feet 2d.	65	Feet 2d.	70	Feet 2d.	75
Arm a.sh.	52	Fingers	82	Fingers	77	Fingers	71
Not Unusual		*Not Unusual*		Proport.	61	Proport.	60
Ear	19	Ear	19	*Not Unusual*		*Not Unusual*	
5 Fingers	46	5 Fingers	48	5 Fingers	38	5 Fingers	27
Proport.	26	Proport.	43	Ear	24	Ear	20
Nostrils	26	Nostrils	17	Nostrils	19	Nostrils	25
Two lips	28	Two lips	21	Two lips	25	Two lips	27
Elbow	19	Elbow	24	Elbow	40	Elbow	45
Exceptional		*Exceptional*		*Exceptional*		Profile	16
Profile	13	Profile	15	Profile	9	*Exceptional*	
Knee	4	Knee	5	Knee	12	Knee	9

Clothing		*Clothing*		*Clothing*		*Clothing*	
0–1 item	16	0–1 item	15	0–1 item	14	0–1 item	9
Not Unusual		Exceptional		Exceptional		Exceptional	
2–3 items	40	2–3 items	35	2–3 items	30	2–3 items	25
Not Unusual		Not Unusual		Not Unusual		Not Unusual	
4 items	44	4 items	50	4 items	56	4 items	66
Not Unusual		Not Unusual		Common		Common	

were in the Exceptional category: good proportion, nostrils, two lips, elbow, profile, arms at shoulder, and knee. It is exceptional to find four or more pieces of clothing on HFDs of six year old girls. Two or three pieces are not unusual, while one or no clothing item is common on drawings at this age level.

Seven year old girls show 11 Expected items on their HFDs: the head, eyes, nose, mouth, body, legs, arms, feet, hair, and two dimensions on arms and legs. Common items are: fingers, neck, arms pointing down, hands, eyebrows, and pupils. The drawing of ears, the correct number of fingers, two dimensions on feet, arms at shoulders, good proportion, and nostrils is not unusual. Four items are Exceptional: elbow, profile, two lips, and knee. For seven year old girls, it is not unusual to find anywhere from zero to four or more pieces of clothing on HFDs.

Eight year old girls differ on only one point on their HFDs from seven year old girls. They include among the Expected items: head, eyes, nose, mouth, body, legs, arms, hair, feet, and two dimensions on arms and legs. Common items are: fingers, neck, arms pointing down, hands, eyebrows, and pupils. It is not unusual to find on the HFDs of eight year old girls ears, the correct number of fingers, two dimensions on feet, arms at shoulders, good proportions, nostrils, and two lips. Only profile, elbow, and knee are Exceptional items. It is not unusual to find anywhere from zero to four or more clothing items on HFDs of eight year old girls.

Nine year old girls draw 12 Expected items on their HFDs: head, eyes, nose, mouth, body, arms, legs, feet, hair, two dimensions on arms and legs, and neck. Common items include: fingers, arms pointing down, hands, eyebrows, pupils, two dimensions on feet, and arms at shoulders. Six items are not unusual: ear, correct number of fingers, good proportion, nostrils, two lips, and elbow. Only profile and knee are Exceptional items. It is not unusual to find anywhere from zero to four or more pieces of clothing on HFDs of nine year old girls.

Ten year old girls can be expected to draw a head, eyes, nose, mouth, body, arms, legs, hair, feet, two dimensions on arms and legs, neck, and arms pointing down. Common items include: arms at shoulder, hands, eyebrows, pupils, feet two-dimensional, fingers. It is not unusual to find on HFDs of ten year old girls ears, correct number of fingers, good proportions, nostrils, two lips, and elbow. Only profile and knee are Exceptional items. It is diagnostically significant to find less than two pieces of clothing on drawings at this age level. Two or more clothing items are expected on HFDs of ten year old girls.

Eleven year old girls do not differ much from ten year old girls on their HFDs. Expected items include: head, eyes, nose, mouth, body, arms, legs, hair, feet, two dimensions on arms and legs, neck, and arms pointing down. It is common to find arms at shoulders, hands, eyebrows, pupils, feet in two dimensions, fingers, and good proportions. The following items are not unusual: correct number of fingers, ear, nostrils, two lips and elbow. Only two items are exceptional: profile and knee. One can expect at least two pieces of clothing on the drawings at this age level; less than two clothing items are diagnostically significant.

Twelve year old girls can be expected to draw: head, eyes, nose, mouth, body, arms, legs, feet, two dimensions on arms and legs, neck, arms pointing down, and arms at shoulders. Common items include: hands, eyebrows, pupils, feet in two dimensions, fingers, and good proportions. Six items are not unusual: correct number of fingers, ear, nostrils, two lips, elbow, and profile. Only knee is exceptional on HFDs of twelve year old girls. At this age level, four or more pieces of clothing on a drawing is common, two or three clothing items are not unusual, while less than two such items are the exception and diagnostically significant.

Comparison of Developmental Items on HFDs of Boys and Girls

A comparison of the data on *Table 2* and *Table 3* reveals some minor but consistent differences between the occurrence of Developmental Items on HFDs of boys and girls. The findings are in accord with the observations of Goodenough, Harris and Machover, all of whom emphasize that drawings of girls in the primary grades are superior to those of boys. There is also a consensus that this difference between the sexes diminishes gradually. By age eight or nine, boys not only catch up with girls but often surpass them in the quality and details of their drawings.

At all age levels, there appear to be some drawing items which are more "masculine" or "feminine" and which occur more often on the HFDs of boys or girls respectively. In the present study, the "masculine" items include profile drawing, knee and ear, while the "feminine" items were hair, pupils, eyebrows, two lips, and clothing. Similar results have been obtained by the other investigators. In fact, these particular differences between the HFDs of boys and girls have been reported so often that they cannot be attributed to chance but must be accepted as real differences between drawings of American boys and American girls.

Developmental Items were earlier defined as items that are primarily related to age and maturation and not to school learning. It is hard to believe that the difference of occurrence of "masculine" and feminine" items on HFDs of boys and girls is biologically determined or linked to the sex genes. These items are developmental in that they are positively correlated with age increase; but at the same time, it is also apparent that they reflect values and attitudes that are generally accepted and fostered in our middle-class Western culture.

From infancy on, girls watch their mother fuss over clothes and hair and facial makeup. A little girl's interest in these things is reinforced by her natural desire to imitate her mother and to gain parental approval by displaying feminine charm. Girls' drawings tend to reflect their awareness and interest in feminine attire and beauty. By contrast, the boys in our society are expected to be more independent and outgoing than girls. The profile drawing is often associated with a turning away from others and a striving toward independence. A boy is also encouraged to participate in active sports and physical activities which draw his attention to body movement and to his limbs and knees. Boys tend to draw figures engaged in physical activity much more often than girls. And, finally, a young boy's short hair makes his ears quite conspicuous and focuses his attention on them. Girls, who are more concerned with the drawing of hair, tend to omit ears from their HFDs, especially when they draw girls or women. Only at age five, when boys and girls rarely make much distinction between their drawings of males and females, are ears shown equally often on HFDs by boys and girls.

One might conclude therefore that specific "masculine" and "feminine" items on HFDs reflect attitudes in children that have been learned unconsciously in early life from the social and cultural environment they live in. The drawing of "masculine" and feminine" items is certainly not learned consciously in the manner in which a child learns to read and write in school. If this be the case, then it can be assumed that the frequency of occurrence of some "masculine" and "feminine" items on HFDs will differ in different cultures with different values.

Just how much the drawing of hair on HFDs is dependent on cultural influences is apparent at the present time when many youngsters draw long-haired male figures in deference to their mop-topped idols the Beatles and others. A few years ago, many clinicians would have considered a boy's drawing of a man with long hair as a sign of sexual maladjustment or sexual confusion and an indication of feminine identification. But in this day of the long-haired folk singers and rock and roll musicians, any child who draws a long-haired male must be regarded as being "with it," as being in tune with his time and generation. For as Dennis (1966) has suggested, most normal and well-adjusted boys draw figures of people whom they admire and who represent the cultural values of their time and place. If many children today draw long-haired singers or astronauts or Batman, yesterday they drew Elvis Presley with the long sideburns, or Davy Crockett with the coon skin cap, or Superman. *Plate 1* shows three HFDs of culture heroes of the 1950's and 1960's whose appearances have greatly influenced the hair styles and headgears worn by boys and presented by them on figure drawings.

In similar manner, the clothing items presented on a HFD reflect the current fashions of a given culture and place. Formerly, girls seemed to draw figures with many more clothing details than today. Several of the brighter eleven and twelve year old girls in the normative population produced figures clad only in a simple shift dress devoid of details or accessories, just like the ones they were wearing themselves. Such drawings tend to score very low on clothing items, yet the styles portrayed were much more fashionable and sophisticated than the more traditional dresses with belts, pockets, jewelry, etc. Because of these observations, it seems advisable not to attribute too much psychological significance to the presence or absence of clothing items and hair on HFDs. Certainly, a child's drawing can only be evaluated if the mode of dress and grooming in his environment is known.

It is interesting to note that none of the "masculine" and "feminine" items on HFDs are among the Expected items for boys and girls at any of the age levels from 5 to 10 years. It appears that the 30 Developmental Items under investigation include two different types. The one kind consists of the basic and essential items which are almost entirely determined by age and maturation and which seem to be little influenced by cultural factors, while the other type of Developmental Item is less essential and is related to age as well as to the social and cultural experiences the child has had.

Validation of Developmental Items on HFDs

A series of studies were conducted by the writer to determine whether the 30 Developmental Items could meet the criteria for such items outlined above (page 9). As was stated earlier, a Developmental Item was defined as a sign on HFDs of children that was: (1) related primarily to age and maturation and that increased in frequency of occurrence as the child got older; (2) that was not markedly affected by the instructions given to the child nor by the drawing medium he used; (3) that was not greatly influenced by school learning, nor (4) by the child's artistic ability.

Increase in frequency of occurrence

The normative data on *Table 2* and *Table 3* show beyond a doubt that the Developmental Items are related to age and maturation and that they increase in frequency of occurrence at successive age levels until a maximum occurrence is reached. Some items are present on practically all HFDs as early as age five, others never appear more often than on relatively few HFDs even at age 12.. But in each case, there is a steady increase in the frequency of occurrence until a plateau is reached at a given age level.

The effect of the drawing medium used and the instructions given on the HFD Test: a comparison of pencil and crayon drawings of young children

This study (Koppitz, 1965) was designed to test the hypothesis that HFDs of kindergarten pupils are but little influenced by the drawing medium used or the instructions given. The subjects for this study were 45 boys and 49 girls who were attending four kindergarten classes in a middle-class suburban elementary school. Their ages ranged from 5 years 6 months to 6 years 9 months. During the last three weeks of the school year, the writer administered the HFD Test individually to each subject in a sectioned-off corner of the classroom.

Observation of the children during the test administration revealed a marked difference in the behavior of the boys and girls. Many of the boys were awkward and shy. Since they were accustomed to using only crayons and heavy primary pencils in class, they lacked experience in the use of the thin No. 2 pencil. Many of the boys had difficulty manipulating the slender pencil. The girls on the other hand were for the most part quite at ease and well poised. They were delighted with the special attention they were receiving and seemed to consider the pencil a challenge. They put forth special effort to show off their drawing skill and to gain approval. Their fine muscle coordination was far better than that of the boys.

On the next to the last day of the school year, the classroom teachers administered a modification of the HFD Test to each of their classes as groups. Each child received a piece of Manila paper, size 8½″ × 11″ and a box with eight crayons. The teachers gave the following instructions: "Now that you are going into the first grade, I would like to have a picture of you to keep. So make me a picture of what you look like. Do not look at anyone else's paper because no two boys and girls look alike." No time limit was set for the drawings. All children were asked to put their names and ages on the back of the paper.

Later, the writer checked all pencil drawings as a group, and then all crayon drawings as a group, for the presence of 23 of the 30 Developmental Items. Since the children were so young, the five most difficult items (i.e., two lips, elbow, knee, profile, and good proportion) were omitted and the three items for scoring clothing were reduced to a single clothing item (i.e., two or more pieces of clothing).

Table 4 shows the results when the pencil and crayon drawings of the boys and the girls were compared. The findings are again presented in terms of the percentage of children who revealed each Developmental Item on their HFDs. It was shown that the seven most basic items (head, eyes, nose, mouth, body, arms, and legs) were included among the Expected items for both boys and girls and on both the pencil and crayon drawings. Hair, feet, two dimensions on arms and legs, fingers, and hands were the next most frequent items on all four sets of HFDs. This suggests that the thirteen basic items on HFDs are truly developmental indicators for young children and are not much influenced by the drawing medium or by the instructions given to the children. On several of the other items, there were some differences between the HFDs of boys and girls and between the crayon and pencil drawings.

Fifteen of the 23 Developmental Items appeared more often on the crayon drawings of the boys than on their pencil HFDs. The crayon drawings showed five items to be Common and only one item (nostrils) to be Exceptional. For the pencil drawings, the reverse was true. Only one item (feet) was Common, while six items were in the Exceptional

Table 4. Comparison of Pencil and Crayon HFDs of Kindergarten Pupils

Boys				Girls			
Crayon HFDs		Pencil HFDs		Crayon HFDs		Pencil HFDs	
Expected %		*Expected %*		*Expected %*		*Expected %*	
Head	100	Head	100	Head	100	Head	100
Eyes	100	Eyes	100	Eyes	100	Eyes	100
Nose	91	Nose	95	Nose	90	Nose	94
Mouth	95	Mouth	95	Mouth	94	Mouth	100
Body	91	Body	89	Body	98	Body	100
Arms	89	Arms	87	Arms	90	Arms	90
Legs	98	Legs	100	Legs	92	Legs	96
Common		*Common*		Hair	94	Hair	88
Feet	84	Feet	62	*Common*		*Common*	
Hair	64	*Not Unusual*		Feet	78	Feet	84
Fingers	58	Fingers	40	Fingers	59	Fingers	55
Arm 2d	53	Arm 2d	44	2 Clothes	53	*Not Unusual*	
Legs 2d.	60	Legs 2d.	33	*Not Unusual*		2 Clothes	23
Not Unusual		Hair	46	Arm 2d.	43	Arm 2d.	50
Hands	42	Hands	31	Hands	31	Hands	40
Ear	29	Ear	18	Leg 2d.	33	Leg 2d.	40
Neck	20	Neck	24	Neck	28	Neck	24
Arm a.sh.	18	Arm a.sh.	27	Arm s.sh.	18	Arm a.sh.	18
Arm down	22	Arm down	22	Feet 2d.	20	Arm down	18
2 Clothes	45	*Exceptional*		Pupils	22	Pupils	24
Eyebrow	22	Eyebrow	12	Eyebrow	28	Eyebrow	32
5 Fingers	29	5 Fingers	12	5 Fingers	33	5 Fingers	24
Feet 2d.	31	Feet 2d.	11	*Exceptional*		*Exceptional*	
Pupils	29	Pupils	12	Ear	6	Ear	10
Exceptional		2 Clothes	7	Arm down	14	Feet 2d.	14
Nostrils	4	Nostrils	2	Nostrils	6	Nostrils	12

category. It would appear therefore that the drawing medium and the method of instructions have a definite effect on the HFDs of 5½ to 6½ year old boys. It seems that young boys who are used to drawing with crayons will do better on the HFD Test when they are allowed to use crayons rather than the unfamiliar pencil.

The girls were very much pleased with themselves and with their pencil drawings. The results justified their attitude. Their pencil drawings were found to be better executed than their crayon drawings. Thirteen of the Developmental Items checked were present more often on the pencil drawings. But with only three minor exceptions, all Developmental Items on the HFDs of the girls fell into the same frequency category on both crayon and pencil drawings. The drawing medium used seemed to have little effect on the HFDs of girls; on none of the essential items did their pencil and crayon drawings differ significantly. (For research or screening purposes, pre-school boys might be better asked to make a HFD with crayons than with a pencil, but girls can be asked to use either pencil or crayon with little difference in the results.)

It is interesting to note that hair and clothing occurred markedly more often on the crayon drawings than on the pencil drawings of both the boys and girls. It stands to reason that the wide, soft, colored crayons lend themselves better to the drawing of bright garments and curly, silken hair than does the sharp, black pencil point. It was mentioned earlier (page 19) that both hair and clothing were among the so-called "feminine" items on HFDs and appeared more often on HFDs of girls than boys. This was also the case in the present study. However it now appears that hair and clothing items on drawings are not only related to the child's age and sex and cultural experiences, but also to the drawing medium used.

The effect of learning and maturation on HFDs

The purpose of this study was to determine whether the changes found on HFDs after a period of time were primarily due to the children's increase in age and maturation or due to learning. In the following study, the writer compared the HFDs of children, matched for age, who either had or did not have a year of kindergarten training.

The subjects for this study were 179 children, 89 boys and 90 girls, representing eight entire kindergarten classes in a suburban elementary school. The HFD Test was administered during the first week of the school year. At that time, the children's age mean was 5 years 3 months. When they were retested nine months later, at the end of the school year, their age mean was 6 years 0 month. No intelligence test scores were available for these subjects, but both the teachers and the writer estimated that the children's range of mental ability extended all the way from the superior level to borderline.

The HFD Test was administered both times by the classroom teachers to each class as a group. Each child was given a piece of Manila paper size 8½" × 11" and a box with eight crayons. It was shown earlier (page 22) that there are no significant differences between pencil and crayon drawings of kindergarten pupils. In fact, it is even preferable to use crayons at that age level since young boys especially often have difficulty manipulating slim pencils.

All HFDs were scored for 23 Developmental Items only; because of the age of the subjects, the five most difficult Developmental Items (two lips, elbow, knee, profile, and good proportions) were omitted and the three clothing items were reduced to one such item (two or more items of clothing). The reliability of scoring these 23 Developmental Items was determined with the aid of another clinical psychologist.* The other psychologist and the writer scored independently of each other 15 HFDs of kindergarten pupils. The two examiners checked a total of 203 and 206 Developmental Items on the 15 protocols. On 199 of the Developmental Items checked, there was complete agreement, i.e., they were scored by both psychologists, while 11 items were scored by only one or the other of the examiners. Thus, there was a 95% agreement by the two psychologists on all items scored.

All the HFDs made at the beginning of the school year were then compared with those produced at the end of the school year. The results of this comparison are shown on *Table 5*. Considerable improvement was revealed on the later HFDs over the first set of drawings. At the end of the school year, 20 of the 23 Developmental Items were found more often on the HFDs than they had appeared at the beginning of the year. The only items which did not increase in frequency of occurrence were the head and eyes which had been present on 98–100% of all HFDs at the time of school entry and therefore could not appear more often, and the ear which was drawn equally often by the subjects before and after one year in kindergarten. The number of items in the Expected category increased from five to seven in the course of the school year, while the items in the Exceptional category decreased from six to two. These findings show that there was a marked improvement on the HFDs, but they do not reveal whether this improvement was the result of maturation or due to a year's training in kindergarten.

The answer to this question was found by comparing two sets of HFDs by 35 pairs of subjects who were carefully matched for sex and for age within one month. The matched subjects included 16 pairs of boys and 19 pairs of girls. One set of HFDs came from 35 children (Group A) who had been the oldest pupils at the beginning of the year. Their drawings were obtained at the time of school entry before they had received any training in kindergarten. The second set of HFDs was taken from 35 children (Group B) who had been the youngest in their classrooms at the beginning of the school year. The HFDs from Group B were collected at the end of the year, after the children had completed a full year of kindergarten training. By this time, the age of Group B was equal to that of Group A at the beginning of the year. The age range for both Group A and Group B was 5 years 6 months to 5 years 10 months, with an age mean of 5 years 7 months.

---

* The writer wishes to express her appreciation to Dr. Margaret G. Lang for her assistance with this reliability study.

Table 5 shows the results when the HFDs of Group A and Group B were compared. The findings reveal remarkably little difference in the frequency of occurrence of the Developmental Items on the HFDs of children who did and did not have one year of kindergarten experience. Head and eyes were present on 100% of both sets of drawings. Of the other 21 Developmental Items tested, one item, fingers, was present equally often on the HFDs of Group A and Group B. Nine Developmental Items were present more often on the HFDs of the school beginners, while 11 items were found more often on the HFDs of those who had completed a year in kindergarten. The HFDs of Group A and Group B showed the identical number of items in each frequency category.

A closer look at individual Developmental Items shows that the following four exhibited the greatest increase after a year of school training: two dimensions on arms and legs, two or more pieces of clothing and the correct number of fingers. There is reason to believe that all four items reflect at least in part some learning experience. Some of the teachers acknowledged that they had encouraged their pupils throughout the year to draw arms and legs on figures in two dimensions instead of drawing stick figures; they also stressed the drawing of clothes. The drawing of five fingers presupposed some knowledge of numbers, which children often

Table 5. Comparison of HFDs of Pupils With and Without Kindergarten Training

179 Unselected Pupils		35 Matched Pairs	
Beginning K Age M 5–3	*End K* Age M 6–0	*Group A (Beginning K)* Age M 5–7	*Group B (End K)* Age M 5–7
Expected %	*Expected %*	*Expected %*	*Expected %*
Head 100	Head 100	Head 100	Head 100
Eyes 99	Eyes 98	Eyes 100	Eyes 100
Mouth 90	Mouth 93	Mouth 94	Mouth 91
Body 90	Body 95	Body 94	Body 91
Legs 91	Legs 95	Legs 94	Legs 97
Common	Nose 90	Nose 91	Nose 94
Nose 80	Arms 89	*Common*	*Common*
Arms 73	*Common*	Arms 74	Arms 80
Feet 72	Feet 82	Feet 77	Feet 74
Hair 66	Hair 80	Hair 63	Arms 2d. 54
Not Unusual	Arms 2d. 56	Fingers 68	Fingers 68
Fingers 49	Fingers 63	*Not Unusual*	*Not Unusual*
Arms 2d. 22	*Not Unusual*	Arms 2d. 34	Hair 43
Legs 2d. 19	Legs 2d. 42	Legs 2d. 26	Legs 2d. 46
Pupils 21	Pupils 25	Pupils 23	Pupils 20
Eyebrows 18	Eyebrows 25	Eyebrows 20	Eyebrows 31
Hands 23	Hands 32	Hands 20	Hands 23
Ears 18	Ears 18	Feet 2d. 26	Feet 2d. 34
2 Clothes 20	2 Clothes 47	2 Clothes 28	2 Clothes 43
Exceptional	Neck 23	Neck 17	5 Fingers 23
Arms down 12	Arm down 21	*Exceptional*	*Exceptional*
Feet 2d. 14	Feet 2d. 26	Arm down 11	Arm down 6
5 Fingers 10	5 Fingers 29	5 Fingers 9	Neck 9
Neck 11	*Exceptional*	Ears 14	Ears 9
Arm a.sh. 5	Arm a.sh. 11	Arm a.sh. 3	Arm a.sh. 6
Nostrils 5	Nostrils 6	Nostrils 9	Nostrils 3

do not acquire until they enter kindergarten. None of the other 19 Developmental Items showed a marked increase in frequency of occurrences as the result of school learning, thus supporting the hypothesis that the basic Developmental Items are primarily related to maturation and are not greatly influenced by school learning.

The findings reported above suggest that the marked improvement on the HFDs of the 179 unselected kindergarten pupils, by the end of the school year, was due primarily to maturation rather than to school training. For if that improvement had been the result of learning, then the same amount of improvement should also have been shown on the HFDs of Group B who had completed a year in kindergarten. The fact that Group A and Group B, matched for age, did not reveal any significant differences on their HFDs despite differences in the amount of school training suggests that school learning at the kindergarten level does not effect the drawing of a human figure to any appreciable degree when the children come from middle-class suburban homes. Whether this would also apply to the drawings of culturally deprived children who never had much opportunity to draw prior to coming to school is not certain. The only items on HFDs that seem to be influenced by training are clothing and the correct number of fingers and possibly two dimensions on the arms and legs.

Further support for the age and maturation hypothesis for the Developmental Items was shown on *Table 5*. It can be seen that the level of maturation of the HFDs of Group A and Group B falls exactly between that of the HFDs of the 179 unselected pupils, made at the beginning of kindergarten, and their drawings, made at the end of kindergarten. The age mean for Group A and Group B was 5 years 7 months which is exactly midway between the age mean of 5 years 3 months of the school beginners and the age mean of 6 years of the children who had completed kindergarten. Thus, the developmental level of the HFDs corresponds to the chronological age of the subjects irrespective of the amount of kindergarten training they had received.

The Influence of high or low performance ability on HFDs

It was earlier hypothesized that the presence of Developmental Items on HFDs is primarily related to maturation and not to the child's artistic ability. It is of course, difficult to determine whether a child has artistic ability or not. However, it might be assumed that a child with such ability would possess among other qualities good visual-motor perception and good fine motor coordination. These are abilities which are measured to a large extent by the Performance Scale on the WISC (Wechsler, 1949). The following study was designed to determine whether children whose WISC Performance IQ scores were considerably higher than their Verbal IQ scores would differ on their HFDs from children with a low WISC Performance IQ score and a higher Verbal IQ score, if both groups of youngsters were matched for WISC Full Scale IQ scores.

It was predicted that if the Developmental Items on HFDs were indeed primarily related to maturation and not to performance ability, then there would be no significant difference in the frequency of occurrence of the

Developmental Items on the HFDs of children with high WISC Performance Test scores and those with low WISC Performance Test scores.

The subjects for this study were 24 pairs of children matched for age, sex and WISC Full Scale IQ score. *Table 6* shows the distribution of the subjects. All of the children were attending public schools, and all of them had been referred to the school psychologist or to a child guidance clinic for psychological evaluation because of learning and/or behavior problems. None of the subjects were retarded or psychotic, and none had any gross motor impairment. Their age range was from 6 years 8 months to 12 years 10 months, and their age mean was 10 years 5 months. One set of 24 subjects had a WISC Performance IQ score that was more than ten points above their Verbal IQ score, while the other set of 24 subjects had a WISC Verbal IQ score that was more than ten points above their Performance IQ scores. A discrepancy of less than ten points between the Verbal and Performance IQ scores on the WISC is usually not considered to be significant, but a discrepancy of 10 or more points is thought to have clinical significance and indicates either higher ability in one of the two areas, or a deficiency in either performance or verbal ability.

The 48 subjects were selected from the writer's clinical file solely on the basis of their IQ scores. All of the HFDs were checked by the investi-

Table 6. **Distribution of Subjects with High and Low Performance IQ Scores**

Ss with High Performance IQ's					Ss with Low Performance IQ's				
Age	Sex	Perf. IQ	Verbal IQ	F.S. IQ	Age	Sex	Perf. IQ	Verbal IQ	F.S. IQ
6–11	M	115	100	108	6–8	M	103	115	110
7–3	M	97	84	89	7–9	M	76	92	83
7–5	M	101	90	95	7–9	M	75	108	91
8–2	M	127	95	109	8–2	M	72	120	97
8–0	F	104	89	96	8–9	F	90	103	96
9–0	M	114	100	107	9–3	M	97	110	104
9–1	M	100	85	91	9–4	M	83	95	88
10–11	M	121	108	115	10–0	M	92	128	112
10–10	M	113	92	102	10–1	M	99	110	105
10–3	M	100	90	94	10–2	M	90	105	98
10–6	F	113	87	99	10–4	M	94	106	101
9–4	M	133	114	125	10–6	M	127	139	137
10–1	M	115	90	105	10–6	M	90	114	103
10–4	F	103	80	90	10–7	F	83	104	93
10–6	M	94	75	83	10–8	M	89	100	94
11–11	M	99	81	88	11–2	M	83	94	88
11–7	F	97	86	91	11–7	F	79	92	85
11–8	F	114	94	104	11–7	F	93	116	106
11–10	F	108	96	107	11–8	F	101	128	117
12–4	M	111	99	105	12–3	M	92	111	102
12–6	M	117	99	108	12–3	M	96	120	109
12–4	M	89	71	77	12–4	M	78	89	82
12–7	M	118	106	113	12–5	M	99	129	116
12–5	F	99	86	91	12–10	F	87	106	97
M 10–5		M 109	M 92	M 100	M 10–4		M 91	M 110	M 100

gator for the presence of the 30 Developmental Items without any knowledge as to which of the two groups a given child belonged to. Thereafter, all HFDs of the subjects with high Performance IQ scores were compared with those of the subjects with low Performance IQ scores. Chi-squares were computed to determine whether there were any statistically significant differences in the frequency of occurrence of any of the Developmental Items on the HFDs of either group of subjects.

Table 7 shows the actual number of subjects in the high and low Performance IQ groups who revealed each Developmental Item on their HFD. None of the Chi-squares values obtained were significant at the .05 level or better. No single Developmental Item differentiated between the subjects with high performance or high verbal ability. There is shown a striking similarity in the relative frequency of occurrence of the various Developmental Items on the drawings of the two groups of matched subjects. The results of this study offer support for the hypothesis that Developmental Items on HFDs are not markedly influenced by a child's performance ability, but are primarily related to age and maturation.

Table 7.   Comparison of HFDs of 24 Pairs of Ss with High and Low Performance IQ's

Developmental Items	Ss w. High Perf. IQ	Ss w. Low Perf. IQ
Head	24	24
Eyes	24	24
Pupils	7	8
Eyebrows	10	10
Nose	24	19
Nostrils	3	2
Mouth	21	24
Two lips	2	2
Ear	7	8
Hair	17	21
Neck	16	16
Body	23	22
Arms	23	21
Arms 2 dimensions	22	20
Arms down	18	16
Arms at shoulders	8	12
Elbow	3	2
Hands	14	10
Fingers	15	13
5 Fingers	4	7
Legs	23	23
Legs 2 dimensions	20	21
Knee	2	1
Feet	20	17
Feet 2 dimensions	11	8
Profile	9	5
Good proportion	6	4
Clothing: 0–1 item	9	11
Clothing: 2–3 items	6	4
Clothing: 4 or more items	9	9

Expected and Exceptional Items on HFDs and IQ scores

The 30 Developmental Items discussed in the preceding chapter were checked on HFDs merely for their presence or absence. They were not meant to represent a scoring system for drawings of children that would yield a specific IQ and Mental Age score. The normative data for the Developmental Items were only intended to show which items on HFDs of boys and girls, of different age levels, one could expect to find, and which items were unusual or rare. However, it was pointed out (page 11) that the absence of Expected items (i.e., items that occurred on 86–100% of all HFDs) might be considered diagnostically significant and would reflect most likely mental immaturity, while the presence of Exceptional items (i.e., items that occur on less than 16% of all HFDs) was regarded as a sign of above average mental maturity. It would seem to follow therefore that the presence and absence of the Expected and Exceptional items on HFDs would be related to a child's level of mental maturity and intelligence.

A study was designed (Koppitz, 1967) to test the following hypothesis: Expected and Exceptional items on HFDs can be used to assess a child's general level of mental maturity even though no definite IQ score is given. A simple method for scoring Expected and Exceptional items on HFDs was devised for this study. A list of the Expected and Exceptional items for the 1856 boys and girls of the normative population at each age level is shown in *Appendix B*. Each Expected and Exceptional item was given the value of 1. Omission of an Expected item was designated as —1, while the presence of an Exceptional item was called +1. In order to avoid negative scores, the value of 5 was added to the sum of all positive and negative scoring points a child received on his HFD. Thus, the omission of one Expected item was counted as —1+5 or a score of 4; the presence of one Exceptional item became +1+5 or a score of 6. The following shows the scores a child may obtain on his HFD if a given number of Expected and Exceptional items are present or absent:

Score	Expected Items	Exceptional Items
8	all present	3 present
7	all present	2 present
6	all present	1 present
or		
6	1 absent	2 present
5	all present	none present
or		
5	1 absent	1 present
4	1 absent	none present
or		
4	2 absent	1 present
3	2 absent	none present
2	3 absent	none present
1	4 absent	none present
0	5 or more absent	none present

This scoring system was applied to the HFDs of 347 boys and girls, age 5 years 11 months to 12 years 11 months, who served as subjects in the present study. All of the subjects had been seen by the writer for psychological evaluation at the child guidance clinic or in school, at which time the HFDs were obtained. The WISC (Wechsler, 1949) or the Stanford-Binet Intelligence Scale (Terman and Merrill, 1960) had been administered to the subjects by the writer or by other qualified psychologists within a year of the HFD Test. The subjects showed a wide range of behavior and learning problems, but none had been medically diagnosed as brain injured, and none suffered from any gross physical disability.

Table 8 shows the distribution of the subjects by age and IQ level. The WISC had been administered to 260 of the subjects, while the remaining 87 children were tested with the Stanford-Binet Scale. The HFD of each

Table 8.   Distribution of Subjects by Age and IQ Scores

Age Level	Level of IQ Scores							
	59 down	60–69	70–79	80–89	90–99	100–109	110 up	Total
6 & 7	3	6	4	14	12	13	15	67
8	3	6	7	13	13	8	5	55
9	1	3	6	13	18	12	12	65
10	0	1	4	7	16	20	7	55
11	1	1	6	19	10	11	10	58
12	6	4	7	8	5	9	8	47
Total	14	21	34	74	74	73	57	347

subject was scored for the Expected and Exceptional items appropriate for his age and sex (*Appendix B*). For example, Eugene's "Beatle" on *Plate 1* would be scored as 5, for he drew all of the items that are Expected for 10 year old boys, but none of the Exceptional items for that age level. Andrew's "Davy Crockett" on *Plate 1* would receive a score of 6 for he not only drew all the Expected items for seven year old boys, but he also drew one Exceptional item: the figure is shown in profile.

Thereafter, the scores from the HFDs were correlated with the WISC Full Scale IQ scores and the Stanford-Binet IQ scores. Separate Pearson's product moment correlations were computed for each age level. Separate correlations were also obtained for the subjects who had been tested with the WISC and those who had been tested with the Stanford-Binet Scale. *Table 9* shows the results of the various correlations. The statistical significance of the correlations was determined by means of *t*-tests. The findings reveal that all of the nine correlations were significant at the .01 level. The results on *Table 9* compare also quite favorably with the correlations between Goodenough Draw-A-Man Test scores and IQ test scores which have been reported in the literature for schoolchildren and young psychiatric patients (Estes et al., 1961; Hanvick, 1953; Harris, 1963, pp. 96–97; Thompson & Finley, 1963; and Vane & Kessler, 1964). It would appear therefore that Expected and Exceptional items on HFDs can be used with some confidence as a quick and easy method of assessing the level of mental maturity of groups of children.

Table 9. Correlations between Expected and Exceptional
Items on HFDs and IQ Scores

Age Level	N	Tests Correlated	Correlations
6 & 7	23	Stanford-Binet & HFDs	.63*
8–10	50	Stanford-Binet & HFDs	.55*
11 & 12	14	Stanford-Binet & HFDs	.62*
6 & 7	44	WISC & HFDs	.60*
8	35	WISC & HFDs	.69*
9	46	WISC & HFDs	.68*
10	44	WISC & HFDs	.45*
11	55	WISC & HFDs	.57*
12	36	WISC & HFDs	.80*

* Significant at the .01 level.

Correlations always deal with groups of subjects and tell very little about the individual child who may vary considerably from the group norms. But practicing clinicians and school psychologists work most often with individual children and not with groups of youngsters. If a test is to be of value for practicing psychologists, it must be able to differentiate and to predict the behavior of any one child. For this reason, the distribution pattern of individual HFD scores and IQ test scores was examined. *Table 10* shows the distribution of the HFD and IQ test scores for all 347 subjects used in the present study. On the basis of these findings, interpretations for each HFD score were devised in terms of the corresponding general level of IQ scores. *Appendix C* shows the interpretation of individual HFD scores.

Table 10. Distribution of HFD and IQ Scores for 347 Subjects, Age 6 to 12

IQ Range	N	HFD Scores from Expected and Exceptional Items								
		0	1	2	3	4	5	6	7	8
59 down	14	3	3	4	1	3				
60–69	21	2	3	6	5	4	1			
70–79	34	1	1	6	13	8	5			
80–89	74		1	9	19	25	18	1	1	
90–99	74		2		9	18	38	7		
100–109	73	1			3	10	47	12		
110 upward	57				1	12	31	9	3	1
Total	347	7	10	25	51	80	140	29	4	1

This method of interpretation translates HFD scores into broad categories of intellectual functioning rather than into specific IQ scores. The broad categories of mental ability are considered sufficient for differentiating between children who are mentally retarded and those who have average or above-average ability. It is felt that placing children into such general categories of functioning is more meaningful than giving them specific IQ scores. This writer has been concerned many times when too much significance was attached to a specific IQ score which may or may not be reliable.

The interpretation of HFD scores presented here was found to be valid for the great majority of subjects in the present study. However, as is always the case, there were some exceptions to this rule. All subjects for whom there was a marked discrepancy between their HFD scores and IQ test scores were examined more closely. It was found that all the children who had an average or above-average score on the IQ tests and a below-average score on the HFD test suffered from serious emotional and personality problems. In each case investigated, the child was actually functioning on the more immature level reflected by his HFD rather than on the level of his more adequate IQ score. It might be said that, in these cases, the HFD revealed the child's actual functioning level while the IQ test score indicated his intellectual potential which he may or may not be able to realize.

In those cases where the level of the HFD score exceeded the IQ test scores, it appeared that the subjects were essentially of normal intelligence but suffered from learning difficulties due to cultural or social deprivation or as the result of problems in hearing, auditory perception or poor memory. In other words, when a child's HFD score is below his IQ score level, one might suspect disturbances in his emotional adjustment and personality, but when the drawing score is higher than the IQ score level, then the chances are that the child is a culturally and socially deprived child with or without specific deficiencies in hearing and memory.

Appendix D shows the Mean scores, Standard Deviations and Quartiles for the Expected and Exceptional items on HFDs at different IQ levels. The data for *Appendix D* were derived from the HFDs of 735 children, age 6 to 12, including both psychiatric clinic patients and youngsters referred to the school psychologist for evaluation because of learning and behavior problems. Among the 735 youngsters were children with and without neurological impairment, but none had any gross motor impairment. The sample used in this study cannot be thought of as representative of the so-called "average" or "normal" elementary school-age population; therefore, the data in *Appendix D* should not be taken as normative data for children as a whole. Unfortunately, it is most difficult for an individual investigator to obtain large samples of WISC or Stanford Binet IQ scores from unselected schoolchildren who have never been referred to a psychologist for testing. However, clinical and school psychologists are unlikely to work with many well-functioning children of normal intelligence, whereas, the subjects used in the present study are quite typical for the population seen by most practicing clinicians and school psychologists. For this reason, the data shown on *Appendix D* can be regarded as being representative for a clinical sample and can be used with confidence in actual work with children.

The following three cases may help to illustrate the practical application of the scoring system for Expected and Exceptional items on HFDs. *Plate 2* shows the HFD of Simon, age 7. Simon's little figure reveals seven of the nine Expected items for seven year old boys (*Appendix B*).

Simon drew: head, eyes, nose, mouth, body, legs and feet. He omitted arms and two dimensions on arms. This means his HFD score is —2+0 +5 = 3 and indicates that he was probably of low average intelligence, i.e., he probably had an IQ between 70 and 90. In fact, Simon obtained an IQ score of 82 on the Stanford-Binet Scale.

The HFD of Max, another seven year old boy, is shown on *Plate 3*. Max drew all nine Expected items for seven year old boys, but none of the Exceptional items. His score on the HFD was therefore —0+0+5 = 5, indicating at least average intelligence, i.e., he probably had an IQ score between 85 and 135. When Max was later tested with the Stanford-Binet Scale, he obtained an IQ score of 103. Then there was Jim, age 9, whose HFD is presented on *Plate 4*. Jim drew all ten Expected items for nine year old boys: head, eyes, nose, mouth, body, legs, arms, feet, and arms and legs in two dimensions; in addition, he drew his figure in profile and depicted a knee, both of which are scored as Exceptional items for this age level. Thus Jim's HFD score is —0+2+5 = 7. A score of 7 indicates high average to superior intelligence, i.e., his IQ score was probably 110 or higher. A look at Jim's clinical record revealed that his WISC IQ score was indeed in the superior range.

The scoring of HFDs for Expected and Exceptional items is quick and easy and seems particularly well suited for the screening of large groups of school beginners to determine which children should be further tested for possible retardation or for . outstanding ability. This method of analyzing HFDs is also useful for the clinician who wants to check his own subjective impression of the child's mental ability against some objective criterion without spending an hour or more for the administration of a full-scale intelligence test. It is surprising how easily an examiner can be influenced by a child's appearance and training or lack of it, and how easily he can over- or underestimate the youngster's ability. Intuitive assessments of children's drawings are often misleading since unessential details may make a HFD look much more mature than it really is. On the other hand, some drawings are regarded as crude and deficient when, in fact, they are quite adequate for a given child's age and sex. This is particularly true for bright, young boys whose HFDs look often quite immature to the casual observer. Six year old boys just cannot and should not be expected to draw figures complete with many details. Even a very crude HFD may reveal all the essential Expected items and may be quite within the range of normal ability.

Developmental Items on HFDs: Summary

Thirty Developmental Items on HFDs were selected and defined (*Appendix A*). Several research studies were presented to demonstrate that these items were primarily related to age and maturation in children. Only a few of the items, notably hair and pieces of clothing, were found to be related to children's age as well as to their sex and social and cultural experiences. The frequency of occurrence of most of the 30 Development Items was not significantly affected by the children's drawing ability, nor by training in kindergarten, or by the drawing medium used. No significant differences were revealed between the basic Developmental Items on pencil and crayon HFDs of pre-school children. At the kindergarten level, either pencil or crayons can be used for the HFD test; for young boys in particular, the use of crayons may be actually preferable to the use of a slim pencil.

Normative data for the 30 Developmental Items on HFDs were given for boys and girls, age 5 to 12. A list of Expected and Exceptional items on HFDs for each age level is shown on *Appendix B*. From the Expected and Exceptional items, a simple scoring system for HFDs was derived. This scoring system was found to correlate significantly with WISC and Stanford-Binet IQ scores and can be used therefore as a rough screening instrument to assess children's mental maturity (*Appendix C*). Some examples of scoring HFDs for Expected and Exceptional items were given.

4. Emotional Indicators on HFDs

IN THIS CHAPTER objective signs on HFDs will be investigated which differ from the Developmental Items that were discussed in the preceding chapter, in that they are not primarily related to a child's age and maturation but reflect his anxieties, concerns, and attitudes. These signs are designated as Emotional Indicators. An Emotional Indicator is here defined as a sign on HFDs which can meet the following three criteria:

(1) It must have clinical validity, i.e., it must be able to differentiate between HFDs of children with and without emotional problems.

(2) It must be unusual and occur infrequently on the HFDs of normal children who are not psychiatric patients, i.e., the sign must be present on less than 16% of the HFDs of children at a given age level.

(3) It must not be related to age and maturation, i.e., its frequency of occurrence on HFDs must not increase solely on the basis of the children's increase in age.

A list of 38 signs on HFDs were selected which were believed to possess all the characteristics of Emotional Indicators. These items were derived from the work of Machover and Hammer and from the writer's own clinical experience. The list consists of three different types of items: The first type includes items that are related to the quality of the HFD; the second group of signs is made up of special features not usually found on HFDs; and the third group consists of omissions of items which would be expected on the HFDs of children at a given age level.

The following is the list of 38 potential Emotional Indicators:

I. *Quality signs*
   broken or sketchy lines
   poor integration of parts of figure
   shading of the face or part of it
   shading of the body and/or limbs
   shading of the hands and/or neck
   gross asymmetry of limbs
   figure slanting by 15 degrees or more
   tiny figure, 2″ or less in height
   big figure, 9″ or more in height
   transparencies

II. *Special features*
   tiny head, 1/10th of total height of figure
   large head, as large or larger than body
   vacant eyes, circles without pupils
   side glances of both eyes, both eyes turned to one side
   crossed eyes, both eyes turned inward
   teeth
   short arms, not long enough to reach waistline
   long arms, that could reach below kneeline

35

    arms clinging to side of body
    big hands, as big as face
    hands cut off, arms without hands and fingers
    hands hidden behind back or in pockets
    legs pressed together
    genitals
    monster or grotesque figure
    three or more figures spontaneously drawn
    figure cut off by edge of paper
    baseline, grass, figure on edge of paper
    sun or moon
    clouds, rain, snow

III. *Omissions*
    omission of eyes
    omission of nose (Boys 6, Girls 5)
    omission of mouth
    omission of body
    omission of arms (Boys 6, Girls 5)
    omission of legs
    omission of feet (Boys 9, Girls 7)
    omission of neck (Boys 10, Girls 9)

The omissions included in the third group of potential Emotional Indicators are actually absences of some of the basic Expected items on HFDs. It was pointed out earlier (page 11) that any Developmental Item that occurs on more than 85 percent of all drawings at a given age level is classified as an Expected item. The presence of Expected items can be taken for granted while the absence of such items is rare and must be considered clinically significant. Such omissions may reflect immaturity or malfunctioning due to retardation and/or emotional disturbances.

All 38 items on the tentative list of Emotional Indicators were defined in detail in a scoring manual. The Emotional Indicators were scored as present or absent in the same manner as the Developmental Items had been scored. The reliability of scoring the Emotional Indicators was discussed earlier (page 10).

Normative study for Emotional Indicators on HFDs

A normative study for Emotional Indicators was carried out to determine whether the items on the tentative list could meet the following two criteria for Emotional Indicators: (1) that they are not primarily related to age and maturation and hence do not increase in frequency of occurrence as a result of the children's increase in age; and (2) that they are rare or unusual and occur on 15% or less of all HFDs at a given age level.

The HFDs of the same 1856 children who had served as normative population (*Table 1*) for the study of Developmental Items were also used for the normative study of Emotional Indicators. The writer scored all HFDs for the presence of the emotional signs.

The normative data for the Emotional Indicators on HFDs of boys are shown on *Table 11*; the results are given in terms of the percentage of the boys who showed each of the items on their drawings. *Table 12* does the same for the girls. It was found that the majority of the items tested could meet the two criteria for Emotional Indicators on HFDs of boys and girls. Most of the items did not increase in frequency of occurrence as the age of the children increased, and most of them were rare or un-

Table 11. Percentage of Boys Showing Emotional Indicators on their HFDs

Emotional Indicator	Age	5	6	7	8	9	10	11	12
	N	128	131	134	138	134	109	105	52
Broken lines*		0	1	0	5	11	12	23	19
Poor integration		16	15	11	7	4	6	2	0
Shading, face		3	3	0	1	1	3	0	0
Shading, body, limbs		30	35	19	12	7	7	4	4
Shading, hands, neck		17	23	11	8	9	9	3	2
Asymmetry of limbs		4	3	2	1	3	1	1	2
Slanting figure		3	2	1	3	5	0	2	2
Tiny figure		5	3	4	2	3	3	3	0
Big figure		11	16	18	10	7	11	11	12
Transparencies		3	6	5	2	3	7	3	0
Tiny head		2	2	1	1	0	0	0	0
Large head*		18	30	23	14	18	11	14	6
Vacant eyes*		25	12	6	17	14	15	14	25
Glance of eyes*		0	2	1	4	2	3	5	2
Crossed eyes		0	1	1	1	1	1	1	2
Teeth		6	8	11	10	9	15	8	12
Short arms		0	2	2	4	1	2	2	4
Long arms		3	5	4	1	2	1	5	0
Arms clinging		3	2	4	6	9	5	10	8
Big hands		2	4	3	0	1	0	0	0
Hands cut off		1	8	10	6	3	6	7	4
Hands hidden*		0	1	1	1	1	2	7	6
Legs together		2	1	1	5	4	6	6	2
Genitals		5	1	1	0	1	0	0	0
Monster, grotesque		1	4	0	1	3	1	0	2
Three figures		5	2	1	1	0	0	1	0
Figure cut off*		2	3	3	4	2	2	2	4
Baseline*		21	27	31	30	22	24	19	23
Sun*		5	9	4	3	0	2	0	0
Clouds, rain		7	5	4	1	1	2	3	2
No eyes		2	1	1	1	0	0	1	0
No nose		—	9	10	6	0	3	3	0
No mouth		8	3	3	5	1	2	3	0
No body		11	3	2	1	0	0	1	0
No arms		—	5	4	4	0	2	1	0
No legs		3	2	1	3	1	1	2	0
No feet		—	—	—	—	10	4	5	6
No neck		—	—	—	—	—	11	7	2

* Item was not able to meet criteria for Emotional Indicators and was therefore omitted from list of Emotional Indicators.

usual. However, there were some exceptions which could not meet one or both of these criteria at one or more age levels. It was shown for instance, that "big figures" are not rare on the HFDs of five to seven year old boys and girls; not until age 8 does this item become unusual and appears on less than 15% of the drawings.

Three items, "big head," "vacant eyes," and "baseline," were present so often on the HFDs of boys and girls at most of the age levels tested

Table 12. **Percentage of Girls Showing Emotional Indicators on their HFDs**

Emotional Indicator	Age	5	6	7	8	9	10	11	12
	N	128	133	125	130	134	108	112	55
Broken lines*		0	0	1	2	7	15	7	5
Poor integration		16	8	4	3	2	1	1	2
Shading, face		2	1	0	0	0	0	0	0
Shading, body, limbs		25	20	11	4	4	2	4	2
Shading, hands, neck		13	20	9	6	3	1	4	0
Asymmetry of limbs		2	4	1	0	1	0	0	0
Slanting figure		5	3	2	3	1	1	2	2
Tiny figure		6	3	2	2	1	1	0	2
Big figure		9	14	17	8	15	10	13	5
Transparencies		6	6	4	3	3	1	3	0
Tiny head		2	0	2	0	0	0	0	0
Large head*		27	28	30	36	26	16	17	16
Vacant eyes*		18	9	11	15	9	6	14	11
Glance of eyes*		2	2	4	6	5	11	10	9
Crossed eyes		1	0	1	0	1	2	1	0
Teeth		9	11	0	5	6	3	1	0
Short arms		2	8	10	10	6	3	5	2
Long arms		2	3	2	2	1	3	1	0
Arms clinging		0	2	2	7	4	5	9	9
Big hands		1	1	2	0	0	0	0	0
Hands cut off		1	8	5	6	6	1	4	2
Hands hidden*		0	0	0	2	4	6	8	11
Legs together		1	2	3	2	4	3	8	13
Genitals		0	0	1	0	1	0	0	0
Monster, grotesque		0	1	0	0	0	1	0	2
Three figures		4	4	2	0	2	1	0	0
Figure cut off*		2	3	2	4	0	2	2	0
Baseline, grass*		18	29	35	21	20	20	16	11
Sun*		10	7	5	3	1	6	1	0
Clouds, rain		6	6	4	3	1	3	2	0
No eyes		0	0	0	0	0	0	2	0
No nose		10	5	8	8	7	5	3	2
No mouth		9	0	0	2	1	1	3	2
No body		9	6	0	1	0	0	0	0
No arms		9	2	1	0	0	0	0	0
No legs		3	7	1	6	1	5	4	4
No feet		—	—	6	10	1	6	4	5
No neck		—	—	—	—	7	6	4	0

* Item was not able to meet criteria for Emotional Indicators and was therefore omitted from list of Emotional Indicators.

that they could not qualify as rare or unusual at any time. These three items were therefore eliminated from the list of Emotional Indicators.

Three other items were found to increase in frequency of occurrence on the HFDs as the children grew older. Thus "broken lines" became not at all unusual on the drawings of eleven and twelve year old boys, while "glance of eyes" and "hidden hands" increased markedly in frequency of occurrence on the HFDs of pre-adolescent girls. These particular items were found to be present on some of the best and most mature drawings of the normative population. It seems therefore that "broken lines," "glance of eyes," and "hidden hands" are more related to sophistication than to emotional problems; consequently, these three items were also taken from the list of Emotional Indicators on HFDs. For a more detailed discussion of these items, see page 69 ff.

This left 32 items on the tentative list of Emotional Indicators. Of these, 24 items seemed to be able to meet the two criteria for Emotional Indicators on HFDs of both boys and girls at all age levels from 5 through 12. The other eight items did not qualify as Emotional Indicators until the children were six years old or older. The following shows the eight items and the ages at which they become Emotional Indicators for boys and girls respectively:

Emotional Indicator on HFD	Valid for boys age	Valid for girls age
Poor integration of parts	7	6
Shading of body and/or limbs	9	8
Shading of hands and/or neck	8	7
Big figure	8	8
Omission of nose	6	5
Omission of arms	6	5
Omission of feet	9	7
Omission of neck	10	9

Before the 32 items could be accepted as valid Emotional Indicators on HFDs of children, it was necessary to show that they could meet the third criterion for Emotional Indicators: their clinical significance had to be demonstrated. Several studies were designed by the writer to determine whether the 32 items could differentiate between HFDs of children with and without emotional problems and behavior symptoms.

Validation of Emotional Indicators on HFDs

The following study was designed to test two hypotheses (Koppitz, 1966 a). The first of these stated that individual Emotional Indicators occur more often on the HFDs of children with emotional problems than on drawings of well-adjusted children. The second hypothesis claims that HFDs of emotionally disturbed children will show a greater number of Emotional Indicators than HFDs of well-adjusted children.

The subjects for this study were 76 pairs of public school children matched for age and sex. Each group included 32 boys and 44 girls; of these 7 subjects were 5 years old, 12 were 6 years old, 10 were 7 years old, 7 were age 8, 6 were 9 year olds, 12 were 10 years old, 18 were age 11, and 4 were 12 years old. *Group A* consisted of 76 patients of a child guidance clinic. The WISC or Stanford-Binet Scale IQ for these Subjects ranged from 90–148, with a Mean score of 110. Thus, all of these subjects were of at least normal intelligence and many of them were of above average ability. The 76 subjects in *Group B* were all pupils of the same suburban elementary school, kindergarten through sixth grade. All of them had been selected by their teachers as outstanding "all around" students with good social, emotional and academic adjustment. No specific intelligence test scores were available for *Group B,* but it may be assumed that most of these youngsters were of high average or superior intelligence.

The HFD Test was administered individually by the writer to each Subject in *Group A* and *Group B*. *Group A* was seen in the guidance clinic, while *Group B* was tested in school. All protocols were checked for the presence of the 32 tentative Emotional Indicators. Chi-squares were computed comparing the number of subjects in the two groups who showed each given Emotional Indicator on their HFDs. In addition, a comparison was made of the total number of Emotional Indicators shown on the HFDs of *Group A* and *Group B*.

Table 13 shows the results of this study. Twelve of the Emotional Indicators were found significantly more often on the HFDs of the clinic patients (*Group A*) than on the drawings of the well-adjusted pupils (*Group B)*. Statistical computations revealed that the Chi-square values for four items (poor integration, shading of body and/or limbs, slanting figure, and tiny figure) were significant at the .01 level; four more items (big figure, short arms, cut off hands, and omission of neck) were significant at the .05 level; and an additional four items (shading of hands and/or neck, asymmetry of limbs, transparencies, and big hands) were able to differentiate the HFDs of *Group A* and *Group B* at the .10 level of significance. Some of the Emotional Indicators occurred so rarely on any of the drawings that statistical analysis was not possible or meaningful (shading of face, no eyes, tiny head, genitals).

Sixteen of the items were present exclusively on the HFDs of the clinic patients in *Group A*. Twelve items were exhibited on HFDs of both groups of subjects, but more often on the drawings of the children with emotional problems. Two items (crossed eyes and omission of legs) were not shown on any of the HFDs. These two items are exceedingly rare, but, in the writer's experience, they reflect emotional problems when they do occur. One item (figure cut off by paper) was present equally often on the protocols of *Group A* and *Group B*, while the last item (sun) occurred actually more often on the drawings of the outstanding pupils than on the HFDs of the emotionally disturbed children. Since both "figure cut off by paper" and "sun" failed to meet the criterion for clinical validity (i.e., they were unable to differentiate between HFDs of clinic patients and well-adjusted students), they were eliminated from the list of Emotional Indicators. This left a total of 30 items that could qualify as Emotional Indicators. All subsequent discussions of Emotional Indicators will be based exclusively on these 30 items. The scoring manual for the 30

Table 13.   Emotional Indicators on HFDs of Clinic Patients (Group A) and Well Adjusted Pupils (Group B)

Emotional Indicators	Group A	Group B	χ^2	P
Poor integration	9	0	7.06	.01
Shading of face	3	0		
Shading of body, limbs	10	1	6.63	.01
Shading of hands, neck	5	0	3.36	.10
Asymmetry of limbs	5	0	3.31	.10
Slanting figure	11	0	9.80	.01
Tiny figure	10	0	8.67	.01
Big figure	7	0	5.55	.02
Transparencies	8	2	2.68	.10
Tiny head	3	0		
Crossed eyes	0	0		
Teeth	5	3		
Short arms	11	3	3.85	.05
Long arms	6	1		
Arms clinging to body	4	2		
Big hands	5	0	3.31	.10
Hands cut off	11	3	3.85	.05
Legs together	3	2		
Genitals	2	0		
Monster, grotesque	3	1		
Three figures	4	0		
Sun*	5	7		
Clouds	6	1		
Figure cut off by paper*	3	3		
No eyes	2	0		
No nose	6	2		
No mouth	4	0		
No body	4	0		
No arms	4	0		
No legs	0	0		
No feet	7	2		
No neck	7	0	5.66	.02

* Item was not clinically valid and was therefore omitted from list of Emotional Indicators.

Emotional Indicators is shown in *Appendix E. Appendix F* lists the 30 Emotional Indicators and the age levels at which they become clinically valid for boys and girls.

The diagnostic significance of the 30 Emotional Indicators appears to be greatly enhanced when the total number of such signs on a given HFD is considered instead of each item separately. *Table 14* shows the number of subjects in *Group A* and *Group B* who had 0, 1, 2, 3, or 4 Emotional Indicators on their drawings. It was found that 58 of the 76 subjects in *Group B,* or three-fourths of all well-adjusted pupils, exhibited no Emotional Indicators at all on their HFDs. Only seven of the clinic patients in *Group A* drew figures without Emotional Indicators (Chi-square 67.19, P< .001). Fifty-five or three-fourths of the children with emotional problems in *Group A* showed two or more Emotional Indicators on their HFDs compared to only four subjects in Group B (Chi-square 69.26, P< .001).

Table 14. Number of Emotional Indicators on
HFDs of Clinic Patients (Group A) and
Well-Adjusted Pupils (Group B)

Number of Emotional Indicators	Group A	Group B
0	7	58
1	14	14
2	23	4
3	22	0
4	10	0
	76	76

The findings in this study offer support for the two hypotheses tested. Thirty of the 32 items investigated were shown to be clinically valid Emotional Indicators. They occurred more often on the HFDs of psychiatric patients than on the drawings of well-adjusted pupils. HFDs of children with emotional problems were also shown to have a significantly higher number of Emotional Indicators than drawings of children without serious emotional problems.

Some Emotional Indicators occur very rarely on any HFDs. This fact may actually enhance their clinical validity. The items "grotesque figure," "omission of mouth," "omission of body," and "omission of arms" are cases in point. Vane and Eisen (1963) found that these particular items were able to predict emotional adjustment in kindergarten. When a HFD shows none of the 30 Emotional Indicators, then it seems likely that the child is free from serious emotional problems. The presence of only one Emotional Indicator on a HFD appears to be inconclusive and is not necessarily a sign of emotional disturbance. An equal number of clinic patients and well-adjusted pupils showed one Emotional Indicator on their drawings. However, two or more Emotional Indicators on a HFD are highly suggestive of emotional problems and unsatisfactory interpersonal relationships. The present study did not explore the degree of disturbance reflected by the different Emotional Indicators, nor did it determine the clinical meaning of each such item. It may be assumed that Emotional Indicators which occur exclusively on HFDs of clinic patients, and not on drawings of well-adjusted pupils, (e.g., tiny figure, big hands, omission of mouth) are diagnostically more significant than those items which are found to some extent on the HFDs of well-adjusted and poorly adjusted children (e.g., teeth, clinging arms, legs together).

Relationship between Emotional Indicators on HFDs and behavior symptoms

The preceding study showed that 30 Emotional Indicators on HFDs (*Appendix E*) can differentiate between the drawings of clinic patients and well-adjusted children. The clinic patients who served as subjects showed a wide variety of emotional problems and symptoms. They had been selected from the writer's clinical file solely on the basis of age, sex and IQ scores in order to match the well-adjusted pupils. In the following study, the subjects were chosen on the basis of their behavior and symptoms. The purpose of this investigation was to discover whether any of the 30 Emotional Indicators on HFDs are related to specific types of behavior or symptoms in children.

The Emotional Indicators on HFDs are believed to reflect a child's attitudes and concerns just as his overt behavior and symptoms reveal much of his underlying attitudes and anxieties. A child who is overtly aggressive may be assumed to be impulsive, frustrated and angry, while an extremely shy and withdrawn child can be assumed to be lacking in self-confidence. The shy child is probably less impulsive than the overtly aggressive child, but he is apt to be anxious, self-depreciating, and unable to reach out toward others. It is hypothesized that the child who directs his frustration and anger toward others and is overtly aggressive will differ from the withdrawn child not only in his behavior but also in the type of Emotional Indicators he will reveal on his HFD. Similarly, it was hypothesized that children who steal from others will show different Emotional Indicators on their HFDs than the children who direct their hostility and anxieties against themselves and develop psychosomatic symptoms.

The subjects for the present studies were 114 psychiatric patients (82 boys and 32 girls) who showed any one of the following symptoms: (1) overt aggressiveness toward others including biting, kicking, hitting, etc.; (2) extreme shyness or depression and withdrawal; (3) neurotic stealing (very deprived children who stole from necessity or youngsters who were members of a gang and who stole to meet their peers' approval were not included in this study); and (4) a history of psychosomatic complaints (including gastrointestinal upsets, asthma, dizzy spells and headaches, etc. and tics). Most of the aggressive youngsters and those who stole had been referred by the juvenile court to a diagnostic center where they were seen by the writer for evaluation. Most of the boys and girls with psychosomatic complaints had been patients at a children's hospital and were referred to the child guidance clinic for psychological evaluation after the physicians had been unable to find any physical basis for the children's problems. The majority of shy children had difficulties at home and in school and were brought to the guidance clinic by their parents for evaluation and treatment.

The age range for all of the subjects was from 5 years 0 months to 12 years 11 months. Their IQ scores on the WISC and the Stanford-Binet Scale ranged from borderline to the superior level. None of them had an IQ score below 70 and none had any gross physical impairment. The subjects represented a wide range of socio-economic backgrounds and included members of various cultural and racial groups.

Within the group of 114 subjects, it was possible to match 31 youngsters who were shy and withdrawn with 31 other children who were overtly aggressive. These 31 pairs of subjects included 20 pairs of boys and 11 pairs of girls; they were matched for age, sex, and IQ scores. Another 35 of the subjects, with a history of stealing, were matched for age, sex, and IQ scores with 35 children who suffered from psychosomatic complaints. The 35 pairs of matched subjects included 27 pairs of boys and 8 pairs of girls. There was some overlap among the two sets of matched pairs. Nine of the shy children also showed psychosomatic complaints, while nine of the aggressive subjects were also among the youngsters who had stolen.

The HFD Test had been administered individually to all subjects by the writer in the guidance clinic or in the diagnostic center at the time of their psychological evaluation. For the present study, the HFDs were drawn from the clinic file and were checked for the presence of the 30 Emotional Indicators. Chi-squares were computed comparing the number of children among the shy and the aggressive subjects who showed each Emotional Indicator on their HFD. The same was done for the youngsters who had psychosomatic complaints and who had stolen.

Comparison of HFDs of shy and aggressive children

Table 15 shows the results when HFDs of shy and aggressive children were compared (Koppitz, 1966b). It was found that no one-to-one relationship exists between any of the Emotional Indicators on HFDs and either shy or overtly aggressive behavior. None of the Emotional Indicators appeared on all of the drawings of either group of subjects. It is therefore not possible to say that the absence of a given Emotional Indicator on a HFD shows that the child is *not* shy or *not* aggressive. However, some of the Emotional Indicators appeared significantly more often on the drawings of the shy or the aggressive children respectively. These particular indicators do seem to reflect attitudes that are associated with these specific types of behavior.

According to the data on *Table 15,* shy and depressed children tend to draw more often "tiny figures" than aggressive children; they also omit more frequently the mouth, the nose, and the eyes, and show more often on their HFDs "cut off hands." These findings seem to illustrate almost literally the shy child's feeling of smallness and insignificance, and his difficulty in reaching out toward others and in communicating with them either verbally or through physical contact. The lack of hands on HFDs underlines the helplessness so often observed in shy and depressed youngsters. In accord with psychoanalytic theory, the omission of the nose on a figure drawing is often interpreted as a sign of castration anxiety. This may be appropriate for some children, but in many cases, the omission of the nose seems to reveal above all withdrawal and fear of "sticking one's nose out," so to speak. The child who omits the nose from his HFD, who "pulls in" his nose may be likened to a snail who pulls in its "feelers" and retreats into its own shell. Whichever way one chooses to interpret the omission of the nose from a HFD, it does seem to reflect anxiety and feelings of inadequacy. *Plate 5* shows an example of a shy child's HFDs.

Once again, it must be emphasized that not all shy subjects in this study drew small figures, nor did they all omit the nose and the mouth or cut the hands from the arms. And not all children who drew small figures or who left off the hands or nose were necessarily withdrawn at all times.

Table 15.   Emotional Indicators on HFDs of Shy and Aggressive Children

Emotional Indicators	Shy Ss	Aggressive Ss	χ^2	P
Poor integration	5	10		
Shading face	0	1		
Shading body, limbs	2	1		
Shading hands, neck	4	3		
Asymmetry of limbs	0	6	4.61	.05
Slanting figure	6	6		
Tiny figure	7	2	2.10	.10
Big figure	0	3		
Transparencies	1	4		
Tiny head	2	2		
Crossed eyes	0	1		
Teeth	0	6	4.61	.05
Short arms	8	5		
Long arms	0	8	7.03	.01
Clinging arms	1	2		
Big hands	0	5	3.48	.05
Hands cut off	15	5	5.98	.02
Legs together	0	1		
Genitals	0	4	2.40	.10
Monster, grotesque	0	1		
Three figures	0	0		
Clouds	1	1		
No eyes	1	0		
No nose	7	2	2.10	.10
No mouth	5	0	3.48	.05
No body	1	1		
No arms	1	3		
No legs	0	0		
No feet	6	4		
No neck	2	3		

These Emotional Indicators were also found on the HFDs of some of the aggressive subjects, though their occurrence was infrequent. Human beings are rarely motivated by only one attitude to the exclusion of all other attitudes; they never act only in one manner, e.g., shy or aggressive. Instead, they combine within themselves many conflicting and contradictory attitudes and needs which may be reflected on their HFDs. Even if one attitude dominates a child at a given time, others may persist in the unconscious and may not become apparent until some time later on. A shy and withdrawn child may at times be quite aggressive and an overtly aggressive child may have periods of withdrawal and depression.

Plate 2 shows the HFD of Simon, age 7, a very anxious and usually shy, brain injured boy of low average intelligence. Simon was rejected by his peers because of a speech defect, awkwardness, and unpredictable behavior. Most of the time, Simon withdrew into a world of fantasy and played by himself. But every now and then, he would try to reach out toward others. Observation and other projective tests showed clearly that Simon was highly ambivalent toward other children. He resented their rejection of him and he was envious of their accomplishments; at the same time he desperately longed to be accepted by them and wanted to make friends with them. At times, Simon would be overwhelmed by simultaneous feelings of affection and hostility which expressed themselves in rather aggressive actions of "loving" other children. On one such occasion, Simon walked up to the unsuspecting Bobby and tried to "love" him; he hugged and kissed Bobby and pinched his arm until it bled and bit a chunk from his ear. Bobby's enraged mother complained bitterly about the "vicious and aggressive" child and was disbelieving when told that Simon was not vicious but rather shy and withdrawn most of the time. Simon himself did not understand all the fuss he had stirred up, he insisted that Bobby was his friend and that he had only wanted to "love" him.

Needless to say, Simon was not included among the subjects of this study because he showed both shy *and* aggressive behavior. All of the children whose HFDs were used in the study showed overwhelmingly one or the other type of behavior and not both. Simon's HFD is presented here to illustrate how conflicting attitudes of shyness and aggression can be revealed in a single drawing. *Plate 2* shows a tiny, heavily shaded figure which reflects intense anxiety, feelings of inadequacy and withdrawal. It also shows a marked slant and poor integration which are associated with a lack of balance and impulsivity which is typical of many aggressive children. Simon's little figure has no arms, a sign which occurred somewhat more often on HFDs of the aggressive children than on the drawings of the shy children. Omission of arms is believed to reflect primarily guilt and anxiety over the misuse or poor performance of the arms and hands.

Slanting of figure and the omission of feet were found fairly often on the HFDs of both the shy and the aggressive subjects of the present study, suggesting that both groups are a bit "off balance" and are lacking in sure footing. However, poor integration of parts and gross asymmetry of limbs occurred more often on the drawings of the aggressive children. Both these signs indicate impulsivity and poor coordination. It may be significant that all of the subjects who revealed these signs on their HFDs also had a history of cortical malfunctioning which may have contributed to their explosiveness and aggressiveness. None of the well-adjusted pupils on *Table 13* revealed poor integration or gross asymmetry of their HFDs. It is believed that these two signs do not reflect hostility or aggressiveness as such, but rather that they reveal a poorly integrated individual who may easily become overtly aggressive when frustrated.

Plate 6 shows the HFD of an aggressive child who drew long arms and big hands. These Emotional Indicators, long arms and big hands, as well as teeth, occurred significantly more often on the HFDs of the aggressive children than on the drawings of the shy children. These three items seem to reflect aggressive and acting out behavior. None of these items were present on the protocols of the shy children. But since a certain degree of aggressiveness is normal and often desirable in our competitive society, it is not surprising that some of the well-adjusted and outgoing children also drew figures with teeth and long arms. (Group B, *Table 13*). These particular items undoubtedly reveal some degree of aggressiveness, but the extent of this aggressiveness and the kind of behavior a child will display in expressing his aggressiveness may vary greatly and cannot be deducted from his HFD.

Genitals and transparencies occurred more often on the drawings of the aggressive youngsters. The presence of genitals on the HFDs of some of the aggressive children is believed to reflect primarily impulsivity and body anxiety. Transparencies on the figure drawings may indicate either a body anxiety or a kind of concretism found so often in young children or in those with neurological impairment. These two Emotional Indicators are not considered to be signs of aggressiveness per se, but may well show underlying impulsivity and anxiety which can contribute to a child's frustration and anger, and hence may become associated with overt aggressiveness.

The total number of Emotional Indicators found on the HFDs of all the aggressive youngsters exceeded that of the shy subjects. The incidence of Emotional Indicators on the individual HFDs was also higher for the overtly aggressive subjects than for the shy ones.

Comparison of HFDs of children with psychosomatic complaints and of those who steal

Table 16 shows the results when the HFDs of 35 clinic patients with a history of psychosomatic complaints were compared with the drawings of 35 youngsters who had been known to steal. The data on *Table 16* indicate that both groups of subjects are poorly integrated, unstable, and anxious. They reveal equally often shading of body and limbs, poor integration, hands cut off from the arms, tiny figure, slanting figure, and omission of feet. However, the children with psychosomatic complaints tend to turn their anxiety and hostility primarily toward themselves and only indirectly toward others who worry about them; whereas, the children who steal direct their aggression toward others and only indirectly toward themselves in that they usually see to it that they get caught and punished.

There were also a few significant differences between the HFDs of the two groups of subjects. The drawings of the children with psychosomatic complaints revealed more often the following Emotional Indicators: short arms, legs pressed together, omission of the nose and the mouth, and clouds. Of course, no single child showed all of these indicators on his drawing. But taken together, these five Emotional Indicators give a very graphic illustration of the kind of child who develops psychosomatic symptoms. We get a picture of a constricted individual who is withdrawn into himself and has "pulled in" his arms and nose; he has pressed his legs together tightly into a posture of defensive immobility and is unable or unwilling to communicate with others; he stands anxiously under a black cloud, that is, he feels threatened by powerful forces outside himself in the environment.

Table 16.   Emotional Indicators on HFDs of Children with a History of Psychosomatic Complaints and Stealing

Emotional Indicators	Psychosomatic Complaints	Stealing	χ^2	P
Poor integration	6	7		
Shading, face	0	1		
Shading, body, limbs	4	6		
Shading, hands, neck	3	6		
Asymmetry of limbs	2	2		
Slanting figure	5	8		
Tiny figure	6	6		
Big figure	0	2		
Transparencies	1	3		
Tiny head	0	3		
Crossed eyes	1	1		
Teeth	2	2		
Short arms	10	3	4.12	.05
Long arms	4	5		
Clinging arms	2	3		
Big hands	0	5	3.45	.05
Hands cut off	8	9		
Legs together	3	0		
Genitals	0	0		
Monster, grotesque	2	3		
Three or more figures	0	0		
Clouds	4	0	2.39	.10
No eyes	2	1		
No nose	4	0	2.39	.10
No mouth	3	1		
No body	0	3		
No arms	1	4		
No legs	0	1		
No feet	4	3		
No neck	0	8	6.91	.01

The HFDs of the children with a history of stealing differed from the drawings of subjects with psychosomatic complaints on the following Emotional Indicators: shading of hands and/or neck, tiny head, big hands, omission of body, omission of arms, and the omission of neck. The tiny head seems to indicate that neurotic children who steal tend to feel more often intellectually inadequate, while the other Emotional Indicators suggest that they experience a great deal of hostility, anxiety, and guilt about their action. Twenty-four of the 35 subjects in this group put special emphasis on the hands of their figures by shading them or by drawing big hands or by cutting them off or by omitting the arms and hands altogether. All of these signs are variations on the same theme. It is important to realize that similar attitudes and anxieties can be expressed in several different ways on HFDs.

The children who stole showed a higher incidence of omission of body and omission of neck on their HFDs. These two items are not thought to be related to stealing as such, but reflect body anxiety and poor impulse control. The findings suggest that children with poor impulse control are more apt to steal, whereas less impulsive children may develop psycho-somatic symptoms when they get frustrated and are angry.

Emotional Indicators on HFDs and school achievement

It was demonstrated (Koppitz, 1966a) that the 30 Emotional Indicators can differentiate between the HFDs of psychiatric patients and of outstanding pupils with good social and emotional adjustment. However, both groups of subjects used in that study were quite atypical and represent only a small percentage of any normal elementary school population. Most youngsters are neither as outstanding as the well-adjusted subjects nor as disturbed as the psychiatric patients. It cannot be assumed, therefore, that the 30 Emotional Indicators can differentiate between the HFDs of the average run of good and poor students in public school as well as they can differentiate between the drawings of children with and without serious emotional problems. Although there is, of course, a positive relationship between emotional adjustment and scholastic achievement, it does not follow that all good students are free from emotional problems while all poor students are emotionally disturbed.

Several studies were designed to determine whether the 30 Emotional Indicators were related to school achievement of pupils in regular elementary school classes and in special classes.

Relationship of Emotional Indicators on HFDs and school achievement in kindergarten through fourth grade

The subjects for the present study were 313 children, age 5 to 10, of whom 180 were good students and 133 were poor students. They attended 23 regular classes, kindergarten through fourth grade, in seven schools in six different areas representing lower, middle, and upper middle-class communities.

During the first month of the school year, the 23 classroom teachers administered the HFD Test to their classes. All HFDs were checked by the writer for the presence of the 30 Emotional Indicators. At the end of the school year, the teachers of five first grades and five second grades administered the Metropolitan Achievement Test (Hildreth, 1946) to their classes, which was then scored by a qualified psychologist. The 49 first graders who obtained a grade placement of 2.4 or higher on the Metropolitan Test were designated as good students, while the 29 subjects with a test score of 1.7 or less were called poor students. The 51 second graders with a grade placement of 3.4 or better were considered to be good students, whereas the 32 children with a score of 2.7 or less on the Metropolitan Test were included among the poor students. The teachers of the remaining 13 classes (two each of kindergarten and first grade, and three each of second, third and fourth grades) were asked to name the six or seven students in their classes whom they ranked highest and lowest in regard to academic achievement and social adjustment.

Thereafter, the HFDs of the subjects with good Achievement Test scores and high teacher ratings were compared with those of the children with

Table 17. Emotional Indicators on HFDs and School Achievement

Emotional Indicators	Kindergarten Teacher Ratings				1st & 2nd Grades Teacher Ratings				1st Grade Met. Ach. Test				2nd Grade Met. Ach. Test			
	Good	Poor	χ^2	P	Good	Poor	χ^2	P	Good	Poor	χ^2	P	Good	Poor	χ^2	P
N	13	13			29	31			49	29			51	32		
Poor integration	—	—			0	5	3.21	.10	—	—			1	7	6.84	.01
Slanting figure	0	2	2.98	.10	1	3			1	5	4.02	.05	0	4	4.28	.05
No mouth	0	4	4.51	.05	1	0			1	2			0	0		
No body	1	7			0	2			0	6	8.34	.01	0	0		
No arms	1	1			0	1			1	5	4.02	.05	2	4		
Monster	0	0			0	1			0	1			0	0		
Three figures	0	0			0	6	4.27	.05	0	7	10.21	.01	0	0		
Number of Emotional Indicators																
0 or 1	10	1	10.09	.01	24	16	5.21	.05	35	11	7.12	.01	47	17	14.85	.01
2 or more	3	12			5	15			14	18			4	15		

low Achievement Test scores and low teacher ratings. Chi-squares were computed for the good and poor students who showed each of the Emotional Indicators on their HFDs and for the total number of Emotional Indicators found on their drawings. *Table 17* shows the Emotional Indicators for whom the Chi-square values were statistically significant and which were therefore found to be related to school achievement. Since the HFDs of three different groups of first and second graders were investigated in this study, a comparison of the data on *Table 17* for the three groups can serve as a cross-validation study. The results can be summarized as follows:

Kindergarten: Only the omission of the body and the omission of the mouth on HFDs distinguished the good from the poor kindergarten pupils. In addition, the total number of Emotional Indicators on the HFDs proved to be diagnostically highly significant. Twelve of the 13 poor students showed two or more Emotional Indicators on their drawings compared to only three of the 13 good pupils.

First and second grades: Five Emotional Indicators (poor integration of parts, slanting figure, omission of the body and the arms, and three or more figures spontaneously drawn) differentiated between the HFDs of the good and poor pupils in the first two grades. Poor integration is, of course, not a valid Emotional Indicator until boys are seven years old and girls six years old (*Appendix E*). Therefore, this item did not apply and was not scored on the HFDs of most of the beginning first graders. However, poor integration of parts was able to differentiate between the drawings of the good and poor second graders.

Slanting figure was found more often on the HFDs of the poor students in all groups of subjects. Only very immature or seriously disturbed young children omit the body from their HFD. This Emotional Indicator is extremely rare among school-age children and was only found on the drawings of poor first graders. Omission of the arms was revealed more often on the HFDs of poor students in both the first and second grades. Three or more figures spontaneously drawn is another immature sign on HFDs and occurred exclusively on the drawings of poor first graders. Monster or grotesque figures were drawn too rarely to make statistical computation meaningful, but this Emotional Indicator was found only on the HFDs of the poor pupils. The HFDs of about half of the poor students exhibited two or more Emotional Indicators, whereas only one-fifth of the good students showed more than one such sign on their drawings.

Third and fourth grades: None of the 30 Emotional Indicators were able to differentiate between the HFDs of the good and poor pupils in the third and fourth grades. All Emotional Indicators were extremely rare on the drawings of these children. There was also no significant difference between the number of Emotional Indicators revealed on the HFDs of the pupils with high and low achievement. Only about one-third of the poor students showed two or more Emotional Indicators on their drawings.

The present findings are in accord with those of other investigators. Vane and Eisen (1962) reported that four items on HFDs could predict adjustment at the end of kindergarten. These four items (omission of the mouth, the body and the arms, and grotesque figure) were also among the seven Emotional Indicators which were found to be related to school achievement among the school beginners in the present study. It appears therefore that the presence of the following seven Emotional Indicators on HFDs can be used with some degree of confidence for predicting difficulty in learning and adjustment in kindergarten and the first two grades: Poor integration of parts on the drawings of second graders reflects poor coordination, poor integrative ability and/or impulsivity, all of which will affect schoolwork. Slanting figure seems to be a sign of instability and imbalance which interferes with academic achievement. Omission of the body and omission of the arms on HFDs of school-age children suggest immaturity, retardation or serious emotional problems. The omission of the mouth indicates feelings of intense inadequacy, resentment and withdrawal. Monster or grotesque figures are only drawn by children with extremely poor self-concepts whose self-depreciation keeps them from doing as well as they might do in school. Three or more figures spontaneously drawn reveal perseveration or immaturity. This Emotional Indicator refers always to the number of figures presented irrespective of the quality of the figures. The individual figures may be quite primitive as on *Plate 7* or more adequate as shown on *Plate 8*.

McHugh (1964) was unable to find any significant differences between the HFDs of good and poor second and fourth grade pupils. She examined four items on the drawings: large head, small figure, short arms, and weak arms. The present study confirms McHugh's findings; these particular items on HFDs are not related to school achievement. There seems to be a consensus that HFDs fail to differentiate between public school-children with high and low achievement above the second grade level. Neither the present study nor Bennett (1964) nor Bradfield (1964) obtained any significant results with drawings of pupils in grades three to six. Thus, it appears that specific signs or Emotional Indicators on HFDs are only of value for predicting school achievement among children at the kindergarten level and in the first two grades. In the higher grades, achievement depends on many factors other than a child's attitudes and self-concept as reflected on HFDs.

These results do not necessarily invalidate Machover's hypothesis for HFDs, as was suggested in the papers of Bennett, Bradfield and McHugh, they rather indicate that hypotheses derived from adult psychiatric patients do not readily apply to normal elementary school pupils. Psychiatric patients are so atypical that it is incorrect to assume that public school-children with low scores on achievement tests or low teacher ratings can be equated with them. The only group of children in public schools who resemble psychiatric patients are the pupils enrolled in special classes for children with emotional and/or neurological problems. Many of these special class pupils are in fact, or should be, receiving psychiatric treatment in mental health clinics or by private clinicians.

Emotional Indicators on HFDs of special class pupils

A special study was conducted to investigate the HFDs of special class pupils. The subjects for this study were 139 children, age 6 to 10, who were attending special public school classes for children with emotional problems and/or brain injury. The IQ range of all 139 subjects was from 70–138 with an IQ Mean score of 94. All of the children were poor students and had serious learning problems. Most of them also had severe behavior disorders and emotional difficulties.

It was possible to match the age and sex of 78 special class pupils with those of 78 good students from the preceding study. The HFDs of these 78 pairs of subjects were compared for the presence of the 30 Emotional Indicators. Chi-squares were computed for each of the Emotional Indicators. In addition the total number of Emotional Indicators on the HFDs of each of the 139 special class pupils was investigated.

Table 18.   Emotional Indicators on HFDs of Special Class Pupils and Good Students

Emotional Indicator	Special Class	Good Pupils	χ^2	P
Poor integration	25	0	27.44	.01
Slanting figure	9	3	2.26	.10
No mouth	6	2		
No body	13	0	12.09	.01
No arms	12	1	8.39	.01
Monster, grotesque	4	0	2.31	.10
Three figures	3	0		
Asymmetry of limbs	7	0	5.39	.05
Tiny figure	9	2	3.52	.05
Short arms	11	3	3.84	.05
Big hands	5	0	3.31	.05
Hands cut off	14	5	3.83	.05
No nose	11	3	3.84	.05
Number of Emotional Indicators				
0 or 1	25	66		
			42.19	.01
2 or more	53	12		

Table 18 shows the results of the first part of this study. The seven Emotional Indicators (poor integration of parts, slanting figure, omission of mouth, omission of body, omission of arms, monster or grotesque figure, and three or more figures) which had appeared significantly more often on the HFDs of poor school beginners than on the drawings of good students (*Table 17*) also consistently occurred more often on the HFDs of the special class pupils. The great frequency of poor integration on the HFDs of all special class pupils is probably related to the high incidence of brain injury among this group of subjects. Poor integration of parts is not unusual on drawings of children with neurological impairment (page 171).

In addition to the seven Emotional Indicators related to school achievement, the HFDs of the special class pupils showed consistently more often six other Emotional Indicators: Asymmetry of limbs, tiny figure, short arms, big hands, hands cut off, and omission of nose. Since these particular items did not differentiate between the good and poor students in regular classes (*Table 17*), it may be assumed that they are not related to school achievement but rather reflect the children's emotional attitudes and problems. By definition, the special class pupils exhibit both learning and behavior problems. It is therefore not surprising that their HFDs reveal many different kinds of Emotional Indicators, some of which are more closely associated with academic achievement and some with emotional maladjustments.

The Emotional Indicators on the HFDs of the 78 special class pupils resemble rather closely the Emotional Indicators on the drawings of the psychiatric patients discussed earlier (*Table 13*). In both cases, the subjects included children with a variety of problems and symptoms; thus it is not unexpected that their HFDs reveal attitudes of both aggressiveness and withdrawal, and of impulsivity as well as timidity.

Table 18 shows that two-thirds of the 78 special class pupils showed two or more Emotional Indicators on their HFDs, while less than one-sixth of the 78 good pupils revealed more than one such indicator on their drawings.

When the HFDs of all 139 special class pupils were analyzed for the number of Emotional Indicators they revealed, the following results were obtained:

Number of Emotional Indicators	Number of Special Class Pupils					
	Age 6	Age 7	Age 8	Age 9	Age 10	Total
0 or 1	7	10	12	9	8	46
2 or more	15	25	22	18	13	93
	22	35	34	27	21	139

At each age level tested, about two-thirds of the special class students exhibited two or more Emotional Indicators on their drawings. In the earlier study (*Table 14*), it was shown that 70% of the clinic patients had two or more Emotional Indicators on their HFDs. In the present study, the same was true for 67% of the 139 special class pupils, compared to 53% of the 133 poor students in regular classes, and 19% of the 180 good students. Two or more Emotional Indicators on a HFD are thought to reveal the presence of some emotional problems. It would appear therefore that emotional problems are found in most clinic patients and special class students, whereas pupils in regular classes with poor achievement may or may not be suffering from emotional maladjustment. About one-fifth of all good students may also show signs of emotional problems.

As was pointed out earlier (page 42), a single Emotional Indicator on a HFD is inconclusive, unless it happens to be one of the seven Emotional Indicators related to school achievement (*Table 17*). The mere presence of one sign of anxiety or aggressiveness on a HFD is not in itself an indication of emotional disturbance. Anxiety and aggressiveness in moderation may actually serve as motivating forces for good achievement, while a total absence of anxiety or aggressiveness may impede the drive for success and achievement. Only when anxiety and aggressiveness are extreme or more than the child can cope with do they become paralyzing and interfere with academic success. Thus, it was found that some signs of anxiety, e.g., shading of figure or clouds, were present to some extent on HFDs of both good and poor students. The same applied to indicators of aggressiveness, e.g., teeth. The diagnostic value of each Emotional Indicator is greatly enhanced when it is combined with one or more other Emotional Indicators on the same HFD.

Interpretation of Emotional Indicators on HFDs

In the preceding sections of this chapter, the clinical validity of the 30 Emotional Indicators was demonstrated by showing their ability to differentiate between the HFDs of groups of children with and without various types of problems. Relatively little has been said about the meaning of each individual Emotional Indicator. At this time, the Emotional Indicators on HFDs will be analyzed for their specific meanings. An attempt will be made to integrate the writer's findings and to relate these to the hypotheses and research data reported by other investigators, notably Machover (1949, 1958, 1960), Levy (1963), Hammer (1963), and Jolles (1952, 1953).

There appears to be a consensus among the experts on HFDs that no one-to-one relationship exists between any single sign on HFDs and a definite personality trait or behavior on part of the boy or girl making the drawing. Anxieties, conflicts or attitudes can be expressed on HFDs in different ways by different children or by one child at different times. This writer can only underscore what others have emphasized again and again: It is not possible to make a meaningful diagnosis or evaluation of a child's behavior or difficulties on the basis of any single sign on a HFD. The *total* drawing and the combination of various signs and indicators should always be considered and should then be analyzed on the basis of the child's age, maturation, emotional status, social and cultural background and should then be evaluated together with other available test data.

The following discussion of the meaning of individual Emotional Indicators on HFDs does not represent an effort to create another handy "cookbook" for the interpretation of drawings. The "cookbook" approach to drawing analysis is considered here deplorable, since it is often employed mechanically by less well trained or less experienced examiners. In the "cookbook" method you look up the meaning of each sign and come up with a ready made diagnosis without regard for the total figure drawn and irrespective of the child's age, sex, intelligence, and social-cultural background. The circumstances under which the drawing was produced are also ignored.

Table 19 summarizes the findings of the various studies on Emotional Indicators presented earlier in this volume along with the results of an investigation of HFDs of brain injured children which follows later on (page 158). A look at the data on *Table 19* shows clearly that some of the Emotional Indicators have greater diagnostic value than others. Each Emotional Indicator will be discussed here separately:

Table 19. Summary of Findings on Emotional Indicators on HFDs of Children

Emotional Indicators	Emot. Probl.	Shy	Aggressive	Psycho-somatic	Stealing	Brain Injury	Poor Sch. Ach.	Special Class
Integration	X		O			X	X	X
Shading face	O							
Shading body	X	O			O			
Shading hands	X				O			
Asymmetry	X		X			X		X
Slanting figure	X				O	X	X	X
Tiny figure	X	X				X		X
Big figure	X		O		O			
Transparency	X		O		O	X		
Tiny head	O				O			
Crossed eyes								
Teeth	O		X					
Short arms	X	O		X				X
Long arms	O		X					
Clinging arms	O							
Big hands	X		X		X			X
Hands cut off	X	X				X		X
Legs together	O			O				
Genitals	O		X					
Monster	O						O	X
Three figures	O						X	O
Clouds	O			X				
No eyes	O							
No nose	O	X		X				X
No mouth	O	X		O			O	O
No body	O				O	X	X	X
No arms	O		O		O		X	X
No legs								
No feet	O	O						
No neck	X				X	X		

X: Item occurs significantly more often on HFDs of group indicated.
O: Item occurs more often on HFDs of group indicated.

Poor integration of parts of figure (Plates 2, 6, 14) is a common phenomenon on HFDs of young and immature children. This sign was not found to be a valid Emotional Indicator before age 7 for boys and age 6 for girls. From then on, poor integration was shown frequently on the HFDs of clinic patients, overtly aggressive children, poor school beginners, special class pupils, and most particularly on the drawings of brain injured youngsters. It did not occur on any of the HFDs of the well-adjusted pupils and the good students. Poor integration appears to be associated with any one or several of the following: instability, a poorly integrated personality, poor coordination or impulsivity. Poor integration seems to indicate immaturity on the part of the child which may be the result of a developmental lag, neurological impairment, regression due to serious emotional disturbance or all of these. It is impossible to determine which of these factors are involved in any given case purely on the basis of this one Emotional Indicator on a HFD.

The present findings are consistent with the results of other investigators who worked with drawings of adult patients. Reznikoff and Tomblen (1956) found that poor integration of figure drawings was associated with organicity in adults. Hammer attributes poor synthesis of HFDs to emotional disturbances, while Machover proposes that it is due either to organicity or mental retardation.

Shading on HFDs, according to all experts, is a manifestation of anxiety, and the degree of shading shown is thought to be related to the intensity of the anxiety within the child. The present findings concur with Machover's observation that shading on HFDs is normal for young children and is not necessarily a sign of psychopathology. But as the children get older, shading on HFDs takes on a considerable diagnostic significance. The only exception to this rule is the shading of the face which is highly significant at all times.

Shading of the face on HFDs is quite unusual at any age level and is therefore a valid Emotional Indicator for all children age 5 to 12. This item was observed mostly on drawings of clinic patients and on some HFDs of the children who were overtly aggressive and who stole. Two different types of shading of the face were noted. The first type consisted of shading of the entire face (*Plates 28 and 96*). In some cases, the shading was so heavy that all facial features were obliterated (*Plate 25c*). Shading of the entire face was invariably produced by seriously disturbed children who were overcome by anxiety and who had a very poor self-concept.

On the second type of HFDs, the shading of the face was limited to only a part of face (e.g., the mouth, nose, eyes). Children who exhibited this kind of shading on their drawings were usually less severely disturbed than the ones who shaded the entire face. Partial shading of the face seems to reflect specific anxieties about those features that are shaded or about their functions. *Plate 3* shows the HFD of Max, age 7, a boy of normal intelligence. Max was the only child of a domineering and ambitious mother who smothered him with affection and overwhelmed him with demands. Max was a very immature and dependent youngster with an infantile lisp. Every time Max opened his mouth to speak, his mother corrected his pronunciation. As a result, Max became very sensitive about his speech and began to stammer. The heavy shading on the lower portion of the face on the drawing on *Plate 3* clearly shows the boy's concern and anxiety about his speech.

Similar drawings were obtained from other children with speech difficulties, who were anxious about their speech problem. Children with speech defects who were not especially bothered by their problem did not shade the mouth area on their HFD. These findings are in accord with Hammer's observation that shading of the face on HFDs indicates discontent with oneself.

Shading of body and/or limbs (*Plates 6, 9, 15, 28*) is common for girls through age 7 and for boys through age 8. This item is not considered a valid Emotional Indicator until age 8 and 9 respectively. The writer concurs with Machover that the implications of shading on HFDs are not altered by the fact that it is so common. Shading of the body on a HFD reveals body anxiety. But such anxiety is normal among school beginners who are just becoming aware of bodily differences and of body functions. Therefore, shading of the body cannot be considered a sign of psychopathology for this age group. However, if shading persists up to and beyond the age of 8 for girls and 9 for boys, then it becomes clinically meaningful. Among the older children shading of the body was found significantly more often on the drawings of clinical patients, of children with psychosomatic complaints, and of youngsters who steal.

Machover hypothesized that the shading of arms reflects guilt feelings for aggressive impulses or masturbatory activity, while she attributes the shading of the legs to anxiety about size and physical growth or concern about sexual impulses. The present test results are not incompatible with these claims, but it is important to remember that these interpretations are only hypotheses. It is safe to assume that shading on HFDs reveals general areas of concern but shading does not indicate the specific cause underlying the manifest anxiety. It is not possible to differentiate on the basis of shading of the arms on a HFD between children who suffer from masturbatory anxiety and those who suffer from guilt over stealing. All that can be said with certainty is that a child who shades the arms of his figure suffers from anxiety because of some actual or fancied activity he engaged in with his arms. The nature of this activity has to be determined through other test results, through questioning, or from his behavioral record.

Shading of hands and/or neck (Plates 4, 6, 45) on HFDs does not become a valid Emotional Indicator until age 7 for girls and age 8 for boys. Thereafter, it was found most often on the drawings of clinic patients and of youngsters who steal, but it also occurred on HFDs of shy and of aggressive children. Shading of the hands does not seem to be related to any specific activity but rather to anxiety over some real or imagined activities involving the hands. Similar hypotheses have been stated by Levy, Machover, and Jolles.

Machover's observations regarding shading of the neck on HFDs were also confirmed by the present research findings. All the children who shaded the neck on their HFDs were engaged in noticeable struggles to control their impulses. Some youngsters managed to maintain a rigid and precarious control over them as long as they were not exposed to too much strain and stress. Other children vacillated between impulsivity and overcontrol and went from one extreme to the other. *Plate 4* shows the HFD of Jim, a 9 year old boy of superior intelligence with serious learning problems. He alternated between impulsive acting-out behavior at home and complete withdrawal and day-dreaming in school.

Gross asymmetry of limbs (Plates 7 (figure 2), 14, 25a) was present quite often on the drawings of the clinic patients, the aggressive children, the brain injured subjects, and the special class pupils. None of the good students or shy children revealed this indicator on their drawings. Gross asymmetry of limbs seems to be associated with poor coordination and impulsiveness. In the present research studies, it was noted that gross asymmetry was exhibited only on HFDs of children who had a history of neurological malfunctioning and who showed a number of organic signs on their test protocols. It is not certain if asymmetry of limbs on a HFD is the result of incoordination and poor fine muscle control or if it reflects the child's feeling of not being well coordinated and of being out of balance. Machover hypothesized that a general disturbance in symmetry on a HFD is a neurotic manifestation but also reflects incoordination, physical awkwardness, physical inadequacy or a confusion of lateral dominance.

Figure slanting by 15° or more (Plates 2, 3, 5) occurred significantly more often on the HFDs of clinic patients, brain injured children, poor students, and special class pupils than on the drawings of good students and well-adjusted pupils. It was present on the drawings of both aggressive and shy children, of youngsters with psychosomatic complaints, and of those who steal. Slanting figure on a HFD does not seem to be associated with any specific type of behavior or symptom; it rather suggests a general instability and lack of balance. Similar observations were made by Machover, who hypothesized that a toppling figure reflects feeling of mental imbalance and a personality in flux. Hammer found this indicator on the drawings of pre-schizophrenic adult patients. In the present studies, slanting figure was observed on HFDs of children ranging all the way from mildly upset to severely disturbed. It is not believed that this Emotional Indicator on HFDs reveals pre-schizoid behavior or necessarily very serious disturbances in children. A slanting figure on the drawings of a child seems to indicate an unstable nervous system or a labile personality; above all, it suggests that the child lacks secure footing.

Tiny figure (Plates 2, 4, 5) was found on the HFDs of the clinic patients, brain injured children, special class pupils and the shy youngsters. Tiny figures were rare on drawings of overtly aggressive children. This Emotional Indicator seems to reflect extreme insecurity, withdrawal and depression. While not all depressed and insecure children draw necessarily tiny figures, it can be assumed with a fair degree of confidence that children who draw tiny figures are timid, withdrawn and probably depressed. But the extent of the shyness and depression will not be revealed on the drawing. Some shy children are able to get along fairly well, whereas others are too depressed or withdrawn to be able to function adequately at home or in school.

The present findings are in accord with the observations of other investigators. Machover, Jolles, Levy, and Lewinson (1964) all agree that tiny figure drawings indicate feelings of inadequacy, a shrunken Ego, concern over dealing with the environment, and above all depression.

Big figure, 9" or more in height, (Plates 16, 29, 37) occurs frequently on HFDs of young children and does not attain clinical significance until age 8 for both boys and girls. At that age level and thereafter, big figures were found most often on the drawings of clinic patients, and especially on the HFDs of youngsters who were aggressive and who stole. Big figures appear to be associated with expansiveness, immaturity, and poor inner controls.

Machover hypothesizes that large drawings by adult patients reflect feelings of narcissism and paranoid delusions of grandiosity which are covering up feelings of inadequacy. Large, empty drawings with poor synthesis have also been said to reveal psychopathic tendencies or organicity. The present findings suggest that the drawing of large figures is less pathological for children than it appears to be for adults. However, it was noted that several of the children who produced large figures were quite immature and had a history of cortical malfunctioning. This would support Machover's hypothesis that large, empty figures may indicate organicity.

Transparencies (Plates 28, 53, 82) were revealed significantly more often on the HFDs of the clinic patients and brain injured children than on the drawings of the well-adjusted pupils. Children who stole and who were overtly aggressive drew transparencies more often than shy youngsters and those with psychosomatic complaints. It would appear, therefore, that transparencies on HFDs are associated with immaturity, impulsivity, and acting-out behavior.

Two different types of transparencies were noted on the HFDs of children. Some of the more immature and concretistic youngsters made the outline of a figure, or a skeleton figure, first and then drew clothes around the figure (see *Plate 43*) as if literally clothing a person. While another group of children made quite ordinary HFDs but then focussed on one particular portion of the figure by means of a transparency of a specific and limited area. Quite often, this area is located in the genital region. This specific type of transparency is believed to be akin to shading and indicates anxiety and concern about the particular part of the body revealed by the transparency.

An example of this specific kind of transparency is shown on *Plate 9* which was drawn by Connie, a 10 year old girl of normal intelligence. Connie had aroused the parents of the neighborhood she lived in by initiating other children into the game of "statues." In this game, some children had to disrobe and pose in the nude to be admired and examined by the others. Similar drawings were obtained from other children who had engaged in sexual activities or explorations, and from youngsters who had fantasized about such activities or who had observed sexual behavior which they did not understand and which confused and frightened them.

Machover claims that the concretistic type of transparencies on HFDs are "normal" for children but reflect poor judgment when they occur on the drawings of adults. The present findings do not support the first claim. Transparencies, as defined in this book, (*Appendix D*), were not normal for school-age children. They are unusual but not necessarily pathological. This primitive type of transparency is usually found on the HFDs of impulsive, concretistic, and immature children and on the drawings of youngsters with cortical malfunctioning. Machover further suggests that the drawing of toes within the outline of a foot or shoe shows pathological aggressiveness. This type of transparency seems to be more significant for adult patients than for schoolchildren. The present findings do not support Machover's hypothesis. None of the overtly aggressive children drew toes on their figures, and of the few other children who made such drawings, none could be regarded as pathologically aggressive. Their case histories rather showed that they were impulsive and concretistic youngsters who showed evidence of cortical malfunctioning. Transparencies on feet appear to be no different from other transparencies and can be interpreted in the same manner as they are interpreted.

Transparencies of specific body areas are very definitely not normal on HFDs of school-age children. They usually point to acute anxiety, conflict, or fear, usually in the areas of sex, childbirth or bodily mutilation. Very often, children who draw such specific transparencies are in effect asking for information or reassurance concerning their impulses or experiences. It is felt that this type of transparency on the HFDs should not be ignored since too often it represents an eloquent plea for help from children who are unable to put their anxieties and questions into words.

Tiny head (*Plates 36, 46, 50*) was found rarely on the HFDs of any of the groups of children tested in the present studies. But when this Emotional Indicator did occur, it was exclusively on drawings of clinic patients and maladjusted children. None of the good students or well-adjusted pupils showed tiny heads on their drawings. The presence of a tiny head on a figure seems to indicate intense feelings of intellectual inadequacy on the part of the child.

The present findings do not support Machover's hypothesis for tiny head on the HFDs of adult patients. She suggested that a small head represents the conscious wish of obsessive-compulsive individuals who want to ignore the control of their brain and long to follow the dictates of their impulses. In the present studies, the children who drew tiny heads on their HFDs were not obsessive-compulsive individuals.

Crossed eyes (*Plates 16 and 107*) on HFDs were rare and were found only on the drawings of a few clinic patients. Crossed eyes seem to be drawn only by children who are quite hostile toward others. This type of drawing is interpreted as a reflection of rebellion and anger. In contrast, the drawing of a sideway glance of both eyes (*Plates 5, 13b,c*) was not found to be a clinically valid Emotional Indicator on the HFDs of children. For a fuller discussion of the glance of the eyes, see page 70. When a child draws a figure with crossed eyes he seems to signify that things are out of focus for him, that he does not view the world in the same manner as others do. He is "so mad that he cannot see straight." He cannot or does not wish to conform to the expected ways of behavior.

Teeth (*Plates 35, 60, 61*) were present to a certain extent on the HFDs of the well-adjusted and the poorly adjusted pupils and on some drawings of all groups of clinic patients with one exception. The one exception were the shy children; none of them revealed teeth on their drawings. Since the presence of teeth on HFDs is relatively widespread, it cannot be considered a sign of serious psychopathology. But since it occurred most often on the records of the overtly aggressive children and not at all on drawings of the withdrawn youngsters, it must be concluded that teeth are a sign of aggressiveness, and not only of oral aggression. It is, of course, recognized that not all aggressiveness is unhealthy. A fair amount of aggressiveness is normal in children and even necessary for leadership and achievement. Hence the occurrence of teeth on a HFD cannot be considered a sign of emotional disturbance if no other Emotional Indicators are present on the drawing. But if teeth appear together with other Emotional Indicators on a drawing, then they become diagnostically meaningful and contribute to the total interpretation of the HFD.

Teeth seem to have more serious implications on the drawings of adult patients than on the HFDs of children. Hammer suggests that the presence of teeth may indicate not only oral aggression but also sadistic tendencies. Machover hypothesized that the drawing of teeth on a HFD reveals infantile oral aggression and is frequently found on drawings of simple schizophrenics, emotionally flat adult hysterics, and low-grade defectives. These hypotheses were not found to be valid for the drawings of children.

Short arms (*Plates 15, 34, 56*) were exhibited significantly more often on the HFDs of clinic patients, children with psychosomatic complaints, special class pupils, and shy youngsters. Short arms were also not entirely absent from some of the drawings of the good students. This Emotional Indicator seems to reflect the child's difficulty in reaching out into the world and toward others. It seems to be associated with the tendency to withdraw, to turn inward toward oneself, and to try to inhibit one's impulses. Children who draw short arms tend to be well behaved; in fact, at times they are too well behaved for their own good. Short arms on HFDs of children cannot be interpreted as a sign of lack of ambition, as was suggested by Machover. Short arms may indicate timidity and a lack of aggressiveness and perhaps leadership, but not necessarily a lack in desire for achievement and success. The present findings concur with those of McHugh (1964) who found that children with high and low achievement did not differ significantly on this drawing item.

Long arms (*Plates 6, 29, 36*) were drawn more often by clinic patients than by well-adjusted pupils. HFDs with long arms occurred frequently among the overtly aggressive children and not at all among the shy youngsters. Thus, it appears that long arms on figure drawings are associated with an aggressive reaching out into the environment. These findings are in accord with those of Hammer and Levy. They observed that long arms reflect externally directed aggressive needs. Machover on the other hand hypothesized that long arms reflect ambition for achievement or for acquisition, including striving for love and affection. The present research data fail to support Machover's specific hypotheses. But on one point, all the investigators seem to agree: long arms on HFDs are associated with a reaching out towards others in contrast to the tendency to withdraw which was revealed by short arms on HFDs.

Arms clinging to the side of the body (*Plates 16, 40, 56*) occurred rarely on the HFDs of the children in the present studies. But when this type of treatment of the arms appeared, it was usually, but not exclusively, on the HFDs of the clinic patients. This Emotional Indicator was not found to be associated with any of the specific types of behavior investigated. It seems that arms clinging to the body reflect a rather rigid inner control on part of the child and a difficulty in reaching out toward others. The case histories of the children who drew clinging arms revealed that they were lacking in flexibility and that their interpersonal relationships were poor. When this Emotional Indicator is found on HFDs alone without any of the other Indicators, then it cannot be considered as a sign of serious psychopathology, but when it occurs together with other Emotional Indicators, then it takes on clinical significance.

It appears that arms clinging to the body have more ominous implications on the HFDs of adult patients than on the drawings of children. Machover reports that paranoid and schizophrenic patients often draw arms pressed to the body, as if to protect themselves from the blows of the environment. She hypothesizes that clinging arms reveal a tendency for reserve and withdrawal. Levy suggests that this type of presentation of the arms reflects a deep-seated conflict and brittle control, and is found in passive and very defensive individuals.

Big hands (Plates 6, 58, 71) were found significantly more often on the HFDs of the clinic patients and special class pupils. This Emotional Indicator occurred particularly frequently on the drawings of the overtly aggressive children and of the youngsters who stole. None of the shy children or those with psychosomatic complaints drew large hands. Thus, big hands seem to be associated with aggressive and acting-out behavior involving the hands, either directly as in overt aggression, or indirectly as in stealing. The present findings show that big hands on a drawing reflect aggressiveness but they do not offer any specific clues as to the underlying factors contributing to the child's acting-out behavior.

Levy claims that big hands reflect compensatory behavior for feelings of inadequacy, manipulatory insufficiency, or difficulty in making contact with others. Machover hypothesizes that big hands are typical for boys who are compensating for physical weakness or who feel guilty over the use of their hands. There may be other reasons as well why a child draws big hands. It seems safest to limit the interpretation of this drawing sign to the demonstrated fact that big hands on HFDs indicate a tendency in children to act out aggressive impulses with their hands. The underlying reason for this aggressiveness has to be determined by additional test data, observations, and from the social histories.

Hands cut off or the drawing of arms without hands and fingers *(Plates 3, 16, 42)* occurred significantly more often on the HFDs of clinic patients, brain injured children, and special class pupils. It was found more often on the drawings of the shy children than on the HFDs of the overtly aggressive children; but cut-off hands were shown equally often on the records of the children who stole and of those with psychosomatic complaints. It appears therefore that cut-off hands on HFDs reflect feelings of inadequacy or guilt over failure to act correctly or over the inability to act at all.

These findings correspond to Machover's observation that omission of hands on a drawing indicates a child's guilt feelings for stealing or for his poor school achievement. She also mentions the possibility of castration anxiety when a child produces a HFD without hands. This particular hypothesis was supported by the case histories of several of the children in the present investigations who drew figures without hands. Since cut-off hands appear to be related to a wide variety of attitudes and anxieties, it is not possible to determine merely from the presence of this Emotional Indicator on a HFD whether a child is suffering from feelings of mental or physical inadequacy and helplessness, from guilt, from anxiety, or from all of these. It is only possible to state that he is troubled and feels inadequate. The cause for his anxiety and disturbance must be determined through additional testing, inquiry, and observation.

Legs pressed together (Plates 40, 54, 66) occurred rarely on any of the HFDs examined in the present volume. It was found most often on the drawings of clinic patients and of children with psychosomatic complaints. A study of the case histories of the children who drew the legs pressed together on their HFDs suggests the following interpretation: This Emotional Indicator seems to indicate above all tenseness in the child and a rigid attempt on his part to control his own sexual impulses or his concern over a sexual attack by others. It seems significant that several of the girls who drew figures with legs together had been exposed to sexual trauma at the hands of older men.

These findings are in accord with Levy's observation that a tight stance on a figure drawing indicates rigidity and brittle control, and with Machover's hypothesis that this sign on adult drawings reflects rejection of sexual approach by others.

Genitals (Plates 27, 59, 94) were rare on the HFDs of all the children tested in the present investigations. When this item did appear, it was invariably on the drawings of clinic patients who were extremely disturbed and who were overtly aggressive. The presence of genitals or symbols for them on HFDs must be considered a sign of serious psychopathology involving acute body anxiety and poor impulse control.

Monsters or grotesque figures (Plates 48, 74, 80) were found primarily on the HFDs of the clinic patients, special class pupils, and poor students. The drawing of monsters or grotesque figures does not seem to be associated with any specific type of behavior, but rather reflects feelings of intense inadequacy and a very poor self-concept. Children who draw non-human monsters or artifacts like robots *(Plate 71)* seem to perceive themselves as being different from others, as not being quite human; children who draw clowns or tramps *(Plate 65)* think of themselves as rather ridiculous individuals who are laughed at and who are not fully accepted by others; while youngsters who draw figures of prehistoric times *(Plate 72)* or members of minority groups of which they are not members *(Plate 47)* feel as though they were outsiders who do not fully belong to the society they live in.

Drawings of grotesque figures occur at all age levels and among children ranging all the way from borderline intelligence to superior ability. A bright child may feel just as inferior in comparison to his brilliant older brother as a retarded child may feel in comparison with a dull normal sister. The drawings of monsters and grotesque figures may be intricate and well executed *(Plate 68)* or they may be crude and quite immature *(Plate 58)*. The present findings do not support Harris' observation (1963, p. 148) that only bright and imaginative children draw grotesque figures.

Examiners will sometimes explain the drawing of a clown or a monster by the fact that the child had just been to a circus or had watched a monster picture on television. Such an explanation overlooks the fact that the child saw also many beautiful or heroic figures in the circus whom he could have drawn, and that the television drama usually includes a hero as well as a villain. In fact, many more children draw positive figures than negative ones. *Plate 1* shows the HFDs of three good students who chose to depict three of the "culture heroes" of their day: Davy Crockett, Elvis Presley, and a Beatle. In the writer's extensive collection of children's drawings, Superman is probably portrayed more often than any other actual or fictional personage *(Plate 33)*.

It seems self-evident that a child will reflect recent experiences in his drawings. But it is always highly significant which of his many experiences he decides to reproduce and is concerned with. Over the years, the names and faces of the heroes and villains on the radio, on television, or in the comic books may change, but the values and qualities they portray rarely change. The meaning attached to monsters and clowns remains the same. The present findings support Levy's observation that a person who draws clowns, cartoons, or silly looking figures reflects contempt and hostility toward himself.

Three or more figures spontaneously drawn (Plates 7, 8, 105) occurred significantly more often on the HFDs of poor students and special class pupils than on the drawings of good students and well-adjusted pupils. Many children will draw spontaneously two figures, a boy and a girl *(Plate 104)*, or a man and a woman, but the drawing of three or more figures is the exception. In the writer's clinical experience, this type of HFD is always associated with poor school achievement. This Emotional Indicator is found almost exclusively on drawings of children of limited ability who come from large, culturally deprived families and/or who are brain injured.

If a child draws spontaneously many figures in response to the request to draw "a whole person," he exhibits a form of perseveration which is not uncommon among very young and immature pre-school children and among neurologically impaired youngsters. Such perseveration is bound to interfere with schoolwork. It was also observed that some of the children who draw multiple figures lack a feeling of identity, of being a person in their own right. They are in reality frequently one of a crowd of children at home and have never received a great deal of individual attention. These children tend to be lost in school since they never learned to function independently. Children who draw more than three figures usually require special help in school if they are to become individualized human beings.

Clouds, rain, snow (Plates 19, 36, 108) appeared, with one exception, exclusively on the HFDs of clinic patients and poorly adjusted pupils. Clouds were found especially often on drawings of very anxious children with psychosomatic complaints, and not at all on the HFDs of the overtly aggressive children. Clouds seem to be drawn primarily by children who do not dare to strike out at others and who instead turn their aggression inward toward themselves. It is hypothesized that the spontaneous addition of clouds on a HFD indicates that the child feels threatened by the adult world, especially by the parents. The child is in effect standing under a cloud, under pressure from above.

Omission of the eyes on HFDs (Plates 7, 12, 18) is a rare phenomenon. The eyes are usually the very first detail a child will add after drawing the head. The omission of the eyes (not just the omission of the pupils or non-seeing eyes) should never be considered an oversight; it always has clinical significance. In the present studies, this sign was found only on the drawings of nonaggressive clinic patients. All the children who omitted the eyes from their figures were found to be socially isolated youngsters. They tended to deny their problems, refused to face the world, and escaped into fantasy. These findings concur with Stone and Ansbacher's (1965) report; they found a significant relationship between the omission of eyes and other "communication organs" on HFDs and poor social interest on part of the child.

Omission of the nose (Plates 5, 15, 34) occurred in the present investigations significantly more often on the HFDs of the special class pupils, the shy youngsters, the clinic patients, and the children suffering from psychosomatic complaints. It appears, therefore, that the omission of the nose on HFDs is associated with shy and withdrawn behavior and a lack of overt aggressiveness. Omission of the nose is related to poor social interests according to Stone and Ansbacher (1965). Traditionally, the nose has been identified as a phallic symbol, and the omission thereof on a HFD has been interpreted by Machover and others as a sign of masturbation guilt or castration anxiety. This may be the case for most adult patients who draw figures without a nose but it is not necessarily valid for children. In the studies reported here, very few of the children who exhibited this Emotional Indicator on their drawings showed castration anxiety. For most of the children who omitted the nose from their HFDs, the nose did not appear to be primarily a phallic symbol, but rather a symbol of forward striving and independence. We "follow our nose" as we venture forth into the world. When a child omits the nose from his drawing, he may be expressing a feeling of immobility and helplessness, an inability to go forward with self-assurance. The omission of the nose seems to reflect most often a tendency to withdraw and shyness, but sometimes, it may also suggest body anxiety or masturbation guilt.

Omission of the mouth (Plates 5, 18, 46) was found most often on the HFDs of the clinic patients, the special class pupils, the poor students, and the children with psychosomatic complaints. It also differentiated significantly between the shy and the aggressive youngsters. Omission of the mouth appears to be always clinically meaningful. It reflects feelings of anxiety, insecurity and withdrawal including passive resistance. This Emotional Indicator reveals either the child's inability or his refusal to communicate with others. The case histories of the children who omitted the mouth from their drawings showed a high incidence of fear, anxiety, perfectionism, and depression. These findings are in accord with Machover's observation that some adult depressed patients omitted the mouth from their drawings. She also suggests that this sign occurs on the drawings of asthmatics. The present investigations did not include enough asthmatic children to either confirm or reject this hypothesis.

Omission of the body (Plates 50, 97, 101a) occurred significantly more often on the HFDs of the clinic patients, the brain injured children, the poor students, the special class pupils, and the children who stole. It is normal for nursery school children to draw "Kopffüssler," that is, to draw figures without bodies that consist merely of a head from which arms and legs are protruding *(Plate 105)*. When kindergarten pupils fail to make bodies on their HFDs, it may be assumed that they are as yet immature and are functioning on the four year old level. At the kindergarten level, this omission may represent an essentially normal but somewhat slower rate of maturation or it may be a sign of retardation and/or neurological impairment. Among school-age children, the omission of the body on HFDs is invariably a serious sign of psychopathology and may reflect any of the following: mental retardation, cortical malfunctioning, severe immaturity due to developmental lag, or emotional disturbance with acute body anxiety and castration fear. It is not possible to tell from a single HFD which of these factors accounts for the omission of the body and whether two or more of these factors are in operation. If a child includes the body on the drawing of a woman but omits it on the drawing of a man *(Plate 104)*, then the presence of emotional problems seems likely. The retarded or brain injured child who is not emotionally disturbed is more apt to omit the body from the drawing of both males and females.

Omission of the arms (Plates 2, 27, 55) was revealed significantly more often on the HFDs of the clinic patients, the poor students and the special class pupils. It was also found that aggressive children and those who steal omitted the arms much more often than the shy children and those with psychosomatic complaints. It appears, therefore, that omission of the arms on a HFD reflects anxiety and guilt over socially unacceptable behavior involving the arms or hands. These findings are in agreement with Machover's observation that the omission of arms on a drawing reflects guilt over hostility or sexuality. But the present research did not support Levy's and Machover's hypothesis that this type of omission is associated with depression and withdrawal from people and the world of objects. This hypothesis may be valid for adult patients, but it did not apply to the HFDs of children. Omission of the arms was exceedingly rare on the drawings of depressed and withdrawn children. In the one instance in which a shy and depressed boy omitted the arms from his HFD, he also had a history of stealing. It is believed that the omission of the arms reflected his guilt and anxiety over his stealing rather than his depression.

HFDs are particularly valuable just because they can reveal conflicting tendencies and attitudes. The classification of children into diagnostic or behavior groups is at best arbitrary and is done here only for research purposes. In real life, children who come to the attention of psychologists are almost never *just* depressed and withdrawn or *just* aggressive. They usually show a variety of symptoms and behavior problems that differ from time to time and at different stages of development and even in different situations, e.g., at home and at school.

Omission of the legs (Plates 10, 16, 65) on HFDs is extremely rare and was found only on the drawings of a few clinic patients and poor students. Legs are usually among the very first parts of a human figure that a pre-school child produces. Legs tend to follow in developmental sequence right after the drawing of the head and eyes, even before the child begins to draw bodies and arms. It may be assumed, therefore, that the omission of the legs on a HFD is never accidental. Machover hypothesizes that the absence of legs reveals conflict in that area. In the present studies, this Emotional Indicator seemed to reflect intense anxiety and insecurity. The specific implications of this sign seemed to be related to the particular way in which the legs were omitted from the drawing.

Plate 10 shows the drawing of Nick, a seven year old boy with muscular distrophy. Walking and running were difficult for Nick. A great deal of attention and concern had been directed toward his legs over the years. It is therefore not surprising that Nick omitted the legs from his HFD entirely, thereby indicating his extreme anxiety about the condition of his legs.

Shirley, a nine year old girl of diminutive size (page 97), made a HFD that was so large that the lower portion of the figure including the legs was cut off by the edge of the paper *(Plate 16)*. In this case, the omission of the legs is directly related to the size of the drawing and seems to reflect the child's acute concern and anxiety over her own small stature and short legs.

Plates 11 and 12 show the HFDs of two seriously disturbed and withdrawn youngsters. In both cases, the figures are drawn in such a way that the legs are hidden from view. This type of omission of the legs seems to show the child's unwillingness or inability to "stand up and be counted," so to speak. The two boys who made the drawings were so insecure and anxious that they sought comfort by withdrawing from reality into fantasy. In effect, their legs were too weak to support them; all they could do was to hide or lie down and escape into daydreaming.

In the present investigations the total number of children who showed omission of legs on their HFDs was too small to permit broad generalizations or to make statistical computations meaningful. The interpretations of the different ways of showing omission of the legs on a HFD should be therefore regarded only as suggestions which require further specific testing and confirmation.

Omission of the feet (Plates 9, 27, 68) on HFDs did not become clinically significant until age 7 for girls and age 9 for boys; that is, until children reach an age at which they begin to be more self-reliant and can stand on their own two feet. In the present studies, omission of the feet was found most often on the HFDs of the clinic patients and the very shy children. It appears that omission of feet on a drawing is not associated with any specific type of behavior or symptom; instead, it seems to reflect a general sense of insecurity and helplessness, a feeling of "having no feet to stand on." These findings concur with Machover's hypothesis that the omission of feet indicate an insecurity of footing.

Omission of the neck (Plates 27, 38, 70) did not become a clinically valid Emotional Indicator until age 9 for girls and age 10 for boys. Thereafter, it occurred significantly more often on the HFDs of the clinic patients, the brain injured children, and the children who stole. None of the well-adjusted pupils or the children with psychosomatic complaints omitted the neck from their drawings. These two groups of youngsters have one thing in common: They tend to display good inner control over their impulses and actions. The omission of the neck on a HFD on the other hand seems to be related to immaturity, impulsivity, and poor inner controls. These findings are in agreement with Machover's observation that the omission of the neck is a common sign on HFDs of immature children and of adult defectives and regressed patients. She hypothesizes that failure to draw the neck on a figure reveals a lack of rational control and poor coordination of impulses and behavior.

Interpretation of signs on HFDs that are not valid Emotional Indicators

In addition to the 30 valid Emotional Indicators discussed above, eight other signs were investigated and interpreted. These eight signs had been considered originally (page 35) as potential Emotional Indicators but were later excluded when they failed to meet the criteria for such items *(Table 11)*. However, since the projective significance of these signs is often referred to in the literature, they will be here briefly discussed in terms of the findings of the present research.

Big head (Plates 5, 14, 34) on a HFD has been variously associated with intellectual striving, brain disease and brain injury, intellectual inadequacy, immaturity, aggression, mental retardation, migraine headaches, and concern over school achievement. It is quite probable that all of these interpretations are correct at one time or another. It may be assumed that a large head on a HFD reflects concern over or preoccupation with some aspect of mental adequacy and functioning. But on the basis of the HFD alone, it is not possible to determine which of the many possible aspects is revealed by the drawing of a large head on a given HFD. It is important to emphasize that not all associations with a large head are necessarily negative or pathological. Many ambitious and striving children with high scholastic achievement show this item on their drawings *(Plate 13c)*. In the present investigations, a large head was found to be not at all unusual on the HFDs of both well-adjusted and poorly adjusted pupils and of clinic patients. This item is present so frequently on the HFDs of children of all ages and both sexes that it cannot be considered either rare or necessarily clinically significant.

Vacant eyes or nonseeing eyes (Plates 2, 10, 13a) have been described on the one hand as a normal sign on the HFDs of children, while on the other hand, they have been associated with guilt feelings over voyeuristic tendencies, with a vague perception of the world, with emotional immaturity, egocentricity, dependency, a lack of discrimination, and depression. In the present studies, vacant eyes were shown so frequently on the HFDs of both boys and girls of all age levels that this sign could not be considered a rare Emotional Indicator. It is quite possible that the interpretations mentioned above are correct for adult patients, but they cannot be considered clinically meaningful for children. Young school-age children are normally egocentric, emotionally immature and dependent. Children have inevitably a vague perception of the world and are curious about happenings, sexual or otherwise. It is normal for children to explore differences and functions of the body. None of these tendencies can be considered as particularly pathological in children, nor can the drawing of vacant eyes on HFDs be considered as such.

Sideway glance of both eyes (Plates 5, 13b and c) on a HFD has been claimed to be a sign of suspicion and paranoid tendencies. The results of the present studies confirm Harris' (1963) observation that this treatment of the eyes on HFDs increases in frequency of occurrence as the children get older. It was found particularly often on the HFDs of the 10, 11 and 12 year old girls, both among the well-adjusted pupils *(Plate 13b)* and the clinic patients. It is not certain whether the glance of the eye reflects the normal self-consciousness and uneasiness of the pre-adolescent child, or if the sideway glance of the eyes on a HFD shows the feminine preoccupation with facial detail and eye makeup or if it is just a display of drawing skill. In some cases, the glance of the eyes seems to be little more than a sign of coyness *(Plate 13c)*, while in a few cases, it may indeed indicate suspiciousness and fear *(Plate 5)*. A look at the total drawing and a check for the presence or absence of the valid Emotional Indicators will usually enable the examiner to determine which of these interpretations is appropriate in a given case. It was noted that a glance of both eyes was drawn most often by the brighter children and that it did not differentiate significantly between well-adjusted and poorly adjusted youngsters. In view of all this, a sideway glance of both eyes on HFDs of children cannot be considered in and of itself a sign of psychopathology.

Hidden hands (Plate 13a, 39, 95) on HFDs have been associated with contact difficulties, evasiveness, guilt, the need to control aggression, and the unwillingness to deal with a situation. The present findings show that hidden hands on HFDs increase in frequency of occurrence as the children get older. This item is not at all unusual on drawings of pre-adolescent boys and girls. Hidden hands did not differentiate between the HFDs of the clinic patients and the well adjusted children. These results concur with the findings of Woods and Cook (1954) who reported that many of the brightest and artistically most gifted children drew figures with hidden hands.

During the administration of the HFD Test, several children *(Plate 13a)* told the examiner that they could not draw hands and chose to avoid the problem by hiding the hands behind the figure's back or by covering them with another object. These children did not reveal any sign of undue anxiety or guilt either on their drawings or in their behavior. They rather showed a deliberate and socially acceptable way of avoiding a difficult task for which they saw no particular need in the first place. Such behavior cannot be considered pathological; it rather reveals good judgment. In several cases, the hiding of the hands on the HFD showed that the child was able to make a realistic assessment of his limited drawing skill and of his inability to meet his own high standards. Objectively speaking, the drawing of hands *is* difficult, and the more intelligent and discriminating children can rarely draw hands well enough to satisfy themselves. Only the less sophisticated child will be content with his drawing of clumsy or incorrect hands.

Hidden hands on a HFD is indeed a sign of evasiveness, but a certain degree of evasiveness is normal in pre-adolescent children. There were, however, cases, especially among the younger children, when the hiding of the hands on a HFD was very definitely connected with extreme withdrawal, anxiety, and guilt *(Plate 95)*. But in each instance where this seemed to be true, there were at least two or more other valid Emotional Indicators on the drawing, e.g., omission of feet, slanting figure, shading, etc. These other indicators revealed the child's problem clearly so that the additional sign of the hidden hands was not needed for a meaningful analysis of the HFD.

Figure cut off by the edge of the paper (Plates 16, 69, 103) has been considered by some investigators a sign of pseudo-self-confidence to aggressive proportions, the compensation of the show-off in an effort to cover weakness, and a reflection of frustration with the environment. In the present studies, this sign did not differentiate between the HFDs of the various groups of children tested. A look at the case histories of the children who exhibited this type of drawing revealed no common denominator. The youngsters showed a great variety of problems, behavior symptoms, and background, and they represented a wide range of age levels, IQ scores and achievement ratings.

It appears that the meaning of a cut-off figure depends at least to some extent on the part of the figure that has been cut off. On drawings where the legs were cut off just above the ankles, the implications appeared to be similar to those of HFDs without feet (page 68). The cutting off of the whole legs seemed to reflect insecurity and a lack of secure footing, in the same way as the omission of the legs from a drawing does (page 68). When the lower portion of the arms were cut off by the side edge of the paper, the drawing resembled a HFD with cut-off hands and should be similarly interpreted (page 63). On some very large drawings, the figure sprawled over the edges of the paper on several sides *(Plates 103)*. In these cases, there did not seem to be any conscious or unconscious attempt to cut off part of the figure; rather, it was found that the child was quite immature and impulsive. His drawing reflected above all poor coordination, weak inner control and poor judgment.

And then there were the HFDs of two very disturbed youngsters with schizoid behavior and a tendency to withdraw into a world of fantasy. These children drew figures with large heads that were cut off on top by the edge of the paper. This type of drawing is very rare and must be considered quite pathological. It would appear, therefore, that each HFD must be considered separately and that the meaning of a cut-off figure will depend on the part that is cut off. There can be no general interpretation of this sign that can be applied to all HFDs.

Baseline or grass (Plates 12, 19, 48) on HFDs has been interpreted as a sign of insecurity, a need for support, and a need for a point of reference. These hypotheses may be correct, but young children, who are living in a world of towering and domineering adults, are by virtue of their size and age naturally insecure and in need of support. This need cannot be considered pathological in young children. It is therefore not surprising that the present investigations revealed a very high incidence of baselines on the HFDs of both boys and girls at all age levels. This item did not differentiate between the drawings of the well-adjusted *(Plate 44)* and poorly adjusted *(Plate 42)* children. The presence of a baseline or grass on a HFD cannot be considered a clinically significant indicator of emotional disturbance among elementary school-age children.

The sun or moon (Plate 12, 19, 108) on a HFD has been associated with parental love and support, and with controlling adult authority. These two parental attitudes are, of course, not mutually exclusive. The present findings seem to offer support for both hypotheses. More well adjusted children than clinic patients drew suns on their HFDs. It was noted that particularly children with psychosomatic complaints added suns to their drawings. The parents of these children were indeed often loving and full of concern while being at the same time quite controlling. The children in turn seemed to feel a great deal of ambivalence toward their parents. But they were able to express only positive attitudes openly, and did not dare to reveal their negative attitudes.

When the HFDs of good and poor pupils were compared, it was found that more pupils with high teacher ratings showed suns on their drawings than did students with low teacher ratings. These findings are in accord with the study of Koppitz, Sullivan, Blyth, and Shelton (1961). The presence of the sun on HFDs seems to be positively related to achievement in the primary grades and is thought to reflect the child's awareness of parental interest in and pressure for achievement. Such pressure, within reasonable limits, may be quite desirable and may serve as a motivating factor for the child to put forth effort in school. Parental pressure for achievement is only harmful if it is extreme; and if the parents expect more from the child than he is able to achieve *(Plate 108)*. It cannot be stated, therefore, that the presence of a sun on a HFD is necessarily a good sign nor that it is invariably a sign of psychopathology or of a disturbed parent-child relationship. A meaningful interpretation of a sun can only be made when the entire HFD is analyzed and after additional information concerning the child and his parents has been obtained.

Broken or sketchy lines (Plates 1a, 13a, 20) on HFDs have been associated with fearfulness, insecurity, feelings of inadequacy, anxiety, stubbornness, and negativism. The present studies revealed a steady increase in the use of sketchy lines on HFDs as the children got older. This concurs with Harris' observation (1963) that sketchy lines are not unusual on HFDs of older children. One might argue that pre-adolescent children as a group tend to be insecure and anxious and that this is reflected by their use of sketchy lines. But it was found that many well-adjusted and quite self-assured children used sketchy lines on their drawings. In fact, many of the most artistically gifted and of the brightest children did so *(Plates 1a, 13a)*.

In addition, it was noted that some of the brain injured children drew figures with sketchy or broken lines (Plate 98a). This observation had been also reported by other investigators. In most instances, there was no problem in distinguishing between the artistically drawn sketchy lines of a talented youngster and the fragmented lines of a neurologically impaired child. But there were some borderline cases where the difference between the two was not apparent. In these drawings, sketchiness of the line was minimal or the fragmentation so slight that no sharp differentiation between the two types of drawings could be made. It appears therefore that sketchy lines on a HFD of children cannot be regarded as a clear sign of psychopathology.

5. Clinical Interpretation of Children's Drawings

A CHILD'S DRAWING is a graphic expression, and as such, it is a statement which is basically no different from any other statement. Just as verbal statements can be analyzed for structure and content, so HFDs can be analyzed for formal structure and signs as well as for content and meaning. In the preceding chapters, HFDs of children were analyzed for their structure and were scored for objective signs and symbols which reflect children's mental maturity and emotional attitudes. At this time, an attempt will be made to interpret HFDs in terms of their clinical meaning and content.

All statements, including HFDs, have some meaning and serve some purpose for the child who makes them. A drawing may represent many different things. It may be an expression of joy or anger, or a cry of fear or anguish; it may be a question, or it may be a demand; it may reflect a wish or a fantasy; or it may be a retelling of something the child has seen or experienced. A HFD can be the expression of any of these and much more. It is the task of the clinician to discover the meaning of HFDs and to find out what the child is trying to communicate through his drawings.

Drawing and painting is a natural mode of expression for young children. They can depict their feelings and attitudes in graphic images and symbols long before they can convey them in abstract verbal concepts. But once a child has mastered the art of communicating his thoughts and feelings by means of the spoken or written word, he will usually give up drawing as a way of expressing himself. By the time most children reach adolescence, they no longer draw spontaneously and are frequently reluctant to draw even when requested to do so. Only the really talented or artistically inclined youngster will continue to draw and paint on his own as he gets older.

However, even nonartistic older children may again revert to the language of drawing and graphic imagery when they are greatly upset and cannot put into words their conscious or unconscious anxieties and conflicts. This writer has observed many times how children who came to the clinic for psychotherapy were at first quite unable to verbalize their problems or anything about themselves but were usually eager and ready to draw and to paint. As these children gained in self-confidence and began to show improvement in their behavior, they would usually stop drawing and painting. They would then begin to act out their problems with the aid of dolls and toys, only to progress to indirect verbal communication by means of puppets or a toy telephone. The children were usually well on their way to recovery when they were able to talk freely to the therapist and could listen without undue anxiety to their own statements which they had recorded on a tape recorder. But whenever a child experienced a setback or showed regression in his behavior, he would usually return to nonverbal means of communication in the therapy session and would once more begin to draw and paint. Thus, it appears that drawing is most meaningful for young children and for children with serious emotional problems.

In trying to analyze children's HFDs clinically, the writer asked herself three questions: (1) *How* did the child draw his figure or figures? (2) *Whom* did the child draw on his picture? and (3) *What* is the child trying to say? In order to discover the answer to these questions, the investigator studied the drawings of many hundreds of children who were well known to her, so that she could check her interpretations of the HFDs against the children's actual behavior and clinical history. It is here maintained that a meaningful analysis of children's drawings presupposes that the clinician not only knows the child's age and sex but also something about the youngster's family and social background. All clinical interpretations of drawings remain speculations unless they can be verified and supported by the child's history and other clinical data.

Based on years of clinical experience and experimentation, the writer would like to suggest three basic principles for analyzing the meaning of HFDs. These principles are believed to be valid for all HFDs of children between the ages of 5 and 12. It is not known if these principles also apply to drawings of older children or adults, and it cannot be assumed that they hold true for drawings that are not HFDs as defined in this volume (page 5). The three principles are outlined below:

(1) *HOW a child draws a figure, regardless of whom he draws, reflects his own self-concept.* The manner in which the drawing is made and the signs and symbols employed, all reveal the inner self-portrait of the child and show his attitude toward himself. If a child draws more than one figure, when asked to make a HFD, then he may show his self-concept on more than one of the figures. On *Plate 51* for instance, Betty indicated her attitudes toward herself in the treatment of both the mother figure and the figure of the girl (page 108).

(2) *The person WHOM the child draws is the person who is of greatest concern and importance to the child at the time he is making the drawing.* In the majority of cases, children will draw themselves for obviously no one is of greater importance to a child than he himself. Usually, children will draw themselves fairly realistically, but some youngsters are so displeased with themselves that they distort their images until they bear little resemblance to their actual appearance or to any other human being. *Plates 48, 68, 74 and 75* are examples of HFDs that show nonhuman or not-quite-human creatures who really represent self-portaits of the children who made them. Other children draw ideal images of themselves in the form of their heroes. Examples are shown on *Plates 1a and c* and *Plate 29*.

But there are exceptions to this rule; some children do not draw themselves. *Plates 14 and 83b* show drawings that represent children's mothers (pages 107 and 133), while *Plate 84* shows a youngster's father (page 133) and *Plate 82* reveals a boy's sister (page 132). In each of the four cases, it was found that the child's primary concern and conflict at that given time centered around the person he drew, that is, around the mother, father or sister respectively. However, the drawing of a person other than oneself need not always indicate conflict with that person. It may also reflect a positive preoccupation with that person, as was the case with Jean who drew a picture of her dream hero Elvis Pressley (*Plate 1b*). It is quite common for young adolescent girls to draw glamorous male figures in response to their awakening sexual impulses and desires.

The principle that a drawing reveals the person who is of most concern to a child differs from Machover's widely accepted hypothesis that the sex of the figure drawn reflects the child's sexual identification. Many studies and investigations of children's drawings have been devoted to the exploration of the sexual identification hypothesis, but the results of these studies have been at best inconclusive (Bieliauskas, 1960; Brown and Tolor, 1957; Butler and Marcuse, 1959; Granick and Smith, 1953; Haworth and Normington, 1961; Jolles, 1952b; McHugh, 1963, 1966; Richey, 1965). While most children do draw figures of their own sex first, a considerable number of youngsters do not follow this pattern and do not necessarily show confused sexual identification. It cannot be assumed that all boys who draw women or girls first are homosexuals or have feminine identification, even though this may be true in a few cases. The same situation applies to girls who draw male figures. Girls who draw males are concerned or preoccupied with boys or men and they may or may not identify with them.

The writer has found consistently that a boy who portrays a girl or woman on his HFD is emotionally involved with a female in his family or environment, but he need not necessarily identify with her. These observations are in accord with Phelan's carefully controlled and executed study (1964). Phelan compared the social adjustment and attitudes of 50 sixth graders who drew a female figure first in response to the HFD Test, with the adjustment and attitudes of 50 boys who drew a male figure first. The two groups of boys were matched for age, IQ level, parental occupation, and religion. The results did not show any significant differences between the two groups in mean total adjustment scores nor on their ratings for adjustment by their teachers. However, a careful analysis of individual test responses of the two groups showed that the boys who drew a female figure first tended to feel more dominated by adults and had a less positive attitude toward their father. It appeared that these boys came more often from mother-dominated homes than did the boys who drew male figures first. It seems quite logical that boys from mother-dominated homes would be more concerned and preoccupied with their mothers and would draw mother figures more often than would boys from father-dominated homes.

Sometimes, children will indicate that the figure on their HFD is not a boy or a girl (themselves) or a man or woman (a parent), but rather that the drawing is supposed to be a picture of the examiner (page 7). This may be flattering for the examiner, but actually it is a very poor sign for the child. In the writer's experience, children who draw the psychologist are very lonely and unhappy youngsters who do not consider themselves worthy of concern and who have no one at home with whom they are involved or preoccupied. These children are social isolates who are starved for attention and affection; they have received so little warmth and recognition from others that they overrespond to the acceptance and friendliness of the psychologist who is a complete stranger whom they have never seen before.

A somewhat different situation is presented by some very concretistic, brain injured children who tend to live completely in any given moment with little reference to the past or future. These children are inclined to draw any person they happen to see in front of them including the examiner, using the other person actually as a model. The drawings are usually quite realistic and are inspired by the situation and not by the child's inner needs or concerns.

(3) *WHAT a child is saying in his HFD may be twofold; it may be an expression of his attitudes and conflicts, or it may be a wishdream, or both.* The choice of the person the child draws and the manner in which the figure is drawn reflect the child's attitudes. These aspects of the HFD represent a statement as to which person is of greatest importance to the child at that moment and as to his feelings about himself. *If a child describes the person he drew, then this description applies to the person drawn*; that is, if he drew himself, the description applies to himself; if he drew someone else, then the description applies to that other person. *Plates 83b and 84* (page 133) offer examples of HFDs by children who drew and described persons who were not themselves. However, *the manner in which the figures were drawn reflects the children's attitude toward themselves.*

If a child tells a spontaneous story about his HFD, then the content of the story represents a wishdream. The HFD on *Plate 14* may serve as an illustration of this hypothesis. The HFD was made by Edith, a seriously neglected and deprived seven year old girl who was disfigured by a badly repaired cleft palate (page 107). The manner in which the figure on *Plate 14* was drawn revealed Edith's self-consciousness about her appearance and her feelings of inadequacy. Edith stated that the figure represents "a lady," that is, her mother. By drawing the mother rather than a girl (herself), Edith indicated that her emotional problems and anxieties at that time were focused on her mother. Edith described the lady (mother) on her picture as "mean" and having a permanent and a "boyfriend." These descriptions applied quite accurately to her mother. Edith perceived correctly that her mother was well-groomed and attractive in contrast to her own disfigurement and neglected appearance; the mother had indeed a "boyfriend" and was in fact "mean" in her treatment of Edith. Edith told the following spontaneous story: "The lady is waiting for her date; she is mad at him. He won't come. She is so mean she wants to go out every night." This story is Edith's wishdream; she is saying in effect: "I wish my mother's boyfriend won't come tonight so that she will stay home with me for a change instead of going out every night."

Many HFDs and family drawings can be analyzed in this way, but it should be stressed here that only spontaneous comments and stories, or stories that were stimulated by a general, open-ended question (e.g., "what kind of a person is this?" and "what is he doing?") are considered valid for this kind of analysis. If a child is asked to answer specific questions about his drawing in a formal interrogation, the results are, in this writer's opinion, often questionable. Children sometimes give responses which they think would please the examiner. While all HFDs offer some insight and information about a child, it is also true that drawings differ a great deal as to the extent of the clinical material they are able to provide. It is quite obvious that many youngsters draw very conventional figures which offer a minimum of clinical information. In such cases, the analysis of the drawing has to be limited to the scoring for objective signs and symbols. No amount of questioning can produce clinically valid material from a HFD if this material is not contained in the drawing in the first place. If the child is trying to communicate with the examiner through his drawings, then he will offer spontaneous clues and comments to his drawing if given the opportunity.

Most investigators of HFDs, including this writer, have studied drawings of large groups of public school children. These drawings are usually obtained in the classrooms by the investigators or by the teachers. With little or no preparation, the children are asked to draw "a man" or "a whole person" or a "picture of yourself." This is about the equivalent of saying to a group of children: "Say something about yourself." The well-trained children will then dutifully perform the required task but rarely will they show any real emotional involvement in their performance. The drawings can then be analyzed for their structure and for signs. But when HFDs of groups of normal school children are examined from the clinical point of view, it is usually found that their content is meager. This is really not very surprising.

Fortunately, the great majority of schoolchildren in middle-class elementary schools are emotionally and socially fairly well-adjusted and are free from serious mental disturbances which might be revealed on HFDs. In addition, most schoolchildren consider the request to make a HFD as little more than another class assignment or a pleasant diversion. Most children will try to do well on the HFD Test in order to gain approval, but they usually do not try to convey to the examiner, consciously or unconsciously, a message concerning their inner conflicts and anxieties. A well-adjusted and poised youngster will not display his innermost feelings if he can help it. Only emotionally disturbed and maladjusted children, who are the exception in a large group of schoolchildren, will reflect their problems unwittingly on their drawings. There is a great deal of difference in the richness of content and meaning, though not necessarily in structure, on the HFDs of large groups of normal, public-school children and the drawings of emotionally disturbed children who are psychiatric patients or who are special class pupils. Children with problems will reveal a good deal of themselves on their drawings, especially if they make their HFDs in a one-to-one situation with an accepting psychologist who is willing and able to listen to their silent but eloquent pleas for understanding and help.

This difference between the HFDs of public-school children and of clinic patients may account for the fact that investigators like Harris (1963), who deal mainly with large numbers of drawings by schoolchildren, tend to underestimate the clinical significance of HFDs, while others like Machover and Hammer, who see almost exclusively drawings of psychiatric patients, tend to overestimate the clinical significance of HFDs. Children's drawings contain usually some clinically meaningful material, but it is incorrect to assume that each and every sign or feature on a drawing is necessarily clinically significant. After all, a certain amount of tension, anxiety and conflict is normal for all children, and it cannot be regarded as pathological when some of these are reflected on HFDs.

It is important to be able to assess a child's intention when analyzing his drawing. Not all drawings serve the same purpose nor should they all be considered equally important or meaningful. A chance sketch produced in a moment of boredom or tension will differ greatly from a drawing executed with careful deliberation. A spontaneous drawing by a child will differ markedly from a HFD made at the request of a psychologist. The drawing instructions may in some instances also affect the clinical content even though the structure of drawings will be little affected. Marcus (1963) shows how differently a child may respond when asked to draw "*a family*" or "*your* family."

Just how different the HFDs of a single child can be in different situations is illustrated by the drawings of Shirley (*Plates 15 and 16*). When Shirley was 8½ years old, the school referred her parents to the child guidance clinic to obtain a psychiatric evaluation of the child. Shirley had failed to make any academic progress in three years of school attendance and was unable to relate to her peers. She was merely tolerated or just ignored by her classmates. Shirley was a tiny child who looked and acted more like a six year old than like an eight year old girl. She was very quiet and invariably cheerful and friendly in a superficial sort of way. To the discerning eye, an underlying depression was evident in her behavior. She was emotionally flat and her social comprehension was poor. On the Stanford-Binet Intelligence Scale, Shirley tested in the low average range. Shirley's mother was a young, attractive, gay, and socially ambitious woman who refused to admit that there was anything wrong with Shirley. She blamed the school for the child's academic failings, and tried to hide her own rejection of her daughter by indulging her with material things.

When first seen at the guidance clinic, Shirley was cheery but remote. She produced the HFD shown on *Plate 15*. She began by drawing the legs, then added the dress, the arms, and finally the head. This particular sequence of drawing the parts of a human figure is usually associated with poor interpersonal relationships. Normally, the head, the area of social perception and communication, is drawn first. Children who draw the head or face last on a HFD tend to have difficulty in relating to others. At first glance, Shirley's finished drawing appears to be quite conventional and not too different from those of other 8½ year old girls. But a closer look at the details shows poor integration of body and head, short arms, the omission of the nose, and shading of the body. All of this suggests that Shirley was a shy, poorly integrated, and anxious child who could not reach out toward others. This impression was further supported by the unusual sequence in which she drew her figure. Thus the HFD on *Plate 15* conveys the impression that Shirley was a superficially conforming, socially isolated, anxious, withdrawn and unhappy child.

Shirley was seen for therapy on a regular weekly basis by the writer. During the first several sessions, Shirley was utterly noncommunicative. She spent her time producing rather stereotyped crayon drawings which were pretty to look at but which were devoid of emotional involvement. Shirley had received praise in the past for her drawing skill and perseverated now in the drawing of "safe" pictures in an effort to avoid painful or unpleasant tasks or an exposure of her underlying difficulties. Shirley imitated her mother's attitude to perfection; she smiled sweetly and denied that she had any problems; yet, it was quite evident that she was unhappy and lonely. Then one day, the writer asked Shirley to draw another "whole person." At first Shirley hesitated, then she looked at the therapist for a long time with a serious, penetrating expression on her face. It was as though she were seeing the therapist for the first time. Shirley seemed eager to tell the therapist something, but she could not utter a single word; instead she drew the figure shown on *Plate 16*. The difference between the HFDs on *Plate 15* and *Plate 16* is striking.

Plate 15 shows the kind of drawing a shy and anxious child will make who is intent on hiding from others her problems, while the HFD on *Plate 16* is the frank drawing of a child who is revealing herself and is asking for help. *Plate 16* shows with startling clarity the intense anger and frustration Shirley was experiencing and her utter helplessness in coping with her feelings. The first drawing says in effect: "Yes, I am miserable and lonely, but so what? It is none of your business and I do not trust you anyway." The second drawing was produced deliberately and for a purpose, and it says quite plainly: "Look, I am hurting, won't you please do something to help me?" This drawing is the plea of a child who cannot put her cry for help into words. *Plate 16* shows the picture of a smiling girl whose crossed eyes betray her underlying anger and frustration. The straight, clinging arms, cut off at the hands, and the omission of the legs, give the impression of helplessness and immobility; they show a desperate attempt on Shirley's part of rigidly controlling her hostile impulses. The large oversized drawing is in marked contrast to Shirley's own diminutive stature and reflects her concern and sensitivity about her failure to grow like other children (page 97).

This chapter will be devoted to the clinical analysis of children's drawings, to *what* the youngsters are trying to say through their drawings rather than to *how* they make their drawings. This content analysis will be carried out on HFDs that are rich in meaning and clinical significance; that is, the analysis will be based largely on the drawings of psychiatric patients and special class pupils rather than on the HFDs of normal public schoolchildren. All children whose drawings are here discussed were personally known to the writer; furthermore considerable background information and additional psychological test data were also available on most of these boys and girls.

Children's approach toward life's problems as reflected on HFDs

Life is difficult at best and even very intelligent, healthy and strong children, who receive a great deal of love and support from their parents, face daily stresses and strains with which they have to cope. A child's ability and success in facing life's problems will depend, of course, on many factors, but not the least of these is the child's attitude toward problems. Some children will struggle hard to master their impulses and will try valiantly to overcome their jealousy of a sibling or to conquer their grief over a lost parent. Some will work with grim determination to learn a difficult task or to tolerate severe frustrations. Other children with equal ability but with less inner strength and motivation may make periodic efforts to meet a challenge only to quit when the going gets rough. Some children vacillate between attempts at solving problems and retreats from them. Again, others have experienced defeat and failure so often that they have stopped fighting and try to avoid all difficulties life presents by offering passive resistance or by escaping into fantasy.

It is important to know and understand a child's approach toward the stresses and strains of life when planning a therapeutic program for him. Especially when working with very passive and nonverbal children, it is essential to determine whether the child is unable or unwilling to apply himself to the task at hand. It is here where HFDs can be of great value in revealing the child's basic attitude toward life and toward the problems facing him.

Ambition reflected on HFDs

On *Plates 17, 18 and 19* are shown the HFDs of three highly motivated and ambitious youngsters who are struggling hard to do well and to please their parents. All three boys can be relied upon to put forth their best efforts and not to give up on a task until it is completed or until they really cannot do any more and are overwhelmed by it. The HFD on *Plate 17* was drawn by Carl, an eleven year old boy of superior intelligence. His ambitious parents set high goals for him. We can see from his drawing that he perceives the tasks before him as a challenge, as a steep mountain which he is willing and able to climb. The drawing is technically awkward and anatomically incorrect, but there can be no doubt that the boy depicted on it has a firm grip on the rock wall with both hands and feet; his expression shows confidence in his ability to reach ultimately the top of the mountain. The task ahead is not portrayed as an easy one, but as one that can be overcome. As might be expected, Carl was a hardworking student who did well in school.

Plate 18 shows quite a contrast to *Plate 17*. This HFD was made by Bill, a 10½ year old boy of high average intelligence. Bill's parents were very ambitious and demanded of their son more than he was able to achieve, no matter how hard he tried to please them. When his schoolwork did not measure up to his parents' expectations, they increased their pressure on him until Bill began to show signs of withdrawal and developed enuresis and unexplained stomach aches. The father insisted that Bill could do the work but was just lazy. Bill's HFD on *Plate 18* tells a different story: Here we see a mountain climber who has reached an impossible impasse; he is desperately hanging on a mountain ledge by his fingertips and is unable to move in either direction. The rope, wound around the rock, is not attached to the climber, it offers him no support. He is all alone, cut off from the rest of the world; there is no use in even calling for help. The situation is so overwhelming that he cannot face it anymore, and so Bill omits the eyes and mouth from his figure on the drawing. In real life too, Bill stopped talking and communicating with others; he withdrew and turned his frustrations and unhappiness inward toward himself; he tried desperately to maintain himself despite his parents' displeasure. He was most unhappy since he wanted to do well but could not. The drawing on *Plate 18* convinced even the father that Bill was not just "lazy" but that he needed help and support if he was to regain his footing and self-confidence.

The HFD on *Plate 19* was produced by David, an eleven year old boy of average intelligence with good social adjustment. But David suffered from a short attention span, distractibility, and a severe memory deficit for sounds and symbols; because of this, he was unable to read. Despite years of scholastic failure, David had not yet given up; he wanted above all to learn to read and was willing to go to any length to accomplish this goal. David drew a tiny figure standing under dark clouds, thus revealing his intense feelings of inadequacy and anxiety over his scholastic failure. He was keenly aware of the premium his parents and society placed on the ability to read, and he perceived this as an ever-present pressure on him. David told the following story with his HFD: "The boy told another guy he would make it over the mountain, and when he made it over the mountain the mountain said: Hurrah!" The way the figure is drawn shows David's poor self-concept, but the story associated with it reveals David's ambition and his wishdream. It is his desire and wish "to make it over the mountain," to learn to read, to conquer his problem; he has not yet given up hope that he will succeed.

Vacillating attitudes toward life reflected on HFDs

The HFD shown on *Plate 20* was drawn by Jerry, a 12 year old boy of high average intelligence. Jerry had suffered from severe emotional and physical neglect and deprivation during the first two years of his life until he was finally removed from his home. Thereafter, he had lived in a number of different foster homes. He had a long history of behavior and learning problems. Jerry was a very moody and unstable youngster who could be most charming one day only to be erratic and unmanageable the next day. Periods of depression alternated with destructive outbursts. He had been suspended from school on several occasions and was about to be expelled when he was seen for psychological evaluation.

Jerry's HFD reflects quite dramatically his uncertainty and instability. He labored hard and long on the drawing and verbalized as he went along: " . . . the boy is running . . . he is playing basketball . . . no, I have an idea, he is walking the rope . . . balancing himself." After completing the HFD, Jerry was suddenly able to discuss freely his anxieties and conflicts. He told the writer that he really wanted to settle down and work hard; he wanted to finish school and then join the Navy; he wanted to make something of himself. But then again, Jerry was convinced that he really was "no good" and that it was all hopeless. He was certain that he was destined to become a "bum." Sometimes, he felt like killing himself. Jerry was painfully aware of his instability and weakness. The HFD showed his wishdream, his desire "to balance himself." However, a few months after the drawing on *Plate 20* was made, Jerry lost his balance completely and had to be referred to a residential treatment center.

In the case of Jerry, the content of the drawing is more clinically revealing than the structure of the figure. Of great importance are his spontaneous comments. He starts out by saying the boy is "running," that is, escaping from his problems; but gradually, he is able to state more precisely his anxieties and uncertainties, and his fervent hope that he can "balance himself." He is saying in effect that he feels as insecure and unstable as a man on a tightrope. In the writer's experience, only very unstable children with a tenuous hold on reality draw tightrope walkers and jugglers. Another example of a tightrope walker is shown on *Plate 99* (page 174), while *Plate 25b* shows a juggler drawn by Frankie (page 149).

Retreat from life's problems revealed on HFDs

In addition to the fighters and strugglers like Carl and David, and the vacillating ones like Jerry and Frankie, there are children who give up when faced with a difficult problem. Jim, Jack, and Jerome, whose HFDs are shown on *Plates 4, 11* and *12*, belonged to this group of youngsters. When faced with difficulties, they either ran away and hid or escaped into fantasy.

Jim was a 9 year old boy of superior intelligence who was a gross underachiever. In school, he spent most of the time sitting passively in his seat daydreaming, whereas, his mother reported, he was impulsive and aggressive at home, especially toward his siblings. Jim's HFD on *Plate 4* reveals three significant features: the figure is small, the neck is shaded, and the boy is running. While making the drawing, Jim spontaneously stated: "He is running, he likes to play and does not want to work or take a bath." Jim expressed likes and dislikes which are not unusual for nine year old boys, but his actual behavior was somewhat atypical. Most boys with similar attitudes register their displeasure but then ultimately conform to their parents' and teachers' demands; in the end they do do their schoolwork and they do take their baths, after a fashion. But not Jim. He had experienced so much frustration and failure in the first two grades that he had become discouraged and had withdrawn from all further efforts at school learning. The tiny figure on his HFD reflects his feelings of inadequacy. The shading of the neck reveals his attempt at controlling his impulsiveness; however, he was not very successful at doing this. He either withdrew completely or rebelled openly. Jim drew a boy "running," thus showing that he was trying to solve his dilemmas by avoiding difficult situations.

A complete psychological evaluation of Jim revealed that he was suffering from a marked difficulty in auditory perception and from a memory deficit which grossly interfered with school achievement. But these problems had not been recognized earlier. Continuous frustration had resulted in discouragement, rebellion, and finally passive withdrawal and escape into fantasy. The HFD helped the examiner to better understand Jim's behavior and pointed to further avenues of investigation and treatment.

Plate 11 was drawn by Jack, another youngster on the run. Neurological impairment and a traumatic early childhood had left their imprints on this hypersensitive child. He was an extremely vulnerable, unstable, eight year old boy of low average intelligence. His level of frustration tolerance was practically nil. Whenever Jack thought he was unable to perform a task or when something unforeseen happened, he would take flight and dash out of the room or hide under a table.

When seen at the guidance clinic, Jack was quite tense and uneasy. Upon the examiner's request, he began drawing a person. He made three circles for the head and the body, then he started to shade the body. As he worked, Jack grew increasingly more anxious and frustrated; he frowned intensely and hid his drawing from the examiner with his hand. He then commenced to draw, almost compulsively, more and more circles. Jack announced: "The boy is looking over a stone fence." The HFD on *Plate 11* is remarkable in many ways. It reflects clearly Jack's own pattern of dealing with problems. Initially, he is most willing to attempt a task; but within minutes, his anxiety and frustration become so strong that he gives up and goes into hiding or withdraws to a safe position. The stone wall in the drawing reflects two conflicting attitudes within Jack: his desire to escape and his longing to participate in social activities. The wall covers the boy so that there is no need for Jack to complete the difficult task of drawing a whole figure; it enables him to avoid the problem. On the other hand, the wall offers a safe place from which the boy can observe all that goes on about him. Jack himself was an alert and observant youngster with good understanding of social situations, even if he could not take part in them. He was painfully aware of his inadequacies which only added to his unhappiness and further contributed to his desire to hide and to run away.

Plate 12 shows the HFD of Jerome, a compulsive eight year old boy with serious emotional problems. Despite superior intelligence, Jerome was a gross underachiever who spent most of his time in school daydreaming and fantasizing. Most children Jerome's age are able to complete a HFD in ten minutes or less. Jerome spent almost one full hour drawing the picture on *Plate 12*. He would have taken even longer if the writer had not finally urged him to complete his masterpiece. Jerome chatted incessantly as he drew, explaining in great detail every stone and every flower he depicted and describing minutely the pattern on the inside of the parasol. In fact, he concentrated on everything but the human figure. He was really planning to omit the human figure altogether and only drew it reluctantly at the very end, when the writer reminded him that he had been asked to draw "a whole person." Jerome's drawing is a vivid illustration of his approach toward life: he was a very sensitive child with almost feminine appreciation of beauty and colors and design, but he could not come to grips with the essential problems of everyday life. He was compulsively preoccupied with irrelevant and minute details. He constantly procrastinated in order to avoid facing difficult tasks and himself. Social interactions were very hard for Jerome; he rather escaped passively into a world of fantasy. His reclining figure in the hammock on *Plate 12* is a nonperson devoid of eyes, nose, mouth, hands and legs; he has no means of communicating with others and cannot engage in any activity or move about. Like his figure on the HFD, Jerome himself had "left the field" and had withdrawn from the real world of people and action into his own world of fantasy.

Children's attitudes toward significant events reflected on drawings

It is the unusual and outstanding event that a child will remember in later life, and that he will tell about in his stories and pictures. The more out of the ordinary and the more disturbing an event in his life is, the greater an impression it will make and the stronger a need the child will have to express his feelings and recations to this event. It is not a matter of chance that most pictures and dreams of children portray traumatic occurrences, but this is not necessarily always the case. Very young children may express both joy and fear or anger in their drawings. Older children tend to communicate their happiness more often through words and action than through pictures, but when they are faced with sad or upsetting events, drawing and painting frequently become their preferred mode of expression.

Happy events reflected on drawings

Plates 21, 22, and *23* show the spontaneous drawings of three young children who were so filled with joy that they had to share their experiences with others; they felt a need to record on paper their big moments of happiness. Since these drawings were produced by the children spontaneously without any instructions, they cannot qualify as HFDs in the strict sense of the term and should not be analyzed as such. But they can serve as illustrations of joyful expressions of children in response to happy events in their lives.

It was a big day for Taneil, not yet five years old, when she was permitted for the first time to sit at the table with her parents and friends to partake of the Thanksgiving Day dinner. The thrill and excitement of the occasion is shown on the drawing on *Plate 21*, which was made right after the completion of the holiday feast. With the normal egocentricity of young children, Taneil presented herself (top left) as the biggest figure of all, larger than the four adults at the table. She drew herself with a big smile and placed the platter with the turkey and the other food dishes right in front of herself. In marked contrast, Taneil put no plate in front of her little sister who was not yet old enough to be seated at the table among the select. The little sister did sit in fact on a high chair a bit apart from the table, right next to the mother. The picture on *Plate 21* records a moment of joy and triumph for Taneil!

One of the highlights in a young boy's life is the day when he receives his first bicycle. *Plate 22* shows Richard's drawing on the memorable occasion. Richard, age 7, began by drawing the bicycle, and only later did he add the boy on the bicycle. It is interesting to note that he only drew those parts of the boy that are needed for the riding of the bicycle. He first drew the hands and arms so that the bicycle could be steered; then followed the head with eyes to guide the bicycle on its course; and finally Richard drew the lower portion of the legs and feet to peddle the bicycle and to make it move. The rest of the figure, the body, was omitted as unessential. The focus of the picture is clearly on the new acquisition, on the bicycle; all else is unimportant.

Plate 23 shows the drawing of Marjorie, age 6, who had recently moved from a large city to a small town. She was experiencing for the first time all the joys of winter in the country. Marjorie was very proud of her newly acquired skill in ice skating and delighted in building snowmen and in riding her sled. Her drawing (made with crayons) is a spontaneous and exuberant account of a memorable winter day. The large white clouds in the bright blue sky on the picture should not be confused with the sinister black clouds found on the HFDs of some very anxious children (*Plates 36 and 108*). The clouds on Marjorie's picture are part of a winter scene; they are welcome signs of more snow to come and more fun to be had.

Reactions to illness and hospitalization reflected on drawings

An operation is a frightening experience for a young child, even when the doctor and the parents assure him that he will be all right. Perhaps the single most upsetting thing about hospitalization is the separation from the parents and home. When Marjorie was 5 years 5 months old, she had to go to the hospital for a tonsillectomy. Her reaction to this event is shown on the quite remarkable drawing on *Plate 24*. This picture reveals better than any words could do Marjorie's feelings as she lay helpless and small in a strange bed completely at the mercy of a big, powerful nurse with a hypodermic needle, a thermometer, and a bedpan. The tiny, frightened face of the patient peeks out from the metal bed which looks almost like a cage. Marjorie's suitcase is standing on the floor, ready to be packed for the trip back home. Is it chance that the handle on the suitcase is broken, or is it an unconscious expression of her fear that she might not get to go home after all? The drawings of most five year old children are full of irregularities and poor integration of parts; since children of that age level are as yet immature and poorly coordinated, it would be a mistake to imbue every line on their drawings with profound clinical significance. But the drawing on *Plate 24* is so outstanding that the failure to connect the handle on the suitcase looks almost deliberate and not as if it had happened accidentally.

Both Taneil (*Plate 21*) and Marjorie (*Plates 23 and 24*) were children of superior intelligence who had an unusual ability to express themselves with crayons and pencils. But it would be wrong to assume that only bright or artistically gifted children can reveal their feelings on drawings. *Plate 25* shows several HFDs by Frankie, a brain injured child of dull normal intelligence who had a long history of illness, hospitalization, and emotional difficulties. In addition to his many organic and behavior problems, he suffered from an odd appearance. Due to a muscle imbalance in his eyes, Frankie had to tilt his head backwards and to one side in order to see. The cocked position of the head resulted not only in teasing and mimicry by peers, but also led Frankie to getting punished by a teacher who thought he was copying work from other children when Frankie was only trying to look at his own paper.

It was finally decided that Frankie should have an operation to correct the muscle imbalance in his eyes. On the day before he went into the hospital for this operation, Frankie came to the guidance clinic for his regular therapy session with the writer. His parents had prepared him for the operation and he knew what to expect. Frankie was even more tense and upset than usual. He did not feel like talking; instead he made clicking noises with his tongue and wanted to draw. *Plate 25c* shows one of the spontaneous drawings Frankie made on this occasion. It shows a "parachute jumper with an air mask." The drawing is crude and primitive but most expressive. It reveals Frankie's acute anxiety about his face and the eye operation. He felt "up in the air," suspended between hope and fear, all alone, without assurance whether he would land again safely or not. The face of the figure is covered with a mask, as if Frankie were seeking protection against the onslaught that is going to be made on it. The fact that the eyes and nose and mouth are covered entirely by the heavily shaded mask reflects Frankie's intense fear, withdrawal and his desire to shut out the real world. The arms and hands of the parachute jumper are reaching upward as if asking for help. *Plate 25c* is a vivid portrait of a very anxious, fearful and upset youngster who is anticipating a traumatic operation.

An even more primitive but equally expressive drawing is shown on *Plate 26*. It was made by Mickey, a retarded, emotionally disturbed, brain injured, six year old boy who attended a special class for children with multiple handicaps. Usually, Mickey was restless but cheerful. He could not follow directions or participate in structured activities, but he would play by himself for periods of time and he usually loved drawing and telling stories to adults. One day, Mickey came to school in a severely disturbed state. He could not talk and was unable to settle down at all. He ran about making peculiar noises and disrupted all other activities in his class. All efforts on the part of the teacher and the writer failed to discover what had upset Mickey. It was assumed that something had occurred in his home which had disturbed Mickey, but the parents could not be reached for confirmation.

As a last resort, the writer placed Mickey on her lap, gently but firmly, presented him with pencil and paper and asked him to draw a picture of his family. Mickey complied by drawing the picture shown on *Plate 26*.

He identified the figures as he drew them and became quite agitated as he scribbled many black lines on his father's body, calling them "blood." Once again, Mickey resumed making his peculiar noises and could not sit still any longer. The drawing was made in but a few seconds, but it provided the answer the writer had been searching for. It was apparent from the drawing that something had happened to Mickey's father and that this was the cause for his upset. The drawing helped the writer to gain some insight into his problem so that she could give him at least a little reassurance and support. The following day, it was learned that Mickey's father had been taken to the hospital with bleeding ulcers. Since Mickey adored his father, his reaction to his father's illness was understandable. Mickey was able to express on his drawing what he could not put into words.

Attitudes toward a new baby revealed on drawings

The birth of a new baby is always a big event in the lives of the other children in the family. The actual arrival of the baby at home is preceded by the pregnancy of the mother and the birth itself which is quite confusing and frightening for many children. And then there is the baby, so very small and yet so demanding. No matter how eagerly a child has anticipated the birth of a sibling, the first reaction to the new arrival is apt to be disappointment and resentment. The baby is not yet much fun; it just sleeps and eats and cries most of the time, and worst of all, it gets so much attention from the adults. In many cases, the birth of a new baby means that the older child is displaced from his favored position; but in some cases, the arrival of a new baby is the fulfillment of a long-standing wish. Obviously then, the attitudes of children toward the birth of a baby in the family will vary greatly and will reveal themselves in many different ways on drawings. *Plates 27, 28, 30,* and *31,* show the reaction of some children to this particular event in their lives.

Plate 27 was drawn by John Willy, a ten year old boy of borderline intelligence. The drawing is startling in its simplicity and directness; it reflects vividly John Willy's confusion and anxiety after the birth of a sister. Both the birth process and the physical appearance of the little girl may have been upsetting for the boy. The drawing shows not only the baby inside the mother but also reveals an oval object between the mother's legs which might represent the vaginal opening for the baby to emerge from or a penis. The HFD reflects considerable confusion about sexual differences and about childbirth. Castration anxiety and fear may account for John Willy's omission of the arms and feet from the mother figure. The drawing on *Plate 27* represents a spontaneous expression of confusion and disturbance on part of the rather dull, inhibited child who did not dare to ask directly for clarification and reassurance. So John Willy drew the picture instead and placed it timidly on the writer's desk while she was out of the room. It was apparent that he wanted information and support.

Another youngster in search of clarification and reassurance was Stephen whose HFD on *Plate 28* reveals a great deal of anxiety, insecurity, and curiosity. When seen by the writer for evaluation and treatment,

Stephen questioned her in detail about human and animal anatomy and professed a great interest in the subject. He drew spontaneously a whole series of pictures of people and animals similar to the one shown on *Plate 28*. He was particularly preoccupied with what he referred to as "mixed food bags and water bags." All this was obviously an indirect way of inquiring about the development and birth of babies. When the writer directed the discussion to that topic, Stephen dropped all pretenses and eagerly asked direct questions about pregnancy and child birth. This in turn led to his statement that his mother was expecting another baby and that he was greatly disappointed that he could not go home and live with her because of it. When Stephen was seen at the guidance clinic, he was living in a children's home.

In Stephen's case the recent birth of a half-brother and the anticipated birth of another baby meant that he had to remain in the children's home. Stephen was a ten year old boy of average intelligence with serious emotional problems. When he was four years old, his father committed suicide and Stephen and his five siblings were placed in the children's home. When the mother remarried a few years later, the children were told that they could come home and live with her and the new stepfather. But the arrival of the baby and the mother's latest pregnancy and ill health changed all that.

Stephen's attitude toward his little half-brother and toward his mother and stepfather was full of resentment and anger; at the same time he was curious about the pregnancies and about child birth, and he longed for a home of his own with his mother and a father. Through his drawings, Stephen was able to reveal his intense anxiety and was able to ask indirectly for information. Many children are too shy or too upset to verbalize their questions. It is then up to the clinician to decipher their questions as portrayed in pictures. By clarifying Stephen's confusion and concern about child birth, it was possible to get him to focus on the much more serious and disturbing feelings of rejection which he was experiencing, and on his ambivalence toward his mother and stepfather. About ten days after Stephen made the HFD on *Plate 28*, he produced the drawing on *Plate 29*. The acute anxiety shown on the earlier drawing had subsided; *Plate 29* shows a gun-toting Davy Crockett, the popular hero of the day, on his way to hunt bears. This picture shows symbolically that Stephen had shifted his concern from pregnancies to a more direct expression of hostility and anger. He was now ready to hunt for big game; Stephen was now able to face his resentment toward his parents.

The birth of a baby can also be a happy event for the other child in the family. Dorothy, age 9, considered her younger brother, age 5, a "pest," but she was overjoyed at the birth of a baby sister. When asked to draw a picture of her family (*Plate 30*), Dorothy first drew herself and then the new baby Kathy. She always referred to Kathy as "my baby." On the drawing, she placed her father right next to herself and added a bit reluctantly the brother on the other side of Kathy. The mother was only drawn as an afterthought and then only at the far righthand side of the paper, apart from the rest of the family. The size and the position of the various family members reveal Dorothy's attitude toward them. (This aspect of the drawing will be discussed in more detail later on (page 141). There can be no doubt that Dorothy loved the baby and wished that the baby were her very own. She awarded the baby the central spot in the picture and placed herself right next to the baby in the natural position of the mother. Her attitude toward the mother's pregnancy and the actual birth process appears to be ambivalent. The way the mother figure is drawn suggests both anxiety and probably envy. In contrast to the other four figures on the drawing, the mother shows a large naval which may stand for the vagina; her abdomen is heavily shaded and reveals transparencies which seem to focus attention on the mother's body. All these features are unusual on the drawings of ten year old girls and are probably related to Dorothy's feelings and concern regarding the mother's pregnancy and the birth of her sister. The total drawing on *Plate 30* suggests that Dorothy wants to put herself in her mother's place; she is very happy to have a new baby in the family but is envious of her mother.

For Henry, the birth of a new baby in the family meant displacement and unhappiness. One of the most-heart rending picture's in the writer's collection of children's drawings is shown on *Plate 31*. It was drawn by Henry, a nine year old boy of average intelligence, who had a history of neurological impairment and who had suffered from physical neglect, deprivation and much instability in his home. Henry was subject to violent temper outbursts, at which time he became unmanageable. The one positive factor in his life had been the warmth and affection his mother had shown him despite her gross deficiencies as manager and provider. The alcoholic, abusive father had left the family some years back. Henry was the youngest of six siblings and his mother's favorite. Henry had been, up to this point, secure in her love, which was reflected in his sunny and warm disposition. He was always dirty and always needed a haircut; his behavior was erratic and at times very explosive; but despite all, the teachers liked him, for Henry always had a ready smile and was responsive and affectionate.

Then one day, Henry lost his smile and became even more aggressive and unmanageable than before. No amount of questioning could elicit from Henry the cause for his sudden change in behavior. Sudden changes in a child's behavior are often related to events in the family circle; therefore, the writer asked Henry to draw a picture of his family. He produced the drawing shown on *Plate 31*. It is a primitive and crude sketch, but most expressive. Henry first drew a figure and said: "That's me, I am yelling because the baby took my lollipop." Then he added a second smaller figure with a lollipop in her hand and announced: "This is my baby sister, she is yelling too because her daddy spanked her." He finally drew a house and began drawing another figure in a window but stopped. "The rest of the family is in the house," Henry said.

There are several noteworthy features about the drawing on *Plate 31*. To begin with, Henry did not have a baby sister. But inquiry revealed that his married sister had given birth to a baby a few days earlier. So this was the reason for Henry's sudden change in behavior; he was no longer the baby, the favored youngest member of the family. "The baby took his lollipop away." The lollipop serves here as a symbol for the sweetest thing in any child's life, for his mother's love and affection. Henry's mother adored all small children but had little feeling or understanding for boys and girls when they were no longer cute and cuddly. She had already begun to lose interest in Henry as he grew older, just as she had done with all her other children. Now the mother had found in her grandaughter a new object for her affection. She spent all day at her daughter's house cooing over the new baby and neglected Henry even more than before. He had to fend for himself after school and had to get his own meals.

Henry was too fond of his mother to express his resentment toward her openly. So he vented his anger and frustration on the new baby instead. The story he told in connection with his drawing represents his wishdream: the baby gets a spanking from her father. The baby is being punished for usurping his privileged position. Henry stated that the father did the punishing. This is of interest; it may reflect Henry's hostile attitude toward his own father who punished him by deserting him. Henry omitted all facial features from the drawing of the baby as if he were trying to blot her out, as if he were denying her reality. He did not specify who the figure in the window was; it too lacks a face and is not communicating with Henry. It would be hard to depict more vividly the impact of a new baby on the life of an older child than Henry did with a few pencil lines and some brief comments regarding his drawing.

Attitudes toward separation from parents reflected on drawings

Ann (*Plate 5*) was overwhelmed and frightened by her mother's sudden and mysterious disappearance. Ann's parents were both quite immature and unstable; they were unable to care for Ann and for her three siblings. The children lived therefore with their grandmother, where their mother joined them periodically. Then one day, the mother left and never returned. No one had thought of telling Ann that her mother was ill and had been taken to the State Hospital. The grandmother who rejected her own daughter also rejected Ann who resembled her mother physically. The other children seemed much less disturbed than Ann since they received much warmth and acceptance from the grandmother. Ann had never been happy in her grandmother's home and missed her mother much more than her younger brothers and sister. After the mother's unexplained disappearance, Ann began to regress in her behavior, she soiled herself, refused to talk, and withdrew from others.

When seen at the guidance clinic, Ann was 7 years and 2 months old. She appeared to be of low average intelligence; her refusal to talk made the administration of formal tests difficult. Ann was entirely uncommunicative until she was asked to draw. *Plate 5* shows her HFD. Ann drew a tiny isolated girl who has lost her balance and who peers with big frightened eyes at a hostile world. The large ears suggest that she might have heard rumors about her mother, or that she is listening for news from her. The omission of the nose and the mouth reflect her withdrawal and refusal to communicate with others. The picture reveals grief, fear, isolation; it is a true portrait of her inner feelings and attitudes. When asked to draw a man or boy, Ann complied by drawing a rather crude but conventional man complete with all essential details including the mouth and nose. Only on the drawing of the girl, herself, did she show her intense anxiety and anguish over the loss of her mother.

Joel (*Plate 32*) was an 11 year old boy of superior intelligence who showed evidence of brain injury. He had a long history of learning and behavior problems. However, while attending special classes for children with emotional and neurological problems, Joel had demonstrated good progress both in his achievement and in his social adjustment. Then quite suddenly, his behavior regressed and Joel began taking things in school and in the community. When seen by the writer, Joel was unable to verbalize the reasons for the change in his behavior and attitudes. When asked to draw a picture of his family, he produced the drawing on *Plate 32*. This drawing reveals what Joel could not put into words: His father is walking away from the family while Joel, the oldest son who feels closely attached to the father, looks back at him in sorrow. Joel had been aware for some time that his father was going to leave the family, but that made the separation no less painful. After years of marital strife, his parents had finally legally separated, Joel had wanted to go with the father, but the court awarded all the children to the mother. Joel was most unhappy.

In the drawing, the father looks quite cheerful, but the figure of the son is mutilated: it lacks arms, nose, mouth; without the father, Joel feels incomplete. On earlier HFDs, Joel had always drawn boys who were completely intact and who did not lack any essential parts of their anatomy. This drawing is different. The picture on *Plate 32* expresses both Joel's feeling of loss of the father and his anxiety and guilt over his stealing (omission of arms) which is, of course, also a reaction to the father's departure.

It is interesting to note that Joel drew the mother and the siblings in frontal view without any distortions and without much emotional involvement on his part. The action and drama in the picture occur between Joel and his father. They are placed at the two opposite ends of the family group as if to stress the distance that has come between them.

Ann and Joel were children who had parents whom they knew and loved and who then suffered the loss and separation from these parents. Timothy, (*Plate 33*) on the other hand, was a youngster who had never known his father but longed for him with all his heart. Timothy was born out of wedlock to a girl of modest intellectual endowment. Timothy lived, with his timid, dull mother, an indifferent unmarried uncle, his stern, domineering grandmother and the meek grandfather. Timothy and his mother were barely tolerated in the grandmother's home. The boy had always been sickly and suffered from a partial hearing loss. He lived a very sheltered and completely isolated life without any playmates. Timothy filled the long and lonely hours with drawing and daydreaming. He was grossly deficient in all social and academic skills, but he could draw quite well and possessed a keen fantasy life.

All of Timothy's drawings and fantasies centered around one topic only: his father. He produced endless variations on the theme. It did not matter what he was asked to draw, he always managed to bring the father into the picture. When he was asked to draw a picture of his family, he announced at once: "I have a Daddy too, but he lives far away on another planet." Then Timothy proceeded to draw his actual family according to their age and importance: on *Plate 33*, the overpowering grandmother leads the procession; she is followed by the grandfather, then come the mother and the uncle, and finally there is Timothy himself. All the family members are lined up, one behind the other; they do not interact. Just when the writer thought that Timothy had finished his drawing, he introduced with bold strokes the object of his dreams, the absent and yet ever-present father. The father appears in this picture as Superman and informs the assembled family with a benign smile (in contrast to the grandmother's grim expression) and a grand gesture that he is going to return to them to stay. Timothy said: "And Superman came from another planet, he is telling them that he is coming to live with them on this planet, his planet is being blown up." In his fantasy, Timothy performs miracles in order to bring home the father whom he longs for. Timothy cannot talk about his father directly beyond saying that he has a father; but in his drawings, he can express most eloquently his dreams and wishes for the idealized father whom he has never known.

Children's attitudes toward themselves as reflected on HFDs

It is difficult, if not impossible, to understand a child's behavior if one does not understand the child's perception of himself. The casual observer and even adults who know the child well may view him very differently from the way the child sees himself. Thus, a child whom others considered to be attractive, intelligent and well behaved, may perceive himself as ugly, stupid, and "bad," and may act accordingly. Whereas, a rather plain and dull child may think of himself as handsome and clever. Objective psychological tests and measurements compare a child with a great many other children and with some mythical "average child," but the youngster himself has no such basis for comparison; he forms his attitudes towards himself from the way the significant adults in his life treat him. If his parents have treated him in early life as though he is a beautiful child, then he will learn to think of himself as such; but if he has been given to understand that he is not up to his parent's expectations, then he will perceive himself as inadequate.

It is often difficult for a teacher or clinician to comprehend why a most likable and capable child is so self-depreciating and lacking in self-confidence until one meets the perfectionistic parents who are never pleased or satisfied with anything the child does and who constantly compare him to his outstanding older sister or brother. On the other hand, the writer has often marvelled at the emotional security and self-acceptance of some children with quite severe physical and mental defects. These children have received so much love and acceptance from their parents that they learned to think of themselves as acceptable and adequate. A child's attitude toward himself is dependent on his parents attitude toward him and not on some objective measure of beauty or intelligence. And the treatment of a child with emotional problems must be geared to his image of himself and not to the therapist's image of the child.

One of the best ways of finding out how a child feels about himself is to have him make an HFD. As was mentioned earlier (page 75), a HFD is a portrait of the inner child, of his attitudes toward himself. This portrait may or may not correspond to his actual, physical appearance. If a child's HFD were nothing but a realistic reproduction of himself, then it would be of little clinical value. The very fact that some HFDs show little or no resemblance to the child's physical image make them clinically so meaningful. As Loewenfeld (1939) and Machover pointed out, a child will emphasize and exaggerate on his drawings those parts of the figure which have special meaning for him. He will change and distort a human figure on his drawing until it resembles or reflects his own perception of himself. Thus, it is not at all unusual for an emotionally disturbed child to produce on his HFD a monster, a clown, or a robot, or to omit or add parts of the figure which may give the drawing a grotesque look. The drawings reproduced in this volume are by no means unique and can be duplicated many times by other drawings in the writer's collection of HFDs.

A child may be concerned about many different aspects of himself. He may worry about his size and consider himself too tall or too short; he may not like his physical appearance or his age; he may be sensitive about some real or imagined disability or mental shortcoming; he may be haunted by feelings of being "bad" and sinful. In this chapter, it will be shown how all of these different attitudes can be reflected on HFDs. The children whose drawings will be presented here vary greatly in age, intelligence, and background, but this has little bearing on their ability to express their attitudes about themselves on HFDs. A five year old boy may be able to convey his anxieties about himself just as vividly as a twelve year old, although the latter may possess more technical drawing skill.

Concern about age reflected on HFDs

Each age level has its own rewards and problems. Most children seem to be satisfied with their actual age and look forward to growing up and gaining more maturity as time goes on. Hence, most children draw figures that are about as old as they are themselves or slightly older. But occasionally a child will draw a figure of a boy or girl who is much younger than he is. The intended age of the drawn figure can usually be determined by asking the child how old the person on his picture is. Sometimes, a child may say a figure is his age or older when he actually draws an infant or toddler. That is, sometimes the child shows in his drawing his unconscious wish of being still an infant even when he consciously denies it.

Clinical experience has shown that those youngsters, who draw children much younger than they themselves are, find little satisfaction in their present life and long for a return to an earlier period when they were younger and happier. Especially, children with learning problems often dream of the pre-school years as the golden years when they were as yet free from pressure for achievement. Children who lack success experiences in school and with peers find little reward in growing up and envy the younger siblings who can stay at home with mother. They often wish that they too could be small and dependent again.

One such child was Tommy, age ten, whose HFD is shown on *Plate 34*. Tommy was of average intelligence but suffered from a speech disorder and learning problems; he was quite immature, emotionally dependent and anxious. His perfectionistic and striving parents had high hopes for their only son and put considerable pressure on Tommy to excel in school. But despite all efforts and special tutoring sessions, Tommy could not meet his parent's expectations. He attended school in a community where the majority of children had high average or superior ability. Tommy just could not compete with them. Each successive year, Tommy's school grades went down a little more while he developed more and more fears, nervous mannerisms, and stomach upsets. He was unable to get along with his little sister and his peers.

When asked to draw a person, Tommy produced the toddler shown on *Plate 34*. He said the boy was three years old, which also happened to be his sister's age. The HFD is quite revealing: The way it is drawn reflects Tommy's feeling about himself, while the indicated age level of the figure shows the age and status he would like to return to. The big head emphasizes his anxiety about scholastic achievement and about his intellectual ability. The Emotional Indicators on the drawing are related to his present concerns: the short arms and legs reveal his feeling of helplessness, passivity, and his inability to move forward toward greater maturity; the omission of the nose may be a sign of his withdrawal as well as an indication of possible castration anxiety. The latter was also suggested by the shading of the body and by Tommy's intense sibling rivalry with his very bright younger sister.

The content of the drawing on *Plate 34* shows Tommy's negative attitude toward growing up and his dissatisfaction with his present age level; it reflects his longing for the time when he was three years old and did not have to go to school and did not have a sister who competed with him. At that time, he could still please his parents and was therefore still happy. Tommy's HFD indicates that he approaches life's problems by withdrawing and escaping in his fantasy to an earlier, happier period in his life.

The normal, healthy child strives toward maturation and adulthood. As children approach adolescence, it can be expected that they will draw ideal images of themselves at a slightly older age level; very often, such figures are shown in uniform or evening dress or in some status-giving attire. The images drawn are usually positive figures in keeping with the social values and mores of the culture in which the child lives. (Dennis, 1966). But every now and then, a child will draw an anti-hero, an older person who rebels against society as they know it. These types of drawings are usually produced by hostile and angry children who have derived little pleasure from childhood and who long to get away from home and school; they dream of being big, independent and powerful.

Eric (*Plate 35*) belonged to this negativistic and hostile group of youngsters. He longed to escape from childhood. Eric and Tommy (*Plate 34*) were almost identical in age; they both had a WISC Full Scale IQ of 103, both had learning problems and poor peer relationships. But that is where the resemblance ended. Whereas Tommy came from a high socio-economic background and was exposed to too much parental pressure and concern, Eric's family led a marginal, unstable existence in a low-income area. Eric had experienced considerable physical and emotional neglect throughout his life and he had learned long since to fend for himself. He spent most of his free time hanging around street corners with older boys. It was a matter of survival for him to be tough and a good fighter. But even an excellent fighter feels pretty small and defenseless in a teen-age world when he is only ten years old. So it was only natural that Eric dreamed of being 18 or 20 years old and of being an even better fighter and tougher guy than he was now. Childhood and school held little satisfaction for Eric. Since his father and older brothers also could not read or write, he was not very upset by his own scholastic failure. His classmates were too immature and childish to be of much interest for him.

Eric showed his contempt for school by making frequent derogatory comments in class and by refusing to participate in class activities. It was not surprising that Eric's teacher found it difficult to interest him in a fourth grade curriculum. Eric's true interests and his ideal are beautifully illustrated on his HFD, shown on *Plate 35*. The content of the drawing reveals Eric's dream image: he longs to be a fully grown tough guy who can swagger in and out of bars and can throw his weight around. The Emotional Indicators on the drawing, the teeth, the omission of the neck, and the long powerful arms, all reflect Eric's impulsivity, hostility, and his aggressive attitude toward himself and the world.

Jonathan, age 7 years 9 months, also had learning problems and longed to escape from school and from parental pressure for achievement. He too wanted to be older than he was, but in contrast to Eric, Jonathan had a positive model to aspire to. When asked to make a HFD, Jonathan produced the picture on *Plate 36;* it represents his older cousin whom he greatly admired. He explained that he wanted to be "a big man like my cousin, he did not go to college . . . he works." Jonathan's ambition to grow up and work with his hands instead of going to college was realistic and his parents were urged to support this ambition.

Tommy, Eric, and Jonathan (*Plates 34, 35, 36*) were all three dissatisfied with their present status and age. Their HFDs show how one of the boys wished he could escape from the presence by regressing to an earlier and happier age, while the other two wanted to free themselves from the confines of childhood by achieving the freedom and independence of adults.

Concern about physical appearance reflected on HFDs

Most children have little awareness of or concern about their bodies or looks as they go about living a full and active life. But once a child's attention is drawn to some unusual feature in his appearance, he may get to be quite self-conscious about it and may develop neurotic preoccupations and anxieties, especially if he is teased about it. Such complexes may be centered around a child's size, body development, skin color or any other feature. Below are given a few examples of HFDs of children which reflect their reactions to specific physical features.

CONCERN ABOUT SMALLNESS. It is tough for a boy to have to compete at all times with a brother who is exactly one year older and who can do everything the boy can do, only better. It is even worse when the brother is tall and good-looking while the boy is unusually short and immature for his age. Such was the case for Peter (*Plate 37*). Peter, eight years old, had the appearance of a six year old child. He bitterly resented it when his brother and his friends called him "peanut" and teased him because of his size. He hated it, that he was always the smallest and weakest in the crowd. Peter longed desperately to catch up with his peers and to be even taller and stronger than his archrival, his brother.

Plate 37 shows Peter's HFD. He made several attempts at drawing a whole figure on one sheet of paper but never succeeded. He finally decided to use two sheets of paper, carefully piecing them together with scotch tape. The drawing which Peter at long last completed reflects quite graphically how intensely Peter felt about his diminutive size and how much he yearned to be tall. The writer has in her collection several HFDs that extend over two sheets of paper. Some of these were made by boys, some by girls; the children who made them varied greatly in intelligence and in their behavior; their age ranged from 8 years to 15 years; but they all had one thing in common: they were all unusually short and they were extremely sensitive about their size. All of them wanted desperately to be taller.

Plate 16 shows the HFD of Shirley whose case was discussed earlier (page 79). Shirley was also a tiny child who was most unhappy about her small stature. She drew a very large figure that extended beyond the edges of the paper; she too would have required a second sheet of paper if she had wanted to complete the drawing. But Shirley left the drawing unfinished, cut off by the edge of the paper; she lacked the determination of Peter who solved his space problem by demanding more paper to draw on. In both cases, the large drawings, whether completed or not, seem to reveal the children's concern about their physical smallness. It should be pointed out, however, that not all children who are small in size draw huge figures. The expansive drawing is a direct expression of concern and anxiety or resentment. Many very tiny children have no strong feelings about their size, some even enjoy the special attention and protection they usually receive because of it. These children do not draw excessively large figures.

CONCERN ABOUT EXCESSIVE HEIGHT. Children vary greatly in body development and height as they approach adolescence. It is not uncommon for some girls and boys to shoot up practically overnight and to find themselves towering half a head above their classmates. These children are usually quite sensitive about height and are often teased because of it. Laura (*Plate 38*), age ten, was one of these excessively tall, skinny girls. She was called "beanpole" by her peers and hardly a day went by without someone making jokes about her size. Laura was extremely self-conscious about her appearance and walked with a stoop in an effort to hide her true height. She refused to get up in class to recite in front of the others and withdrew more and more. Prior to her growth spurt, she had been an average girl who was outgoing and socially well adjusted. But more recently, she had become sullen and unhappy.

When asked to make a HFD, Laura produced the tiny figure shown on *Plate 38*. The size and the slant of her figure reflect her insecurity and intense concern about her height. The figure looks as if someone had pushed the head down into the body to shorten it. The head, arms, and legs are all in good proportion to each other, only the body is squeezed together and the neck is omitted. The HFD seems to show what Laura wishes she could do with herself, namely, to reduce herself to a smaller size so that she won't be so conspicuous among her peers.

CONCERN OVER SECONDARY SEX CHARACTERISTICS. Along with an increase in height and weight, the budding adolescent begins to develop secondary sex characteristics. A child's reaction to body changes will depend to a large extent on the attitude of the important other people in his life. Bodily maturation is a normal process and need not cause any emotional disturbances in the child if the parents prepare him wisely for the change. But if a child is taught that his developing body and the growing impulses, associated with this development, are evil and sinful, then he will most likely react to them with anxiety and guilt.

Debrah (*Plate 39*) belonged to the group of girls who mature early. When she was 11 years and 8 months old, she was a tall, fully developed young lady of striking appearance. She could easily have passed for 15 or 16, although she was emotionally still quite immature. But Debrah's good looks caused her much agony and brought her eventually to the guidance clinic for help. Her stern and rather plain stepmother was a staunch member of a fundamentalist church which considered the body evil and all matters related to sex sinful. She viewed Debrah's physical development with alarm and never missed a chance to preach to the girl on the evils of sex. She accused Debrah of being "oversexed just like her older sister" whom Debrah resembled in appearance. This sister had eloped at age 16 primarily in order to escape from the home and the stepmother. But the stepmother was unable or unwilling to admit that this was the case. She was now making life impossible for Debrah in a misguided attempt to prevent her from following in her sister's "evil" ways.

Debrah reacted to her stepmother's preaching and nagging with open defiance at home and in school. But when she was seen at the guidance center, she confided to the writer that she was quite worried lest she really was "oversexed." Debrah's HFD (*Plate 39*) reflects both her rebelliousness and her acute anxiety about her body development and her stirring impulses. The bold pencil lines on the figure on *Plate 39* and the defiant expression of the face are in marked contrast to the hidden hands and stubby feet. The grossly exaggerated breasts and the heavily shaded, contracted waistline of the figure reveal her desperate attempt at controlling her normal drives and desires, and show her very real concern and fear of her sexuality.

Debrah's HFD is a good illustration of how a child draws his feelings about himself and not a portrait of his actual physical self. After she had been seen by the writer for several months of guidance and therapy, Debrah was asked again to draw a whole person. This time, she produced a well proportioned teenage girl in an evening gown. This drawing was neither unduly large nor very small, and it showed none of the exaggerated features of the earlier HFD. It was obvious that Debrah had not changed physically in that time, but she had changed her attitude toward her body and toward her very normal sexual development.

CONCERN ABOUT HAIR. It has been said that "the hair is a woman's crowning glory" and most girls spend many hours each week washing, setting and combing their hair. They probably devote more time and attention to their hair than to anything else. It is therefore not surprising that most maturing girls also devote special attention and effort to the drawing of the hair on their HFDs. Machover has suggested that glamorous treatment of hair on drawings connotes sensuality, while rumpled and disorderly hair indicates sexual excitement. These interpretations may be correct for adolescents and adults, but they do not necessarily hold true for younger children.

Hair can be the source of joy and pride, but it can also be the cause for embarrassment and anguish. With the rapidly changing hairstyles of our time, it is inevitable that the girl with long, stringy hair will be miserable when short and curly hair is in style, while the curly-haired youngster will suffer agonies when long, straight hair is in vogue. And then there are children like Dorothy, age nine, whose hair is one big "mess." *Plate 30* shows Dorothy's family portrait. The single most outstanding feature on this drawing is the treatment of her own hair. None of the other family members on the drawing show as much wild hair as the figure of Dorothy does. If nothing else were known about the girl, it might be assumed that this treatment of the hair reflects sexual precocity. But the writer is inclined always to look first for the most obvious and simple explanation of drawing signs before making deeper symbolic interpretations thereof. In Dorothy's case, the most obvious thing was to look at the child herself. Beyond a doubt, the most outstanding physical feature of Dorothy was her hair. She had a mass of extremely heavy, curly, ill-kempt hair. In addition, Dorothy usually showed also much neglect in her total appearance; along with a bath and clean clothes, she was most of the time badly in need of a shampoo, a haircut and just plain grooming. But Dorothy was as yet too young and too poorly trained to care for herself, and her immature, unstable mother was quite unable to provide adequate care for her children.

Dorothy was very sensitive about her hair, particularly since her peers would not let her play with them and called her among other things "ragmop." About one week after Dorothy drew the picture shown on *Plate 30*, she was asked to fill out an Incomplete Sentence Blank. Among the sentences she completed were the following:

Sometimes I........hate myself.

Other kids........hate me, they don't like my hair.

People think that I........am terrible because of my hair, and because
                              of my behavior.

I need........a new set of hair.

Thus we find Dorothy's well-founded concern over her hair expressed on both her family drawing and on the Incomplete Sentence Blank. There can be therefore no doubt as to the meaning of the exaggerated treatment of the hair on the drawing. In view of Dorothy's strong feelings about her hair, steps were initiated to teach Dorothy to care for her own hair which resulted in a big improvement in her appearance and in a gradual change in her self-concept.

While Dorothy was unhappy because she had too much hair, Odetta *(Plate 40)*, a ten year old colored girl of normal intelligence, was very self-conscious because she did not have enough hair. Odetta's hair was extremely short and did not grow despite extensive treatments with oils and creams. She labored hard over her hair in an effort to straighten it and lengthen it. Odetta had very poor interpersonal relationships and a long history of behavior and emotional problems. She attributed most of her problems to her own "ugliness," especially to her short hair. This was, of course, a vast oversimplification and distortion of the actual situation; but to Odetta, it was real and she hated herself and her appearance—above all, she hated her hair. When Odetta was requested to make an HFD, she asked for permission to use crayons. *Plate 40* shows the HFD she made with crayons. She drew with utmost care a girl with long, straight blond hair and big blue eyes. This was her dream image! She longed to be blond and blue-eyed and to have beautiful long silky hair that could be worn in a ponytail.

Unfortunately, Odetta was not unique. It is not uncommon for Negro children to reject their own appearance. Dennis (1966) reports that almost all of the drawings he obtained several years ago from Negro boys in Mississippi and in Brooklyn, New York, represented Caucasian men with Caucasian hair. Only a very small percentage of the boys drew figures with Negroid features and Negroid hair. Dennis hypothesized that children draw the kind of persons whom they admire. He interprets his findings as rejection by the Negro youngsters of their racial identity and appearance and a desire on their part to look like white people.

The writer's own experiences with Negro children several years back in Tennessee, in Ohio, and in New York State, were similar to those of Dennis. Ten or even five years ago, it was rare to find a colored child who would depict a Negro on his HFD. However, at present the situation seems to be changing. When the writer collected recently several hundred HFDs from two schools with predominantly colored pupils, a sizable number of the drawings unmistakably revealed figures with Negroid features and Negroid hair. These figures were for the most part drawn in a positive and accepting way without denial or self-rejection. *Plate 41* shows the HFDs of three colored girls of normal intelligence who drew figures of

Negro girls. The treatment of the hair on these drawings is particularly interesting. The three hair styles depicted represent actual hair styles worn by the girls and by their older sisters. One drawing even shows the exaggerated beehive hairdo which is sometimes achieved with the help of a wig or a hairpiece. This hairdo may look rather grotesque to a staid middle-class, middle-aged adult, but it was regarded as the height of fashion and sophistication among the younger, faster set. All three HFDs on *Plate 41* represent figures and hairdos to which the girls could actually aspire and are not unrealistic dream images like the one Odetta produced on *Plate 40*.

This greater acceptance of Negro children of themselves and of their appearance, as reflected on HFDs, is probably a direct result of their new-found pride in the emergent African nations and in the civil rights movement in this country. It is, of course, not possible to say how widespread among Negro children this change in self-concept is, since the writer's experience is at present limited to the drawings of youngsters in one small Northern industrial town.

CONCERN ABOUT OBESITY. Obesity in children may result from several different causes, and children's reaction to their own overweight also varies greatly. Some obese children are quite pleased with themselves, which is understandable when one meets their obese parents and siblings. But the neurotic child who overeats is an unhappy child. And the unhappier he is, the more he will eat and the heavier he will get. These children tend to be quite sensitive about their appearance; they would like to lose weight, but are usually unable to control their appetites.

Benjie *(Plate 42)*, age 9, was one of these unhappy, overweight children. He was of average intelligence, but very sensitive, excitable, and restless. His school achievement was poor and he showed impaired visual-motor perception. Benjie had been a sickly baby who presented feeding problems throughout his early childhood. His anxious mother used to coax him to eat and spoon-fed him until age six. When Benjie started going to school, he began eating on his own and never stopped eating after that time. He put on a great deal of weight and was mercilessly teased by his peers, which only increased his anxiety and his appetite. *Plate 42* shows Benjie's HFD.

He started out by drawing a head and a coonskin cap and announced: "It's Davy Crockett." But then he drew the body of the figure and added: "No, it's Jackie Gleason, because he is so fat." In his subconscious or even conscious mind, he probably added: "just like me." Benjie was too honest to delude himself into thinking that he would ever be an heroic figure like Davy Crockett, but by saying that his figure was Jackie Gleason, he seemed to try to convince himself that even fat guys can be famous and successful. Once again, the subject matter or content of the HFD reveals the child's dream and aspiration, while the details of the drawing reflect Benjie's actual feeling about himself. The poorly integrated plump fellow on the drawing is Benjie himself, unable to act or to reach out, he lacks hands. He is also uncertain where he is going, since his feet are pointing in both directions at once.

CONCERN ABOUT SKIN COLOR. The young child who is fully accepted in his family and neighborhood will have little conscious concern about his skin color. But when he enters school and moves out into the larger community, he will become more and more aware of racial differences and of the reaction of others to his complexion. A child's pigmentation may become a matter of great concern to him and as such it will be reflected on his HFDs.

Keith *(Plate 43)*, age seven and a half, had always been a lively and outgoing youngster. Then when he was in the second grade, his behavior seemed to change; he became more and more aggressive and defiant both at home and in school. Keith was constantly in fights with other children and was generally considered a troublemaker. His mother and teacher were at a loss to explain this change in behavior. The school psychologist referred him for psychiatric help to the guidance clinic.

When Keith was asked to make an HFD, he produced the figure shown on *Plate 43*. He completed the drawing rather rapidly and then added quite carefully and deliberately the circles on the boy's face and neck. In response to questioning, Keith said that the boy "has measles." But further inquiry revealed that Keith had never had the measles nor did he know anyone who had the measles at that time; he also stated that he had recently neither heard nor read anything about measles. As Keith put it: "I just felt like drawing measles." A check with his mother confirmed his claim that he had had no recent contact with or exposure to measles in any form. What then is the meaning of the "measles"?

The writer is inclined to consider the "measles" on the drawing a form of shading and an indicator of anxiety and self-consciousness about his skin color. It so happened that Keith had a lovely, smooth, café-au-lait complexion. He was the child of a blond Caucasian mother and a dark-skinned Negro father. The family had moved not long ago to a racially mixed urban community where conditions were tense and steadily deteriorating as more unskilled Southern Negroes and backwoods hillbillies moved into the area and competed for the same jobs and houses. In school and in the community, Keith found himself caught between the two racial groups, not being fully accepted by either one of them. He rebelled openly against the rejection he suffered and tried to fight for his place in society. The HFD on *Plate 43* shows Keith's self-consciousness and concern over his skin color. He was being treated by his peers as if in fact he did have the "measles," as if he were one to be avoided. Perhaps Keith wished that his dark coloring would vanish just as the red blotches of the measles disappear in due time. Keith's drawing showed clearly that he was in need of counseling and guidance to help him achieve better acceptance of himself. At the same time, plans were worked out with the teacher to help bring about greater tolerance and cooperation between the various students in the class.

Danny, age eleven, was another Negro child who was concerned about his skin color. *Plate 76* shows his HFD. He depicted Frankenstein and the Apeman. Danny shaded the Apeman's face with many short pencil marks that were probably meant to represent fur, but the total effect is that of a Negro boy and reflects undoubtedly his concern about his own dark complexion.

The HFDs on *Plates 14, 27, 40, 56, 65 and 66* were all drawn by Negro children with serious emotional problems, but none of these drawings reveal a particular preoccupation with skin color. This is not to say that these children were indifferent about their pigmentation; but at the time they made their HFDs, skin color was not the thing they were most concerned about. A child will emphasize on his HFDs those attitudes and anxieties that are uppermost in his mind at that given moment. These particular children had many other problems, fears, and anxieties which were of greater importance to them at that time and which were therefore reflected on their HFDs.

Plates 41 and 44 show the HFDs of well-adjusted Negro children who were good students in school and who had a positive self-concept. They drew figures that are unmistakably Negroid in appearance. Skin color is no major issue for these children. Some children left the faces and limbs of their figures blank or white, while Manuel *(Plate 44)* shaded the face, hands and legs of his figure smoothly and evenly, showing realistically his own dark complexion. The shading on *Plate 44* is in marked contrast to that on *Plate 43 and 76*. Manuel drew deliberately and comfortably an attractive colored girl with Negroid features and skin color like his own whereas the shading on Keith's figure and on Danny's Apeman reflects above all anxiety and concern about their racial identity. It is of utmost importance to study the quality and intensity of shading of the face and limbs on a HFD, since the meaning of such shading can vary greatly.

CONCERN ABOUT PHYSICAL STRENGTH. Anyone working with growing boys is bound to spend many hours each year feeling and admiring the sprouting biceps of the young "supermen" who are eager to display and demonstrate their first visible sign of physical strength and power. This small bulging muscle stands for so much more than just the ability to beat up the next fellow; it is almost a status symbol among third and fourth graders and symbolizes budding manliness and independence. And woe unto the youngster who lags behind in his physical development, whose skinny arm is one more obvious sign of his weakness and insignificance. At least, that is the way it looked to Philip, the eight year old boy whose HFD is shown on *Plate 45.*

Philip was a small, hypersensitive and anxious boy who felt overwhelmed by his environment. His striving, highly articulate parents expected a great deal from their five children, and all of them except Philip excelled in school and in the community. Philip was constantly exposed to parental pressure for greater achievement, while his older siblings lorded over him and made him feel utterly small and unimportant. The only one smaller than he in the family was his younger sister who was the undisputed darling and pet of them all. She received more attention and affection than all the rest of the children. Philip felt like a "nobody" at home and in school. His clumsy attempts at gaining recognition from his peers usually ended by his being beaten and outright rejected. He annoyed the other children by his silly and disturbing behavior.

The HFD on *Plate 45* reveals both Philip's poor self-concept and his ideal dream image. The skinny, poorly integrated arms and legs and the small head with the foolish grin reflect Philip's feelings of weakness and inadequacy, while the content of the drawing shows his desire to be a strongman with bulging muscles who can lift great weights with one hand. Philip emphasized the muscles both in shape and by shading. The large size of the muscles expresses his wish for power and manliness, whereas the shading indicates his anxiety about his own lack of muscles and strength. These two attitudes were also contained in his spontaneous comments about his HFD: "This is a strongman . . . he is happy, he can beat up everyone, even Albert, he is the strongest in our class . . . I am the weakest."

Concern about specific disabilities reflected on HFDs

Machover (1949) and others who accept the body image hypothesis for HFDs (page 4) have concluded that a person with a specific disability or bodily impairment would reflect the same on his HFD. When research studies failed to support this hypothesis (Centers and Centers, 1963), it was suggested that children with physical handicaps who fail to show body distortion or conflict signs on their HFDs were either denying their problem or were drawing a wish-fulfilling image.

In the present volume, neither the body image hypothesis nor the implications drawn from it are accepted as necessarily valid. Once again, it should be stated that this writer maintains that HFDs reflect a child's *attitude* toward himself and his body. Therefore, the drawing need not bear any resemblance to the child's actual appearance. A perfectly healthy, well-developed child, whose overprotective mother has fussed over him for years, may have become a hypochondriac and may perceive himself as an invalid and a cripple. On his HFD, he may portray himself as such. While another child, physically handicapped from birth or early childhood but fully accepted and loved by mature and stable parents, may have made a very good emotional and social adjustment and may not actually think of himself as being different from other children. When this youngster draws a figure without any visible handicap or conflict signs, he is portraying his feelings about himself which need not be at all defensive.

HFDs of children with disabilities are just as varied as those of children without disabilities (Silverstein, A. B. and Robinson, H. A., 1956; Wawrzaszek, I., Johnson, O.G. and Sciera, J.L., 1958). Children with handicaps who are concerned about their disabilities will reflect these concerns on their HFDs just as they would any other concern or anxiety. A child's attitude toward his disability will depend, of course, on many factors in addition to the actual severity of the handicap. Some youngsters may feel impaired and handicapped long after their disability has been corrected, while others may learn to overcome their initial anxieties and may develop a positive self-concept even when there is no objective evidence of improvement in their physical condition. In some instances, a child's concern about his handicap may increase as he gets older; in other cases it decreases with age. There is no one way in which children react to their disabilities, nor is there any one way in which their reactions are reflected on HFDs. The following HFDs and case histories are presented to illustrate how some children reveal their concerns about disabilities on their drawings. The HFDs shown are by no means unique and can be readily duplicated by other drawings from the writer's collection.

CONCERN ABOUT SPEECH DISORDERS. Max (*Plate 3*) was a seven year old boy with a mild articulatory speech disorder; when he got excited, he stammered. Max's case history was discussed earlier (page 57). He was very self-conscious about his speech although it was quite intelligible and did not interfere with his communication with other children. Max' concern about his speech resulted from his mother's constant nagging and fussing about his articulation. He was particularly embarrassed when she corrected him in front of other people. Just how intense Max' anxiety and concern was is shown on his HFD on *Plate 3*. The figure he drew exhibits heavy shading around the mouth and the lower portion of the face. This type of shading has been found by the writer only on HFDs of children who worry about their speech problems. Children with equally severe or worse speech disorders who do not worry about them do not show on their HFDs shading of the mouth and the lower portion of the face.

In Max' case, the speech disorder was mild and there was every reason to believe that he would overcome this difficulty with greater maturation and with continued speech therapy. The situation was very different for Sammy, who was also a seven year old youngster of normal intelligence. Sammy *(Plate 46)* was an aphasic child who suffered from an expressive type of speech disorder. He could hear and understand what others said to him, but because of a disturbance in his feedback mechanism, he could not hear and correct his own voice. He was unable to pronounce certain sounds correctly and his speech was for the most part unintelligible. Sammy could not comprehend why others did not understand him. It annoyed him a great deal when people asked him to repeat a word or sentence and then still failed to understand him. In addition, Sammy suffered from serious malfunctioning in visual-motor perception.

But Sammy was a friendly and imaginative boy, who was well liked by his peers in the primary grades. They readily included him in their games, since he was quiet and gentle and did not pose a threat to other children. *Plate 46* shows Sammy's HFD. The most outstanding features of this drawing are the small head and the omission of the mouth. Sammy's drawing of a girl is larger, well proportioned and free from omissions. The drawing of a boy clearly reflects Sammy's concern about his speech problem. His HFD reveals that Sammy thought of himself at that point as a rather inadequate human being.

As time went by, Sammy gained in size but his speech did not improve despite speech therapy. His academic progress was exceedingly slow. Sammy began to show more and more signs of frustration and communication with others became increasingly more difficult. Young children rarely engage in long conversations, but as children get older, verbal communication gets to be more important. Gradually, his peers became less patient with Sammy and did not have as much time and consideration for him. With each succeeding year, Sammy developed more signs of emotional problems and anxieties. His self-concept deteriorated; he began to think of himself as being no longer a full member of society but rather an outsider *(Plate 47)* and finally as being ludicrous and not quite human *(Plate 48)*. For a more complete discussion of Sammy's case, see page 156.

CONCERN ABOUT HEARING LOSS. Donald *(Plate 49)* had attended the school for the deaf since he was three years old, and he had worn a hearing aid since he was four years old. Donald had always been a very difficult child whom the mother could not control. He had always suffered from sleep disturbances, restlessness, an insatiable appetite, and temper outbursts. He frequently truanted from home and school. When seen at the guidance clinic, Donald was seven years old. He seemed starved for affection and was very eager to communicate with the examiner. He was an excellent lipreader and had no difficulty understanding what the writer said to him. But it was also quite apparent that Donald was a strong-minded child who wanted his own way. He did not wish to work or to perform required tasks; instead, he wanted to play and to be loved.

When asked to draw a whole person, Donald at first refused, but when the examiner insisted, he reluctantly agreed and produced the HFD on *Plate 49*. Donald drew a tiny stickfigure lacking in all detail with the exception of the hearing aid and the battery. A stickfigure is usually a sign of avoidance. In Donald's case, the stickfigure represents something of a compromise. He was saying in effect: "I really do not want to draw, I do not know how to draw, but if you insist, I will draw a stickfigure which requires little effort." The tiny stickfigure reveals withdrawal and evasiveness, just as in real life, Donald ran away from home and school when he could not get his way or when the frustrations got to be unbearable. The omission of the hands shows his feeling of helplessness and of inadequacy. The prominent treatment of the hearing aid and the wide, heavily drawn mouth suggest that Donald would like to communicate with others and is troubled by his handicap. Thus, we find that even a noncooperative, brain injured child of dull normal intelligence can convey unwittingly his anxieties and concerns about his handicap on his HFD.

CONCERN ABOUT IMPAIRED VISION. Mickey *(Plate 50)* was born with cataracts and glaucoma which necessitated two eye operations during the first year of his life. The operations were successful. Later, Mickey was fitted with glasses with thick lenses which adequately corrected his vision. There was good evidence that Mickey could see quite well with his glasses and he was proud of them. It was unlikely that Mickey consciously recollected the operations he underwent in infancy. Nevertheless, the early trauma left its mark on Mickey. He retained an acute anxiety about his eyes and his glasses and revealed it dramatically on his HFD on *Plate 50*. This HFD was made when Mickey was six years old. The crudeness of the drawing is largely due to the fact that Mickey was a mentally retarded youngster with neurological impairment. What was remarkable about his HFD was the sequence in which he drew it and the treatment of the face and the eyes. Mickey started out by drawing eyes and glasses; only after that did he add the head, the nose, the mouth, and finally the rest of the figure. The shading on the face further underscores Mickey's anxiety and concern about his eyesight (page 57).

CONCERN ABOUT A CLEFT PALATE. Edith (*Plate 14*) had been a premature baby who weighed only three pounds four ounces at birth. She was born with a cleft palate and only half a nose. Her unstable, immature mother was unable to accept the disfigured child and boarded her out with neighbors and friends. When Edith was five years old, her palate and nose were badly repaired. Rejection, instability, and neglect had all contributed to Edith's poor emotional and social development and to her extremely negative selfconcept. By the time she entered school, she presented serious emotional and behavior problems. Because of her disruptive behavior, she was several times suspended from kindergarten and from the first grade. When finally seen at the child guidance clinic, Edith was seven years old. At that time, she was living with her mother and her 18 months old brother. It was discovered that Edith was suffering from multiple problems resulting from various factors in her life, but her disfigured face had been one of the major reasons for the treatment she had received from others and for her distorted feelings about herself.

Plate 14 shows Edith's HFD. It is a remarkable drawing in many ways. The treatment of the nose and mouth are unusual and reflect vividly Edith's concern about her malformation and speech problem. She was painfully aware of her appearance. Her feeling of mutilation and incompleteness is further shown by the asymmetry and poor integration of the arms and hands and by the omission of the foot, which may symbolize the partially missing nose. In marked contrast to the HFD on *Plate 14*, Edith's drawing of a man is much more conventional and does not show any omissions or unusual treatment of the nose and mouth.

The way in which the figure was drawn on *Plate 14* reflects the anxieties and concerns Edith experienced because of her physical handicap. The content of the drawing and the story she told about it show Edith's attitude toward her family and her wish-dream (page 77). The "lady" on the HFD may be assumed to be her mother who indeed went out practically every night, leaving Edith at home to look after the little brother. In her story, Edith contrasts the mother's good looks with her own disfigurement and she protests against the mother's "meanness' and expresses the wish that the boyfriend would not come, so that the mother would stay home with her for a change.

CONCERN OVER CEREBRAL PALSY. Betty (*Plate 51*), an eight year old girl of superior intelligence, was a hemiplegic youngster who had little use of her right hand and leg. But this did not stop her from participating fully in most activities at home and in school. With the aid of a brace, she got around fairly well. She had many friends among her classmates and in the community. Betty was blessed in that she was born into a close-knit, warm, stable, and devoutly religious family. The parents accepted Betty without reservations on the same basis as their other children and gave her much support and affection. The mother observed correctly: "Betty likes people and people like her." Betty's attitude toward other people and toward herself reflected the parent's attitude toward her.

When asked to make a HFD, Betty produced the drawing shown on *Plate 51*. She spontaneously drew her whole family "going to church." She drew herself as the smallest child sheltered under the mother's protective garments. It is interesting that she drew herself complete and intact, while displacing her own handicap onto the mother. The mother is shown with one two-dimensional leg and one stick leg: one leg functions correctly, and one leg that is impaired. Betty seems to be saying in her picture: "I do not want to grow up, I want to remain little since I cannot stand up for myself alone. But as long as my mother lovingly protects me and shelters me, and as long as she carries my burden for me, I will not worry but will enjoy life to the fullest." The content of the drawing on *Plate 51* shows Betty's wish-dream: she wants to be the youngest in the family, she wants to remain immature and dependent. She not only likes people, but she needs people for her security and protection. In actuality, Betty was not the smallest and youngest child in her family. She had two younger brothers. By drawing the entire family, Betty reveals her complete reliance on her family. Betty's drawing does not show any resentment or undue anxiety over her impairment, but it does express a strong need for continued support and protection. The transparencies on Betty's drawing are typical of those found on drawings of neurologically impaired children and indicate above all concretistic thinking (page 60).

Dennis (*Plates 52a and b*) was less fortunate than Betty. He too was a hemiplegic child who wore a brace on his right leg and had little use of his right hand. In addition, Dennis was quite immature for his age and showed evidence of mild mental retardation. His mother found it very difficult to fully accept Dennis and his impairment. Intellectually, she accepted the fact that he was a handicapped child. She dutifully took Dennis twice a week for physical therapy and exercised his leg for several hours each day. But the mother had to force herself to do this; it was a painful task for her. Inevitably she transferred some of her own anxieties and fears about Dennis' limitations to the child himself. He was grossly lacking in self-confidence and soon showed active resistance to going to the treatment center.

Dennis was seen at the guidance clinic when he was six years old. The HFD he made at that time is shown on *Plate 52a*. The heavily shaded face of his figure lacks all features while the hands, fingers, and feet are grossly distorted and also shaded. The asymmetry and size of the hands reveal Dennis' concern about them. His intense anxiety and insecurity was also verbalized as he drew. Every other moment he would ask: "Am I doing right?" He seemed most eager for reassurance and support. When Dennis finished his drawing, he asked if he could take it home to his daddy. He never once mentioned his mother. The drawing on *Plate 52a* reveals Dennis' acute anxiety and concern over his physical handicap and a marked lack in self-confidence and self-acceptance.

When Dennis' mother enrolled in a therapy group at the clinic, she gradually began to change her attitude toward Dennis. Instead of feeling primarily sorry for herself, she began to see her son as a person in his own right and began to realize what his condition meant to him. This change in the mother's attitude soon brought forth a change in Dennis; he became much happier and freer. Where he had formerly resisted going for physical therapy, he now actually looked forward to these sessions at the treatment center. His whole outlook changed and he began to develop a more positive attitude toward himself. He no longer scowled and frowned most of the time, but instead learned to smile.

Four months after the first HFD was obtained, Dennis was asked to draw another whole person. This second HFD is shown on *Plate 52b*. The difference between the two drawings is striking. Not enough time had elapsed between the drawing of the first and second HFD to attribute the improvement primarily to an increase in age and maturation. What had greatly changed in these four months was the mother's attitude toward Dennis and Dennis' attitude toward himself. The second HFD is complete with eyes, nose, mouth, hair and ears. The figure has a body and legs with feet. Only the arms are missing. The drawing as a whole suggests much less anxiety and a better self-concept than was the case for the earlier HFD. The omission of the arms probably reflects Dennis' lingering concern over his inability to use his hands. But since his mental age was only five, when he drew the figure on *Plate 52b*, the omission may also be a sign of his general immaturity and mild retardation. It is not uncommon for dull five year old boys to omit the arms from their drawings. Whichever interpretation one prefers, there can be no doubt that the second drawing of Dennis reveals a marked change and improvement in his attitude regarding himself and his disability. On the first HFD, Dennis depicts himself as a nonperson, while on the second drawing, he portrays himself as a human being, albeit an incomplete one.

CONCERN OVER A COLOSTOMY. Jennifer *(Plates 53 and 54)* had suffered from ulcerative colitis for several years. When she was eleven years old, surgical intervention became necessary. After a successful operation, Jennifer was sent to a convalescent home to recuperate and to learn to take care of herself, now that she had to use a colostomy bag. Jennifer seemed to adjust to her new condition fairly well until it was time for her to go home and return to school.

Since her home was a considerable distance from the hospital and from the convalescent home, Jennifer was sent to the child guidance clinic for supportive therapy during the difficult period of readjustment to the community. When first seen by the writer, Jennifer produced the HFD shown on *Plate 53*. One of the most striking features on this drawing is the large, wary eye. It looks as if the girl on the picture is watching uneasily people's recation to her, even though she herself has turned her head away as if trying to avoid meeting people face to face.

A second unusual sign on *Plate 53* is the transparency of the skirt. The treatment of the skirt differs markedly from the transparencies shown on *Plate 43* and *Plate 51* which reflected above all a concretistic approach to figure drawing and to life. On Jennifer's drawing, the transparency is akin to that on *Plate 9* and *Plate 30*. In these cases, the transparency focused on a specific portion of the figure. This type of transparency serves to emphasize and highlight the area of the body on which the child's main anxiety and concern are centered (page 60). In the case of Connie (*Plate 9*), the transparency reflected her anxiety over her sexual activities and investigations. In the case of Dorothy (*Plate 30*), the transparency revealed her concern over the mother's pregnancy and her sister's birth. In Jennifer's case, the transparency on *Plate 53* shows her anxiety about her colostomy. These differences in concerns and anxiety are not apparent from the transparencies as such. The transparencies merely pinpoint the location of the concern but the specific cause for the anxiety must be deducted from the child's total situation and experiences.

At first, Jennifer was reluctant to return to school, whereupon the writer arranged a meeting with the school nurse and the principal so that they would know and understand Jennifer's problems. A place was provided for Jennifer in school where she could go any time to attend to her needs in private when necessary. Thereafter, Jennifer returned willingly to school and participated in most school activities. Her adjustment was quite satisfactory. She was seen on a weekly basis for continued support at the guidance clinic for some time to come. When Jennifer was twelve years old, she was again asked to make a HFD. The result in shown on *Plate 54*.

At first glance, the HFD on *Plate 54* looks like the drawings of countless other pre-adolescent girls who produce wishdream images of well-shaped ballerinas or glamour girls. Jennifer drew a girl on tiptoe wearing ballet slippers. The treatment of the face is quite conventional; there is no longer any sign of suspicion or evasion. The only noteworthy signs on this HFD are the heavy, reinforced lines on the sides of the body and at the lower end of the garment, and the failure to separate the thighs with a line. By omitting the dividing line between the legs, Jennifer seems to try to blot out the area of her concern. Whereas she formerly drew attention to this area by means of the transparency *(Plate 53)*, she revealed her anxiety now through heavy shading and the omission of lines. It is only natural that Jennifer should feel continued concern about her condition, but the drawing on *Plate 54* shows that she had learned to accept her handicap and was no longer defensive about it. Jennifer's second drawing is much more mature and sophisticated than the earlier one, just as her behavior and social adjustment was more mature and confident than it had been before.

Concern about school achievement reflected on HFDs.

In our middle-class society, much value is placed on academic achievement. Parents who never went to college themselves are eagerly striving toward the day when their son or daughter graduates from college. Practically from the day a child enters kindergarten, he is imbued with the idea that he must go to college and that scholastic success equals "goodness," whereas the child who fails a grade or gets poor marks is made to feel that he is "bad." Such parental striving is in keeping with the American dream and has spurred many youngsters on to accomplish great things. Parental ambition and pressure for achievement can serve as a motivating force and can be quite useful for the well-integrated, intelligent and healthy youngster. But such pressure can also be extremely harmful and upsetting for the child who lacks the mental maturity and ability to live up to his parents' expectations. This is particularly true if the child's failure to do well in school results from factors that are not readily apparent to teachers and parents. For lack of any better explanation, these children are often considered "lazy," or "stupid," or "bad." As a result, many youngsters with minimal impairment suffer intense guilt feelings which only intensify their learning difficulties.

Kenneth (*Plate 55*) was unable to learn to read and write despite average intelligence. His parents had had little education themselves and were determined that their children should have all the advantages they had never had. They were going to see to it that Kenneth and his brothers finished high school and went to college, even if it meant that the parents had to hold down two jobs each and had to save and skimp every penny. It was incomprehensible to them that Kenneth did not learn. His three siblings were good students. The parents spent hours working with Kenneth; they pleaded with him, they threatened him, they tried to bribe him, and they punished him, but it was all to no avail. After one year in Kindergarten and one year in the first grade, Kenneth still could not write his name nor could he read a single word. Yet to all outer appearances, he was a perfectly normal and healthy boy with only a slight speech defect.

At the beginning of the second grade, Kenneth was transferred to a special public school class for children of normal intelligence with specific learning problems. His parents were very much opposed to this move and kept insisting that there was nothing wrong with Kenneth. They felt that he was "lazy" and that he should be *made* to learn. Kenneth was overwhelmed by guilt feelings and by resentment toward his parents and school. He was torn by ambivalent emotions and anxiety. When he entered the special class, he was extremely withdrawn and showed signs of serious emotional disturbance. He was convinced that he was stupid and bad. Psychological test results and an EEG clearly revealed evidence of neurological impairment which had not been recognized earlier.

At first, Kenneth panicked at the sight of a book or any material related to schoolwork. After several weeks of free play and games, Kenneth began to relax a bit in school; but at home, the situation became worse. A "war" was on between Kenneth and his parents. In his drawings and paintings and in his play, Kenneth relived this war day after day. *Plate 55* shows his HFD. The drawing reveals a pathetic little figure without nose, without mouth, without arms and without feet. These omissions reflect Kenneth's intense feelings of inadequacy and guilt. They also show his tendency to withdraw in the face of parental pressure. The content of the drawing is even more illuminating. The boy on the picture appears to be in a cage or cell. Kenneth commented while he drew: "A stupid boy, a crazy boy; he would not do anything in school so they sent him to a reform school. He is in a bomb shelter. The army put him there. There is a war on."

Kenneth describes the boy on *Plate 55* as a "stupid boy" and a "crazy boy;" these are his feelings about himself. His reference to the "reform school" shows how much he had been influenced by his parents' view of the special class. Despite much effort on part of the clinical staff and the teacher to explain the therapeutic and positive features of the small special class, Kenneth and his parents thought of it in punitive terms. But the second part of Kenneth's comment is not merely a description of himself but a story, and as such it represents his wish-dream. The "reform school" changes into a "bomb shelter," that is, Kenneth has learned from actual experience that the special class is not a place where children are punished but that it is a safe and secure place where he finds protection and shelter during the "war" that rages on the outside. Kenneth seems to be saying that he wants the army (i.e., the teacher and clinicians) to fight for him and to make his parents understand his problem. The "war" between Kenneth and the school on the one side and his parents on the other side raged on for the better part of the school year before it was finally possible to convince the parents that Kenneth was not "stupid" or "lazy" or "crazy," but that he was a boy of normal intelligence who could not learn to read and write because of a brain injury which affected his auditory and visual-motor perception and which interfered with his memory for sounds and symbols.

Jonathan (*Plate 36*), age 7 years 9 months, was repeating the first grade but still lagged behind in his achievement. His parents were college graduates and professional people who took it for granted that Jonathan would also go to college. His mother bought special books for him and worked with him diligently every day after school; but despite her effort, Jonathan failed to show much academic progress. His extreme restlessness, distractibility, and serious perceptual problems interfered with his schoolwork. His conceptualization was also poor.

When asked to make an HFD, Jonathan produced the picture on *Plate 36*. The tiny head on the figure reflects Jonathan's acute concern over his mental ability or lack of it. The clouds above the figure indicate that he feels under pressure from the parents which only intensifies his anxiety and sense of failure. The story Jonathan told about the drawing reveals his wish-dream. The HFD represents his hero, the cousin whom he greatly admires and in whose footsteps he wants to follow: "I'll make my cousin. He is a big man. He did not go to college. He works on the house, he is soldering . . . I like what my cousin likes." Later Jonathan added: "I like school but not too much, I want to be 19 like my cousin and work, he did not go to college."

Plate 36 reveals thus both Jonathan's concern about his poor achievement and his wish to be grown-up (page 96), to escape from school and to go to work like his cousin. Actually, Jonathan's appraisal of his ability and his goals for the future were quite realistic. It was now up to the school psychologist and the teacher to help the parents to readjust their expectations for Jonathan so that the threatening clouds above him could be lifted and so that he could be himself without having to feel anxious or guilty.

Concern about behavior reflected on HFDs

Two children may engage in the same kind of activity and yet may have very different motivations for and reactions to their behavior. Playing hooky, for instance, may be a matter of prestige and status for one child, while it is a sign of severe disturbance, depression, and withdrawal for another child. There is no one-to-one relationship between a given activity and children's attitudes. But whenever a child engages in activities that arouse anxiety and concern in him, then these activities will be reflected in his drawings. HFDs can be of great value in helping therapists and clinicians to understand how a child feels about his activities. For a child who steals and reveals strong guilt feelings and anxieties will require a different mode of treatment from the child who steals but lacks all indications of concern and guilt.

CONCERN OVER STEALING. It was shown earlier (page 48) that many children who steal exhibit their guilt feelings about their actions by placing special emphasis on the arms and hands of their HFDs. This emphasis may take the form of the omission of the arms or hands, it may result in the drawing of very large or heavily shaded hands, or it may be found in the presentation of very weak and short arms. Some examples of HFDs of children who steal are presented below. *Plate 32* shows the HFD of Joel who began stealing when his parents separated. Joel omitted the arms altogether from the figure of himself. Eddie, a nine year old boy of normal intelligence, was a severely deprived youngster with a long history of stealing and fighting. He drew excessively long, heavily shaded arms with huge hands on his HFD which is shown on *Plate 6*.

Carla (*Plate 56*) was nine years old when she came to the child guidance clinic for evaluation. She was of normal intelligence but had taken things since she was three years old. Her mother had fed her and had clothed her well, but had had little time or affection for the child. Carla had been left frequently with strangers in rooming houses or in beer gardens while her mother worked as a waitress. After the birth of a sibling, Carla intensified her stealing and started to truant from home and school. The HFD on *Plate 56* shows a girl with very short, clinging arms without hands or fingers, reflecting thereby Carla's intense feelings of inadequacy, helplessness and anxiety. The drawing also discloses her difficulty in reaching out toward others, whom she regards with a suspicious glance, and her tendency to take flight when the situation gets to be intolerable. The figure on the HFD appears to be tense and wary, ready to run off at any moment. Never having known emotional security and affection, Carla had substituted objects and food for love and took these things when she felt neglected and left out.

And then there was Jeff, whose HFD is shown on *Plate 57*. Jeff was a ten year old boy of low average intelligence with a psychopathic personality. He was superficially friendly and gay but emotionally flat. He denied having any problems. Jeff had suffered severe deprivation and multiple placements prior to age five when he and his sister were placed in their current foster home. The fostermother greatly favored the sister over

Jeff. Jeff was impulsive, aggressive, and had a history of stealing and firesetting. He had been in difficulty in school from the time he entered kindergarten. Jeff's HFD (*Plate 57*) shows extremely poor integration of parts, gross asymmetry of limbs, and transparencies, all of which are frequently found on drawings of children with cortical malfunctioning. Not enough was known about Jeff's early life and medical history to confirm a diagnosis of brain injury. His behavior however, was not incompatible with such a diagnosis.

Jeff drew a girl who may well represent the favored sister. But the expression Jeff put on the figure, the foolish grin on her face, corresponds to Jeff's own bland cheerfulness, and to his denial of all problems. The weak, short, and clinging arms suggest a feeling of helplessness and an attempt at rigidly controlling his impulses. Jeff deals with his problems by suppressing them from his consciousness and by acting out his conflicts and anger in socially unacceptable behavior. Jeff's figure on *Plate 57* is disconnected, the upper and lower part of the girl are not joined. This sign on the drawing seems to reflect Jeff's disassociation of his hostile and aggressive impulses from his conscious awareness and intellectual control. His drawing lacks any indication of shading or omissions which would reveal anxiety or guilt. The absence of these indicators make the prognosis for Jeff less positive and success of treatment more difficult.

CONCERN OVER FIRESETTING. Firesetting, like stealing, may be symptomatic of a variety of problems and may reflect many different attitudes in the youngsters involved. It was mentioned in the preceding section that Jeff had engaged not only in stealing but also in firesetting. His HFD on *Plate 57* shows a marked lack of guilt and anxiety. The figure turns her head away and smiles happily. In reality too, Jeff cheerfully denied any problems even while setting his house on fire. There is nothing in his drawing that is specifically related to concern over firesetting. Jeff's HFD shows in general many signs of maladjustment; it is indicative of a poorly integrated, immature, bland personality with psychopathic tendencies.

Mel (*Plate 58*), a five year old boy of high average intelligence, represents a very different picture from Jeff. Mel's parents separated before he was born. He suffered much insecurity and instability at home during the first years of his life. Mel bitterly resented his mother's marriage to the stepfather and the subsequent addition of two more boys to the family. Mel expressed his jealousy of the stepfather and of the half-siblings by setting the baby's crib on fire. His exasperated and misguided mother tried to correct Mel's ways by burning his hands and neck with a red-hot knife. This punitive and brutal treatment only increased Mel's feelings of rejection, guilt and anxiety.

Plate 58 shows Mel's HFD. He commented while drawing: "It's an Indian with two feathers—and the hands." The small size of the drawing reflects Mel's insecurity and acute anxiety. The large hands indicate both hostility and guilt over his actions. By making his figure an Indian, Mel reveals his feelings of not belonging to the family, of being an outsider (page 125). But just like an Indian brave, he is willing to fight for his place in society if he has to.

CONCERN ABOUT MASTURBATION AND SEXUAL ACTIVITIES. A certain amount of sexual play and masturbation is normal in developing children and need not cause any undue anxiety and guilt on their part. However, too often the significant adults in a child's life impress on him their own sexual anxieties and problems, so that the child begins to feel "bad" and guilty because of his perfectly normal impulses and activities. Most children learn sooner or later to control their impulses and to adapt to socially accepted patterns of behavior. But there are exceptions. Especially very lonely, isolated, or unhappy children often find comfort in masturbation and may develop the habit of excessive and compulsive masturbation, which meets with disapproval from adults and which then leads to more anxiety and guilt in the children.

Timothy (page 92) whose family picture is shown on *Plate 33* was a compulsive masturbator. During long months of illness when he was confined to bed, he amused himself by playing with himself or drawing. On his family portrait, Timothy drew on each of the three male members of the family pants with pockets and with oblong objects below the pockets. These objects might be thought of as knees, if it were not for Timothy's behavior. In school he would spend hours each day with his hand in his pocket masturbating. The shape and position of the oblong objects on the drawing show that they are in all likelihood phallic symbols. The presence of two phalluses on each of the male figures merely emphasizes the importance Timothy attached to them and the intensity of his castration fear. Another way of revealing his masturbation guilt and anxiety was his preoccupation with elephants and their trunks; he made countless drawings of such animals.

Philip (*Plate 59*), an eight year old boy of normal intelligence, was also a compulsive masturbator. His constant masturbation seemed to be an attempt to reassure himself that he was all there and to relieve his tensions and guilt feelings. Phillip was a very unhappy and emotionally disturbed youngster. *Plate 59* shows his HFD. Philip informed the examiner that his crude and primitive drawing represented "a boy holding a pipe." This picture is a very direct and frank statement of Philip's castration anxiety and masturbation guilt. The "pipe" in the boy's hand has become detached from the boy's body. Philip was a youngster with many problems; masturbation anxiety was only one of his difficulties. It just so happened that this particular problem was uppermost on his mind when he made the HFD shown on *Plate 59*, hence masturbation guilt and fear are the dominant theme on this drawing. On an earlier drawing, shown on *Plate 45*, Philip expressed primarily feelings of physical and mental weakness and inadequacy (page 104). On that HFD, Philip drew a wishdream image: a strongman. A closer look at the strongman on *Plate 45* shows a small scribble or squiggle of a line at the bottom of his sash. This might be considered a chance doodle, but in view of Philip's habits and anxieties, it may actually represent a phallic symbol. This impression is further enhanced by the shading of the strongman's hand, another sign of anxiety and guilt which is often associated with masturbation. Thus, it now appears that Philip makes two statements on the drawing on *Plate 45*: one statement concerns his feelings of inadequacy and his longing to be strong, and the second one concerns his masturbation guilt and anxiety; the two are, of course, interrelated.

Doris (*Plate 60*) was five years old when she was brought to the guidance clinic for evaluation. Since the birth of her sister, Doris had engaged in excessive masturbation and body manipulation which was very upsetting to her parents. When asked to draw a whole person, Doris produced the HFD on *Plate 60*. She commented spontaneously as she drew: "My sister, these are her teeth . . . there is a window by her side, she is going to pull it up when she feels like it." Without these explanations, the drawing might be regarded as just another primitive drawing of an anxious five year old child. The rectangular object might have been easily mistaken for a box or a house. When analyzing children's HFDs for their structure only, it is immaterial to know the meaning of all the objects on the drawing. But it is quite risky to try to interpret children's HFDs clinically without knowledge of what the child was trying to draw, of what his intentions were. It would have been very difficult, for instance, to attribute clinical meaning to Doris' drawing on *Plate 60* without her explanations. But with these elaborations, the meaning seems clear. Doris drew her sister who is her chief object of concern and jealousy. But the way she drew the figure of her sister reflects Doris' own attitudes. The teeth show her resentment and anger. The body is omitted; instead Doris places heavy, amorphous shading in the area where the body should have been, thereby revealing intense body anxiety, far in excess of what is normal for five year old girls (page 57). The omission of the nose further emphasizes her anxiety. That this anxiety is related to her masturbation seems clear if one assumes that the "window" on the drawing is a symbolic representation for the vaginal opening, which she "pulls when she feels like it." The drawing on *Plate 60* shows therefore that Doris' primary concern and problem is sibling rivalry, while the masturbation is only a secondary symptom which she engages in for comfort, but which in turn produces more anxiety and guilt.

Burt (*Plates 61 to 64*) was an 11 year old boy of normal intelligence. He was referred to the mental health clinic because of bizarre and inappropriate behavior in school and at home. When first seen, Burt made the grotesque HFD shown on *Plate 61*. The slanting figure with the shrivelled body has a huge head which is supported by a long, snakelike neck from which protrudes a big, heavily shaded Adam's apple with a worm in it. Burt volunteered: "That is a man with a worm coming out of his Adam's apple." He seemed very much pleased with his picture. The Adam's apple, the worm, the goatee, and the mustache are all generally acknowledged symbols of masculinity and sexual striving. The fact that all these symbols are so heavily shaded and exaggerated, while the man's body, the seat of sexual impulses, is so tiny, suggests concern, anxiety, and guilt about sexual thoughts or activities. Since the figure on *Plate 61* has the exaggerated feeling and quality of a cartoon character, the writer asked Burt to make another drawing representing himself. The result is shown on *Plate 62*. Although the second HFD differs greatly from the first one, the attitudes and anxieties expressed are remarkably similar. Burt drew himself as a devil to show his "badness." Once again, the head of the figure is enormous, and is endowed with heavily shaded phallic symbols: horns, a big nose, a mustache, and a goatee. Once again, the neck is greatly emphasized: on *Plate 61* it was excessively long and thin, on *Plate 62* it is extremely broad and heavy. The body which was shrivelled and small on *Plate 61* has all but disappeared on *Plate 62*. The minute stickbody and limbs are hardly recognizable; the only conspicuous feature are the big feet. Thus we find that Burt's self-portrait shows essentially the same indications of masturbation anxiety and guilt as did his drawing of "a person," only that these signs are possibly more intensified. Both drawings show beyond a doubt that Burt was a seriously disturbed and troubled youngster.

Burt was seen by the writer on a regular weekly basis for psychotherapy. Further projective material and information gathered from Burt during the therapy sessions disclosed that he had engaged in considerable masturbation for which he had been severely punished by his puritanical parents who threatened him with hell and purgatory. So Burt had stopped masturbating but thought about it continuously. He was overwhelmed by anxiety and guilt for being so "bad." The more he tried to suppress his impulses and to banish his "evil" thoughts, the more tense and disturbed he became, until he could concentrate no longer on his schoolwork or anything else. He giggled, made funny noises, and rolled on the floor when he could not contain himself any more.

Four months after the first two drawings were made, Burt was again asked to make an HFD. His drawing is shown on *Plate 63*. This picture is not nearly as bizarre as the earlier ones and reflects his general improvement in behavior and attitudes. But even so, the drawing still reveals unmistakable signs of masturbation anxiety. The boy on the drawing is holding a huge "screwdriver" and has grotesquely large feet and heels. Burt commented "A boy....he had just been using a screwdriver." The implications are obvious.

After another four months of therapy, Burt produced the HFD shown on *Plate 64*. This drawing shows a marked improvement over the earlier HFDs and corresponds to his drastically changed behavior in school and at home. Both the parents and the teacher reported that Burt was once again able to concentrate and to finish his assignments; he no longer displayed any disruptive or bizarre behavior and seemed in general much happier. His social relationships had also improved a great deal. The drawing on *Plate 64* reveals however still considerable impulsivity and suggests that Burt had not yet completely overcome his masturbation anxiety even though it had greatly decreased. The excessively large feet reflect still some concern and anxiety about his sexual thoughts and activities. But the drawing is free of schizoid signs. Burt continued to improve during the next few months; he was able to discontinue his treatment shortly thereafter.

On Burt's four HFDs (*Plates 61 to 64*) is shown how a child can reveal masturbation guilt in many different ways by exaggerating portions of the figure, by diminishing or omitting parts of it, by adding grotesque symbols and signs, by distorting some aspects of the figure, or by heavily shading those parts of the figure that bear a relationship to the problem. Burt used all of these methods in different combinations and to different degrees.

Curiosity and awakening of sexual impulses in children frequently result in sexual explorations and sex play with other youngsters. Such activities may be accompanied by intense feelings of anxiety and guilt. *Plate 9* shows the HFD of Connie, age 10, who tried to satisfy her sexual curiosity by involving other children in the games of "statues" and "doctor." In the former, the children had to pose in the nude and were admired by their peers, whereas in the latter game, the "patient" had to disrobe and was then carefully examined by the "doctor." Connie's anxiety and guilt are shown in the transparent treatment of the skirt on the HFD, by the omission of the hands, and by the slant of the figure.

Ernie (*Plate 65*), a ten year old boy of low average intelligence, was quite preoccupied with sexual matters. His mother had deserted him when he was only an infant. Ernie had been raised by his father who took him along to pool halls and bars and let him roam the streets at will. Ernie worshipped his father and tried to imitate his ways. The father remarried when Ernie was nine years old. The boy bitterly resented his stepmother and her attempts to keep him at home and to discipline him. Ernie considered himself a man. He openly defied the stepmother and began involving little girls in the neighborhood in sex play. When his father expressed disapproval of this activity, Ernie was both angry and upset. On his HFD, shown on *Plate 65*, he displayed guilt as well as resentment. Ernie drew a clown with whiskers but without arms and legs. The whiskers, the treatment of the neck, and the heavily reinforced lines on the crotch testify to his preoccupation with masculine striving and sexual activities; the missing limbs reflect his anxiety and guilt. Ernie depicted himself as a ludicrous person, as a clown; he felt that his father was laughing at him and was treating him like a naughty little boy just when Ernie thought that he was a man and was acting like the father.

Julian (*Plate 66*) was born out of wedlock. When he was 18 months old, his mother was hospitalized and Julian was placed in a foster home where he remained henceforth. Later, his mother returned home and married. She stayed married just long enough to give birth to two more children before divorcing her husband. Julian bitterly resented the fact that his half-sisters could live with the mother while he had to live in a foster home. He became moody, withdrawn, displayed temper outbursts in school and in the home. Above all, Julian began to investigate little girls and induced them with threats and bribery to let him play with them sexually.

Julian was nine years old when he was brought to the juvenile diagnostic center. When asked to make a HFD, he produced a picture of a boy in rags with holes and patches on his clothes and with a big rake in his hand. But since Julian's activities and problems involved girls and his mother, he was also asked to draw "a whole girl or woman." This second HFD is shown on *Plate 66*. There are several interesting features on this drawing. The body of the woman is shaded and the skirt is slit at the hemline in a very suggestive way. On the one hand, Julian seems to draw deliberate attention to this symbolic opening while at the same time he shows intense anxiety; on the picture, the woman's legs are pressed together tightly and her feet are crossed over. In this way, Julian expresses both preoccupation with sexuality and fear of it. On both of his drawings, Julian reveals signs of masculine striving and castration anxiety. His figure of a boy carries a big rake, a phallic symbol, while his pants are full of holes, which suggests castration fear. The figure of the woman smokes a phallic cigarette while wearing a slit skirt.

Julian seems confused and frightened by body differences of males and females. After all, his sisters, whose bodies differed from his, were allowed to live with the mother, whereas he, the boy, was cast out of the family circle like the beggar boy on his drawing. Julian seemed to perceive his sisters as mutilated boys and exhibited intense castration anxiety on his part. He was evidently afraid that he too would have to give up his masculinity before he would be allowed to go home to his mother. Much of his sexual activity with little girls appeared to be an attempt by Julian to clarify the mystery of girls and females whom he viewed as privileged and threatening creatures.

When asked to tell something about his drawing on *Plate 66*, Julian replied: "She is singing: 'ain't she sweet.' She is a housewife and has a boy and a girl and a husband." Once again, we find that the drawing reveals the child's anxieties while the story he tells about the drawing represents his wish-dream. Julian wants nothing more than to have a mother who is an ordinary housewife who takes care of her family which consists of a father, a boy (himself) and a girl.

Odetta, whose HFD is shown on *Plate 40*, was a ten year old girl of normal intelligence with intense feelings of inadequacy. She had suffered from severe early deprivation and neglect and had been subjected to numerous placements during her lifetime. Odetta had never experienced the warm affection of a loving mother in a stable home. As a result, Odetta never learned to accept herself as a person who was lovable and worthwhile; she hated herself and blamed most of her difficulties on her looks (page 100). Being starved for attention and recognition, she had permitted an older man to play with her sexually in return for money and candy.

Plate 40 shows a very feminine and attractive girl who represents Odetta's dream image. But the treatment of the arms and legs on the drawing show her difficulties in interpersonal relationships and her anxiety and guilt feelings. The rigidly clinging arms reveal her inability to reach out toward others; the legs are tightly pressed together and are displaced; they do not support the body and reflect Odetta's insecurity and lack of stability. The tight stance of the legs seems to indicate her uneasiness about her sexual activities and an attempt to ward off sexual advances.

Concern about being "different" reflected on HFDs

The pre-school child will look primarily to his parents for approval and reassurance. But once a child has entered school, he will begin to long for recognition and acceptance by his peer group as well. His "buddy" or his "gang" will gain in importance as the child gets older and will provide him with a sense of belonging and security. A youngster who is not accepted by his peers is likely to feel left out and will perceive himself as being "different." Parents and teachers may not always be aware of how inadequate and rejected children feel who are "on the outside." To the casual observer, these children look just like any other children, but in their own eyes they look "different." They may consider themselves unlovable, ridiculous, or even grotesque and not quite human. Most children are unable to discuss such feelings about themselves, but they can usually express them quite vividly on HFDs.

The following case histories and HFDs are presented here to show how children, who feel that they are "different" from others, can reflect this attitude on their drawings. It is interesting to note that children who differ greatly in age, sex, mental ability, behavior symptoms and place of residence may still use very similar images to reveal their feelings about being "different." In part, these images are determined by the specific culture the children live in; but in part, they seem to hark back to almost universal symbols that are accepted the world over. The HFDs presented here are by no means unique; they were selected from a much larger number of similar drawings in the writer's collection of children's drawings.

CONCERN ABOUT BEING NONHUMAN. A *scarecrow* is a poor substitute for a human being. It is nothing but a bundle of old clothes and some sticks. It cannot move about or talk or do anything but scare birds, and sometimes it cannot even do that. In that case, the scarecrow is nothing but a pathetic and ridiculous contraption. That is exactly the way Sammy saw himself *(Plate 48)*. Sammy was an aphasic youngster whose speech was all but unintelligible. But there was nothing wrong with Sammy's reasoning. With each successive year, Sammy became more and more aware of his handicap and frustrated by it. Difficulty in communication cut him off from his peer group and interfered with his school progress. When he tried to talk to other children, they looked at him bewildered and did not understand him. To make matters worse, Sammy's father ridiculed him because he did not comprehend the cause and severity of Sammy's problem.

Sammy's feeling of utter helplessness and sadness is tellingly revealed on his HFD shown on *Plate 48*. He drew a scarecrow with a very unhappy expression on its face. Even the crows seem to be making fun of the scarecrow as they fly off with ears of corn in their beaks. If this picture had been drawn during the month of October, one might have suspected that is was inspired by Halloween, but such was not the case. The drawing on *Plate 48* was made in the springtime and was not influenced by the season but by Sammy's own feelings about himself. In the writer's collection are several HFDs showing scarecrows. One of these was drawn by a 16 year old retarded girl who differed from Sammy in every conceivable way with one exception: she too, thought of herself as being an absurd "thing," something less than human.

Puppets and marionettes are popular toys. Most children have either owned them or seen them on television or in a show. The experience of seeing puppets is shared by many youngsters, but only the exceptional child will identify himself with a puppet. Very few children draw puppets when asked to draw an HFD. Jay (*Plate 67*), an eleven year old boy of average intelligence, was one of the children who drew a puppet. Jay was the son of extremely rigid and domineering parents who adhered strictly to a fundamentalist religion. As long as Jay was small and docile, all went well. But as he grew older and began to develop a mind of his own, difficulties arose between him and his parents. They could not tolerate any signs of rebellion or independence on their son's part and denied him permission to participate in activities with his peers. As Jay's frustration and anger mounted, he sought relief by blowing off steam in school. He began to develop serious behavior problems and was referred to the school psychologist.

When asked to make an HFD, Jay produced the puppet shown on *Plate 67*. The small size of the figure and the omission of the mouth reflect Jay's feeling of helplessness and inadequacy, and his tendency to withdraw at home when faced with his parents' overwhelming power. He did not dare to speak out openly. Jay's HFD conveys in a most telling way that he felt trapped. He did not see himself as a free and independent human being, but merely as a puppet, a toy, who was completely at the mercy of his parents. They were the ones who pulled the strings, and the puppet had to jump at their beck and call. Jay commented as he drew: "He is a sailor, a sailor for Columbus—but he does not look that way." While the actual drawing reflects Jay's attitude toward himself, the stated content of the drawing reveals his wish-dream. Jay would like to be a sailor and leave home; he would like to set out to discover new worlds for himself where he can be free from parental domination and restriction. The fact that he said the sailor was "for Columbus" only underscores his desire to rebel and to escape from home to some far-off place.

Robots have fascinated boys of all ages for a long time. In their imagination, boys usually dream of building robots whom they can control and who will do what they want them to do. It is only the very unhappy children, who feel overwhelmed by domineering and usually disapproving fathers, who will identify themselves with the robot and not with the robot's creator. They will feel as though they were in fact a machine, a robot, who has no identity of its own and who is functioning only at the whim of its lord and master.

Plate 68 shows the robot drawn by Joe, an 11 year old boy with poor verbal ability and learning difficulties. Joe was a very insecure, seriously disturbed youngster who bitterly resented his stern father's punitive ways. But Joe could not express his anger at home; instead he displaced his hostility and frustration onto his siblings and peers. He openly defied authority in school and annoyed other children, who rejected him. Joe had extremely poor interpersonal relationships and moved in a world of his own. His peers frequently commented that he did not seem to be quite human; they referred to him as the "zombie." Joe seemed to share their feelings, for when he was asked to make an HFD, he did not draw a human being but a robot. It is significant that Joe's robot lacks feet. The omission of the feet from an HFD of an 11 year old child of normal intelligence is most unusual and clinically meaningful. It reflects not only insecurity but most likely also intense castration anxiety.

Plate 71 shows another robot. This one was drawn by Elliott, an eight year old boy with superior verbal ability but serious malfunctioning in the visual-motor area. Elliott had a very strict father who had high goals for his only son. When Elliott's achievement did not meet the father's expectations, the father exerted considerable pressure on Elliott and ridiculed him for his clumsiness and reading difficulty. Since Elliott did not dare to express his resentment toward his father openly at home, he either acted out his frustrations in aggressive attacks on his siblings and peers, or he escaped into fantasy. Elliott spent many hours each day dreaming about a robot who destroyed his master and blew up the universe. When he was asked to make an HFD, Elliot complied by drawing a robot, the hero of his daydreams. The way he drew the robot on *Plate 71* reflects Elliott's feelings about himself. The tiny head reveals his concern over his poor school progress, while the long arms and powerful pincer-hands show his aggressive reaching out into the world about him. Elliott felt like an outcast in his family, like someone who was not a member of the human race. Then Elliott proceeded to tell a vivid story about the destruction the robot is about to inflict on the world and on the human beings who rejected him. This story is, of course, Elliott's wish-dream; this is what he wishes he could do himself.

CONCERN ABOUT FEELING NOT QUITE HUMAN. Puppets, scarecrows, and robots are artifacts made by humans; they have no real existence of their own. They move and talk and act only at the command of others and are at the mercy of their masters. But in the realm of the myths, science fiction, and in fantasy, there are many creatures who are alive and have some human characteristics yet are not quite human. Usually, these creatures are asocial or antisocial. Many children who feel like outsiders and who do not consider themselves as quite human will identify with these asocial or antisocial creatures and will portray them on their HFDs.

Kevin *(Plate 74)*, a ten year old boy of low average intelligence, had been showing increasingly disorganized behavior prior to coming to the child guidance clinic for evaluation. Kevin had been running the streets since he was eight years old and had a long history of truancy, stealing, and vandalism. Kevin lived with his immature, unstable, mentally limited mother in "an atmosphere of immorality and irresponsibility" according to the social worker's report. Kevin had suffered from severe emotional deprivation and physical neglect all his life. Since he had no family life at home, he looked toward his peers for acceptance and support, but they teased him because of his odd appearance. Kevin was unusually homely. He had a lopsided head, prominent buck teeth, pale nondescript eyes, and ill-kempt, stringy, mouse-colored hair. Scorned and rejected by his peers, Kevin held much to himself. Outwardly, he was usually submissive and withdrawn, while seething with anger and frustration on the inside. Much of the time, he engaged in aggressive fantasy and muttered to himself. When the frustrations overwhelmed him, he acted them out and stole or destroyed things. Kevin had difficulty at times separating fact from fancy.

Plate 74 shows Kevin's bizarre HFD. According to Kevin, it represents a creature who is *"half robot and half giant,"* thereby reflecting Kevin's inner conflicts and disorganization. He felt that he was not all of one piece. Kevin perceived part of him as not being really alive at all, while the other part of him was something less than human. Kevin felt that he did not have entire control over himself and his actions, since the robot half of him was controlled by forces outside of him. But he thought of the other part of himself as big and strong like a giant. This part wanted to act out his anger and longed to take revenge on his peers who rejected him. The huge hands and long arms of his monster show Kevin's hostility and aggressiveness, whereas the poor integration of the arms and the omission of the neck reveal his impulsivity and his poor personality integration.

Chuck drew a *"wolfman"* who is shown on Plate 75. Chuck, a seven year old brain injured boy of superior intelligence, was exceedingly clumsy and had very poor coordination. He also suffered from serious malfunctioning in visual-motor perception and his frustration tolerance was minimal. Every time other children teased him or called him names, he flew into a rage. Chuck was exceedingly stubborn and wanted his own way at all times. He was engaged in an ongoing power struggle with his parents. Chuck was a very angry and frustrated young man who succeeded in making life difficult for himself, for his family, for his teachers, and for his peers.

When asked to make an HFD, Chuck produced the picture shown on Plate 75. He elaborated spontaneously: "He is a wolfman, he is a bad person." The drawing reveals Chuck's attitude toward himself: He perceived himself as being not quite human, as being a monster who is bad. The shading of the body and the omission of the nose suggest intense anxiety and withdrawal; the asymmetry of the arms reflects his impulsivity, while the long, heavy neck indicates his unsuccessful attempt at controlling his impulses. The bold, large drawing of the wolfman also suggests defiance and a wish to get even with his parents and teachers; if others did not accept him, Chuck would show them how "bad" he really was and would scare them with his behavior.

Danny (Plate 76) was another child who was at odds with the world about him. His mother had died when he was an infant. His father remarried a few years later, but his stepmother never fully accepted Danny. He started running the streets with older boys from the time he entered school. Danny had a long history of truancy, stealing, and molesting of other children. Danny was a very unhappy and hostile boy of borderline intelligence. When he was 11 years old, he was placed in a children's home and was brought to the diagnostic center for evaluation. *Plate 76* shows his HFD.

Danny drew *"Frankenstein and the Apeman."* Like many other children, Danny was fascinated by the Frankenstein movies. But the majority of youngsters do not identify themselves with Frankenstein; they visualize themselves as the good guys; they identify with Superman *(Plate 33)* or with Davy Crockett *(Plates 1 and 29)* or with Batman, or with whoever happens to be the hero of the day. In the writer's experience, it is only the hostile and unhappy child who will draw Frankenstein and the likes when drawing an inner self-portrait. In Danny's case, it would appear that he perceived himself more in the role of the Apeman than in the part of Frankenstein. Danny was a very dependent youngster who seldom acted alone. He was usually in the company of older boys whose orders he followed. He both admired and feared these older boys; they were his Frankenstein.

The way Danny drew his figures reveals his attitude toward himself. Both Frankenstein and the Apeman have sad expressions, and their faces are accentuated by a scar in one case and by heavy shading in the other. Both faces actually resemble Danny's own face and reflect his sensitivity about his appearance. Danny was a very dark-complexioned Negro boy with a mournful expression and a big scar across his forehead, which he had obtained in an accident. Both figures on *Plate 76* have arms without hands or fingers, thereby indicating Danny's feeling of inadequacy and guilt; the omission of the neck reveals his impulsivity. By making Frankenstein so large and the Apeman so small, Danny shows his own dependency on the older boys. Both figures symbolize aggressive and destructive power and reflect Danny's desire to be powerful and to get even with the hostile world he lived in.

Burt *(Plate 62)*, a very disturbed 11 year old boy of average intelligence, was overwhelmed by his feeling of badness. When asked to draw a picture of himself, he drew the devil on *Plate 62*. Burt was not overtly aggressive like Chuck and Danny, and he did not draw hostile and destructive monsters like the other boys. Burt had a strict religious upbringing and a strong sense of right and wrong. He was convinced that his evil thoughts and actions made him something less than human, and that he was wicked like the devil. Burt wrestled with his problems of guilt and anxiety within himself and directed his feelings toward himself. For a more detailed discussion of Burt's case, see page 116.

CONCERN ABOUT FEELING LIKE AN "OUTSIDER." Feeling "different" from others is not an all-or-nothing proposition, it is rather a matter of degree. It seems safe to assume that a child who perceives himself as the "Wolfman" feels more alive and human than one who thinks of himself as an inanimate scarecrow or a puppet. On the other hand, children who draw themselves as not quite human creatures have a stronger feeling of being different than do youngsters who draw themselves as figures who are human beings, but who are not fully accepted members of society. They may depict themselves as "outsiders;" that is, they may draw themselves as members of a minority group (e.g., an Indian, *Plate 58)*, as a citizen from a different country (e.g., a Frenchman, *Plate 69*), as a person from a different planet (e.g., a spaceman, *Plate 77*), or as a man from a different era (e.g., a caveman, *Plate 72*). It was found that children who presented "outsiders" on their HFDs tend to feel "different" and apart from their social environment but still regard themselves as members of the human race.

Michael *(Plate 77)*, age six, suffered from neurological impairment. He was quite immature and poorly coordinated though his intelligence was within the normal range. His school achievement was poor as were his interpersonal relationships. When his father and the school brought more pressure to bear on Michael than he could tolerate, he withdrew into fantasy. He cut himself off from the world around him. Michael spent many hours each day talking to himself, gesticulating with both hands, masturbating openly, and showing generally bizarre and inappropriate behavior. Michael was referred to the clinic for evaluation. *Plate 77* shows his HFD. Michael drew a *"spaceman up in space,"* thereby revealing his feeling of being "up in the air" like a person from a different planet who is neither understood nor accepted on earth. Michael's spaceman lacks a mouth and is therefore unable to communicate with other human beings. Michael attached all sorts of wires and antennas to his spaceman so he could receive messages from outer space and could communicate with other beings, just as Michael himself was forever talking to people who were not there. The anxious look on the spaceman's face, the omission of his nose, and the cord connecting the spaceman with a "plug" suggest concern on Michael's part about masturbatory activity and body intactness.

After about a year of therapy and remedial instructions, Elliott, age nine, made the HFD shown on *Plate 72*. Whereas he had drawn a robot earlier *(Plate 71)*, he now drew a *caveman* with an axe. Elliott showed in effect that he had rejoined the human race, but that he still felt like an outsider. He still perceived himself as a very primitive person who was not yet a fully civilized, accepted member of society. Elliott explained his picture: "He is a story character who lives in a cave and hunts sabertooth tigers and wild horses." Perhaps Elliott was really expressing the wish that he could be free to roam about and could hunt tigers instead of having to study all the time. It is also possible that his story of the hunter reflects his wish for greater physical prowess and skill, since his father, who was a good athlete, taunted Elliott because of his lack of athletic ability.

The *Indian* has an ambiguous place in our society. On the one hand, he is described in books as a brave and heroic warrior; on the other hand, he is the guy who always loses and gets shot on television and in the movies. In real life, he is treated as a second-class citizen who is often restricted to reservations and is treated as an outsider in his native land. This is hardly a desirable status for children to aspire to. Yet it is not unusual for children to identify with the Indians, especially if they feel like the underdog and are not fully accepted by others.

Plate 58 shows an Indian brave drawn by five year old Mel (page 114). He felt like an outsider in his own home when he was displaced by a new stepfather and two half-brothers. The drawing of the Indian reveals that Mel perceived himself as an outcast but that he is also ready to fight for his place in the home. However, the tiny size of Mel's figure seems to show that he had little confidence in his ability to succeed against the overwhelming odds he had to face.

Plate 47 shows a very elaborate Indian with a teepee who was drawn by Sammy, an eight year old aphasic boy with unintelligible speech (page 105). It seems rather incongruous that the Indian brave in full regalia with a war bonnet should be sitting down while shooting his bow and arrow. It seems almost as if Sammy did not really believe in his Indian's fighting ability, nor in his own. The shooting of the arrow is just a pose or an empty gesture. The Indian on *Plate 47* is really too weak to get up and fight; he has all but given up. This reflects quite accurately Sammy's own attitude at the time. He was hostile, resentful, and frustrated, but he was unable to fight or to do anything about his minority status in his peer group. He was on the outside; he could not communicate with others since he could not make himself understood.

A *foreigner* usually speaks a different language and has different customs from the people who are native in a given land. The foreigner may be tolerated or even welcomed because he may be interesting and different; but even at best, he remains an outsider. So when 12 year old Joe *(Plate 69)* portrayed a "Frenchman" on his HFD, he was saying in effect: "Yes, I am a human being, but I do not quite belong to my family, I am different." Joe's drawing on *Plate 69* reflects intense feelings of insecurity and castration anxiety. The Frenchman has no feet to stand on and he reveals a big scar on his face. Joe commented as he drew: "It is a Frenchman with a cut on his face . . . he cut himself, no he got wounded in the war."

CONCERN ABOUT FEELING RIDICULOUS. A *clown* is a person who acts silly so that other people will laugh at him. Everybody loves a clown, but nobody takes him seriously. Quite often, a child will feel as if he were a clown, for adults laugh at him but do not really respect him or listen to him. A child who feels that he is ridiculous like a clown and not worthy of respect will perceive himself as an outsider. Some children, who are usually overlooked and ignored at home, may resort to acting the part of a clown just to get some attention from others. But the clown in the circus who makes others laugh never laughs himself; he is really a sad figure, and the child who tries to gain attention by acting silly tends to be an unhappy and lonely child.

When Scotty *(Plate 80)*, an eight year old boy of average intelligence, was requested to make an HFD, he asked: "Can I make a clown?" Then he proceeded to draw the picture shown on *Plate 80*. "It's a clown dressed up like a hobo," he explained. Scotty had good reason to feel that he was ridiculous; he was a social misfit. He was unusually tall and heavy for his age and looked more like a 10 or 11 year old boy than like an eight year old. Yet emotionally, he was quite immature and resembled more a six or seven year old. His parents and teachers always expected more of him than he could do and were then disappointed when he did not act as mature as he looked. When Scotty played with children his own age, he was accused of being a bully because he was so much bigger and stronger than they were. Scotty was clumsy and poorly coordinated; when he touched things, they usually broke, and when he played with children, he hurt them unwittingly. He was constantly in trouble and the parents of other children would not let their youngsters play with him. Scotty was made to feel that he was different; he was a misfit in any group of children. In addition, he had serious learning problems and could not read or write as well as most six year old children who were a good head shorter than he was. All this contributed to his feeling of being ridiculous. When his frustrations and hostility mounted, he would vent his anger on other children in school which only led to further difficulties. Scotty was a very unhappy youngster who was in need of psychiatric help. His HFD clearly reflects the low opinion he had of himself and his anger at others. *Plate 80* shows a "hobo clown" who is so grotesque that he is funny; he is a tramp, an outcast, someone people laugh at.

Eight year old Frankie *(Plate 25)* was another youngster who felt ridiculous. Other children laughed at him and imitated him. Frankie held his head at an angle in order to see better since he suffered from a muscle imbalance in his eyes. He also had a number of nervous mannerisms that made him "different." *Plate 25b* shows Frankie's "clown juggling balls." In this HFD, Frankie vividly reflects his feelings about himself. He portrays himself as a juggling clown who is desperately trying to hang on to his balls, i.e., he was trying to retain his grip on reality which he could lose any moment (page 149). Frankie made this drawing when he was in a state of great agitation and emotional upset. A clown and a juggler may entertain others, but it is not a happy experience to feel like a clown who is juggling balls.

Ernie *(Plate 65)*, age ten, felt that he was being laughed at by his family and peers. All his efforts at demonstrating his manliness were ridiculed by them. He met with failure at home, in school and in the community. He was a ludicrous figure whom no one took seriously; he was nothing but a fool. So when asked to make an HFD, Ernie drew the clown shown on *Plate 65*. A more detailed discussion of Ernie's drawing was given on page 118. A clown was also drawn by Anthony *(Plate 98b)* whose case history is presented on page 173.

6.   Children's Attitudes toward Their Family Reflected on Drawings

A CHILD IS A SOCIAL BEING who can never be fully understood in isolation apart from his social environment. In order to make a meaningful psychological evaluation of a child, one has to know not only his social background, but also how the child perceives himself, his family, and his place within the family.

A young child is dependent on his parents for food and shelter, for emotional and social support, and for security. No matter how inadequate or limited his parents may be, a child needs them and will therefore usually show some attachment to them. They are his parents for better or for worse; he has no choice in the matter. It is sometimes amazing to observe children's loyalty to parents who are actually rejecting and neglectful. Young children tend to accept their parents as they are without any questioning. Subconsciously, a child may feel ambivalent or hostile toward his parents, but on the conscious level, he will rarely criticize them. To admit consciously that his parents are inadequate is profoundly disturbing for a child and threatens his basic security. There is an unwritten law in our society that children defend and protect their parents' name and reputation whether the latter deserve it or not.

Even a deprived and abused child will rarely if ever denounce or accuse his parents when seen initially for a psychiatric interview. When asked by an examiner to tell something about his mother, the child will often say "she is nice" or he will say nothing at all. These are two ways in which a child can express indirectly his negative attitudes toward his parents without feeling threatened, or even without being aware of it. The child who is hostile toward his mother will refer to her as "she" rather than "mother" or "Mommy" or the like; while the child who only speaks of "him" has a negative attitude toward his father. The same is true for the child who omits mentioning his father or mother entirely, even when he is specifically questioned about them.

But if children are unwilling or unable to put their hostile attitudes toward parents into words, they can and do express them quite readily on drawings. On a drawing, a child can reveal unconsciously negative attitudes toward his family by disguising the shapes of his parents and siblings and by using signs and symbols he himself may not be aware of. Drawings can frequently offer insights into a child's interpersonal relationships which other psychological techniques or methods fail to provide. There are three different types of drawings that can reveal a child's positive and negative attitudes toward his family. These are: (a) spontaneous drawings; (b) HFDs, and (c) family portraits. In the following sections, each of these types of drawings will be discussed and illustrated.

Spontaneous drawings reflecting children's attitudes toward their family

Children who draw a picture of their family spontaneously tend to have a warm and positive relationship with one or both parents. These

128

children feel emotionally secure enough to express their attitudes openly and directly; they have no need to hide or to disguise their feelings.

Plate 21 shows an example of a spontaneous family picture. It was drawn by Taneil, a happy, well-adjusted, bright four year old girl. Taneil drew herself in the center of her family while partaking of a joyous Thanksgiving dinner. The drawing suggests that Taneil had a warm and loving attitude toward her family and friends. The irregularities and disproportions of the figures on the picture must be attributed largely to Taneil's tender age and lack of drawing skill. *Plate 21* was discussed more fully on page 85.

Another child who drew a spontaneous family picture was Michael *(Plate 79)*. He was then seven years old. When first seen by the writer, Michael had been a very disturbed youngster whose behavior was on occasion inappropriate and who lived much of the time in fantasy (page 125). Throughout the school year, Michael and his parents were seen for therapy and guidance at the clinic. Michael used his therapy sessions well and made good progress. About one year after his treatment began, Michael came to the clinic for his regular session on a Monday afternoon. He seemed to be very upset. The writer knew from experience that the weekends, when the father was home, were sometimes difficult for Michael. Michael asked for pencil and paper and began drawing a series of spontaneous pictures which he accompanied with a running commentary. These drawings culminated in the one shown on *Plate 79*. Michael's face was flushed, his eyes shone, his voice trembled, and he laughed almost hysterically as he elaborated on his drawing.

The drawing on *Plate 79* is quite remarkable in its vividness. Michael was only able to draw it because he felt at that point secure in the affection of his mother and sister, and because he had learned that he could express his feelings freely in the therapy session without having to fear criticism or punishment. But perhaps most important of all was the fact that Michael's attitude toward his father was not entirely negative but rather ambivalent. He both feared and admired his father; therefore, Michael represented him both as a monster and as a hero, as Superman. Michael verbalized as he drew: "Father with a big mouth says: 'shut up!' He is mean. Everybody (Michael and sister) is fighting, he does not want that, he is Superman. He pushes your sister, I punch him back. He falls to the ground; he's gone cuckoo. His ears went down." Michael's story is first an account of a squabble between him and his sister and his father's intervention. But then Michael indulges in wishful thinking; he "punches" the father and knocks him down; he gets even with him for his "meanness." Michael expresses resentment toward the father's authoritarian ways, while at the same time revealing his fondness for his sister whom he defends in this story against the father, even though he had just been fighting with her. The way the figures are drawn shows Michael's feeling of awe and envy toward the big he-man father and his own feeling of insignificance and smallness. The content of the story indicates that Michael wishes he were as big and strong as the father so he could defeat him.

HFDs reflecting children's attitudes toward their family

When children are asked to make an HFD, they usually draw one person who represents some aspect of themselves. But there are exceptions to this rule. On occasion, a child will draw not himself but a member of his family or even his whole family. In such a case, it may be assumed that the family member or members portrayed on the HFD are of particular importance to the child at that given time. In general, a child will draw a fairly faithful likeness of himself and others if his attitude toward the people on the drawing is positive. If the attitude is negative, he will distort and disguise the figures. As was pointed out earlier, it just is not "nice" to express openly hostile feelings toward one's family, so some disguise becomes necessary.

Plate 51 shows the HFD of Betty, an eight year old hemiplegic girl. When asked to draw "*a* whole person," she drew her entire family. Betty's drawing clearly reflects her closeness to her family and her affection for it. But *Plate 51* also reveals Betty's strong need for support and protection from the family, especially from the mother. Betty drew herself in the center of the family group, sheltered by her mother's clothing. By drawing herself quite tiny, even though she was not really the smallest in the family, Betty seems to express her desire to remain small and dependent in the secure circle of her family (page 107).

Christopher *(Plate 81)*, a ten year old boy of normal intelligence, also drew his entire family when asked to make an HFD. But Christopher's attitude toward his family was much less positive than Betty's attitude toward her family. So instead of drawing the members of his family realistically, Christopher disguised them in the form of animals, thereby hiding his feelings from himself and others. He could not openly admit that he hated his stepfather and that he was angry at his real father who had deserted him, nor could he accept his own ambivalence toward his mother who had left him for long periods of time in the past and who devoted at present too much time to the younger siblings. Christopher could express such feelings only indirectly on his drawing which is shown on *Plate 81*. A meaningful interpretation of this drawing is only possible if one is acquainted with Christopher's family background. Without such knowledge, the picture on *Plate 81* would appear to be nothing more than a hunting scene. But when it is related to Christopher's own history, then it takes on considerable clinical significance.

When Christopher was a year old, his father left the family; for three years, Christopher was boarded in a children's home or lived with his grandparents until his mother remarried. The stepfather was a very stern and demanding person who had little understanding of Christopher. When the latter developed learning problems in school, both parents put considerable pressure on him to improve his achievement. Christopher felt rejected by the parents, particularly since they greatly indulged his two younger half-siblings. Christopher developed into a very restless and unhappy youngster with many fears, anxieties, and nervous mannerisms. He had difficulty getting along with his peers and could not concentrate on his work in school. Christopher daydreamed much of the time; he was only happy when he could withdraw from people and could play with his animals. Above all, he loved turtles.

Christopher told the following story as he made the HFD on *Plate 81:* "This two-headed mother dragon is friendly toward the turtle and tries to help him. This lizard is trying to eat the turtle, he is poisonous. The man is hunting a great long sea serpent. The sea serpent is sticking his head out of his house. The man has a revolver, a rifle, and a knife. Back here is his car with all his equipment." With Christopher's own history in mind, the meaning of this story and the drawing seems clear; Christopher himself is represented by two of the characters on the HFD. First there is the turtle whom he dearly loves in real life and with whom Christopher identifies in the story. The turtle is a small, shy, fearful creature just like Christopher; it cannot fight, its only defense is withdrawal in the face of danger. The turtle in the picture is being threatened by a poisonous lizard who wants to eat it, just as Christopher felt that he was being threatened by his stepfather. The poisonous lizard represents therefore the step-father, while the two-headed mother dragon represents Christopher's mother. She is shown as two-headed since she was in effect two-faced; on the one hand, she takes care of Christopher and is the only mother he has; on the other hand, she did desert him in the past and has now displaced him with new children. But since spontaneous stories represent wish-dreams, we find here that the mother dragon is kindly disposed, she is "friendly" and she "tries to help him." That is, Christopher is looking toward his mother to protect him against the stepfather.

There is a second part to Christopher's story and drawing. The man on *Plate 81* represents Christopher's ideal dream image: a strong, active, well-equipped hunter who is out to find the "sea serpent." The elusive sea serpent is most likely Christopher's natural father who has vanished from his life. Christopher wants to find his real father and is at the same time fearful of him and resents him. The drawing clearly shows Christopher's ambivalence toward this father. The sea serpent has big threatening teeth and the hunter has armed himself just to be on the safe side in case he should meet him. At the same time, the sea serpent is "sticking his head out of his house," he is not hiding, but rather puts himself into a position where he can be seen and found. The weapons the hunter is carrying, the revolver, the rifle, and the knife, are all usually thought of as phallic symbols. In this particular case, they may have a double meaning; they may stand for protection and safety, as well as for masculine identification. Since Christopher feels threatened and rejected by his stepfather, he may be searching for his real father in order to identify with him.

Matthew *(Plate 82)*, an eight year old boy of normal intelligence, was another child who revealed his attitudes toward his family on his HFD. Once again, it is necessary to know something about Matthew's family situation in order to fully understand the meaning of the drawing shown on *Plate 82.* Matthew was a neurologically impaired youngster who was hypertalkative, distractible, and quite immature. He suffered from serious perceptual malfunctioning and had very poor coordination. His school progress was minimal and his interpersonal relationships were poor.

Matthew's only sibling was a nine year old sister who excelled in everything; she was attractive, socially popular and an outstanding pupil. The sibling rivalry between Matthew and his sister was intense. He deeply resented his sister and blamed much of his difficulty on her. The parents were inconsistent and unstable individuals, who had too many problems of their own to be able to give Matthew the support he needed.

With this background in mind, the meaning of the HFD on *Plate 82* becomes clear. Matthew drew an underwater scene, extending over two sheets of paper, with a sunken boat and a girl who is being attacked by a fish. He accompanied the drawing of his picture with the following story: "This is a swordfish eating a nine year old girl, also a tinfish and the boat they sunk. All the captains and the crew are dead." The nine year old girl in the story is, of course, the sister, although the way she is drawn reflects Matthew's own impulsivity and instability. On the drawing, Matthew himself is disguised in the form of the swordfish who attacks the sister. The sunken boat is probably his home or the school with all the teachers and peers. The content of the story is Matthew's wish-dream; he wants to devour and destroy his archrival, the sister, and he wants to sink and remove from his life all the demanding, disapproving, and threatening "captains" (parents and teachers) and the "crews" (peers). In real life, Matthew was much too passive and timid to express his resentment and hostility toward others openly and directly, but he succeeded very well in showing his attitudes indirectly on his HFD.

An even more subtle and indirect way of revealing sibling rivalry was illustrated on the HFD of Benjie (page 101). Benjie's HFD is shown on *Plate 42*. He first stated that he was drawing "Davy Crockett" but then decided that this figure really represented "Jackie Gleason," because "he is so fat." But in addition to the human figure, Benjie drew a tiny racing car, apparently a toy car. Benjie commented: "A little car is coming along and is going 'toot.' I go out of the way because I think it is a big car." It might seem hazardous to interpret the meaning of the little car and Benjie's statement, if one did not know that Benjie had a younger brother who excelled in all areas where Benjie had problems. There is no doubt in the writer's mind that the little car on Benjie's HFD represents his brother who is coming along from behind and who is bypassing him. The brother may be younger than he is, but Benjie regards him as a "big car," so he steps aside. Benjie gives up, he is no fighter. He internalizes his problems instead: he overeats, suffers from tension headaches, and cries a great deal at home and in school when the frustrations get to be too great.

It is even more anxiety-provoking for a child to acknowledge and to express hostile feelings towards his mother or father than toward a sibling. Sheilah *(Plate 83)*, a 12 year old girl of high average intelligence, was quite resentful and hostile toward her domineering, restrictive, and coercive mother. She was particularly disturbed by her mother's constant nagging at the weak, ineffectual father. But Sheilah was afraid to express her feelings since she was a good girl who did not think it was right for a child to be angry at her mother and she also feared her mother's punitiveness and her sharp tongue. So Sheilah suppressed her hostility and turned her feelings inward. As a result, she suffered from severe headaches and other psychosomatic disturbances. When the physicians were unable to find any physical basis for Sheilah's complaints, they referred her to the guidance clinic. There Sheilah was seen by the writer for therapy (page 153).

At the beginning of therapy, Sheilah was quite evasive in her verbalizations and in her drawings (Plate 83a). After five months of treatment, Sheilah was asked to make another HFD. The result is shown on Plate 83b. Sheilah drew a witch on a broomstick which looks at first glance like a traditional Halloween drawing. If this picture had been made in October, no special meaning could have been attached to it. But the HFD on Plate 83b was drawn in March, when spring was in the air and when most 12 or 13 year old girls were drawing figures of glamorous boys and girls; therefore, the content of Sheilah's HFD must be regarded as highly significant. Sheilah commented as she drew: "She is a real mean old witch who haunts people all the time and who scares them to death." There can be hardly any doubt that Sheilah's drawing reveals her attitude toward her mother; thus, it represents a significant clinical accomplishment on her part. For the first time, Sheilah was able to express her resentment toward her mother, albeit indirectly through an HFD. It is not a coincidence that Sheilah's physical symptoms had disappeared by the time she made the drawing on Plate 83b, and that she was well on the road to recovery. In the week after she drew the witch on the broomstick, Sheilah was able to discuss her feelings toward her mother directly with the therapist.

Alfred (Plate 84) had a long history of behavior and learning problems in school. He was an extremely hyperactive, impulsive, distractable nine year old boy of low average intelligence. Alfred had suffered from a convulsive disorder since early childhood, he also had a slight hearing loss and many allergies. He came from a socially and economically marginal family that was dominated by a very punitive and unreasonable father. The mother was meek and mild; she was completely overwhelmed by her six children and by her abusive husband. All discipline in the family was handled by the father.

When asked to make an HFD, Alfred produced the picture shown on Plate 84. It reveals Alfred's attitude toward himself and his concern about his father. In fact, Alfred drew his father and labeled the picture: "My father is 38 years old." He then drew a loop in the father's hand and said: "This is his belt, he licks the kids." Alfred stated this very matter-of-factly, merely reporting the kind of behavior that was common in his home. Yet the very fact that he drew the father and the belt shows that he did not like the treatment he was receiving and that he was preoccupied with and afraid of his father. Alfred was unable or unwilling to discuss his father directly, but the drawing seemed to be in effect an indirect plea for the examiner to please stop the father from beating the children.

The way Alfred drew the figure on Plate 84 is of interest; it shows a continuous outline of the body and limbs. In the writer's experience, con-

tinuous outlines on HFDs are found primarily on drawings of brain injured children (*Plate 98c*) or of very disorganized children who are
desperately trying to control themselves and are attempting to put a
boundary around their scattered and poorly integrated personality. By
drawing a continuous outline, the children try to establish firm limits
for themselves and hope thereby to prevent complete disorganization or
deterioration. The omission of the eyes and the very short arms of the
figure on *Plate 84* reveal Alfred's difficulty in reaching out toward others
and in communicating with them.

Family portraits reflecting children's attitudes toward their family

The "Draw-a-family" or "Draw-your-family" technique is not new; a
number of clinicians have written about it. Hammer (1958), Hulse (1952,
1956), and Reznikoff and Reznikoff (1958) have suggested that family
drawings reveal a child's attitude toward other members of his family
and his perception of his own role within the family. Family relationships
are expressed by the relative size and placement of the figures on the
drawing and by the omissions, substitutions, or exaggerations of the
figures or parts of them.

In the writer's opinion, the drawing of a family portrait is of great
clinical value. It is important to emphasize that a family portrait, just
like an HFD, reveals a child's attitude toward his family and is not a
faithful reproduction of the child's actual family, although it may be this
too. But if a child's family drawing were nothing but an attempt at a
realistic portrait of the family, then it would be of little clinical significance. In order to obtain the greatest projective value from a family
drawing, it is important not to restrict the child as to whom he should
or should not draw, even if the results are bizarre. The "family" portrait
on *Plate 89* for instance, contains nothing but the crude drawing of a
dog; while the delightful family scene on *Plate 86* includes mostly imaginary family members and excludes the child's real family. The omission
of parents and siblings is always highly significant and may be more revealing than their presence.

It is recommended that the following instructions be used for obtaining
a family portrait: "I would like you to draw a picture of your whole family;
you can draw it any way you want to." That is all. Anything the child
chooses to draw or not to draw is accepted without questioning or comments until the picture is completed. If the child does not volunteer the
names and the identity of the figures he is drawing, he is asked to identify
them afterwards. Omissions of members of the family or of the child
himself are not very unusual on such drawings: they are always significant.
Such omissions should never be considered accidental or unimportant.
Some psychologists insist that a child draw *all* members of his family and
ask the child to correct any omission he might have made. This seems
unfortunate, since it dilutes the clinical significance of the drawing and
interferes with the child's free and spontaneous expression of his feelings.

A child may reveal on a drawing his attitude toward family members who may or may not be actually living with him. It is not surprising therefore that Lawton and Seechrest (1962) found no significant differences between the family drawings of boys who came from homes in which the father was present, and boys who came from homes in which the father was absent. A boy's attitude toward a father who is in the home may be just as positive or negative as the attitude of a boy whose father is absent.

In the preceding section of this chapter, it was shown that children sometimes disguise the appearance of family members on HFDs so that their expression of hostility or aggression toward them is not apparent and therefore not threatening. But when a child is asked specifically to draw his "whole family," then disguises of the figures are not possible and an expression of socially unacceptable attitudes by this means is no longer safe. On a family drawing, a child has to resort to omissions, substitutions, or the changing of size and position of figures as ways of revealing his underlying negative attitudes toward family members.

Some children omit themselves from family drawings. The writer found that this occurs most often on drawings of children who do not consider themselves an important or integral part of the family. Such omission is never deliberate; it reflects the child's unconscious feeling of insignificance and rejection. A socially and emotionally well-adjusted child is usually quite pleased with himself and has a healthy respect for himself. More often than not, a happy young child will draw himself first and will place himself in the center of the family group. Taneil's spontaneous family picture on *Plate 21* is a good example of such a drawing. Taneil not only drew herself first and in the central position, but she also made herself larger than anyone else (page 85).

Mickey's family drawing is shown on *Plate 26*. It reveals the father, the mother and his little sister, but not himself. One can only speculate whether the pencil scribble on the left hand side of the paper represents Mickey. One might hypothesize that Mickey, who was very upset at the time he made the drawing (page 87), lost patience and became too frustrated to be able to draw another person, even himself. But if this was the case, then the fact remains that he left himself to be drawn last, and this in itself is significant. But one might also hypothesize that the scribble on *Plate 26* reflects Mickey's attitude toward himself; it might indicate that he considers himself a mere nothing and not worthy of representation. He may be saying that he perceives himself not as a human being but merely as a formless blob.

Norman, a six year old brain injured boy of normal intelligence, produced the family portrait shown on *Plate 85*. With hasty, impulsive strokes he drew his father, his two sisters and himself. Then he stopped, looked at the drawing for some time and remarked: "I forgot my mother—no room for her here." Some psychologists might attribute this omission to Norman's impulsivity and to his poor spatial planning ability. But such an explanation seems hardly adequate. It is quite unlikely that a six year old child of normal intelligence will "forget" his mother. After all, the mother is the most important person in a young child's life. Norman's verbal statement is a rationalization for his indirect expression of unconscious hostility toward his mother. What he is saying in his family drawing on *Plate 85* is in effect: "I am mad at my mother but I cannot say that or admit that even to myself, since I need my mother and love her. So rather than say something that I cannot accept, I will not talk about her at all and I will not draw her either."

Norman's social history showed that he had reason for such an attitude toward his mother. She was a very unstable, inconsistent, disorganized person who indulged her children one day, only to neglect or abuse them the next day. It is no coincidence that Norman's ten year old sister also omitted the mother from her family drawing. The mother was quite unpredictable and was therefore threatening for the children; they never knew what to expect from her. The father on the other hand was quite consistent in his behavior. He was strict but had a great deal of affection for his children. His punishments were at times severe, but the children felt that he was fair and they knew where they stood with him; they could depend on him.

Henry (*Plate 31*), a nine year old boy of average intelligence, lived with his mother and three older siblings. Two other sisters were married and had homes of their own. The father had deserted the family when Henry was four years old. When Henry was asked to draw a picture of his "whole family," he produced the drawing shown on *Plate 31*. This picture was made at a time when Henry was extremely upset. On the drawing, Henry omits all members of his family with the exception of himself and "his baby sister who took his lollipop." But Henry had no "baby sister;" he was the youngest child in his family. Through this drawing, Henry expressed his resentment over the arrival of a new baby in his oldest sister's house. The new niece had displaced him from his position as the baby of the family and his mother's favorite; she had in effect taken "his lollipop away." Thus, Henry's family drawing focuses on the two persons in his larger family group who were at the center of his emotional conflict and upset; all other members of the family are omitted. The omission of the mother and siblings may be regarded as a sign of Henry's anger and resentment toward them. Henry felt rejected and deserted by them, since they devoted all their attention to the new baby. For a more detailed discussion of Henry's drawing see page 90.

While Henry omitted all the members of his immediate family with the exception of himself and his niece, some children add nonexistent or imaginary family members to their drawings. Such substitutions or additions have always considerable clinical significance. *Plate 33* shows Timothy's family portrait. Timothy's family history and his drawing were discussed in some detail earlier (page 92). He was an illegitimate child who had never known his father. But since Timothy was a very lonely and unhappy youngster, he spent much of his time dreaming of the unknown father. When asked to draw his family, Timothy portrayed the actual members of his family with amazing faithfulness in the order of their age and importance, but then he added with bold strokes his father in the form of Superman. The size and the position of the figures on *Plate 33* clearly reflect Timothy's attitude toward them. On the one side is the greatly idealized dream image of the father, on the opposite far side of the paper is Timothy himself, a small and insignificant figure who is kept apart from Superman by the other adults. There can be no doubt that the grandmother is the dominant force in Timothy's actual family; she lords over all the others.

When Shirley was nine years old, she was asked to draw a picture of her "whole family." The result is shown on *Plate 86*. Shirley's history was presented earlier (page 79). She was a girl of low average intelligence who was grossly undersized. She tried to hide her loneliness and unhappiness behind a bland and superficial smile. Shirley had no friends and was unable to relate to others or to express her emotions and attitudes openly. But Shirley loved to draw. On drawings, she could reveal what she did not dare to put into words.

Plate 86 shows a very charming family group. Shirley explained: "This is my little brother in his cradle, that's me, and this is my big sister, she is 14." The way Shirley drew the figures is significant. She started by drawing the legs first, then added the bodies and the arms, and finally completed the figures by adding the heads. Children who draw human figures in this sequence usually have been found to have difficulty in interpersonal relationships. Shirley devoted much time to the drawing of the dresses; she copied her own dress in detail, including the design on the pocket. The heads of the two girls on the other hand were drawn quite rapidly and mechanically in a stereotyped way as if Shirley were drawing dolls and not individuals.

The most interesting aspects of Shirley's family portrait on *Plate 86* are the people she represented. In real life, Shirley did not have a little brother nor did she have an older sister. Thus, we find that the family drawing contains two non-existent family members and Shirley herself, while her actual family had been omitted. This drawing tells a great deal about Shirley's attitude toward her parents and her little sister. When questioned about the people on her drawing, Shirley insisted that she really had a little brother and a big sister. There was no indication that Shirley was out of touch with reality or that she was confusing fact with fancy; she was not hallucinating. What did finally emerge was that neighbors of hers had a new baby boy whom Shirley was allowed to hold and feed on occasion. So she had "adopted" him in her own mind as a brother. It was also learned that Shirley was very fond of a teenage girl in the community whom she longed to have for a sister. Shirley's drawing shows therefore her wish-dream, the family she would like to have. Since she felt unwanted in her own family, she had substituted an older sister who was warm and maternal, and a little brother who was so small that he presented no threat or competition. He was someone Shirley could take care of and who would look up to her.

The drawing on *Plate 86* indicated a serious disturbance in the relationship between Shirley and her parents and sister. Efforts were made to change the situation. Shirley's parents were persuaded to participate in a parents' therapy group and were seen for counseling, so as to better understand and accept their daughter. Both Shirley and the parents benefited from this experience. About a year later, Shirley was again asked to draw her whole family. At that point, she seemed to be much happier and more outgoing than she had been earlier. Her second family portrait is shown on *Plate 87*. The contrast between *Plate 86* and *Plate 87* is striking. Instead of drawing substitute family members, Shirley now produced an accurate picture of her actual family: mother, father, younger sister and herself. On *Plate 87*, the mother is still a bit apart from the others who are holding hands, but she is present and accepted. The two sisters are shown in matching dresses, hand in hand, side by side like twins, no longer competitors and enemies. Shirley was in fact beginning to interact and to play with her sister, and she was discovering that her sister was not so bad after all. Shirley perceived herself, perhaps for the first time in her life, as an integral part of a family group. On her drawing, she expressed mainly positive attitudes toward her family and toward herself. Much of the credit for this change in Shirley's attitudes belonged to the parents who were able and willing to change their own attitudes and behavior toward Shirley in the course of the year.

Shirley's drawings on *Plates 86 and 87* show that two family portraits, obtained some time apart, can reveal a child's change in attitude toward his family. Even very crude and primitive drawings of young and impaired children are sensitive mirrors of family relationships. Unfortunately, not all changes in a child's attitudes toward his family and himself are in the positive direction. *Plate 88* shows the family portrait of Bobby, a six year old brain injured boy of low average intelligence. Because of marked immaturity, serious perceptual problems, and gross incoordination, Bobby was placed in a small special class for children with neurological impairment. Bobby seemed to be quite happy in his new class, but his parents were bitterly opposed to this placement. They were unwilling or unable to accept the fact that Bobby had learning difficulties and blamed his scholastic failure on the kindergarten teacher.

When asked to draw his whole family, Bobby produced the primitive picture shown on *Plate 88*. It includes his parents, his dog, his bird and the bird cage, and Bobby himself. Since Bobby was an only child, he substituted his pets for siblings, which is not uncommon. The crudeness of the drawing is the result of his impulsivity and very poor coordination. It may be significant that Bobby drew himself so much smaller than his dog, thereby showing his feeling of inadequacy and insignificance. Yet, the drawing is complete; that is, no one is omitted, and Bobby clearly reflects his feeling of belonging to his family group.

When Bobby returned to school in the fall, after the long summer vacation, he seemed like a changed child. He was more tense and restless than before; his ever-ready smile and cheerful chatter had disappeared. He did not even ask for constant reassurance and attention as he had done before. Bobby seemed defeated. He was obviously unhappy and troubled but he could not state the cause for his unhappiness. Once again,

Bobby was asked to make a family portrait. Bobby was very tense and anxious as he began to draw "Spot, the beagle," then he stopped and announced that the picture was finished. This "family" portrait is shown on *Plate 89*. Bobby was praised for his drawing of the dog, but was then gently urged to make another drawing of his "whole family." Bobby was by now extremely agitated and disturbed. He refused to draw another picture and the matter was dropped. The implications are clear. Bobby's inability to draw himself or his parents reflected a marked deterioration in his attitudes toward them and himself. Bobby was so threatened by his hostility toward his parents that he could not even express it indirectly on paper; his intense guilt feelings and his low opinion of himself prevented him from drawing a picture of himself. The only member of the family who was not threatening was Spot, the dog; therefore, Bobby was able to draw him without much difficulty. The bird, shown on the earlier picture, had died in the meantime. It is quite rare that children omit from a family portrait *all* members of the family, including themselves. When this does occur, it is invariably a sign of serious emotional disturbance and of acute anxiety. Such a child is always in need of psychiatric help.

The following information was later obtained from the parents: they had remained unconvinced that Bobby had any neurological problems or that he was any different from any other child. They still maintained that his poor academic achievement was the fault of the school. They had hired a tutor for Bobby who worked with him every morning during the summer months, while the mother worked with him every evening. When Bobby failed to make the expected progress under this regime, the parents expressed much disappointment and disapproval and increased their pressure on him. As a result Bobby became extremely anxious and not only failed to learn new skills but also forgot what he had learned during the previous year. When Bobby returned to school in September, he was not only a child with learning problems but also a youngster with serious emotional disturbances.

The omission of family members from a family portrait reflects strong negative attitudes on part of the child toward the omitted family member. The same is true when a child attempts to draw someone in his family but is unable to finish the figure of that particular person. Quite often, a child will have no difficulty depicting one parent or sibling but will be unable to complete the drawing of the other parent or another brother or sister. Whenever this occurs, it is a good indication that the child is hostile toward that particular parent or sibling. Sometimes, a child tries to make a family portrait but is unable to complete any of the figures; fortunately this is rare, for it is invariably a sign of serious disturbances in the relationship between the child and his family.

When Douglas, an eight year old boy of normal intelligence, was asked to make a picture of his family, he hesitated and volunteered to draw a car instead. After some gentle urging by the examiner, Douglas tried to comply with the request. "Must I draw everyone in the family, even my dog and cat?" he asked. Douglas was told that he could draw his family anyway he wanted to draw it. Douglas announced: "I will draw my father, he is the biggest." He started drawing a pair of cowboy boots with spurs, then he added legs and a body. Douglas had difficulty drawing the arms, erased them several times and decided that he was really drawing his brother. Again he was dissatisfied and erased most of the figure and said that he was drawing the father after all. Now Douglas tried drawing the head but again he did not succeed. During this entire time, he exhibited acute anxiety and much frustration. After erasing and redrawing the figure or parts of it four times Douglas gave up: "I can't draw my father, but I can draw my mother real good." Thereupon, Douglas began drawing a woman's head on the remnants of the male figure only to get disgusted and to erase it all again. Finally, Douglas decided to make a fresh start with the figure of his mother. He drew a lady's skirt, turtleneck sweater and one leg, and that was as far as he got. No matter how hard he tried, he could not complete the head or the other leg.

Many of the brightest and best-adjusted children erase parts of their drawings in order to correct them. Erasures as such are not necessarily a negative sign on children's drawings. But excessive erasing and the inability to improve or to complete a figure on a drawing are invariably a sign of intense anxiety and reveal hostility toward the person who is being drawn. In the case of Douglas, it was apparent that the relationship with his parents was grossly disturbed and that he could not cope with it. The examiner suggested therefore that Douglas stop drawing his family and make a different picture instead. She asked him to draw on a new sheet of paper "a whole person, any kind of a person you want to draw." "O, that is easy," Douglas exclaimed, "I can draw *just any* person." Douglas set about at once to produce a very tiny but complete figure. Encouraged by this success, he drew a second figure that was slightly taller though still very small. After studying his picture, Douglas announced: "That is me, I am taking my little brother Ted for a walk, he is two years old."

From the incomplete family drawing, it was apparent that Douglas was a most insecure and anxious boy who felt very hostile toward his parents and toward the brother next to him. On the second drawing, it was shown that Douglas felt comfortable only with one member of his family and that was the youngest brother. Children never seem to have difficulty drawing the people whom they like. The smallness of his figures discloses once again Douglas' extreme insecurity and feeling of inadequacy.

From an interview with Douglas' mother later on, it was learned that the parents had recently separated, and that she was unable to accept her oldest son in the same way as her other children. Douglas resembled his irresponsible and immature father physically and always reminded the mother of the father. The mother freely admitted that she "could not stand the boy." She also complained that Douglas was constantly fighting with his brother Peppy, who evidently was the mother's favorite. In view of these family relationships, it was not surprising that Douglas was unable to portray his whole family.

The child who is happy in his family group tends to draw all members of his family more or less in the order of their age and in correct size to each other. But most children with emotional problems are ambivalent toward their parents and siblings; they have both strong positive and strong negative feelings toward them. This ambivalence is often shown by a change in the size and position of the family members.

Plate 30 shows the family drawing of Dorothy, a nine year old girl of average intelligence. Her history was presented in some detail on page 89. Dorothy drew herself as large as her father and placed herself right next to him. In this picture, Dorothy occupies the righful place of the mother, while the mother is placed apart from the rest of the family at the far end of the paper. The mother was drawn last and smaller than the other family members. As was mentioned earlier, this family portait was made shortly after the birth of Dorothy's baby sister Kathy. Dorothy was delighted to have a new sister and claimed that Kathy was "her baby." The placement and size of the figures reveal her attitude toward her family. Dorothy felt quite close to her father and adored the baby. She placed herself right between them and was thus competing for her mother's position in the family. Dorothy tolerated her brother, he was included in the "inner family circle." Only the mother was placed apart from the others; this showed Dorothy's strong ambivalence toward her mother. Dorothy's attitude toward her mother was both positive and negative to a strong degree; if she had felt only hostility toward the mother, she would have omitted her most likely altogether from the drawing.

Joel (*Plate 32*), an eleven year old boy of superior intelligence, was very much upset when his parents separated. Joel had always been close to his father and was torn by ambivalent feelings when the latter left the home. Joel's family portrait is shown on *Plate 32*; it was discussed more fully earlier on page 92. It suffices here to point out how the placement of Joel and the father on the drawing reveals the special relationship between the two: they are shown at the opposite ends of the family group as if to emphasize the distance that has come beween them. The father walks away with a smile; Joel, small, forlorn, and mutilated, is walking in the opposite direction while looking back at the father mournfully. The heavy shading on the father's neck seems to reflect Joel's attempt at controlling his conflicting attitudes and impulses. The remaining members of the family are presented in frontal view without any signs of undue emotional involvement; Joel accepts them without much ambivalence or reservation.

A family is more than just a number of people who are related and who happen to live under the same roof. A family is a unit, a group of individuals who are bound to each other with strong emotional ties and loyalties, who care for each other, and who communicate and interact with one another. But not all parents and children living together form a family unit in this sense of the word. Homer, a nine year old boy of superior intelligence, was an only child. He lived with his emotionally unstable parents who had engaged in much strife and violent discord ever since Homer was born. The parents were much too much involved in their own problems to pay much attention to Homer. He was a lonely and unhappy child and his self-concept was extremely poor. He could not get along with other children and was a social isolate. When asked to make a family portrait, Homer drew grotesque caricatures of "my Frankenstein mom," "my crazy monster dad," and himself as "Vampire Batman." Homer insisted on drawing the mother on one side of the paper, the father on the other side of the paper, and himself on a second sheet of paper. These drawings clearly show that Homer did not perceive his family as a unit, but rather as three grotesque creatures who were separated and apart from each other. Each family member was placed on a separate side of the paper just as in real life the mother and the father and Homer lived in separate worlds. They could not relate to each other or communicate with each other.

Duane *(Plate 90)*, age 11, lived in the same house with his parents, his two brothers, and his two sisters. But he did not live in a warm, close-knit family unit. To the casual observer, Duane's family looked ideal. All the children were attractive and healthy, and they were physically well cared for. The parents were hardworking, respected citizens of their community. But something was lacking. Duane was referred to the school psychologist because of lethargy in the classroom, a complete lack of interest in school activities, failure to complete his assignments and an inability to relate to other children. The teacher questioned his intellectual adequacy. Psychological tests revealed that Duane was of normal intelligence, but that he suffered from perceptual malfunctioning, which could account at least in part for his learning difficulties. But this did not fully explain his poor interpersonal relationships and his utter lack of spontaneity and enthusiasm.

Plate 90 shows Duane's family portrait; it is a rather frightening picture. It reveals a group of seven people lined up according to size, but there is no differentiation between males and females and between adults and children. None of the figures have facial features, nor do they have any feet to stand on. Without eyes, noses or mouths, they are unable to see each other or to communicate with each other. Duane drew a family of "zombies." The figures on *Plate 90* have human form but lack human spirit or personality. In this drawing, Duane indicated quite dramatically that he did not perceive himself as a member of a real family and that he considered himself, his parents, and his siblings as something less than human; they were mere things, just numbers. Duane presented his family as nameless, sexless, faceless creatures who were nobodies. On *Plate 90*, Duane showed neither affection nor hostility or anger toward his family; he displayed a marked absence of feelings. Duane reflected his own isolation within a group of unrelating persons. And since he never learned to feel or to express affection and anger within the family circle, he also failed to show such attitudes towards others in the community and school.

In an interview, Duane's mother reported that he was the oldest of five children who followed one another so closely that Duane and the youngest child were less than seven years apart. The mother never had a chance to spend much time with each individual child. Duane's father was a retired Army man who was very strict and authoritarian. He ruled over his family like a master sergeant with little regard for individual differences or abilities. The mother, a gentle and frail woman, was not in good health; she barely managed to keep her brood clothed and fed; she just did not have the energy for more. Long before Duane was ready and able to do so, he was called upon to look after the younger children. He was too immature and too insecure to rebel against his father's harsh rule and against the heavy responsibilities that were put on him, so he just gave up and became a nobody.

Michael's *(Plate 78)* home background was radically different from Duane's. If anything, there was too much interaction and emotional involvement between the members of Michael's family. His mother, an imaginative and warm woman, devoted much of her time and energy to her two children. Michael and his older sister Monica were very fond of each other and had been inseparable until just recently. Nine year old Monica was beginning to prefer the company of her girl friends and at times excluded her little brother from their gatherings. Michael resented this bitterly. Michael's father expected a great deal from his son and was often impatient with the latter's immaturity, slow school progress, and awkwardness. There could be no doubt about the father's real interest and affection for his family even though he was very authoritarian and did not tolerate any signs of defiance or aggression. Since Michael was denied the normal expressions of hostility and anger, he was frequently frustrated. Michael sought relief and comfort by withdrawing into aggressive fantasy. There was a time when Michael had retreated so completely into his imaginary world that he was for periods of time out of contact with reality (page 125). At that point, he had been referred to the child guidance clinic for treatment.

Michael was seen by the writer for regular playtherapy sessions. He used much of this time for drawing and painting. As he gained in self-confidence, his drawings became much freer. *Plate 78* shows a family portrait by Michael which he made on request of the therapist when he was seven years old. Michael was only able to draw this delightful picture because he felt quite comfortable in the writer's presence and because he wanted to share his feelings with her. The drawing reveals much fondness for the mother, and strong ambivalences toward his father and, to a lesser degree, toward his sister. Michael no longer had to suppress his negative attitudes but could acknowledge them on the family portrait in a direct and humorous fashion.

Michael began his picture on *Plate 78* by drawing himself in a central position and then his sister; thereafter, he added the mother, and finally the father. Michael verbalized as he drew: "That's me, here is Monica. She has only one star, she has to obey me. I have four stars. This is my mommy. We are bigger than she is, she has a big egg head. She is an angel with wings and a halo. Dad is the tiniest, winiest, he has a big head." Here Michael almost choked laughing. He then added two horns to Monica's head; "Monica is a devil," Michael exclaimed with bursts of laughter. The therapist asked Michael if he was an angel or a devil. Michael replied truthfully: "In between," and drew a halo and horns on the figure of himself, then he added, "but Dad is the biggest devil, he is lighting a match with my foot." Michael adorned his father with some horns and made him give Michael "a hot foot."

The drawing on *Plate 78* expresses quite freely and accurately his affection for his mother; both his fondness of and annoyance at the sister who is trying to exclude him from her social groups, and his resentment of the father who gives him a rough time. On the picture, Michael makes himself a four star general so that all others have to obey him. This is his wish-dream; in reality, he has to follow the wishes of his father, mother, and sister since he is the youngest. He reduces the father in size so that he can give the father orders for a change. This drawing shows clearly that Michael is having fun and is consciously engaging in a fantasy; he knows fact from fancy and is no longer "up in the air" removed from reality as he was when he drew the picture on *Plate 77*. With much accuracy, Michael describes himself as neither totally good nor totally bad. The quality of the drawing suggests considerable warmth and affection even toward the father whom he both resents and admires. All the figures on *Plate 78* are smiling; this is basically a picture of a close-knit family group. For further growth and development of Michael's attitudes toward his family and his ability to express them, see *Plate 79* and the discussion on page 129.

7. Psychotherapy and Children's Drawings

IN THE PRECEDING CHAPTERS, it was shown that HFDs and family portraits can be used for the evaluation and understanding of children's self-concepts and of their interpersonal relationships. It was also repeatedly pointed out that such drawings are quite sensitive to changes in a child's attitudes toward himself and others. A youngster can often reveal feelings on a HFD which he could not or would not put into words. And because HFDs reflect both conscious and unconscious attitudes and concerns, the process of making HFDs can be quite therapeutic. It enables the child to express anxieties and conflicts in a constructive, nonthreatening way. It follows therefore that drawing can serve both as a means of therapy and as a method for evaluating the progress made in treatment by children with emotional problems. The present chapter will be devoted to the exploration of these two aspects of HFDs and of other drawings.

Drawing as a therapeutic technique

Naumburg (1958) and Kramer (1958) have ably demonstrated the value of art therapy with psychiatric patients and with emotionally disturbed children in a treatment center. Both writers have used in their work free art expression, above all painting. The writer's own clinical experience with children strongly supports their claims regarding the value of painting and free art expression in therapy. However, at this time the discussion will be limited to the use of HFDs and related pencil drawings as a therapeutic technique in order to remain within the scope of this book. The writer has been unable to find any one technique or method (e.g., doll house and doll family, puppets, painting, etc.) that seems to be appropriate for the treatment of all children who are referred for therapy. She has therefore endeavored to offer her patients a wide range of materials and modes for self-expression, so that they can select the technique best suited to their particular needs at a given time. Inevitably, there are some children who spontaneously choose drawing with pencils or crayons as their preferred means of communication in some or most of their treatment sessions.

It was found that two different groups of children will draw in their therapy sessions if given a free choice of activities. One group consists of the very young and/or retarded, nonverbal youngsters for whom drawing is a natural way of expression. The other group of children includes seriously disturbed youngsters who can express themselves through graphic signs and symbols at a time when direct action or verbal communication is still too threatening. Most of the children who were seen for treatment by the writer went through a diagnostic workup first, at which time they were asked to make an HFD. It is often difficult to say where diagnosis ends and therapy begins. For obviously a good diagnostic procedure should be and is also therapeutic. It is quite possible and even probable that the experience of producing an HFD in the initial session serves as motivation for some children in wanting to make further pencil drawings in subsequent therapy sessions. These children have discovered that making HFDs is enjoyable and nonthreatening. Some youngsters will draw in the first few hours of treatment until they feel comfortable enough to use other materials or to communicate verbally. Others persist in drawing during most of their treatment. Burt *(Plates 61 and 62)* and Butch *(Plates 91 to 93)* may serve to illustrate the two different types of children who use pencil drawings as a therapeutic technique.

The history of Burt, an eleven year old schizoid boy of normal intelligence, was discussed earlier (page 116). When Burt was first referred to the guidance clinic, his behavior had regressed to an infantile level; he crawled on the floor in class, made peculiar noises and showed quite inappropriate affect. *Plate 61* and *Plate 62* show the HFDs he made at the time of his initial interview. The figures presented are quite bizarre and reflect serious emotional disturbances. Burt returned to the clinic for regular weekly therapy sessions. During the first three sessions, Burt wanted to do nothing but draw. He spontaneously produced one grotesque figure after another; each time, he accompanied his drawings with giggles and verbal outbursts and much emotional involvement. He started to draw again at the beginning of the fourth session, but his figure was now much less bizarre. Burt quickly lost interest, he stopped drawing and turned to the doll house instead. In subsequent sessions, as his behavior improved in school, Burt used toys, puppets, and the tape recorder; he never again returned to spontaneous drawing. On one occasion, he suffered from a temporary crisis and showed regression in his behavior; during this time, he painted and used clay in his therapy session. This lasted for only one week.

It was apparent that drawing had been most helpful for Burt in the beginning of his therapy. But as he regained a more mature level of functioning, he stopped drawing in favor of direct action and verbalization. Thus Burt's recovery followed the normal developmental sequence of a child: the immature child draws until he reaches pre-adolescence, then he turns from indirect graphic expression to verbal modes of communication and to action.

Butch *(Plates 91 to 93)* differed greatly from Burt. He was a nine year old brain injured boy of borderline intelligence who had very poor co-ordination and who was hypersensitive. He was usually cheerful and out-going, but if anything unexpected or unusual occurred, Butch responded with a strong gastrointestinal reaction. Butch was not a verbal child; it was difficult for him to express his thoughts and feelings in words. When he was in a good mood, he enjoyed making polite conversation with adults by repeating a few stock phrases he had learned. But when he was upset, he could not speak at all.

One day, Butch's teacher asked the school psychologist to see the youngster since he seemed to be unusually disturbed. He had thrown up on the school bus and had been sick to his stomach off and on throughout the morning. The school nurse had been unable to contact the mother, but she did not think that Butch was physically ill. He had no fever nor any aches and pains, whereas he was obviously emotionally very upset. Butch could not say what bothered him. He went readily with the writer to her office and tried to smile feebly, but he did not utter a word. It was suggested to him that he might like to make an HFD. When presented with a pencil and paper, Butch began to draw at once. *Plate 91* shows the result. Butch drew two houses sideways and explained with a great deal of agitation, flushing, and emotional involvement that the picture presented: "Two houses stuck together, a snake comes out of one house and ties them together." This highly suggestive drawing was accepted quite matter-of-factly by the writer, who then asked Butch who lived in the houses. Butch did not answer, but instead made a second drawing which is shown on *Plate 92.* Once again Butch explained his picture with a great deal of anxiety and excitement: "Two people, a man and a woman, they are lying on top of each other, they are touching, they are fighting." Thereupon, Butch jumped up and was about to dash out of the office, when the writer caught hold of him and suggested that he might like to hang his pictures up on the office wall. Butch did this with satisfaction; he sighed deeply as if greatly relieved, then he returned to his classroom.

The meaning of the drawings seems rather obvious, but it was felt that Butch was too upset to be able to tolerate any interpretation of his drawings at that time. The following day, Butch was waiting for the writer in the school hallway. He begged to be allowed to go with her. With the teacher's permission, Butch returned to the psychologist's office on this day and on the following eight school days. Each time he only stayed for 10–15 minutes. He always admired his drawings on the wall first, then he spontaneously drew more pictures. Butch made a series of drawings of "upside-down submarines," "fighting man and woman," "boy with knife in his foot," or just "big knives." There could be no doubt that Butch had observed or been exposed to sexual intercourse which he perceived as an act of violence and which greatly frightened him. Yet even the suggestion of an interpretation or discussion of his pictures by the writer produced panic in Butch, so all attempts in this direction were abandoned. Above all, Butch seemed to want to draw, he wanted the opportunity to express his thoughts and fears in the presence of an accepting adult. Whenever he completed a drawing Butch would look at the writer as if for assurance and each time he sighed deeply before leaving the office. It was as though the process of drawing in front of a witness had lifted a burden from him. His teacher reported that he was always quite relaxed when he returned to the classroom.

On the tenth day in the psychologists office, Butch drew a picture of "dogs in bed" which is reproduced on *Plate 93.* He then made a picture of a huge knife covering the full length of the paper. Butch commented spontaneously: "He takes a knife and sticks it into another dog again and again, he cuts him up." Butch said this with much finality and smiled at the writer. Then Butch got up and left; he did not ask to return. According to the teacher, Butch had shown no more undue anxiety in class and there had been no more stomach upsets after the initial session with the psychologist. A hypersensitive child like Butch is likely to have numerous emotional upsets in the course of his lifetime, but for the time being, he seemed to be quite comfortable and there was no need to continue seeing him on a regular basis. Butch had somehow resolved his problem. The writer was never able to discover just what had actually happened to Butch to cause his upset; she could only guess that he had had a traumatic sexual experience. There is also no certainty that drawing per se was the main cause for his rapid recovery from this traumatic episode. In this instance, drawing served as a means by which Butch could communicate with the writer; through his drawings, he could share his anxieties and fears and thereby reduce them, even though no interpretations or explanations were given to him. What little verbalization occurred during these brief sessions came from Butch's side. The writer has often noted that verbal interpretations are not always necessary or helpful in the treatment of young children. Drawings can serve as a nonverbal means of communication between the child and the therapist, which can be more meaningful and reassuring than the use of words would be.

Assessing progress in treatment through HFDs

Therapists working with emotionally disturbed children must learn to be patient and enduring; they have to tolerate much frustration, and they have to give a great deal of themselves. Most of them will go to great lengths to help their patients especially if they can see some signs of success resulting from their efforts. There can be no greater satisfaction for a therapist than to see a youngster under his care improve and regain good mental health. However, the wish for success makes it sometimes difficult for a clinician to be an objective judge of his patients' progress.

It is important to take a long-range view of a child's improvement in therapy and not to be misled by day to day minor fluctuations in the youngster's behavior and moods. Sometimes, therapists will get discouraged by some relatively minor crisis or upset on part of the child, thinking it to be a serious setback or a sign of regression, when in fact the child is making good progress. Too often, therapists forget what the child was like when he first started treatment. Some psychologists think they see marked improvement in their patients when in fact the children have not improved but have just changed their symptoms or have matured a bit as a natural consequence of getting older. Clearly then, there is a need for methods to assess objectively a child's progress in psychotherapy. Experience has shown that HFDs can often be used in this capacity if the psychologist is trained and experienced in the interpretation of such drawings. HFDs are objective and reliable indicators of children's self-concepts and of their attitudes toward others, and these in turn are central to children's emotional adjustment. Successive HFDs of a single child, taken over a long period of time, will reveal any change or lack of change in the child's attitude toward himself and others. Needless to say, the HFDs of some youngsters are more revealing than those of others.

The following case histories are presented to illustrate the way in which HFDs can show progress and growth of children in treatment. Burt's gradual success in overcoming his acute masturbation anxiety and guilt feelings was revealed on *Plates 61 to 64*, and was discussed in detail earlier on pages 116–118. Compared to the earlier HFDs, the drawing on *Plate 64* shows a marked lessening of anxiety and a considerable growth in self-confidence; however, it also indicates that Burt had not yet resolved all of his problems and that he needed supportive therapy for a while longer.

The progress of Frankie, a seven year old brain injured boy of average intelligence, is shown on *Plates 25a to 25d*. As was mentioned above (page 87), Frankie had a long history of illness. He was a rather odd-looking child who held his head tilted backward at an angle, so that he could see better. His eyes were turned up in their sockets due to muscle imbalance. Frankie was a social isolate who was rejected by his peers because of his unpredictable behavior and immaturity. His mother was a very unstable woman who favored the younger daughter. She had little warmth and affection for Frankie. The father was sincerely interested in his son, but he was a rigid, coercive and restrictive person. Frankie was a good boy who tried hard to please his parents, especially his father. In school, Frankie presented no serious problems while he was in kindergarten other than being somewhat restless and immature. But in the first grade, Frankie had difficulty with his schoolwork. He was seriously handicapped by his visual problem and by his hyperactivity.

When Frankie was first seen by the writer at the guidance clinic, he produced the HFD shown on *Plate 25a*. It reveals a poorly integrated figure of an unhappy looking boy. The asymmetrical treatment of the arms and legs and the placement of the arms reflect emotional imbalance, immaturity, and signs of neurological impairment. Frankie and his father were seen on a regular weekly basis for treatment and guidance. By the end of the school year, the father and the writer agreed that Frankie had made good progress and was more relaxed and outgoing. After several weeks of summer vacations, Frankie returned to the clinic to continue with playtherapy. He had matured quite a bit during the summer and everyone concerned was pleased. But after a few weeks in the second grade, Frankie's problems reappeared in intensified form. He tried desperately to keep up with his schoolwork but could not. In addition, his new classmates were less tolerant of him than the first graders had been. The younger children had just ignored Frankie. But the second graders teased him because of his appearance, and as a result, Frankie regressed in his behavior and showed new symptoms.

By midyear, Frankie's condition had deteriorated even more. When asked to make an HFD, Frankie produced the "clown juggling balls" shown on *Plate 25b*. As was pointed out earlier, clowns are drawn primarily by children who feel that they are ridiculous and are being laughed at by others (page 126). Jugglers are in a precarious position; they put on a show which even a slight mishap or error can bring to naught. Children who draw jugglers usually perceive themselves as being in a very unstable situation (page 83). Frankie's drawing was not a happy one and showed that his emotional adjustment had markedly worsened since he made the HFD on *Plate 25a* some ten months earlier.

The parents, the teacher, and the therapist were all quite concerned about Frankie. It was decided that a complete physical and visual re-examination of Frankie was in order to determine if Frankie could be given relief from his constant headaches and his visual difficulties. The reevaluation resulted in a recommendation that Frankie undergo surgery to correct the muscle imbalance in his eyes. His parents prepared him for the impending operation. On the day before Frankie was to enter the hospital, he came to the clinic for his regular therapy session. Frankie was extremely upset. *Plate 25c* shows the HFD he produced on that day. It represents "a parachute jumper with an airmask." This drawing vividly shows that Frankie felt as if the ground had dropped out from under him and he was floating in the air helplessly, uncertain if and where he might land. The parachute jumper wears an airmask to protect his face from any onslaught that was being planned against it. This mask, i.e., the heavy shading of the face, reveals the acute anxiety Frankie was experiencing in anticipation of the operation. Every effort was made to reassure him and to support him at this time.

The operation was a complete success and vastly improved Frankie's vision and appearance. Frankie and his parents were quite pleased with the change. Three months after the operation, Frankie drew the cheerful little man shown on *Plate 25d*. The size of the drawing and the absences of hands indicate that Frankie was still somewhat insecure and timid, while the primitive character of the drawing reflects primarily his neurological impairment which of course persisted. But despite these features, the drawing is a fairly positive one. The shading of the limbs is not unusual on HFDs of eight year old boys and cannot be considered a sign of pathology (page 57), whereas the shading of the face on the previous HFD (*Plate 25c*) was very unusual and a sign of serious disturbance. The figure on *Plate 25d* shows considerable progress on Frankie's part and shows for the first time a well-integrated, cheerful human being. Frankie had definitely improved even though his drawings still reflected some evidence of anxiety. In fact, Frankie continued to make such good progress that therapy was discontinued after six months.

Elliott (*Plates 71 to 73*) and Joe (*Plates 68 to 70*) had a great deal in common: Both were of superior intelligence, yet suffered from serious learning problems due to cortical malfunctioning. Both came from solid, upward-striving, middle-class families with warm, accepting mothers and ambitious, hardworking, demanding fathers who were emotionally cold and remote. Both fathers were quite critical and punitive in their attitudes toward their sons. In both cases, the fathers favored the scholastically and socially successful siblings over the youngsters here under discussion. Elliott and Joe were both so intimidated by their fathers that they were quite unable to express their resentment and hostility toward them openly. Instead, the boys directed their anger and frustration against their siblings and peers. Both boys were unhappy and disturbed youngsters who were seen for therapy at the guidance center. In both cases, the mothers participated in the boy's treatment, while the fathers refused to get involved.

Plate 71 shows Elliott's initial HFD, made when he was eight years old. Elliott presented himself as a nonhuman creature, a robot. The significance of a robot on an HFD was discussed in detail on page 121. The drawing indicates that Elliott perceived himself as being different, as being not an independent individual but rather a mechanical thing that was manipulated and controlled by others. Elliott was seen for remedial reading lessons and for individual playtherapy. After eight months of treatment, Elliott showed marked progress in his behavior in school and at home. *Plate 72* shows the HFD he produced at that time. It reveals that Elliott no longer saw himself as a nonhuman artifact, but rather as a human being, albeit on outsider on the fringes of society. He drew a "caveman" rather than a member of a civilized community (page 125). There can be no doubt that the drawing on *Plate 72* demonstrates considerable change and improvement in Elliott's self-concept compared to the earlier drawing on *Plate 71*. But it also shows that Elliott still had a long way to go before he could be considered a well-adjusted youngster.

During the next ten months, Elliott continued to make progress in all areas. When he was ten years old, he was asked to produce another HFD. This drawing is shown on *Plate 73*. At first glance, the tiny, much-erased figure on the drawing seems to contradict the observation that Elliott made progress in treatment. A more careful look at *Plate 73* is both reassuring and sobering. Elliott commented as he drew. "the boy is reading a book." The fact that Elliott drew "a boy" and not a robot or a caveman, as before, is an indication that he considered himself at that point not only human but a member of the real world and present-day society. He accepts his own limitations and position; he is a little boy. The fact that Elliott drew a boy who is reading reflects considerable growth on his part. When Elliott first came to the clinic, he was a nonreader who shied away from all books and reading material. Now, he took pride in his ability to read simple books, and emphasized this skill on the drawing. The drawing on *Plate 73* does not depict Elliott's wishful thinking but records a fact; it is not a story but a description: he is a boy who can read. However, the size of the drawing and the omission of the facial features betray continued insecurity and vulnerability. His relationship with his father, though improved, was still precarious and his peer relationships were far from good. The drawing showed quite clearly that Elliott, though much improved, still required supportive therapy for some time to come. But in view of his good academic progress and his general improvement so far, there was reason to believe that his long-range prognosis was good.

Joe also drew a robot when first seen at the clinic. His HFD is reproduced on *Plate 68* and was discussed more fully on page 121. After six months of treatment, Joe showed considerable improvement in his behavior and attitudes. Once again he was asked to make a HFD. This picture is shown on *Plate 69*. Like Elliott, Joe revealed on his second drawing that he no longer considered himself a nonhuman artifact but rather a human being who was an outsider, who was not a full-fledged member of his community. Joe drew a "Frenchman," a foreigner. Elliott's caveman was socially farther removed from our American society than Joe's Frenchman. But Elliott's caveman was complete and intact, while Joe's drawing shows a badly castrated and mutilated figure (page 126).

During the next six months of therapy, Joe continued to show improvement in school and at home, although he remained a social isolate and an outsider. When he was 12 years old, Joe made another HFD. He drew another "Frenchman" who is reproduced on *Plate 70*. This drawing shows both an improved self-concept and the continuing feeling of being different from others and of not being fully accepted. But in contrast to the Frenchman on *Plate 69*, the second Frenchman on *Plate 70* is well-integrated. Some concern over developing impulses is still evident on this drawing but this is not extreme and is, in moderation, common among pre-adolescent youngsters. The drawing reflects Joe's actual situation quite accurately. He had become a fairly well-functioning but impulsive youngster who stood apart from others. Not all children are destined to be socially popular, red-blooded American boys and football players. There is room in our society for the quiet ones and the lone wolves, provided they can function fairly successfully within the framework of their community and do not disturb others unduly nor are hurting themselves too badly. Joe had reached this point; he could manage after a fashion. He decided on his own to discontinue therapy. When last heard from, he was still a social isolate who maintained himself valiantly on the fringes of his peer group.

The history of Jennifer, an 11 year old girl with a colostomy, was discussed at some length earlier on pages 109 and 110. Her two drawings, shown on *Plates 53 and 54*, are other examples of how a child's progress in therapy is reflected on his HFDs. At the beginning of treatment, Jennifer was very self-conscious, anxious, and extremely uncomfortable with strangers. She always feared that her "secret" would be found out and that she would be exposed in public. She was constantly watching the reaction of others and was afraid of returning to school or going out into the community. Her first HFD (*Plate 53*) clearly reflects Jennifer's wariness and anxiety; it also shows her tendency to withdraw and to turn away from others.

After five months of guidance and support at the clinic, Jennifer showed a remarkable growth in self-confidence. She was attending school regularly and was doing quite well in all subjects. She had gained considerable poise and assurance. *Plate 54* shows Jennifer's second HFD, which she produced at that time. The drawing depicts a girl who looks the observer straight in the eye without undue self-consciousness or uneasiness, just as Jennifer herself was able to do. The figure on the HFD reveals feminine poise and charm appropriate for a young girl, thus reflecting Jennifer's positive attitude toward herself. Only two signs on the drawing betray her lingering anxiety about her physical condition. Jennifer omitted the line between the girl's thighs and she reinforced the outline of the body as if drawing attention to her own body and its lack of intactness. The drawing on *Plate 54* offered support for the clinic staff's recommendation that Jennifer terminate individual therapy and join instead a group of teenagers and young adults who also had colostomies and who met regularly to give each other support and to share information. It was felt that Jennifer had developed considerable self-confidence and was doing as well as she could; however, it was recognized that because of her physical condition, she would require ongoing support and guidance for a long time to come, and this could be supplied best by others who shared her difficulties.

A child's change in attitude and progress in treatment may reveal itself in different ways on HFDs. Usually, these changes are evident in changes on the child's drawing of himself. But in Sheilah's case, growth in therapy was reflected in a change of the person whom Sheilah presented on her HFD (*Plate 83*). When Sheilah, age 12, first came to the guidance clinic, she drew herself (*Plate 83a*) with her head turned away as if she were trying to avoid facing others. The arms of her figure are thin, weak and ineffectual. This drawing vividly reflects Sheilah's approach toward her conflicts and anxieties. She denied her hostility toward her nagging and domineering mother. Sheilah turned her head away from the facts and internalized her feelings so that her anger and frustrations could only find expression through psychosomatic complaints.

But Sheilah was an intelligent youngster who wanted help; once she gained insight into her difficulties, she was willing to work hard on her problems. After five months of treatment, Sheilah's physical symptoms had all but disappeared. Her attitudes toward herself and her family gradually changed. When asked to make another HFD, Sheilah produced the witch shown on *Plate 83b*. Sheilah commented spontaneously: "She is a real mean old witch who haunts people all the time and who scares them to death" (page 132). It was not hard for Sheilah to discover the true identity of her witch. The fact that she could express her feelings toward her mother in the image of the witch showed the extent of her progress. Once Sheilah had been able to reveal her feelings on the drawing, she was also able to discuss her ambivalence toward her mother openly in the next therapy sessions. Following the drawing of the witch, Sheilah continued to improve so rapidly that therapy was soon discontinued.

The six children discussed so far in this chapter were all seen for individual therapy and all of them showed improvement in the course of treatment. But unfortunately, improvement in therapy is not inevitable nor is it necessarily enduring; it may be only temporary. Too often, factors beyond the control of the therapist, affect a child's life and prevent any positive changes from occurring or wipe out whatever gains have been made. Even more frustrating is the situation school psychologists frequently have to contend with. They may recognize serious problems in a child but are then unable to get the kind of help that the child needs. In such cases, the psychologist can do nothing but watch helplessly while the child regresses or deteriorates in his attitudes and behavior. The following two cases illustrate how HFDs can reflect a child's lack of progress and deterioration. In one case, the youngster was in therapy; in the other case, the child did not receive individual treatment but attended a special class in school.

George (*Plates 94 to 97*), a nine year old boy of average intelligence, was brought to the clinic by his father. George had been suspended from

school because of bizarre and disruptive behavior that could not be controlled in the classroom despite much effort on part of the teacher and
school psychologist. George was a very unhappy, tense, restless, hyperactive, and anxious child who was haunted by fears and fantasies of death
and destruction. He vehemently denied having any problems and tried
very hard to prove that he was superior to his peers. Since his classmates
rejected him, he attached himself to older boys and tried to imitate their
behavior. However, most of the time he stayed by himself and talked to
himself while moving about and playing with small toys, rubber bands,
and pencils.

When first seen at the clinic, George made an HFD shown on *Plate 94*.
This drawing clearly shows that George was a very disturbed child who
was in need of psychiatric help. George said of his figure: "It's a policeman with two poisonous snakes, they bit off his arms." The drawing expresses extreme impulsivity, castration anxiety, fear and guilt. The figure
lacks arms and a neck, the legs are pressed together tightly as if to ward
off sexual attack or body injury. The snakes, usually associated with
masculinity and power, are here poisonous and dangerous; they bring
about mutilation and possibly death. The drawing is supposed to represent
a policeman, an authority figure who offers control and protection, but
who also punishes for wrongdoing. One might suppose that the policeman
represents George's need and desire for control of his impulses and
anxiety, and the feeling that he should be punished for his badness. All
of George's other projective test responses revealed again and again a
sense of being evil, intense guilt feelings and castration anxiety.

A review of George's social history showed that the youngster had a
very unstable, emotionally disturbed mother who had been intermittently
hospitalized. His father had been overseas with the armed services for
several years during George's early childhood. The birth of a younger
sister had coincided with the onset of George's more serious problems
and had undoubtedly contributed to his castration anxiety and paranoid
tendencies. But George also had a long history of physical illnesses and
always had been a very vulnerable and labile child. His school attendance
had been so irregular that he had to repeat a grade. There was reason to
believe that George had been involved in sexual activities with older boys.
In view of all these negative factors in George's life, it is not surprising
that progress in therapy was slow and uneven. He had good and bad days.
For a while, it almost looked as though some slow but steady growth and
improvement was taking place. But perhaps this was just wishful thinking
on part of the therapist.

When George returned to the clinic after a two-weeks absence due
to illness, there could be no doubt that all progress, if there had been any,
was lost. George appeared more upset than ever before. It was impossible
for him to sit still for more than a few seconds. His actions and his speech
were quite bizarre and there were indications that he was hallucinating.
With some persuasion, it was possible to get George to make an HFD. The
result is shown on *Plate 95*. The drawing on *Plate 95* was done three
months after the first HFD on *Plate 94* was produced. On the first drawing,

George expressed freely his fears and anxieties; it represents a plea for help. The picture on *Plate 95* reveals a withdrawal and a desperate attempt at controlling his impulses and maintaining his balance. The figure on this drawing is about to topple over; the arms are held tightly and rigidly against the body, the hands are hidden, the legs are pressed together. The figure looks tense and constricted; despite all efforts, he is doomed to fall over since he is unable to reach out for support or to step forward to break the fall and to balance himself. The shaded body indicates acute body anxiety, while the heavily shaded ear looks like an earmuff and suggests that George was trying to shut out the voices he heard. The figure looks out into space and is not in touch with his immediate environment. The omission of the mouth emphasizes George's inability to communicate with others. The bushy mustache is a symbol for masculine striving, but the figure lacks masculine strength. Once again, George called his figure a "policeman," but he did not elaborate any further.

There can be no doubt that the drawing on *Plate 95* shows an intensification of George's difficulties and a desperate effort on his part at maintaining a hold on reality. It was later learned that, just prior to George's return to the clinic, his mother had another mental breakdown and had to go once again to the hospital. There was little the therapist could do to counteract the traumatic events George was experiencing at home. Thereafter, George seemed more disorganized each time he came for treatment. It was apparent that George needed much more intensive therapy than he was getting and that a period of residential treatment was indicated. But his father was too upset by the mother's illness to be able to fully appreciate the condition George was in.

Another month passed; George continued to become more and more disturbed. *Plate 96* shows the progressive disorganization that was taking place. The control George had tried so hard to maintain on the two earlier drawings had disintegrated. The drawing on *Plate 96* shows the break-through of George's aggressive impulses; it also depicts his fears and his helplessness in the face of inner forces that were overwhelming him. The civilized policeman of the earlier HFDs has been displaced by a monster. His shaded face, the grotesque tusks, the huge ears, the omission of hands and feet, the poorly integrated arms, and the tight stance of the legs, all point to a serious mental disturbance and a lack of inner controls. George said the drawing represented "Maurice," a boy in his class in school whom he blamed for all his difficulties. Since George could not admit that he had any problems, he had to project them onto someone else. But the way the figure on *Plate 96* is drawn reveals his own attitude toward himself.

Several more weeks had to pass until the slow process of referral and placement finally got into motion. George was seen as often as possible for supportive therapy until he could enter a residential treatment center. On his last visit to the clinic, George produced the HFD on *Plate 97*. His disorganization was now almost complete; George had regressed to a very primitive level of functioning and was out of contact with reality.

Sammy (*Plates 46 to 48*) was a youngster who suffered from an expressive type of aphasia. He attended a special class for brain injured children and received speech therapy. But Sammy was not able to benefit from the special class nor from the speech therapy. It is not certain if another type of class could have met his needs better. When the writer first met Sammy, he was seven years old. Sammy could understand all that was said to him, but his own speech was for the most part unintelligible. He also showed serious malfunctioning in visual-motor perception and in the ability to associate sounds with visual symbols. But Sammy was a friendly, quiet and cheerful boy who was well liked by his peers. They were protective of him. He had one friend in particular who was devoted to him and who could understand him better than anyone else.

Plate 46 shows Sammy's HFD which he made when he first entered the special class program. The omission of the mouth and the small size of the figure reflect his concern over his speech and communication difficulties (page 105). But the drawing also reveals that Sammy regards himself as a member of society, as a human being, although a rather weak and helpless one.

A year later, Sammy showed little growth academically, emotionally, or socially. The difference between him and his classmates had increased markedly. His speech had not improved and Sammy failed to make any appreciable school progress, even though his reasoning ability was good. Sammy was unable to read or write. Gradually, Sammy lost his cheerfulness and became more and more frustrated as communication with teachers and peers got to be increasingly more difficult. It was a sad day for Sammy when his very close friend moved to another community. There was no other child who could take his place. *Plate 47* shows Sammy's HFD which he produced at that time. He was then eight years old. Sammy drew an Indian (page 126). He now perceived himself as an outsider, as a member of a minority group. He depicted an Indian brave, a warrior in full regalia. This Indian brave is sitting down; he raises his bow and arrow as if to shoot, but he poses only, he seems too weak and scrawny to get up to fight. The Indian is putting on a show of being courageous and having a fighting spirit, but he is in fact defeated and has all but given up the fight, just as Sammy had done. Sammy surrounded his Indian with "Indian corn" as with a wall; it shut him off from others. The Indian is as isolated as Sammy was. The tiny figure on *Plate 46* shows a healthier self-concept than the lonely outsider, the defeated Indian on *Plate 47*.

Despite much effort on part of the teachers and the speech therapist during the following year, Sammy did not make much progress in academics nor did his speech improve. During Sammy's early years, he had the advantage of having an understanding and accepting mother who devoted much time to him. But when Sammy was nine years old, his father became seriously ill and the mother had to go to work to support the family. Sammy was left alone much of the time without siblings or peers to play with. He became increasingly more moody and unhappy. He expressed his frustrations in temper outbursts, stubbornness and truancy. When Sammy was ten years old, he was again asked to make an HFD. The result is shown on *Plate 48*. This time Sammy drew a scarecrow. He now perceived himself as a ludicrous contraption that was only an imitation of a person but not a real human being; even the crows were laughing at him. For a more detailed discussion of *Plate 48*, see page 120.

In Sammy's three drawings (*Plates 46, 47, and 48*), we see the steady deterioration of the self-concept of an intelligent, but severely handicapped child whose needs have not been met by his environment. At age seven, Sammy still felt like a full-fledged member of society; by age eight, he perceived himself as an outsider of his community; and by age ten, he had ceased to think of himself as a human being; he portrayed himself as a mere thing, a ridiculous object of little value.

8. Brain Injury and HFDs

BRAIN INJURED CHILDREN are often evaluated and treated as if they were in a class by themselves, apart from other children. Yet brain injured children are above all children and all of their behavior is human behavior which occurs at some time and to some extent also in children who are not brain injured. What distinguishes the brain injured child from the non-brain injured child is primarily a malfunctioning of his integrative capacity and/or his control mechanism. Such malfunctioning may result in a slower development, or incomplete or distorted functioning of perception, conceptualization, movement, expression and social behavior, and in a lowering of the threshold to withstand even the normal stresses and strains of living. A brain injured child may exhibit any one or several of these characteristics to a lesser or greater degree depending on the location and the extent of the neurological impairment and on the child's age when it occurred. It is obvious then that brain injured children vary greatly from one another and that there is no such thing as *the* brain injured child. Hence, it stands to reason that there is also no such thing as *the* "organic" HFD.

One can assume, therefore, that drawings of neurologically impaired children vary greatly from each other depending on the child's age, emotional adjustment and the amount and the type of brain injury the child suffered. HFDs are expressions of the mental development and interpersonal attitudes of non-brain injured and brain injured children alike. It seems likely then that the same signs and symbols will appear on the HFDs of both groups of children. Any significant differences that might be found between the drawings of children with and without neurological impairment should occur in the frequency of occurrence of the various signs and symbols, but not in the signs as such.

HFDs are sometimes used as an aid in diagnosing brain injury. The question presents itself whether HFDs are valid instruments for such a purpose. Many experienced clinicians will label the HFDs of some individuals as "organic" and are often able to support their claims with developmental, social, and medical evidence of brain injury in these patients. The interpretation of drawings as "organic" is usually based on clinical intuition. Only a limited amount of research data is available to back it up. The handful of controlled studies with HFDs of brain injured subjects, that are reported in the literature, use mostly the drawings of adult patients. Their findings are at best inconclusive.

Berrien (1935) investigated the drawings of post-encephalitic patients and found them to be primitive and inconsistent in quality. Buck (1948) and Jolles (1952) developed hypotheses of "organic" signs on the House-Tree-Person Test. But these hypotheses failed to find support in the studies by Michal-Smith (1953) and Bieliauskas and Kirkham (1958). Michal-Smith reported that only "line quality" differentiated the drawings of the organic from the nonorganic patients. Bieliauskas and Kirkham failed to find any significant signs on the drawings of their patients. The most often quoted "organic" indicators on HFDs were suggested by Machover (1949). She observed that drawings of brain injured patients were often "large, empty, poorly proportioned and weakly synthesized" and that they frequently showed "heavy lines and a disproportionately large head." But Machover stated that these signs appear on the drawings of both the organic and the mentally retarded patients. She does not claim that these signs are present on the HFDs of all organic patients nor that they appear exclusively on drawings of brain injured subjects. No mention is made whether these "organic" signs are considered valid for HFDs of adult patients only or also for the drawings of neurologically impaired children.

Reznikoff and Tomblen's (1956) carefully designed and well-executed research study tested fourteen of Machover's (1949) and Vernier's (1952) hypotheses regarding "organic" signs on HFDs. They found that none of these signs occurred exclusively on the HFDs of their organic patients, but five of them were able to differentiate significantly between the drawings of organic and neurotic patients and between the organic and schizophrenic patients. The five items were: weak synthesis, part missing, shrunken arms and legs, parts other than head or extremities distorted, and petal or scribbles fingers. Since Reznikoff and Tomblen used adult patients for subjects, it cannot be assumed that their findings automatically also apply to the HFDs of brain injured children. A careful investigation of the relationship of HFDs and brain injury in children seems therefore in order.

A casual glance at the HFDs of some brain injured children of normal or near normal mental ability shows an amazing variety of types and styles of figure drawings. Just how different the HFDs of a single child with cerebral malfunctioning can be is demonstrated by the four drawings on *Plate 98* and *Plate 99*. The four HFDs were made by Anthony, a boy of average intelligence. Anthony had suffered from a severe case of measles followed by encephalitis at age four which resulted in medically diagnosed brain pathology. Anthony's four HFDs vary greatly from each other although they were made within a relatively short time. Each of the four drawings has a different but distinct "organic" quality about it and is in some way inappropriate or unusual for seven to nine year old boys of normal intelligence. A detailed analysis of these drawings follows on page 166.

Plate 25 shows four HFDs by Frankie whose brain injury can be traced back to a very difficult birth. But in addition, Frankie suffered in infancy from several serious illnesses with high fever and convulsions which probably further contributed to his neurological impairment. Frankie's four HFDs differ greatly from one another; they not only reflect "organicity" but also reveal emotional instability and disturbances (page 149).

Anthony and Frankie were both very sensitive and labile youngsters whose behavior and functioning varied as much as their drawings. But if unevenness in behavior is typical for some brain injured children, others are characterized by rigidity and perseveration in their thinking and behavior which grossly interferes with their growth and development. *Plate 100* shows six HFDs by Leonard, a boy of low average intelligence who suffered brain injury at birth. *Figure a* on *Plate 100* was drawn when Leonard was seven years two months old, *Figure f* when he was nine years eight months old. This means that the six tiny, crude drawings on *Plate 100* were produced during the two and a half year age interval when most children show the greatest improvement and maturation on their HFDs. The minimal amount of growth and change on Leonard's drawings is striking and reflects graphically his perseverative behavior pattern and personality.

In contrast to Leonard's drawings, the HFDs by Gordon on *Plate 101* show a steady improvement from *Figure a*, made at age six, to *Figure c*, drawn at age eight. Gordon had suffered a head injury at age three. He later developed Grand Mal epilepsy and serious learning difficulties. His WISC IQ scores were in the Low Average range. Patrick, a brain injured child of average intelligence, also showed a steady improvement on his HFDs. *Plate 102* exhibits four of his drawings which he produced between age 11 and 13. The last of these drawings is so adequate, apart from a slight asymmetry and the omission of one finger, that it cannot be readily recognized as the HFD of a brain injured child. This is even more true for the HFDs shown on *Plate 35* and *Plate 70*, both of which were produced by children of good intelligence who were medically diagnosed as brain injured. Eric *(Plate 35)* had sustained a prenatal brain injury when his mother suffered from toxemia during the last month of pregnancy. Joe *(Plate 70)* was hit by a car at age seven and acquired a skull fracture and concussions which resulted in brain pathology and a change in personality.

From the various examples of HFDs presented above, it can be seen that diagnosing brain injury from HFDs is difficult and complex. Most of the so-called "organic" drawings are produced by children of limited mental ability or with such obvious neurological impairment that a differential diagnosis seems hardly necessary in order to understand the child's problems. Much more difficult is the case of the child with the so-called "minimal brain injury." Some neurologically impaired youngsters, like Eric for instance *(Plate 35)*, make HFDs that reveal no "organic" signs at all. This may be misleading and the child may then be diagnosed as *not* being brain injured. This kind of conclusion can be quite harmful for the child since unrealistic demands may be made of him and less obvious symptoms, e.g., poor auditory perception or memory deficits, may be overlooked; the child's learning difficulties may be incorrectly attributed to "emotional blocks" or neurotic problems. It is never safe to rule out the possibility of brain injury in a child just because his HFD does not *look* "organic."

A number of studies were designed by the writer to explore objectively the relationship between HFDs and brain injury in children, age six to twelve. More specifically, an effort was made to discover whether the Developmental Items *(Appendix A)* and the Emotional Indicators on HFDs *(Appendix E)* could differentiate between the drawings of children with and without brain injury.

Subjects

Clinicians often fail to agree whether a child is or is not neurologically impaired. Many youngsters have an uneven and slow developmental history, show behavior typical of brain injured children, exhibit perceptual malfunctioning and learning problems, and reveal a performance on psychological tests that is usually associated with cerebral malfunctioning; yet despite all of this, they may fail to show any positive signs on a neurological examination nor any abnormality on the EEG. Many physicians recognize that behavior observations, the developmental history, and psychological test results can be used effectively to demonstrate the probable presence of neurological impairment in children even when this is not apparent from the medical examinations. Others insist on medical evidence before they are willing to diagnose a child as brain injured. A psychologist can merely hypothesize and suggest that a child suffers from neurological impairment, but since brain injury is a medical diagnosis, it can only be made by a physician. For this reason, the subjects for the present studies were limited to children who had been diagnosed as brain injured by a child neurologist and/or child psychiatrist.

The subjects included 231 brain injured (BI) children, age six through age twelve, with an IQ range from 42–138. None of the children had any gross motor impairment. The medical histories of these 231 BI children showed a variety of factors which had most likely contributed to their neurological malfunctioning. As might be expected, some children revealed several events in their lives which could have resulted in or intensified the brain injury. Thus, a child may have suffered from a prenatal and birth trauma as well as from serious illnesses with high fever in infancy; quite often it is the hyperactive, brain injured child who falls and hurts his head, or who runs into the path of a car and sustains a skull fracture or concussion which may result in more brain pathology.

Below are listed some of the factors which were revealed in the case histories of the 231 BI children and which probably contributed to their neurological impairment. Most of these factors are not mutually exclusive and any one child may have experienced two or more of them:

Traumatic Event	N	% of BI Ss
Mother ill during pregnancy (German measles, toxemia, severe hemorrhaging)	44	19
Premature birth (birth weight less than 5 lbs. and time spent in incubator)	24	10
Difficult birth, birth injury, bruised head	64	28
Congenital abnormalities (hydrocephalus or microcephalus 4, Mongoloid 4, mild CP or hemiplegic 15, RH baby, blue baby 5, Aphasia with unintelligible speech or no speech 5)	33	14
Illness at birth (prenatal syphilis, congenital jaundice, hypothyroidism)	8	3
Serious illness with very high fever in infancy (pneumonia, measles, scarlet fever, etc.)	37	16
High fever with convulsions in infancy or early childhood	29	12
Encephalities or meningitis	16	7

Head injury due to fall	26	11
Skull fracture in car accident	12	5
Concussion, coma, long period of unconsciousness	9	4
Hematoma, brain or skull surgery	12	5
Grand Mal or Petit Mal epilepsy	14	6

Not all of the 231 children were given an EEG or a neurological examination. But of those who had such tests, 56 youngsters or 24% of the subjects showed some cerebral dysrhythmia and abnormality on the EEG, while five children revealed positive signs on their neurological examination.

Most of the 231 BI children were seen by the writer for psychological evaluation at which time the HFDs were obtained. However, some of the youngsters were patients of another clinical psychologist* who very generously put their drawings at the writer's disposal. A number of the BI children were seen by the writer more than once for reevaluation or treatment, so that more than one HFD could be collected from them. When this was the case, two or even three HFDs of a given child were included in the present study, provided the drawings were obtained at different age levels. For instance, in the case of Leonard, whose six HFDs are shown on *Plate 100*, only *Figures a, c.* and *e,* drawn at ages seven, eight and nine respectively, were included in the study. If several HFDs of one child were available from a single age level, then the most adequate drawing was selected for inclusion in this study. *Plate 25*, for example, shows three HFDs that were drawn by Frankie at age eight, but only *Figure 25d* was used in this study. This particular HFD was selected because it reflected Frankie's potential ability, while *Figures 25b* and *25c*, drawn at a time of crisis (page 150), reflect above all emotional disturbances.

Following this procedure, a total of 388 HFDs were selected from the 231 BI children for inclusion in the following investigation. Hereafter, therefore, the total number of BI subjects referred to will be 388 even though only 231 different individuals are involved. Some children will be counted twice or even three times, but never at the same age level. *Table 20* shows the distribution of the 388 BI subjects by age, sex, and IQ score levels. The latter were derived from the WISC or the Stanford-Binet Intelligence Scale. It can be seen from *Table 20* that most BI subjects were between the ages of seven and nine and that most of them had an IQ score somewhere between 80 and 100. The ratio of boys to girls for all BI subjects was five to one. The proportion of girls among the BI subjects increased at the lower IQ levels. At the borderline and retarded level, the ratio of boys to girls was three to one. Since all of the BI subjects were psychiatric patients with behavior and learning problems, it might be concluded that BI girls who are of average or above-average intelligence are more likely to compensate for their difficulties than BI boys of equal mental ability, and that they come therefore less often to the attention of the psychologist. In our middle-class society, girls are usually more

---

* The writer is grateful to Dr. David D. Blyth for contributing some HFDs of BI children to the present investigation.

Table 20. Distribution of 388 BI Subjects by Age, Sex, and IQ Scores

Age Level	Sex	69 down B	G	70–79 B	G	80–89 B	G	90–99 B	G	100–109 B	G	110 upward B	G	Total B	G
6		0	0	7	1	12	2	0	0	7	1	5	0	31	4
7		9	1	10	3	17	2	13	6	8	1	9	0	66	13
8		5	3	8	3	21	1	14	0	11	2	9	0	68	9
9		4	1	8	5	19	3	15	0	11	2	9	0	66	11
10		3	2	7	4	11	4	11	0	4	1	6	0	42	11
11		2	1	3	1	8	3	6	0	6	3	5	1	30	9
12		4	0	6	0	4	1	4	1	5	0	2	1	25	3
Total		27	8	49	17	92	16	63	7	52	10	45	2	328	60
Grand Total		35		66		108		70		62		47		388	

indulged and protected than boys, particularly if they are vulnerable and "nervous." The demands on and expectations from boys also tend to be higher than from girls. In the eyes of most parents, low school achievement is less cause for concern in a girl than in a boy; more pressure to excel in academic achievement is put on boys than on girls. In addition, girls tend to be strivers and are likely to work harder than boys when they have difficulties. And finally, girls tend to mature socially and physically a bit earlier than boys. A BI girl who is somewhat immature and slow in her development may still be on par with the younger boys in her class and therefore will not be as conspicuous as the BI boy who tends to be noticeably more immature than his classmates. The BI boy is in a much less favorable position than the BI girl of equivalent age and intelligence.

Developmental Items on HFDs and BI in children

A study was made to discover if any single Developmental Item on HFDs can differentiate between the drawings of BI and non-BI subjects, who are not mentally retarded. The subjects for this specific study included the 282 BI boys from *Table 20* whose IQ scores were above 75. The 803 6 to 12 year old boys from the normative population (*Table 1*) served as controls (non-BI subjects). Chi-squares were computed comparing the number of BI and non-BI subjects at each age level who showed each of the 30 Developmental Items on their HFDs. *Table 21* shows the eleven Developmental Items which occurred significantly more often on the HFDs of either the BI or the non-BI subjects at one or more age levels.

The eleven Developmental Items which were able to differentiate between the HFDs of the BI and the non-BI subjects are listed below:

The body is an Expected item for HFDs of six year old boys. The BI boys age six omitted the body from their drawings significantly more often than did the non-BI boys. By age seven and beyond, the omission of the body from a HFD was extremely rare in either group of subjects. When it did occur, it was always of considerable diagnostic significance (*Plate 101a*).

Table 21. Developmental Items Differentiating Between HFDs of BI and Non-BI Boys

Developmental Items	6 years		7 years		8 years		9 years		10 years		11 & 12 years	
N (BI / Non-BI)	25 / 131		53 / 134		61 / 138		58 / 134		37 / 109		48 / 157	
	χ^2	P	χ^2	P	χ^2	P	χ^2	P	χ^2	P	χ^2	P
Body	16.31	.001	—		5.24	.01	23.06	.001	—		6.22	.02
Pupils	—		6.81	.01			19.28	.001	5.95	.02	17.99	.001
Neck	—		6.05	.02	—		19.01	.001	6.48	.02	7.29	.01
Arms 2 dim.	5.06	.05	20.34	.001	45.86	.001	19.01	.001	13.70	.001	10.22	.01
Arms down	6.03	.02	17.10	.001	28.28	.001	18.65	.001	8.69	.001	23.78	.001
Arms at shoulder	—		11.73	.001	19.37	.001	18.98	.001	3.65	.05		
Hands	3.41	.05	4.27	.05	7.43	.01	—		4.41	.05	9.45	.01
Five fingers	—		4.38	.05	4.61	.05	5.59	.05	4.41	.05	10.15	.01
Legs 2 dim.	17.95	.001	19.90	.001	41.05	.001	16.66	.001	17.05	.001	8.51	.01
0–1 clothes	—		13.14	.001	20.46	.001	13.81	.001	4.41	.05	2.87	.10
4 p. clothes	—		6.67	.01	2.86	.10	18.09	.001	12.91	.001		

Pupils were quite rare on HFDs of both BI and non-BI boys age six. Most young children draw merely dots or circles for eyes. But by age seven and thereafter, many more non-BI boys drew eyes with pupils than did BI boys. At all age levels, most BI boys made immature presentations of eyes (*Plate 98a to c, Plate 100b to f, Plate 101a and b*).

The neck was shown but rarely on HFDs of six year old boys, both BI or non-BI. But by age seven, most non-BI boys produced figures with clearly defined necks. BI boys age seven and older continued to omit the neck significantly more often. By age ten, necks get to be Expected items on HFDs of boys but only half of the ten year old BI subjects showed necks on their drawings; even at age eleven and twelve, only two-thirds of the BI boys drew necks on their HFDs (*Plate 99, Plate 100a to f, Plate 101 b and c*).

Arms in two dimensions were drawn by two-thirds of the six year old non-BI boys. By age seven, two dimensions of the arms on a HFD is an Expected item. At all age levels, BI boys tend to persist significantly more often in drawing immature stick arms on their figures (*Plate 100a to c, Plate 101 a to c*).

Arms pointing down differentiated between the HFDs of BI and non-BI boys at all age levels. By age seven, more than half of the non-BI boys drew arms pointing downward, and by age ten, this item gets to be an Expected item. At all age levels, BI boys persist in drawing arms horizontally or pointing upward which is characteristic of very immature or very young children. (*Plate 98b, Plate 100 a to f, Plate 101 a to c, Plate 102 a and b*).

Arms correctly attached at shoulder differentiated the HFDs of BI and non-BI boys at all age levels. The drawing of this item requires a considerable degree of mental maturity and integrative capacity. At age six and seven, it rarely occurs on the drawings of non-BI boys. Not until age nine was it Common for the non-BI boys to draw arms that were correctly attached at the shoulder. Among BI boys, age six to eight, arms were seldom if ever drawn in correct position at the shoulder. It was not unusual to see, even among the HFDs of 9 to 12 year old BI boys, incorrectly attached arms (*Plate 98b, Plate 99, 100, 101, Plate 102 a, b, and d*).

Hands were found on the HFDs of the majority of non-BI boys from age six on. But at no age level are hands Expected items. The BI boys, age six to eight and ten, tended to omit hands from their drawings significantly more often than did the non-BI boys. Most BI boys drew figures with arms and fingers without any indication of hands or they produced merely arms with neither hands nor fingers (*Plate 100 a to c, Plate 102a*).

The correct number of fingers was rarely shown on the HFDs of the six year old boys, whether BI or non-BI. But by age seven and thereafter, significantly more non-BI boys drew figures with five fingers on each hand. At each age level, more than half of the non-BI boys produced the correct number of fingers on their HFDs compared to only one-third of the BI boys. On drawings of the BI boys, it was not unusual to find hands with too many or too few fingers (*Plate 98a and b, Plate 99, Plate 100 a to c*).

Two dimensions on legs occurred significantly more often on the HFDs of the non-BI boys at all age levels. Stick legs were extremely rare on the drawings of non-BI boys, age eight or older, while more than half of all the BI boys, age six to eight, drew one dimensional stick legs. Many of the older BI youngsters also persisted in this primitive type of presentation of the legs on their HFDs (*Plates 100a, c, e, f, Plate 101, Plate 102*).

Only one or no piece of clothing belongs into the Common category on HFDs of six year old boys, both BI and non-BI. But by age seven and beyond, this item differentiated significantly between the HFDs of the BI and the Non-BI boys. The great majority of seven year old non-BI boys drew more than one piece of clothing on their figures, whereas the omission of clothing persisted on the drawings of most BI boys until age ten and was not uncommon even thereafter (*Plate 98, Plate 100 a to f, Plate 101 a to c*).

Four or more pieces of clothing are quite rare on HFDs of six year old boys, both BI and non-BI. For BI boys, four pieces of clothing on a drawing remained exceptional at all age levels. For non-BI boys, this item increased in frequency of occurrence as the children got older; by age twelve, almost half of all the Non-BI boys depicted four or more clothing pieces on their HFDs.

Obviously, no single BI child will show on his drawing all of the items which differentiated between the HFDs of the BI and non-BI boys. But most BI youngsters will reveal one or more of these items on their drawings. A typical representative of the BI subjects in the present study is Leonard whose six HFDs are shown on *Plate 100*. Leonard was between seven and nine years old when he made these drawings and his IQ scores were in the 80's. All of Leonard's HFDs show an absence of clothing items and an omission of the neck. Five of the figures display only dots or vacant circles for eyes and omit the pupils. *Figures a, b, and c* reveal stick arms and all but *Figure d* exhibit stick legs. On none of the six drawings are the arms correctly attached at the shoulders and on none of them are the arms pointing downward. On *Figures a, b and c*, the hands are omitted and the number of fingers is incorrect. Thus, each of Leonard's six HFDs on *Plate 100* shows at least six or more items that differentiated between drawings of BI and non-BI boys.

Each of Anthony's four HFDs on *Plate 98* and *Plate 99* reveals some items that were characteristic for drawings of BI boys, but these items differ for each of the drawings. *Figure a* on *Plate 98* lacks pupils, has an incorrect number of fingers, and shows only one piece of clothing. *Figure 98b* shows an absence of pupils, the arms are extending upward rather than down, they are incorrectly attached to the body, and some of the fingers are missing. On *Figure 98c*, a clearly defined neck is omitted, so are pupils and clothing items. The HFD on *Plate 99* shows a considerable improvement over Anthony's other three drawings on *Plate 98*. But here, too, the neck is missing, the arms are incorrectly attached to the body, and several fingers are omitted.

Once again, it must be emphasized that the 11 Developmental Items, which differentiated between the HFDs of the BI and non-BI boys, do not occur on any one drawing of a BI child, nor do they occur exclusively on the HFDs of BI children. It is, therefore, not possible to make a diagnosis of brain injury merely on the basis of Developmental Items on a HFD. However, if a child is being evaluated for possible organic involvement, and if his developmental history, and his psychological and/or neurological test results are suggestive of brain injury, then the presence or absence of the significant Developmental Items on the HFD can lend weight to a positive diagnosis. A HFD should only be used as one in a battery of tests when making a differential diagnosis of a child's behavior and symptoms.

Expected and Exceptional Items on HFDs and IQ scores of BI children

It was demonstrated earlier (page 29) that scores derived from the Expected and Exceptional Items on HFDs (*Appendix B*) can be used as an easy and reliable means of assessing a child's general level of mental ability. The HFDs scores of young psychiatric clinic patients and of elementary school children with behavior and learning problems were found to be significantly correlated with their WISC and Stanford-Binet IQ scores (*Table 9*). However, Bender (1940) reported that most of her postencephalitic patients obtained M.A. scores on the Goodenough Draw-A-Man Test that were two or more years below their M.A. scores on the Stanford-Binet Scale. Bender suggested that a large discrepancy between the Stanford-Binet and the Draw-A-Man IQ scores might be a diagnostic sign for brain pathology. One might expect, therefore, that the correlations between the HFD scores and WISC or Stanford-Binet IQ scores will be considerably lower for BI subjects than for non-BI children. On the other hand, the HFD scoring system deals only with basic Expected and Exceptional Items and is not much influenced by details on the drawings. BI children often omit details which are scored by the Goodenough-Harris system but not by the HFD scoring system. Therefore, it was hypothesized that HFD scores and IQ scores of BI children would show a positive correlation that was statistically significant, and that the Expected and Exceptional Items on HFDs could be used with equal confidence for the assessment of the mental ability of non-BI and BI children.

A study was carried out to test this hypothesis. The 388 BI subjects (*Table 20*) were divided into age groups: The first group included 115 children age six and seven. Sixty-eight of these subjects had been tested with the WISC, while the remaining 47 children had been given the Stanford-Binet Intelligence Scale. The second group was made up of 206 children between the ages of eight and ten. Of these, 165 had been tested with the WISC and 41 with the Stanford-Binet Scale. The 67 11 and 12 year old subjects made up the third group. All of them had been given the WISC with a few exceptions who had been tested with the Stanford-Binet Scale. Pearson product-moment coefficients of correlation were computed between the HFD scores and the IQ scores of each group of subjects. The level of significance of the correlations was determined by means of the *t*-Test. The following results were obtained:

Age of Ss	N	Tests correlated	Correlation	Level of Siginificance
6 and 7	68	WISC & HFDs	.56	.005
6 and 7	47	S-B & HFDs	.50	.005
8 to 10	165	WISC & HFDs	.51	.005
8 to 10	41	S-B & HFDs	.57	.005
11 and 12	67	(WISC & S-B) & HFDs	.35	.005

The results show that all five correlations between the HFD scores and the IQ scores of the BI subjects were statistically significant at the .005 level and compare favorably with the correlations between the HFD and IQ scores of the non-BI subjects shown on *Table 9*. The present findings support the hypothesis tested and indicate that the Expected and Exceptional Items on HFDs can be used as a rough measure of mental maturity with equal confidence for children with or without brain injury. *Appendix D* shows the Quartile scores, the Mean scores, and the Standard Deviations for all children, age 5 to 12, whether BI or non-BI. The interpretation of individual HFD scores is the same for all youngsters whether they are neurologically impaired or not *(Appendix C)*.

Table 22 illustrates how the HFDs of four BI boys, whose drawings are shown on *Plates 98 to 102*, would be scored for Expected and Exceptional Items. Also shown are the levels of mental maturity the HFD scores fall into and the WISC Full Scale IQ scores the four boys had obtained. The scoring of most of the HFDs on *Plates 98 to 102* is simple and obvious. Some of the drawings exhibit all the Expected Items and none of the Exceptional Items listed in Appendix B for a given age level. These drawings are therefore scored as $-0+0+5 = 5$. When one or two of the Expected Items are missing from the HFD and no Exceptional Item is present, then the scores are 4 or 3 respectively. Only *Figure c* on *Plate 98* represents a somewhat unusual situation. This HFD displays three

Table 22.   Comparison of HFD Scores and WISC IQ Scores of BI Boys

Plate	Child's Name	Child's Age	Scoring of HFD	Mental Maturity Level of HFD	WISC IQ Score
98a	Anthony	7–11	$-0 + 0 + 5 = 5$	Ave. to High Ave.	107
98b	Anthony	8–2	$-0 + 0 + 5 = 5$	Ave. to High Ave.	107
98c	Anthony	8–7	$-3 + 2 + 5 = 4$	Low Ave. to Ave.	107
99	Anthony	9–5	$-0 + 0 + 5 = 5$	Ave. to High Ave.	107
100a	Leonard	7–2	$-1 + 0 + 5 = 4$	Low Ave. to Ave.	89
100b	Leonard	7–10	$-1 + 0 + 5 = 4$	Low Ave. to Ave.	89
100c	Leonard	8–3	$-2 + 0 + 5 = 3$	Low Average	85
100d	Leonard	8–10	$-0 + 0 + 5 = 5$	Ave. to High Ave.	85
100e	Leonard	9–3	$-1 + 0 + 5 = 4$	Low Ave. to Ave.	85
100f	Leonard	9–8	$-1 + 0 + 5 = 4$	Low Ave. to Ave.	85
101a	Gordon	6–0	$-1 + 0 + 5 = 4$	Low Ave. to Ave.	83
101b	Gordon	7–10	$-1 + 0 + 5 = 4$	Low Ave. to Ave.	83
101c	Gordon	8–2	$-2 + 0 + 5 = 3$	Low Average	83
102a	Patrick	11–8	$-2 + 0 + 5 = 3$	Low Average	98
102b	Patrick	12–6	$-1 + 0 + 5 = 4$	Low Ave. to Ave.	98
102c	Patrick	12–10	$-0 + 0 + 5 = 5$	Ave. to High Ave.	98

omissions of Expected Items for eight year old boys (no arms, arms not in two dimensions, no feet); at the same time, the drawing shows two Exceptional Items for this age level (profile drawing and knee). The score for *Figure 98c* is therefore $-3+2+5 = 4$.

With two exceptions, all of the HFD scores of the BI Subjects on *Table 22* fall within the same level of mental maturity as their WISC IQ scores. One of the exceptions is *Plate 102a*. Patrick's score for this HFD is only 3 or Low Average (legs not in two dimensions, arms not pointing down) while his WISC IQ score was 98 or Average. However, when Patrick made another HFD a year later, it showed good improvement. *Plate 102b* reveals the absence of only one Expected Item (arm not pointing down); it was scored as 4. *Plate 102c* was without any omissions of Expected Items and was scored as 5. This increase in HFD scores reflects accurately Patrick's improvement as the result of therapy. At the beginning of his treatment, Patrick could not function at the average level despite his IQ score. A year later, his school achievement had greatly improved and his behavior was much more mature.

It was noted that BI children who show a marked discrepancy between their HFD score and their WISC or Stanford-Binet IQ scores were usually also seriously emotionally disturbed. These children were usually functioning on the more retarded level indicated by their HFD score and not on the higher level shown by the IQ test score. IQ test scores may reveal the child's intellectual potential, but many emotionally disturbed and brain injured children do not or cannot live up to their intellectual potential.

Emotional Indicators on HFDs and BI children

A study was made to determine whether the 30 Emotional Indicators on HFDs (*Appendix E*) could differentiate between the drawings of BI and non-BI boys age 6 to 12. The 282 BI and 803 Control subjects used in the earlier study on Developmental Items on HFDs of BI children (page 163) served also as subjects for the present investigation. Chi-squares were computed for the number of BI boys and Controls at each age level who showed each given Emotional Indicator on their HFDs.

As might be expected, none of the Emotional Indicators occurred exclusively on the HFDs of the BI subjects, nor did any of the Emotional Indicators appear on all of the drawings of the BI boys. But eight of the Indicators were found significantly more often at one or more age levels on the HFDs of the neurologically impaired youngsters than on the drawings of the Controls. *Table 23* shows the results of this study. The eight Emotional Indicators that were significantly associated with brain injury in children are listed below:

(1) *Poor integration of parts of figure* is not an unusual sign on HFDs of both BI and non-BI boys at age six. But from age seven on, this Emotional Indicator differentiated significantly between the HFDs of the BI and the non-BI subjects. It was found on 44 percent of the drawings of the BI boys, age 7 to 12, compared to only 5 percent of the HFDs of the Control subjects. These findings are in agreement with Machover (1949) and Reznikoff and Tomblen (1956) who reported the presence of "weak synthesis"

Table 23. Emotional Indicators Differentiating Between HFDs of BI and Non-BI Boys Age 6 to 12

Emotional Indicator	6 years χ^2	6 years P	7 years χ^2	7 years P	8 years χ^2	8 years P	9 years χ^2	9 years P	10 years χ^2	10 years P	11–12 years χ^2	11–12 years P
N — BI	25		53		61		58		37		48	
N — Non-BI	131		134		138		134		109		157	
Integration	12.05	.001	48.53	.001	55.13	.001	33.73	.001	34.36	.001	46.99	.001
Asymmetry	m.o.†		5.00	.05	m.o.		m.o.		m.o.		m.o.	
Slanting figure	n.d.‡		4.64	.05	m.o.		m.o.		5.44	.05	22.31	.001
Transparencies			m.o.		11.76	.001	m.o.		m.o.		13.32	.001
Tiny figure	4.82	.05	3.25	.10	9.68	.01	m.o.		m.o.		5.01	.05
Hands cut off	9.94	.01	3.77	.05	5.97	.05	4.79	.05	8.15	.01	8.22	.01
No body	16.31	.001	n.d.		n.d.		n.d.		n.d.		n.d.	
No neck	n.v.*		n.v.		n.v.		n.v.		5.95	.05	17.99	.001

* n.v.: Emotional Indicator *not valid* for that age level.

† m.o.: Item occurred *more often* on HFDs of BI boys but too rarely for statistical computations.

‡ n.d.: *No difference* in frequency of occurrence of item on HFDs of BI and Non-BI boys.

on the drawings of their brain injured patients. Poor integration of parts of the figure seems to reflect a poor integrative capacity, immaturity, impulsivity, and/or poor coordination all of which are very common in children with neurological impairment (*Plate 98 a and b, Plate 100, Plate 101*).

(2) *Gross asymmetry of limbs* occurred most often on the HFDs of very immature children. This item differentiated significantly between the HFDs of the BI and the non-BI boys at the six and seven year age level. By age eight and thereafter, gross asymmetry of limbs was not present often enough to make statistical computations meaningful, even though it appeared consistently more often on the drawings of the BI boys. Eight percent of the HFDs of all the BI subjects showed gross asymmetry as against 2 percent of the drawings of the control group. A detailed analysis of the drawings of these 2 percent of the Control subjects gives reason to suspect that these children also suffered from some kind of cortical malfunctioning; their drawings look just like HFDs made by BI children. This suspicion could not be verified since no additional information was available on the Control subjects. However, it stands to reason that any large group of unselected schoolchildren will include a small number of neurologically impaired children who may or may not come to the attention of the school psychologist. Gross asymmetry of limbs seems to reflect an imbalanced, impulsive, poorly coordinated individual. This Emotional Indicator seems to be akin to the "shrunken limbs" which Reznikoff and Tomblen (1956) found to be associated with brain injury in their patients (*Plate 14, Plate 74, Plate 75*).

(3) *Slanting of figure by 15° or more* occurred on 11 percent of the HFDs of the BI subjects and only on 2 percent of the drawings by the Control group. Although this item was present more often on the drawings of the BI boys at all age levels, this difference in frequency of occurrence was statistically significant only at ages seven, ten and eleven. It is not certain whether the slanting of the figure is the result of poor coordination or if it reveals above all a lack of emotional balance or both. Slanting figures seem to occur most often on drawings of insecure and unstable children (*Plate 2, Plate 98a, Plate 102b*).

(4) *Transparencies* were found consistently more often on the HFDs of the BI boys, age seven and older, than on the drawings of the Control group. But this difference was statistically significant only at the eight and eleven and twelve year old level. At the six year old level, BI and non-BI boys did not differ in the number of transparencies they depicted on their HFDs. A total of 11 percent of all the BI subjects and 4 percent of the Controls exhibited transparencies on their drawings. BI subjects revealed primarily the primitive type of transparencies in which the child first draws a stickman which he then surrounds with a body and clothing. This type of transparency is usually associated with immaturity and concretistic thinking which is of course typical of many neurologically impaired children (*Plate 98a and b, Plate 100d, Plate 102a to c*).

(5) *Tiny figures less than 2" in height* were found on 12 percent of the HFDs of the BI subjects while only 3 percent of the Control subjects drew tiny figures on their pictures. At all age levels, tiny figures occurred more

often on the drawings of the BI youngsters than on the drawings of the non-BI boys; this difference was statistically significant at ages 6 to 8 and 11 and 12. However, there is nothing to suggest that the drawing of tiny figures is a sign of neurological impairment as such, or that it reflects attitudes specifically related to brain injury. An earlier study (page 44) showed that tiny figures on HFDs indicate an attitude of timidity, withdrawal and depression. It is believed that the relatively high incidence of tiny figures on the HFDs of the BI subjects is an expression of their reaction to the neurological impairment. Since most BI children experience considerable difficulty and frustration in school and at home, they tend to feel inadequate and shy, and many BI youngsters show signs of depression. Some BI youngsters use withdrawal as a means to control their own impulsivity. Simon who was discussed earlier (page 45) is a case in point. His HFD is shown on *Plate 2*. Additional examples of tiny figures are shown on *Plate 100*. Five of Leonard's six HFDs on *Plate 100* are less than 2″ in height.

(6) *Cut-off hands*, or arms with neither hands nor fingers differentiated significantly between the HFDs of the BI and the non-BI subjects at all age levels. This item was found on 17 percent of the drawings of the BI boys compared to 5 percent of the HFDs of the non-BI boys. The interpretation of cut-off hands is believed to be similar to that of tiny figure. There is no reason to assume that this Emotional Indicator is a direct reflection of neurological impairment as such but rather that it is an indication of helplessness and anxiety on part of the BI child in the face of his own limitations and many failure experiences. Cut-off hands seem to indicate a general attitude of concern and/or guilt over doing wrong or failing to achieve with one's hands (*Plate 25d, Plate 100d*).

(7) *Omission of the body* was extremely rare on HFDs of school-age children of normal intelligence. At the six year old level, significantly more BI boys drew figures without bodies than non-BI subjects. Thereafter, omission of the body appeared so infrequently on the HFDs of both the BI and the non-BI subjects to make any sort of comparison meaningless. On the rare occasions when this item did appear on a drawing, it was always clinically significant. In the case of a BI child, it may reflect either immaturity and slow maturation or mental retardation. Gordon, whose HFDs are shown on *Plate 101*, is an example of an immature and slowly developing BI child of low average intelligence. *Figure 101a*, drawn at age six, displays a figure without a body. But by age seven and eight, Gordon drew figures with bodies as shown on *Plate 101b and c*. These drawings represent a marked improvement over the earlier HFD. Mickey, a retarded brain injured child on the other hand, failed to show such an improvement on his drawings. *Plate 50* shows the HFD Mickey made at age six; it lacks a body. On drawings obtained from Mickey at age seven and eight, he continued to omit the body.

(8) *Omission of the neck* on a HFD does not qualify as an Emotional Indicator for boys until age ten (*Appendix E*). At that age level, omission of the neck differentiated significantly between the drawings of the BI and the non-BI subjects. Twenty-nine percent of the 10 to 12 year old BI

boys drew figures without necks as against 7 percent of the Control subjects. Omission of the neck is believed to reflect impulsivity and poor mental control over one's impulses. Since many neurologically impaired children are extremely impulsive and show a malfunctioning of inner controls, it is not surprising that so many BI subjects omitted the neck from their drawings (*Plates 35 and 70*).

Clinical Interpretation of HFDs of BI children

HFDs reflect children's interpersonal attitudes regardless of whether the children are neurologically impaired or not. When Frankie's drawing (*Plate 25c*) was selected to illustrate how a child might reveal his feelings about an impending operation on his HFDs (page 87), no particular significance was given to the fact that Frankie was a brain injured youngster. A child without brain injury might have disclosed similar attitudes on his drawing. The drawings of BI children can be clinically interpreted in the same way as the HFDs of non-BI children.

The case of Anthony may serve as an example of how the drawings of a neurologically impaired boy can reflect his problems, his attitudes, and his progress in therapy. *Plates 98 and 99* show four HFDs made by Anthony. As was mentioned earlier (page 159), Anthony obtained a brain injury as a result of a serious case of measles followed by encephalitis at age four. According to his parents, he underwent a complete personality change by the time he entered school. Despite average intelligence and a stable and loving home situation, Anthony developed learning and behavior problems. He was a very perceptive youngster who was painfully aware that he could not meet the standards of his home and school environment. His father was a successful professional man and his two older brothers were honor students in high school. As Anthony's failures and frustrations increased, his behavior became more disturbed and disturbing. The parents finally brought Anthony to the child guidance clinic to seek help for the boy and for themselves in order to be better able to understand and help Anthony.

Figure a on Plate 98 was drawn by Anthony at the time of his initial interview at the clinic. The drawing shows poor integration of parts, slanting of the figure, gross asymmetry of arms, and transparencies, all of which are found significantly more often on HFDs of children with emotional problems and are also associated with brain injury. *Figure 98a* indicates that Anthony was a very unstable, poorly integrated, impulsive child who seemed in danger of losing his balance despite great efforts at self-control, as was shown by the treatment of the long, prominent neck on the drawing. In the interview, Anthony expressed a keen desire to learn and to achieve scholastic success so that he could obtain his father's approval. At a clinic staff conference, it was decided to offer Anthony remedial therapy twice a week while the parents were seen for guidance sessions.

Initially, Anthony responded well to the remedial therapy sessions and made good progress. Then three months later, his mother gave birth to a baby girl which upset Anthony very much. All of the attention Anthony had received during the past months was now lavished on the new arrival. Anthony suffered from intense sibling rivalry and once again his behavior deteriorated and his schoolwork regressed. *Figure b* on *Plate 98* shows Anthony's HFD at that time. The drawing is much cruder and more primitive than his earlier HFD and reflects his regressed state. Poor integration and transparencies are still in evidence but the slant and the asymmetry of limbs on the first HFD have disappeared. Instead of making an ordinary boy or man as before, Anthony drew a grotesque figure, a clown, whose head seems to be "unstuck." Anthony now perceived himself as a ludicrous outsider (page 126). He no longer felt like a fully accepted member of the family since he had been displaced by the baby. Anthony saw himself as someone who was laughed at by others and who was not taken seriously. The presence of teeth on the clown show the anger and hostility Anthony was feeling.

Figure b on *Plate 98* served to confirm the impression gained from Anthony's behavior. It was therefore decided that Anthony needed more intensive therapy and support at this time, in order to improve his self-concept and to help him work through his resentment toward the baby. Thereafter, Anthony was seen for playtherapy as well as for remedial lessons. Five months later, Anthony was asked to make another HFD. The result is shown on *Plate 98c*. This time he drew an armless girl in profile. The fact that he drew a girl reflects his preoccupation with and concern over his sister. The hostile image of the disintegrating clown has given way to a helpless, withdrawn female figure. The drawing shows that Anthony still had many problems but also that he had made some progress. The drawing is no longer as poorly integrated as before and clearly represents an improvement. Anthony no longer felt that he was an outsider but rather that he was a member of his family, though a very weak and helpless one. The girl on the HFD represents Anthony's sister, but the *way* she is drawn reflects his attitude toward himself. Anthony's feeling of anxiety and helplessness is shown by the figure's lack of arms and feet and by the fact that the girl is sitting down, as if she were too weak to stand on her own feet. The drawing is in profile, thereby suggesting that Anthony is withdrawing, turning away from others. The continuous outline of the figure shows Anthony's attempt at controlling his hostile impulses (page 133).

Treatment continued for Anthony throughout the next year. He made slow but steady progress in his emotional adjustment and in academic achievement. When he was nine years old, Anthony was asked to make another HFD. *Plate 99* shows the drawing he made on this occasion. Anthony said it was "a man walking a tightrope." A tightrope walker is at best in a pretty precarious position and has an uncertain footing. This type of figure is usually drawn by very insecure children who are trying hard to maintain their balance or to gain control over themselves. In Anthony's case, the HFD reflected his strong effort and motivation to regain his stability. It also revealed his lingering feeling of uncertainty and anxiety about his adequacy. It is a sign of progress that Anthony's tightrope walker is a male and that he is well integrated. He lacks neither arms nor feet and he meets the problems head-on without evasion. This HFD can be scored for only one Emotional Indicator, and that is "grotesque figure." A tightrope walker is an acrobat and a circus performer and, as such, he is akin to clowns, and drawings of tightrope walkers are interpreted in a similar way as pictures of clowns. But acrobats entertain by displaying their skill in contrast to clowns who make themselves ridiculous in order to amuse. The former suggest therefore a somewhat more adequate self-concept than the latter. A change in attitude toward himself was also evident in Anthony's behavior and in greater self-confidence in social relationships. When last heard from, Anthony was continuing to make gains in all areas.

From the discussion of Anthony's four HFDs on *Plates 98 and 99,* it can be seen that the emotional attitudes of a brain injured child are just as clearly revealed on his drawings as are those of non-brain injured children.

HFDs and brain injury in children: Summary

Children with neurological impairment are above all human beings whose mental growth and development follow the same general pattern as those of non-BI children, albeit at a somewhat slower and often uneven pace. BI children's reactions to external and internal stimuli are similar to other children's reactions and the attitudes they develop toward themselves and others are just like those of other youngsters although they may be more exaggerated. It is therefore not surprising that HFDs reflect the mental maturity and the interpersonal attitudes of BI and non-BI children alike. No single Developmental Item or Emotional Indicator on HFDs was found to occur exclusively on the drawings of one group of youngsters or the other, nor was any single sign or symbol present on the HFDs of all the BI children or of all the non-BI children.

A comparison of HFDs of BI and non-BI boys of normal intelligence did show however, that some of the Developmental Items and some of the Emotional Indicators tend to occur significantly more often, or less often respectively, on the drawings of the youngsters with neurological impairment (*Appendix G*). Thus is was found that 11 omissions of Developmental Items on HFDs may have diagnostic implications for brain injury at one or more age levels. These items are (*Table 21*):

Omission of body
Omission of pupils
Omission of neck
Omission of two dimensions of arms (stick arms)
Arms not pointing downward (arms horizontal or up)
Arms incorrectly attached at shoulder
Omission of hands
Incorrect number of fingers
Omission of two dimensions on legs (stick legs)
Less than two pieces of clothing
Less than four pieces of clothing

HFDs of BI children can be scored for Expected and Exceptional Items in the same manner as the drawings of non-BI youngsters. The HFD scores thus obtained were found to correlate significantly with the WISC and Stanford-Binet Scale IQ scores of the BI youngsters. The HFD scores can be used therefore as a quick and easy means of assessing a brain injured child's mental ability (page 168).

Eight of the 30 Emotional Indicators were found to occur more often on the HFDs of the BI boys than on the drawings of the Control subjects. These eight Emotional Indicators are (*Table 23*):

Poor integration of parts of figure (age 7 to 12)
Gross asymmetry of limbs
Figure slanting by 15° or more
Transparencies (age 7 to 12)
Omission of body (age 6)
Omission of neck (age 10 to 12)
Tiny figure less than 2″ in height
Hands cut off

The first six of these Emotional Indicators reflect immaturity, poor integrative capacity, impulsivity, and instability, all of which are so characteristic for many of the BI children. The last two of the Emotional Indicators seem to reflect above all the BI child's poor self-concept and his feelings of inadequacy and helplessness.

The omission or presence of any of the Developmental Items and the Emotional Indicators, that were associated with brain injury, cannot be considered by themselves signs of cerebral malfunctioning since all of these signs also occur to some extent on the drawings of non-BI children. But the presence of several of these signs on a HFD may be regarded as an indication that brain injury *may* be present. The HFD Test should never be used alone for differential diagnosis; it should only be used as one in a battery of tests. A diagnosis of brain injury or cerebral malfunctioning cannot or should not ever be made solely on the basis of a HFD, however, a drawing can be used effectively to support a diagnosis. The presence of several significant items on a HFD can serve to supplement other psychological, medical and social data.

The clinical interpretation of HFDs is the same for BI and non-BI children. Neurologically impaired children can reveal their attitudes on HFDs just as vividly and in the same manner as children without neurological impairment.

9. Using HFDs in Combination with Other Psychological Tests

ON SEVERAL OCCASIONS in the past, it was suggested (Koppitz, 1959, 1960, 1962), that the diagnostic usefulness of the HFD Test is greatly enhanced when it is used in combination with the Bender Gestalt Test or as part of a test battery. The following studies are presented as examples of how the HFD Test can be combined with other tests for the purpose of screening school beginners and as a way of helping to identify children with emotional and/or neurological problems who need special class placement.

Predicting first grade achievement with the HFD Test and the Bender Gestalt Test

The Bender Gestalt Test (Bender 1938, 1946) and the HFD Test are both paper and pencil tests and both reflect the mental development of children. However, they differ significantly in some aspects and can supplement each other in a meaningful way. The Bender Test measures primarily a child's functioning in visual-motor perception and is only to a lesser degree a projective test. The HFD Test on the other hand is particularly sensitive to a child's emotional attitudes and to his self-concept and gives a good indication of the child's mental ability. A meaningful and valid prediction of a youngster's school achievement must be based always on all three of these: the child's mental ability, his perceptual functioning, and his emotional adjustment. Together, the HFD Test and the Bender Test can assess all three of these areas.

The present study was designed to determine how well the Bender and the HFD Test together can predict academic achievement of school beginners. The subjects for this study were 128 children who attended five first grade classes in five different schools, representing a socio-economic cross-section. The subjects ranged in age from 5 years 9 months to 6 years 11 months. None of the children were repeating the first grade. During the first month of the school year, the Bender Gestalt Test was administered to each child individually by a qualified psychologist. But there is really no reason why this test could not have been administered as a group test, as was demonstrated by Keogh and Smith (1960) and Ruckhaber (1962). The HFD Test was administered to each class as a group by their teachers. At the end of the school year, the teachers gave the Metropolitan Achievement Test, Primary I Battery, Form R (Hildreth, 1946). The Metropolitan Achievement Test was scored by the psychologists. All Bender protocols were scored by the writer according to the Koppitz system (1964), while all HFDs were checked for the presence of the *eight* Exceptional Items for six year old children (*Appendix B*) and for the *six* Emotional Indicators which are related to school achievement in the first grade (page 51). These six items are: slanting figure, omission of the mouth, omission of the body, omission of the arms, monster or grotesque figure, and three or more figures spontaneously drawn. The eight Exceptional Items included:

nostrils, two lips, profile, elbow, knee, good proportion, arms correctly attached at shoulder, and four or more pieces of clothing. The presence of any of the Exceptional Items on a HFD was believed to show above-average intelligence, while the presence of any of the six Emotional Indicators was thought to reflect emotional problems which would interfere with school achievement.

The subjects were divided into five groups according to their grade placement on the Metropolitan Achievement Test. All those with an Average Achievement Score of 2.8 or higher were considered to be *outstanding* pupils; those with an achievement level of 2.4–2.7 were designated as *good* students; those with achievement scores of 1.8–2.3 were called *average* pupils; a grade placement of 1.5–1.7 was considered *poor;* while a score of 1.4 or less was regarded as *very poor.* The Bender scores were divided into five categories: *Good* (scores more than one Standard Deviation below the Mean score), *High Average* (scores falling between the Mean and minus one Standard Deviation), *Low Average* (scores falling between the Mean and plus one Standard Deviation), *Poor* (scores between plus one Standard Deviation and plus two Standard Deviations), and *Very Poor* (scores greater than plus two Standard Deviations from the Mean score.) The Bender Mean scores and Standard Deviations were obtained from the normative data in *The Bender Gestalt Test for Young Children* (Koppitz, 1964, p. 188). *Table 24* shows the Bender Test scores for different age levels in the five categories used in this and the following investigations.

The results of the present study are shown on *Figure 1.* It was found that, with a few exceptions, the outstanding and good pupils showed at least Low Average Bender scores and displayed a marked absence of Emotional Indicators on their HFDs while exhibiting Exceptional Items

Table 24. **Distribution of Bender Gestalt Test Scores at Different Age Levels**

| Age Level | Bender Gestalt Test Scores* | | | | | |
	Very Good	Good	High Average	Low Average	Poor	Very Poor
5	0–5	6–9	10–13	14–17	18–21	22 up
5½	0–2	3–5	6–9	10–13	14–17	18 up
6	0–1	2–3	4–8	9–12	13–17	18 up
6½	0	1–2	3–6	7–10	11–14	15 up
7	0	1	2–4	5–8	9–12	13 up
7½	0	1	2–4	5–8	9–11	12 up
8	0	0	1–3	4–7	8–11	12 up
8½	0	0	0–2	3–5	6–9	10 up
9	0	0	0–2	3–4	5	6 up
9½	0	0	0–1	2–3	4–5	6 up
10	0	0	0–1	2–3	4–5	6 up
10½	0	0	0–1	2–3	4–5	6 up

* Since the Bender Test is scored for errors a high score indicates poor performance while a low score reflects a good Bender record.

on their drawings. That is, the outstanding and good pupils showed for the most part above-average mental ability (Exceptional Items on HFDs), an absence of emotional problems (no Emotional Indicators on HFDs), and at least low average perceptual maturity (Low Average or better Bender scores).

The average pupils revealed a variety of test response patterns. Some youngsters showed good perceptual maturation (above-average Bender performance) but presented signs of emotional problems (Emotional Indicators on their HFDs which seemed to interfere with above-average achievement. Others exhibited quite poor Bender scores along with Exceptional Items on their HFDs. These youngsters were apparently able to overcome or to compensate for immature visual-motor perception since they were of good intelligence and were not handicapped by serious emotional problems. But most of the average students had just average Bender scores, and revealed neither Exceptional Items nor Emotional Indicators on their HFDs; they were apparently of average ability with average perceptual maturation.

Most poor and very poor pupils had below-average Bender performance and they exhibited on their HFDs one or more of the Emotional Indicators, that are related to school achievement, while failing to show any Exceptional Items. In other words, children who fail in the first grade tend to have immature or malfunctioning visual-motor perception *as well as* emotional problems. They usually do not show above-average mental ability.

The findings from this study clearly demonstrate that the Bender and the HFD Test together are much better in predicting the achievement of school beginners than either test alone. In general, it seems safe to predict that school beginners will be average or above-average students in the first grade if they show an Exceptional Item on their HFD, an absence of the six significant Emotional Indicators, and if their Bender Test score is at least within the Low Average range. Children who reveal one or more of the six Emotional Indicators on their drawings may possibly be average students, but more likely they will be below-average pupils. Youngsters who display Low Average or Poor Bender scores together with one of the six Emotional Indicators on their HFDs can be expected to be poor students. Children who omit the body from their drawing or who produce three or more figures spontaneously were found to be poor students irrespective of their Bender score.

Predicting achievement of second grade pupils

This study is a follow-up of the preceding investigation and is an attempt to determine whether school achievement in the primary grades can be more accurately predicted when a brief verbal test is added to the HFD Test and the Bender Gestalt Test. As far as possible, the same subjects were used in the present study as in the previous one. Some changes among the children included were unavoidable. Thirteen of the poor and very poor first graders were automatically eliminated from this study since they were repeating the first grade and were not among the second graders.

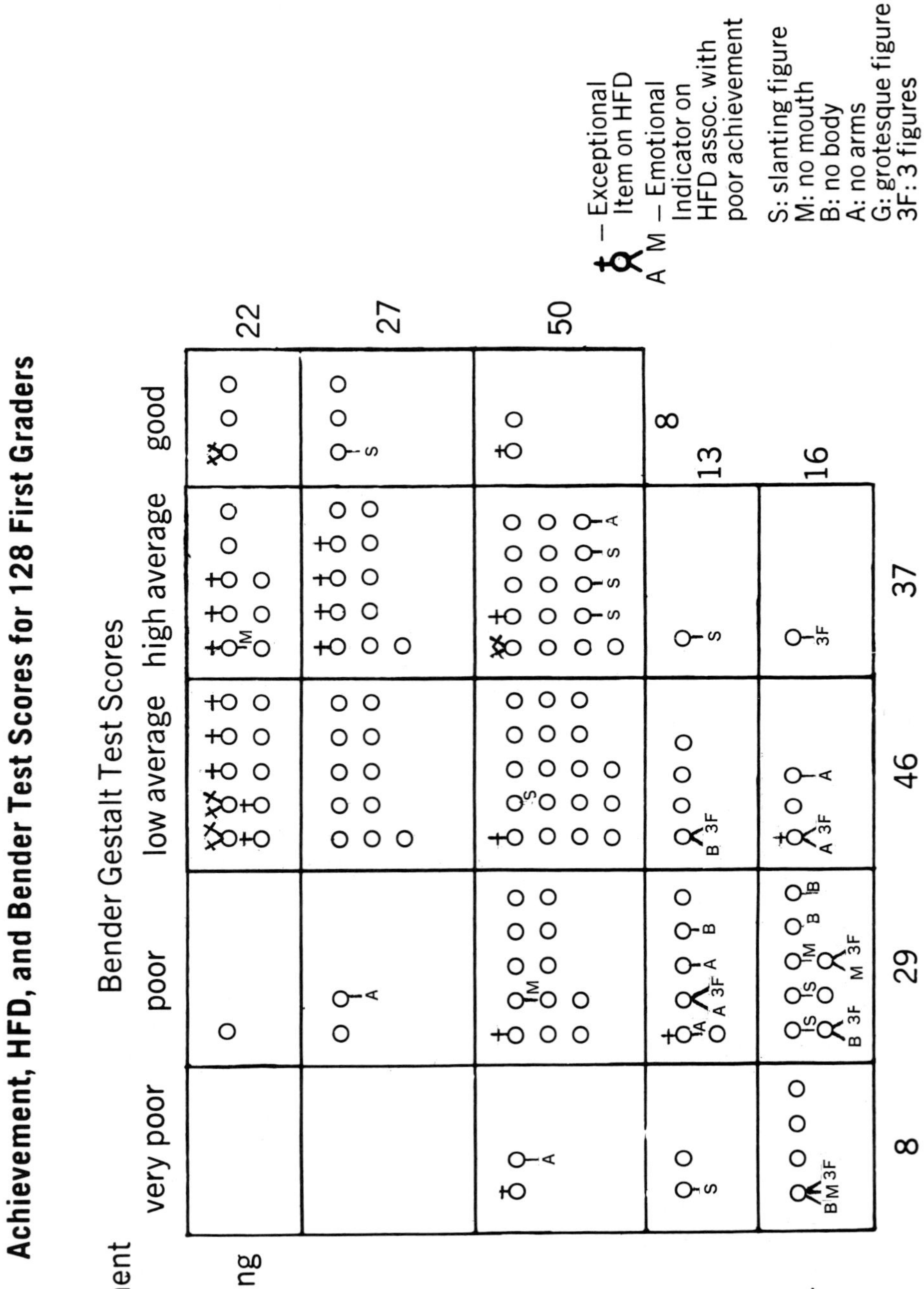
Achievement, HFD, and Bender Test Scores for 128 First Graders
Bender Gestalt Test Scores
Achievement Level
very poor
poor
low average
high average
good
Outstanding
Good
Average
Poor
Very Poor
22
27
50
8
13
16
8
29
46
37
— Exceptional Item on HFD
A M — Emotional Indicator on HFD assoc. with poor achievement
S: slanting figure
M: no mouth
B: no body
A: no arms
G: grotesque figure
3F: 3 figures

Figure 1.

Twelve other children had either moved away or were not present at the time of testing in the second grade. Instead, ten new subjects were included in the present investigation who had not been present in the first grade. The total number of second graders participating in this study was 113. The subjects ranged in age from 6 years 9 months to 7 years 10 months.

The procedure followed in this study was the same as in the preceding investigation, with a few minor changes. All subjects were tested at the beginning of the school year with the Bender and the HFD test as before. Only now, the HFDs were scored for the *six* Exceptional Items that are valid for seven year old children (nostrils, two lips, profile, elbow, knee, and good proportions) and for the *seven* Emotional Indicators that were related to school achievement in the second grade (poor integration of parts, slanting figure, omission of body, omission of mouth, omission of arms, monster or grotesque figure, three or more figures drawn). Poor integration of parts was added to the list for the second graders; this item is not valid for boys prior to age seven. The Information Subtest of the WISC was added as a third test to get some measure of the children's verbal ability. This test was administered to each subject individually by a psychologist along with the Bender Test. The Information Subtest was selected since it correlates well with the total Verbal IQ score on the WISC, and since it is quick and easy to administer and to score. All subjects who obtained a Raw Score of 10 or more on the Information Subtest were considered to have above-average verbal ability. A Raw Score of 10 is equivalent to a testing age of 8½ years or one year above the average age of the second grade subjects.

The Metropolitan Achievement Test was again administered at the end of the school year. The children whose Average Metropolitan Achievement score was 3.8 or better were considered to be *outstanding* pupils; those with a grade placement of 3.4–3.7 were included among the *good* students; those with achievement scores between 2.8 and 3.3 were called *average* pupils; those with an achievement at the 2.5–2.7 level were designated as *poor* students; and finally all those whose achievement scores were 2.4 or less were labeled as *very poor* students.

The results of this study are shown on *Figure 2.* The findings are not dissimilar to those of the preceding study. The outstanding and good students revealed for the most part good verbal ability (i.e., Information score of 10 or higher) and/or above average intelligence (i.e., one Exceptional Item on their HFDs); their Bender Test performance was at least at the Low Average and more often at the High Average level or better. Their HFDs tended to be free from the seven significant Emotional Indicators, thus showing that their school achievement was not depressed by emotional problems.

The average students revealed once again a wide range of Bender Test scores. Some of them showed quite poor Bender performance but seemed to be able to compensate for their immature visual-motor perception by virtue of good intelligence (Exceptional Item on HFD) or good verbal ability (high score on Information Test). Most average students did not show any of the seven Emotional Indicators on their HFDs.

Achievement, HFD, Bender and Verbal Scores for 113 Second Graders

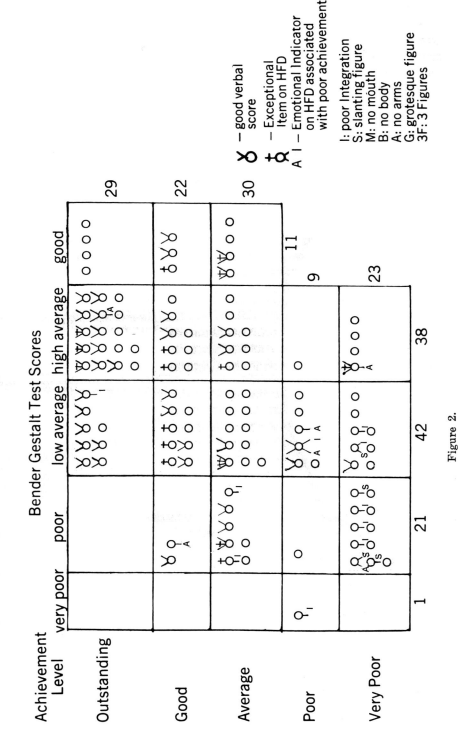

Figure 2.

The poor and very poor pupils showed again a high incidence of malfunctioning or immaturity in visual-motor perception (Low Average and Poor Bender scores) as well as emotional problems (Emotional Indicators on HFDs) with an absence of above-average intelligence (no Exceptional Items on HFDs) or good verbal ability (no high scores on the Information Test). In the few cases where poor students revealed good verbal ability and average scores on the Bender Test, the children's achievement level was depressed by emotional problems.

The results of this study clearly show that the three tests, the Bender Gestalt Test, the HFD Test, and the Information Subtest of the WISC, together are better able to predict second grade achievement than any one or two of the tests alone. The Bender alone can predict fairly accurately that all youngsters with High Average or better Bender performance will be most likely average or better than average students. But it is not possible to tell from the Bender Test alone what the achievement of those children will be who obtain Low Average Bender scores. Depending on their intelligence, verbal ability and emotional adjustment, these children may reveal anywhere from outstanding to very poor achievement. A Poor or Very Poor score on the Bender Test suggests poor school achievement unless the child is able to compensate for his perceptual deficiencies by means of good verbal ability; in that case, his achievement may yet be average despite the poor performance on the Bender Test.

The HFD Test by itself can predict that children with one or more Exceptional Items on their drawings will tend to be at least average and probably better than average students, while youngsters who show on their HFDs one of the seven Emotional Indicators that are related to achievement, will be most likely below average students. However, only 31 children or 27 percent of the second grade subjects showed either an Exceptional Item or one of the seven Emotional Indicators on their drawings. This means that it was not possible to make any predictions about the achievement of 73 percent of the second grade subjects from their HFDs.

A high score on the Information Subtest of the WISC by itself can predict with some assurance average or better than average achievement among second graders. But this does not imply that children who do not obtain a high score on the Information Test are necessarily poor students. The subjects whose Information score was not outstanding displayed a wide range of achievement scores, all the way from outstanding to very poor.

Test patterns of children admitted to special classes

More and more public schools are establishing special classes for children of normal intelligence who are unable to profit from regular classroom attendance. These youngsters have usually serious learning problems and behavior difficulties due to emotional disturbances and/or neurological impairment. Such classes may be designated as EH classes (Educationally Handicapped), LP classes (Learning Problems), NH classes (Neurologically Handicapped), ED/BI classes (Emotionally Disturbed and/or Brain Injured), or by any other name. They are all similar in that they offer children who are not mentally retarded (IQ 75 or higher) the chance to be in a small class with individualized instruction geared to their particular needs without undue pressure or competition. Since these special classes are still relatively new in most public school systems, there is still a need to determine a way of identifying children who would profit most from these classes.

The following study was carried out as a step toward developing a screening battery for the selection of special class students. It was hypothesized that the test patterns of children who had profited from special classes would show the way for the screening of potential candidates for such classes in the future. The two preceding studies showed that poor students in regular first and second grades tended to have perceptual malfunctioning as well as emotional problems and an absence of high intelligence. By definition, all special class pupils are poor students and can therefore be expected to show the same problems as other poor students only more intensified. For this reason, it was decided to administer to students in the special classes the Bender Gestalt Test as a measure of their maturation in visual-motor perception, the HFD Test as an indicator of their intellectual ability (Exceptional Items) and their emotional adjustment (Emotional Indicators), and a verbal test. The Information Subtest of the WISC was able to discriminate the good pupils in the second grade, but not the poor ones. A verbal test that would reveal difficulties in the verbal area was needed for the present study. Many special class students were known to suffer from poor auditory perception; it was decided therefore to use the Wepman Test of Auditory Discrimination (Wepman, 1958) as a third test.

The subjects for this study were 139 public-school children, age six to ten, who were admitted to the ED/BI classes of the Board of Cooperative Educational Services in Yorktown Heights, New York, between the fall of 1961 and the spring of 1965. All subjects in this study were supposedly of "normal intellectual potential"; they had an IQ range from 69–138. The 139 special class pupils included 22 children who were six years old; 35 children were seven years old; 34 were eight years old; 27 youngsters were age nine; and 21 children were ten years old. All subjects were seen by the writer within the first month after entering the special class program, at which time the Bender and the HFD Tests were administered. Unfortunately only about two-thirds of the children were tested with the Wepman Test. The results with this test are therefore incomplete.

The Bender records were scored according to the Koppitz system and were grouped as indicated on *Table 24*. The HFDs were checked for those Exceptional Items which were appropriate for each subject's age level. The drawings were then scored for the presence of all 30 Emotional Indicators which differentiated children with emotional problems from well-adjusted children *(Appendix E)*. It was assumed that special class pupils would suffer from a great variety of emotional problems, not all of which would be necessarily related to school achievement. Therefore, all of the Emotional Indicators were included in this study. The Wepman Test was scored according to the published instructions. All children whose error score fell one year below their chronological age level were considered to have poor auditory perception.

Figure 3 shows the pattern of the test performances for the 139 special class pupils according to their age levels. The following results were obtained when each of the three tests (the Bender, HFD and Wepman Test) was considered separately for all of the subjects as a group:

	Test performance	Number of Subjects	%
1. Bender Test:	poor or very poor visual-motor perception	85	61
2. Bender Test:	low or immature visual-motor perception	39	29
3. Wepman Test:	poor auditory perception (including 3 aphasics and 1 hard-of-hearing child)	32	23
4. HFD Test:	two or more of 30 Emotional Indicators	93	70
5. HFD Test:	one Emotional Indicator related to poor school achievement	75	54

When these signs of perceptual and emotional problems were combined the results were as follows:

	Number of Subjects	%
poor or immature visual-motor *and* poor auditory perception *and* emotional problems	21	15
poor or immature visual-motor *and* poor auditory perception	7	5
poor or immature visual-motor perception *and* emotional problems	78	56
poor auditory perception *and* emotional problems	1	1
poor or immature visual-motor perception *only*	18	13
poor auditory perception *only*	3	2
emotional problems *only*	7	5
no perceptual *or* emotional problems	4	3
Total	139	100

This means that the test performances of 77 percent of the special class pupils revealed two or more signs of perceptual and/or emotional problems; 20 percent of the students showed positive signs on at least one of the three tests used, while only 3 percent or four of the 139 special class subjects failed to exhibit any significant indicators of perceptual malfunctioning or emotional disturbance on either the Bender or the Wepman or the HFD Test.

Twelve of the subjects drew Exceptional Items on their HFDs. This is not surprising since many of the special class pupils were of high average or superior intelligence. However, with one exception, all of the bright youngsters with Exceptional Items on their drawings also showed signs of perceptual malfunctioning and/or emotional problems. Because of these, they were unable to progress in school satisfactorily despite their good mental ability. Thus, good intellectual potential by itself is not sufficient to assure good academic achievement. The absence of perceptual problems and of emotional disturbances, or the ability to overcome these, is required before a child can begin to live up to his intellectual potential.

Test Score Patterns for 139 Special Class Pupils

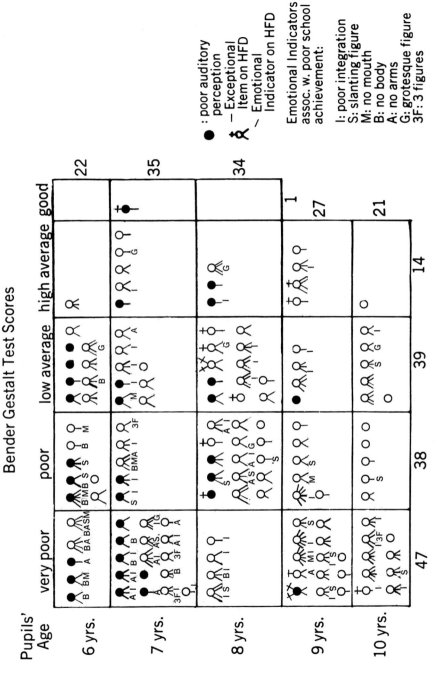

Figure 3.

The findings of this study show that most special class pupils suffer from multiple problems. Some educators and clinicians still advocate that emotionally disturbed and brain injured children be separated into different classes. Yet any such separation is at best arbitrary since most special class pupils exhibit *both* neurological impairment *and* emotional problems to varying degrees. It is often difficult to determine where one lets off and the other begins. This writer strongly advocates that special class pupils be grouped according to their age, size, level of maturation and above all according to their mental and social functioning and *not* according to diagnostic labels. This study shows that the HFD Test together with the Bender Test and the Wepman Test can be of value in the screening process of pupils for special classes and in the placing of children in class groups.

10. Practical Application of Findings on HFDs

In the preceding chapters, different aspects of the HFD Test were explored and discussed separately. The drawings of children, age five to twelve, were examined for Developmental Items and for Emotional Indicators, they were analyzed for clinical implications and for signs of brain injury, and they were combined with other tests for the screening of school beginners and of special class pupils. At this time, an attempt will be made to integrate all these findings and to apply them to individual HFDs of youngsters who were seen for psychological evaluation by the writer in the child guidance clinic or in a school. The children chosen for this presentation are considered to be rather typical of the kind of youngsters who are normally seen by clinical or school psychologists. The case histories and the HFDs of each child will be discussed in detail in order to demonstrate the wide range of usefulness of the drawings as well as their limitations. It will be seen that the HFDs offer insight into the children's mental ability and interpersonal relationships to varying degrees; some drawings are much more revealing than others.

Case 1: JoAnn, age six

JoAnn *(Plate 103)* was brought to the child guidance clinic by her mother who complained that the child was enuretic, restless, hypertalkative, very stubborn, and controlling. JoAnn did only what she wanted to do and threw temper tantrums when she did not get her way. It was learned that JoAnn's parents were separated and that the little girl and her mother lived with the grandparents. JoAnn, who was attending kindergarten, was also rebellious in school. Her behavior and her work were less than satisfactory even though she appeared to be of at least average intelligence. When JoAnn was seen for her initial interview at the clinic, she was six years and two months old. She was found to be a very attractive, well-developed, curly-haired girl who seemed eager for attention and approval. She appeared to be at ease and spoke freely. JoAnn was very cooperative during the testing session. She readily produced the HFD shown on *Plate 103* and chatted spontaneously as she drew: "That's a teenager—I want to be a teenager, I don't want to be a little girl anymore."

The following is a detailed analysis of JoAnn's HFD on *Plate 103:*

EXPECTED AND EXCEPTIONAL ITEMS (APPENDIX B). The drawing reveals all the Expected Items for six year old girls, as well as two of the Exceptional Items: Two lips and four or more pieces of clothing (blouse, skirt, socks, and shoes). Thus JoAnn's HFD score is $-0+2+5 = 7$. This indicates that she is most likely of high average or superior intelligence *(Appendix C)*. This hypothesis was confirmed when JoAnn obtained later in the session a WISC Full Scale IQ score of 120. Her verbal IQ score was 119, and her Performance score was 115.

EMOTIONAL INDICATORS (APPENDIX F). JoAnn's drawing shows only one Emotional Indicator: transparency (on sleeves and feet). The type of transparency exhibited on *Plate 103* is typical of immature and concretistic children and does not indicate any specific anxiety or disturbance. The presence of only one Emotional Indicator on a HFD is inconclusive (page 42) and cannot be regarded as a sign of psychopathology.

SCHOOL ACHIEVEMENT (PAGE 51). JoAnn drew none of the Emotional Indicators that are related to poor school achievement in the first grade. Since she appears to be of above-average intelligence, as shown by the Exceptional Items on her HFD and does not seem to have any serious emotional disturbance, it is predicted that she will be an average or probably above-average pupil in the first grade.

ORGANIC SIGNS ON HFD (APPENDIX G). There is nothing on JoAnn's HFD that would suggest brain injury. Only one item that occurred more often on the drawings of the neurologically impaired children appeared on JoAnn's HFD; this was the omission of hands. However, it is common for six year old children to draw either only hands or only fingers, so that this item by itself cannot be regarded as being diagnostically significant.

CLINICAL INTERPRETATION OF HFD. JoAnn depicted a teenager on her drawing, thereby indicating that she was dissatisfied with both her past and her present situation. She wanted to escape from home and from her dependent and helpless situation. She wanted to grow up. "I don't want to be a little girl anymore," JoAnn said. Being a little girl held no satisfaction for JoAnn; it may be assumed therefore that her needs were not being met in the home and that her relationship with her parents and grandparents was not good.

The way the figure on *Plate 103* is drawn reflects JoAnn's impulsivity, her determination and her attitudes. The large size of the drawing may be a result of her immaturity and her expansiveness, but it may also express her desire to be big. The girl on the picture is drawn so large that one arm and part of the skirt are cut off by the edge of the paper. It almost looks as if the figure was too confined on the page and is bursting out of the restrictions imposed on it by the boundaries of the paper, just as JoAnn was rebelling in real life against the restrictions placed on her. The large mouth of the figure might be thought of by some clinicians as a sign of oral needs which had not been met, but the large mouth may also be a sign of JoAnn's awareness of and concern over her hypertalkativeness. JoAnn was a very verbal child and much of her defiance and rebellion was expressed verbally. Her constant talking got her into much difficulty at home and in school. Aggressiveness is also suggested by the long fingers of the figure.

SUMMARY OF ANALYSIS OF HFD ON PLATE 103. From the drawing, it was hypothesized that JoAnn was a child of high average or superior intelligence with no indications of neurological impairment or serious emotional disturbances. However, she seemed to be dissatisfied with things as they were at home and was engaged in active rebellion against authority figures. She longed to escape from her dependent position as a little child and wanted to be grown-up, free and independent. She seemed to express much of her defiance verbally. JoAnn had the potential to be a good student in the first grade.

In a later interview with the mother, it was learned that JoAnn had reason to be dissatisfied with her situation at home, and had cause to rebel against the adults in her life. Her father had deserted her; her mother was quite cold and rejecting; and her grandparents were coercive and overly restrictive. The mother and grandparents did not agree on how to handle JoAnn, and JoAnn used this conflict to play the mother and the grandparents against each other and to defy all of them. At the same time, she longed for affection and recognition as was shown in the testing session. But there was no one in her home who could offer her warm and satisfying support and acceptance. So JoAnn registered her unhappiness and dissatisfaction in her rebellious behavior. Clearly, the problem lay in the family relationships and not in JoAnn as such.

Arrangements were made to see the mother and the grandmother for guidance on a regular basis. They were helped to agree on a reasonable way to handle JoAnn which was then followed by both of them. JoAnn was given more freedom and responsibilities within firm limits. She was treated with respect as an intelligent, independent human being who was in turn expected to conform to the household rules. Within a relatively short time, JoAnn responded to her mother's and grandmother's firm, consistent actions and changed her own attitude and behavior; she no longer wet the bed and was more cooperative in school and at home. JoAnn seemed happier and her schoolwork markedly improved. As a consequence, her mother could admit that now for the first time she was able to enjoy her daughter.

Case 2: Jake, age seven

Jake was one of those unhappy youngsters who are unusually tall and heavy while being extremely immature emotionally and socially. Jake had considerable difficulty in the first grade. He could not follow directions and was unable to read or to comprehend number concepts. He was a tense and anxious child with a very short attention span and much restlessness. In school, Jake was considered to be a disturbing influence; he upset the other children by running about, calling out and annoying them. The school principal and the teacher referred Jake's mother to the child guidance clinic for help. Jake's mother went along with this suggestion since she too had considerable trouble with him at home. Jake was constantly fighting with his younger sister, he exhibited many fears, was a fussy eater, cried easily, and wet the bed.

When Jake was seen at the child guidance clinic, he was seven years two months old. He was shy and tense but very cooperative. His appearance resembled more that of an eight year old than a seven year old boy, while his behavior was more like that of a six year old child. When asked to make an HFD, Jake produced the picture shown on *Plate 104*. He drew two figures, "a girl and a boy," but did not choose to discuss his HFD. Since Jake appeared to be quite anxious at this point, no attempt was made to probe any further into the meaning of his picture. The drawing speaks for itself.

The following is a detailed analysis of Jake's HFD on *Plate 104*:

EXPECTED AND EXCEPTIONAL ITEMS (APPENDIX B). Jake drew two figures which differ greatly from each other. For the scoring of the Expected and Exceptional Items, the more adequate of the two figures was selected so as to reflect the highest level of Jake's mental ability at that given time. Since the picture of the girl on *Plate 104* is more complete than the figure of the boy, the former was scored. Jake's girl showed none of the Exceptional Items and revealed an absence of one Expected Item (two dimensions on arms). The HFD score is therefore $-1+0+5 = 4$. This means that Jake was probably of low average to average intelligence (*Appendix C*) which concurs with his WISC IQ score of 86.

EMOTIONAL INDICATORS (APPENDIX F). When analyzing a drawing with more than one figure on it for Emotional Indicators, it seems logical to select for scoring the one figure that reveals the most emotional signs and concerns. For this reason, the figure of the boy on *Plate 104* was chosen as the one on which the Emotional Indicators were to be checked. It was found that Jake's boy showed two Emotional Indicators: omission of body and short arms. The presence of two Emotional Indicators on a drawing is regarded as a sign of emotional problems (page 42). Since the figure of the girl on Jake's drawing has a body while the boy does not, it must be concluded that this omission is a sign of castration anxiety. The short arms reflect withdrawal and helplessness.

SCHOOL ACHIEVEMENT. Jake's HFD shows an absence of the body on the figure of the boy. This particular Emotional Indicator was found to be associated with poor achievement in the first grade *(Table 17)*. In addition to emotional problems, Jake also seemed to have poor visual-motor perception since his performance on the Bender Gestalt Test was very poor. In view of his emotional and perceptual difficulties, it was predicted that Jake would show poor school progress (page 179).

ORGANIC SIGNS ON THE HFD (APPENDIX G). The better of the two figures on *Plate 104*, i.e., the drawing of the girl, was selected for the scoring of organic signs. It was considered essential that the drawing which best reflected Jake's mental potential be chosen for this analysis. Jake's drawing of the girl showed six items that had been found significantly more often on the HFDs of the brain injured children. These six items were: omission of neck, stickarms, arms horizontal, arms not at shoulder, sticklegs, and less than two pieces of clothing. On the basis of these findings, the possibility of brain injury cannot be ruled out for Jake and requires further exploration. This was particularly true since Jake's Bender Gestalt Test protocol also showed several indicators suggestive of neurological impairment.

CLINICAL INTERPRETATION OF HFD. Jake drew "a girl and a boy." It may be assumed that these figures represent his sister and himself. Since he drew the girl first and larger than the boy, it was hypothesized that much of Jake's anxiety and concern was centered around his only sister, who was five years old. Jake depicted the figure of the sister complete with a body but omitted the body from his own picture; it is therefore believed that Jake suffered from intense castration anxiety which was probably associated with the birth of his sister in some way. The figure of the boy was drawn with a large, open mouth as if he were crying out for help. The short arms suggest shyness and an inability to reach out toward others. The placement of the boy on the page indicates that he is "up in the air" compared to his sister who is placed closer to the bottom edge of the paper and who seems to have a slightly more secure footing.

SUMMARY OF ANALYSIS OF HFD ON PLATE 104. From the HFD on *Plate 104*, it was concluded that Jake was an unhappy, emotionally disturbed boy of low average to average intelligence who appeared to be suffering from intense castration anxiety and sibling rivalry. There was reason to predict that Jake's school achievement would be poor since he showed emotional and perceptual problems and lacked outstanding mental ability which might have helped him to overcome these difficulties. The HFD also suggested that Jake may be suffering from brain injury; however, this hypothesis needed confirmation from other test results and from his developmental and medical history.

From Jake's social history, it was learned that his birth had been traumatic and that his development in speech and walking had been unusually slow. At age three, he fell on his head and suffered a concussion. When Jake was four years old, his immature, coercive and punitive mother found him in the process of exploring his little sister's body. Jake was severely beaten on this occasion. In a later interview, the mother was able to trace Jake's fearfulness, his body anxiety and his enuresis back to this event. Jake had always been a fussy eater. Usually, he was a quiet and withdrawn child, but he was also subject to temper outbursts, especially when his sister got into his way. Jake's developmental, medical, and social history all point in the direction of neurological impairment, along with strong indications of emotional disturbance. This diagnosis was subsequently confirmed by a child psychiatrist, thus offering support for the impressions gathered from Jake's HFD.

Case 3: Craig, age seven

Craig was referred to the school psychologist to help determine his class placement. He was attending the first grade but was unable to do any of the work and found it difficult to conform to classroom routine or to participate in group activities. When seen for evaluation by the writer, Craig was seven years and two months old. He was most cooperative and eager to please, although he appeared to be a bit confused and bewildered and sought constant reassurance and support from the psychologist. Craig seemed to enjoy the testing session and the attention he was getting. He was completely unaware of his errors and his poor test performance. Craig was a well-developed, attractive, and friendly youngster. His speech was immature and it was noted that he had a strong tendency to perseverate. Whenever he received the least bit of encouragement or praise for an answer or action, he would repeat it over and over again until he was stopped.

Craig's HFD is shown on *Plate 105*. The following is an analysis of the HFD on *Plate 105*:

EXPECTED AND EXCEPTIONAL ITEMS (APPENDIX B). Craig drew no less than five figures on his HFD. The last of these was selected for scoring since it is much better than the other four. This figure, in the lower left-hand corner of *Plate 105*, exhibits none of the Exceptional Items and omits five of the Expected Items (nose, mouth, body, feet, and two dimensions of arms). Thus Craig's HFD score is $-5+0+5 = 0$ and suggests *(Appendix C)* that Craig is most likely a mentally retarded child.

EMOTIONAL INDICATORS (APPENDIX F). The little figure in the lower left-hand corner of *Plate 105* was also selected for the scoring of specific Emotional Indicators. This figure was the only one that was nearly complete, but even so it is grossly inadequate. The HFD shows no less than six Emotional Indicators: poor integration of parts, tiny figure, omission of nose, omission of mouth, omission of body, and three or more figures drawn spontaneously. Such a large number of Emotional Indicators occurs almost exclusively on the HFDs of children with serious emotional problems; it was, therefore, hypothesized that Craig was an emotionally disturbed child. The Emotional Indicators indicate that Craig was a very immature, poorly integrated, insecure, impulsive youngster who had a strong tendency to perseverate and who had difficulty communicating with others.

SCHOOL ACHIEVEMENT. Craig's HFD contained three of the Emotional Indicators (omission of mouth, omission of body, and three or more figures spontaneously drawn) which are specifically associated with poor achievement in the first grade *(Table 17)*. This alone would indicate that he was not yet ready for the first grade. Aside from that, Craig's HFD suggests mental deficiency and emotional disturbance, while his Bender Gestalt Test reflected gross malfunctioning in visual-motor perception, all of which made it most unlikely that Craig could benefit at that time from first grade attendance (page 179).

ORGANIC SIGNS ON HFD (APPENDIX G). Craig's drawing displays a total of ten items that occurred significantly more often on the HFDs of brain injured boys. These ten items are: no pupils, no neck, stickarms, arms horizontal, arms not at shoulder, incorrect number of fingers, sticklegs, no clothing items, poor integration of parts, and tiny figure. Judging from the HFD, there is a strong likelihood that Craig was a brain injured child. His performance on the Bender Gestalt Test was also highly indicative of neurological impairment.

CLINICAL INTERPRETATION OF HFD. *Plate 105* as a whole suggests that Craig was a very immature, poorly integrated, timid child who was groping toward finding himself as an individual. It is interesting that each of the five figures on the page differs from the others. On each figure, he added a little more than on the preceding one. First eyes, then eyebrows, then the mouth. On the fourth figure, Craig drew hair and a mouth but was unable to add the rest of the figure. On the fifth and last figure, Craig drew a head with arms and legs, but omitted the nose, mouth, and hair. It is as if Craig could only concentrate on one feature of the figure at a time; he did not perceive himself as a whole integrated person. The big, vacant eyes on the figures look out at the world in a vague, nonseeing way; the absence of the nose and the smallness of the figure suggest insecurity and withdrawal; the omission of the mouth on three of the five figures reflects Craig's difficulty in communicating with others. The drawing strongly indicates that Craig was as yet a "nonperson," an incomplete human being who needed a great deal of support, guidance and nurturance.

SUMMARY OF ANALYSIS OF HFD ON PLATE 105. From Craig's HFD, it is hypothesized that he was a mentally retarded, brain injured child with emotional problems who was in no way ready for formal schoolwork. He seemed to be grossly misplaced in the first grade.

Further psychological testing and information gathered from Craig's record offered support for the hypothesis stated above. It was learned that Craig had spent much of his kindergarten year in the hospital with a brain tumor and had undergone brain surgery because of it. The clinical record indicated that Craig was probably of normal intelligence prior to the development of the tumor and the brain operation. When the WISC was administered, Craig obtained a Verbal IQ score of 72, a Performance IQ score of less than 44, and a Full Scale IQ score of 55. There was considerable intertest scatter on the WISC. Most of the Subtest scores were on the defective level, but the Weighted Score on the Comprehension Subtest was 11 or normal, thereby supporting the report that Craig had been most likely of average intelligence prior to his brain pathology. Craig seemed to have retained the common sense, everyday reasoning ability he had had previously, while the higher mental processes of conceptualization, memory, and perception had been affected and had deteriorated. There was no doubt that Craig had suffered considerable brain injury as a result of his operation and that he was functioning at this point at the retarded level. It was not possible to predict if and how much of his former mental ability he might recover in time. It was obvious that he did not belong at this time in a first grade class.

Craig's teacher reported that his lack of judgment and his inability to follow directions made him something of an outsider with peers. Since Craig was a quiet, nonthreatening boy, other children did not bother him; they tolerated him good-naturedly or ignored him. They did not include him in their games. Craig was described as being a lonely child who was constantly in search of adult attention; he wanted to please but did not know how. In school, he faced constant frustration and failure which only added to his insecurity and restlessness. In view of Craig's HFD, all his other test results, and his medical and social history, it was recommended that Craig be transferred to a class for educable retarded children where his needs could be better met and where he would not be required to do work he was not able to do.

Case 4: Hubert, age eight

Hubert was brought to the child guidance clinic by his distraught mother because of severe behavior and learning problems. Hubert was said to be a moody child; some days he was very aggressive and at other times he was withdrawn. At no time was he able to complete his assignments in school and his peer relationships were always poor. Hubert had repeated the first grade and was now failing in the second grade.

When seen for psychological evaluation, Hubert was eight years and two months old. He was rather small for his age, but well-groomed and obviously well cared for. Hubert had a somewhat vague expression on his face and gave the impression of being a very unhappy, anxious, and disorganized child. Hubert answered all questions put to him with either yes or no. He offered no spontaneous comments and seemed to have difficulty concentrating and following directions. *Plate 106* shows the HFD Hubert made at the writer's request. The analysis of Hubert's HFD on *Plate 106* follows:

EXPECTED AND EXCEPTIONAL ITEMS (APPENDIX B). Hubert drew one Exceptional Item (nostrils) and omitted two of the Expected Items (feet and two dimensions on legs). His HFD score is therefore $-2+1+5 = 4$, which indicates that his mental ability is probably in the low average to average range *(Appendix C)*.

EMOTIONAL INDICATORS (APPENDIX F). The drawing on *Plate 106* shows three Emotional Indicators (poor integration of parts, big figure, and big hand). Three Emotional Indicators are usually a sign of serious emotional difficulties. The specific Emotional Indicators drawn suggest that Hubert had poor personality integration along with a tendency toward expansiveness and overt aggressiveness.

SCHOOL ACHIEVEMENT. The presence of three Emotional Indicators on the HFD reveals that Hubert had emotional problems. One of these Emotional Indicators (poor integration of parts) is specifically related to poor achievement in the second grade *(Table 17)*. Hubert's performance on the Bender Gestalt Test showed that he had also very poor visual-motor perception. The combination of emotional and perceptual problems is apt to interfere with academic progress and is highly suggestive of learning problems in school, despite average or near average intelligence (page 185).

ORGANIC SIGNS ON HFD (APPENDIX G). The HFD on *Plate 106* shows six signs that appeared significantly more often on the drawings of the eight year old brain injured boys. These signs are: omission of pupils, arms horizontal, arms incorrectly attached, stick legs, only one piece of clothing, and poor integration of parts. In view of the large number of organic signs on *Plate 106*, the possibility of cortical malfunctioning could not be ruled out and further testing for brain injury seemed indicated.

CLINICAL INTERPRETATION. Hubert's HFD looks quite grotesque although there is no indication that he intended to make a grotesque figure or monster. Rather it is believed that Hubert's drawing reflects a disorganized mental state and his feeling about himself. The most outstanding feature on the HFD on *Plate 106* is the treatment of the head. The head is not clearly separated from the body; it is merely an extension of the body and ends in a point. This type of drawing is not too common and has been found by the writer only on HFDs of very disturbed, disorganized and schizoid children with intense feelings of mental inadequacy. The pointed head seems to be akin to the tiny head and reveals that Hubert thought of himself as being mentally inadequate and as having no brain. Hubert appeared to be ruled by his impulses which had overwhelmed his intellectual controls. Much insecurity is also shown in the drawing of the short, weak legs and by the omission of the feet. The legs are hardly big and strong enough to support the massive body of the figure. The arms on *Plate 106* represent quite a contrast to the legs. They are enormous and suggest considerable overt aggressiveness. The eyes on Hubert's HFD are mere slits. It is as if he were blinded by the bright light of day around him and were reluctant to face it. Just as pupils contract when light is too strong, so Hubert himself seems to contract and to withdraw from an overpowering surrounding. Thus Hubert's HFD displays signs of both aggressiveness and withdrawal.

SUMMARY OF ANALYSIS OF HFD ON PLATE 106. From Hubert's drawing, it was hypothesized that he was a seriously disturbed, very insecure, impulse-ridden child of low average to average mental ability who felt intellectually grossly inadequate and who could not cope with the world about him. He appeared to be ambivalent in his attitudes since he exhibited signs of both withdrawal and overt aggressiveness. The quality of the drawing showed very poor integrative capacity and possible personality disorganization and neurological impairment. It was predicted that his school achievement would be poor.

The impressions gained from the HFD were supported by Hubert's social and clinical record. Hubert was so disturbed at the time of testing that the IQ score he obtained at that time could not be regarded as valid. His score on the Stanford-Binet Scale was only 70. A week later, the Raven's Progressive Matrices were administered to Hubert. On this test, he obtained an IQ score of 81. It was felt that Hubert's true IQ level was probably in the low 80's or the low average range.

From the parents, it was learned that they had adopted Hubert when he was about 10 months old after he had been found abandoned in a parking lot. At the time, he had shown many signs of neglect and deprivation and was grossly undernourished. The adoptive parents were warm and stable people who provided a comfortable home for Hubert and offered him many cultural and social advantages. The adoptive parents were devoutly religious people who firmly believed that love and prayer could overcome all the bad effects of Hubert's early life. Hubert had always been small for his age, but after a year of loving and tender care, Hubert appeared to be a happy and normal child. When he entered school it became, however, soon apparent that he could not hold his own with the other children of the neighborhood. The average IQ of pupils in the school Hubert attended was well above average. No matter how hard he tried, he just could not meet the demands of the school. Although Hubert showed no medical evidence of brain injury and despite a negative EEG, Hubert's behavior and his learning difficulties were highly suggestive of neurological impairment. It is quite possible that his severe early deprivation might have resulted in some permanent cortical malfunctioning. Hubert was a good child who wanted to please his parents, but he could not succeed in school. As his frustrations increased, he had become more and more aggressive and more and more disturbed. It was apparent that Hubert was grossly misplaced in his school where much more was expected of him than he could possibly produce. Recommendations were made for playtherapy and for transfer to a special class for children with emotional problems or to a private school with less academic emphasis.

Case 5: Juan, age nine

The teacher referred Juan to the school psychologist as she was puzzled by his behavior and wanted help in understanding the boy. Juan appeared to be of normal intelligence but he just could not learn to read and seemed to have difficulties retaining what little he did learn. Juan had been kept back in kindergarten since he was much smaller and more immature than his peers at that time. Now he was in the third grade and was still small for his age and immature; his speech was infantile. Juan presented no behavior problems, but he fatigued easily and was stubborn at times. It was difficult to hold his attention.

Juan was nine years six months old when he was seen by the psychologist. He was subdued but cooperative. Juan only spoke in response to direct questions and volunteered no information other than that he did not like school. Juan's HFD is shown on *Plate 107*. The analysis of Juan's HFD on *Plate 107* is given below:

EXPECTED AND EXCEPTIONAL ITEMS (APPENDIX B). Juan's drawing reveals all of the Expected Items and one of the Exceptional Items (nostrils). His HFD score is therefore —0+1+5 = 6, and indicates that Juan is probably of average to superior intelligence *(Appendix C)*.

EMOTIONAL INDICATORS (APPENDIX F). The drawing on *Plate 107* exhibits three Emotional Indicators (crossed eyes, teeth, and clinging arms) thereby suggesting that Juan has serious emotional problems. It is interesting to note that the three Emotional Indicators reflect conflicting tendencies. The crossed eyes and the teeth reveal hostile and aggressive attitudes, while the clinging arms show rigid self-control and difficulty in making contact with others.

SCHOOL ACHIEVEMENT. It is not possible to predict the school achievement of a nine year old boy solely from his HFD (page 51). But when the HFD is combined with other tests, it takes on predictive ability. Juan's responses to the HFD Test, the Bender and Wepman Test reveal a pattern that is similar to that of special class pupils (see *Figure 3*). The HFD shows that Juan has adequate intelligence but that he suffers from emotional disturbances; his performance on the Bender Gestalt Test and the Wepman Test of Auditory Discrimination both reflected perceptual malfunctioning. The dual handicap of emotional and perceptual problems is apt to interfere with school achievement irrespective of the child's mental ability (page 187).

ORGANIC SIGNS ON HFDS (APPENDIX G). Juan's HFD shows three signs that occurred significantly more often on the drawings of the brain injured boys. The signs are: omission of neck, wrong number of fingers, and less than four pieces of clothing. The possibility of neurological impairment cannot be ruled out therefore and further exploration in this regard was indicated.

CLINICAL INTERPRETATION OF HFD. Juan said of his drawing: "A man, he works—he is 30 years old." This is a description and not a story; therefore, the drawing does not constitute a wish-dream. The man Juan drew represents most likely his father, thus indicating that his chief concern and anxiety focused on his father. The way the figure was drawn reveals Juan's own attitudes. The teeth and the crossed eyes show considerable anger and hostility, probably directed toward the father. Juan was a small and frail youngster who could not stand up and fight even if he wanted to do so, so instead he tried to control his hostile impulses as is shown by the rigidly clinging arms on *Plate 107*. The big ears may reflect Juan's uneasiness about not always understanding what others are saying due to his poor auditory perception. The drawing of the big pocket and the treatment of the right foot on the HFD suggest that Juan might have sought relief from his tensions through masturbatory activity.

SUMMARY OF ANALYSIS OF HFD ON PLATE 107. Juan's drawing suggests that he was a child of average to superior intelligence with serious emotional problems. He appeared to be suffering from considerable anger and hostility which was apparently directed toward his father but which he could not express openly. Juan found it difficult to relate to others and probably sought relief from his anxieties in masturbation. The HFD also suggested the possibility of neurological malfunctioning. This hypothesis was supported by Juan's poor performance on the Bender Gestalt Test and the Wepman Test of Auditory Discrimination. In view of all these signs of emotional and perceptual difficulties, it was predicted that Juan would show poor academic progress despite good intelligence.

Further testing and information gathered from Juan's social history confirmed the impressions gained from Juan's HFD on *Plate 107*. At age seven, Juan's Full Scale IQ score on the WISC had been 103 or average. A more recent WISC IQ score was only 90. This indicates that Juan had indeed average mental potential but that emotional and perceptual problems were interfering with his intellectual functioning and with his school achievement. It was learned that Juan's mother was weak and ineffectual, while his father was quite authoritarian and punitive. The father blamed the boy's poor school progress on his "laziness" and tried to coerce Juan into doing better. The mother reported that Juan was stubborn and sullen at home; he did not rebel openly against the father, but on occasion, he threw a temper tantrum and once he set a fire in the home. Juan's slow early development and lingering immaturity pointed to neurological impairment but no results from an EEG or a neurological examination were available. It was therefore not possible to either confirm or reject the hypothesis of possible brain injury.

Case 6: Mary, age nine

Mary had a history of epilepsy. She had suffered from numerous Petit Mal seizures each day until a year ago when it had been possible to bring the seizures under control with the aid of medication. For many months, Mary had rarely shown more than one or at most two attacks a day. Her parents became alarmed when Mary showed again a marked increase in the number of daily seizures and when she burst into tears at the least provocation. Mary appeared to be troubled and unhappy. The family physician referred the family to the child guidance clinic for consultation.

Mary was seen for evaluation by the writer at the clinic. At the time, she was nine years and five months old. She appeared to be a bit vague, but was very friendly, cooperative and quite chatty. Mary produced the HFD shown on *Plate 108*. The following is the analysis of the HFD on *Plate 108*:

EXPECTED AND EXCEPTIONAL ITEMS (APPENDIX B). Mary's drawing shows none of the Exceptional Items and omits four of the Expected Items for nine year old girls: nose, arms, arms in two dimensions, and hair. Her HFD score is $-4+0+5 = 1$ and suggests *(Appendix C)* that Mary was either a mentally retarded child and/or that she was so seriously disturbed that she was functioning on the retarded level.

EMOTIONAL INDICATORS (APPENDIX F). *Plate 108* exhibits five Emotional Indicators: transparency, legs pressed together, clouds, omission of nose, and omission of arms, thus disclosing that Mary had serious emotional problems. The Emotional Indicators presented on the HFD are suggestive of withdrawal, helplessness, acute anxiety and guilt and a feeling of severe pressure from above.

SCHOOL ACHIEVEMENT. HFDs alone are not good predictors of school achievement for nine year old girls, but together with other tests, they can predict such achievement. Mary's responses to the HFD Test and the Bender Test are quite similar to those of special class pupils *(Figure 3)*. On her HFD, Mary revealed mental retardation and/or serious emotional problems. Her performance on the Bender Gestalt Test was indicative of gross malfunctioning in visual-motor perception as well. The combined test pattern suggested that Mary would have poor school achievement (page 185).

ORGANIC SIGNS ON HFDs (APPENDIX G). Mary's HFD shows only one of the organic signs for nine year olds: less than four pieces of clothing. The quality of the drawing is poor and suggests poor fine muscle coordination; the lines of the legs and feet overlap but this cannot be really scored for poor integration of parts. Mary's drawing is inconclusive for the diagnosis of brain injury. It is not possible to make any generalizations from Mary's HFD concerning drawings of epileptic children. Nothing was found in the literature regarding figure drawings of youngsters with Grand Mal and Petit Mal seizures, and the writer's experience with drawings of epileptic children is limited. One can only speculate whether these youngsters as a group tend to reveal the "typical" organic signs on their HFDs or not.

CLINICAL INTERPRETATION OF HFD. The HFD on *Plate 108* indicates considerable anxiety on Mary's part. The figure on the drawing was described by Mary as "a girl." To the casual observer, the figure on *Plate 108* looks like a boy, yet Mary stated specifically that it was a girl. This points up the danger of determining the sex of a figure on a drawing without inquiring into the child's intention. Nowadays, the wearing of pants and slacks is commonplace for both boys and girls, and both males and females wear their hair either long or short. It is often difficult to separate the sexes on the basis of their appearance both in real life and on drawings.

The girl on Mary's HFD is walking under a black cloud and under a heavily shaded black sun. The girl looks as though she were floating helplessly in the air without secure footing. She seems immobile since her legs are pressed together and she cannot step forward; she cannot reach out toward others since she lacks arms; she has retreated into herself and has "pulled in" her nose, unable to forge ahead. The girl on *Plate 108* looks constricted and frozen, with a foolish grin on her face, in a big threatening world. On her drawing, Mary expresses the feeling of being under much pressure from authority figures at home and/or in school (the black clouds and the black sun). She appears to feel guilty because of her poor achievement (omission of arms) and would like to withdraw in the face of the overwhelming demands that are made on her; Mary would like to retreat to the time a year or two ago when less was expected of her. The girl on the HFD was said to be only eight years old while Mary was actually 9½ years old.

Mary said of her HFD: "It's a girl, eight years old, walking. She is going to her friends house. Her mother said she could go. She is happy when she can play and play." Mary clearly indicated her anxiety and unhappiness about her condition and her desire to escape from hard work and to play instead. She seems to look for comfort and support to her peers; being a good girl, she longed for her mother's permission to play instead of having to work.

SUMMARY OF ANALYSIS OF HFD ON PLATE 108. From Mary's drawing, it was concluded that she was probably a mentally retarded girl with serious emotional problems. Or else that she was so disturbed that she was functioning on a retarded level. Mary seemed to feel overpowered by demands made on her by authority figures at home or in school or both. She showed signs of acute anxiety and guilt and displayed on the drawing a desire to withdraw from the situation she was in at present. From her HFD and from her Bender Gestalt Test results, it was predicted that she would have considerable difficulty in school and could not be expected to perform up to grade level.

On the basis of Mary's HFD it was hypothesized that she felt under considerable pressure from her environment and that the increase in Petit Mal seizures might be a direct response to the undue strain and anxiety she was experiencing. On the WISC, Mary obtained a Verbal IQ score of 70, a Performance IQ score of 64 and a Full Scale IQ score of 64. It was therefore recommended that the parents request the school to transfer Mary from a regular class to a class for slow learners or a class for educable retarded children. The parents were also urged to reduce their expectations for Mary. Within days after such a transfer was put into effect, Mary seemed greatly relieved and was once again her cheerful self. The number of daily seizures diminished again to their earlier infrequent rate and Mary rarely cried.

Case 7: Roger, age ten

Roger was referred to the school psychologist because of his disruptive behavior in the classroom. The teacher reported that he was constantly trying to get attention; he told "whoppers," took things from other children, was impulsive and showed poor inner controls. Roger did not like to be corrected and cried when he had to do an assignment over again. His schoolwork was usually carelessly done, and much of the time, Roger was somewhere "off in space;" he fantasized out loud and moved about noisily.

Roger was ten years and nine months of age when he was seen by this psychologist. He was a tall, attractive, but poorly coordinated youngster. He related easily to the examiner and was most cooperative. Roger seemed to enjoy the attention he was receiving and tried hard to please. But his attention span was short and he was subject to mood swings, vacillating between enthusiastic outbursts and angry withdrawal. When asked to make an HFD, Roger produced the large figure shown on *Plate 109*. The following is an analysis of Roger's HFD on *Plate 109*:

EXPECTED AND EXCEPTIONAL ITEMS (APPENDIX B). *Plate 109* reveals one Exceptional Item (knees) while two of the Expected Items for ten year old boys (neck and arms pointing down) are missing. Roger's HFD score is therefore $-2+1+5 = 4$ and indicates that he is probably of low average to average intelligence *(Appendix C)*.

EMOTIONAL INDICATORS (APPENDIX F). Roger's HFD shows four Emotional Indicators (big figure, teeth, short arms, and omission of neck) and thereby reflects the presence of emotional problems. The four Emotional Indicators drawn by Roger suggest that he was an impulsive and expansive youngster with hostile attitudes which he was unable to act out overtly.

SCHOOL ACHIEVEMENT. The school achievement of ten year old boys cannot be predicted from HFDs alone; however, when the drawings are combined with other tests, they have predictive value. Roger's intellectual potential appeared to be within the normal range (Exceptional Item on HFD); however, the presence of emotional disturbances (Emotional Indicators on the HFD) and malfunctioning in visual-motor perception (poor score on the Bender Gestalt Test) are apt to interfere with his school achievement (page 187). It was therefore hypothesized that Roger would be a poor student in school.

ORGANIC SIGNS ON HFD (APPENDIX G). Roger's drawing on *Plate 109* exhibits six signs that occurred more often on the HFDs of the brain injured boys; these six signs are: no pupils, no neck, arms horizontal, arms incorrectly attached, incorrect number of fingers, and less than four pieces of clothing. In view of the relatively high incidence of organic signs on Roger's HFD, the possibility of neurological impairment must be considered and warrants further investigation.

CLINICAL INTERPRETATION OF HFD. Roger commented as he drew the figure on *Plate 109*: "He's a general . . . he is mad . . . U.S. cavalry . . . in the fort walking down stairs . . . attack by Indians . . . he commands the Army . . . takes them to victory . . . he is the hero!" This drawing clearly shows that Roger, who had met with much failure and frustration in school and real life, sought satisfaction in fantasy. The drawing and the story associated with it represents a wishdream. In his imagination, Roger depicted himself as a person of importance and power, as an angry and victorious general. Roger seems to be saying in his drawing: "I am mad and angry at the Indians (siblings and peers?) who attack me and give me a rough time. I will make war on them and show them who I really am. I will defeat them. I am a hero."

The way the general is drawn reflects Roger's feelings toward himself and others. He perceived himself (accurately) as being big and clumsy. The enormous mouth with the ferocious line of teeth on the drawing and the relatively large hands reveal Roger's hostile and aggressive attitudes toward others, but the short, stubby arms suggest that he is unable to reach out and to act out his hostility and anger. The absence of the neck and the merging of the head with the huge body of the figure on *Plate 109* show that Roger is overwhelmed by his impulses and lacks strong cortical control over his actions and thoughts. Expansiveness and poor inner control are also reflected by the size of the figure and by the poor differentiation of its details and parts.

SUMMARY OF ANALYSIS OF HFD ON PLATE 109. From his HFD, it was concluded that Roger was a very impulsive, poorly controlled boy of low average to average intelligence who had emotional problems and suffered also most likely from neurological impairment. This latter hypothesis was also supported by his poor performance on the Bender Gestalt Test. In view of Roger's many indicators of emotional problems on the drawing and his poor Bender Test record, it was predicted that he would have considerable difficulty with school achievement. Roger appeared to have a very poor self-concept. He had much hostility and anger which he was evidently not able to express overtly; instead, he seemed to find relief and satisfaction in wish-fulfilling fantasies and imaginative stories in which he was the conquering hero.

When the WISC was administered to Roger, he obtained a Verbal IQ of 99, a Performance IQ of 97, and a Full Scale IQ 98, thereby confirming the conclusion from the HFD that he was of average intelligence. Roger gave the impression of being very insecure and of wanting acceptance and recognition desperately. It was learned that he was the youngest of six siblings. He was the only boy in the family and as such was often teased and bossed by his five older and more adequate sisters. The father and mother often compared him unfavorably with his sisters, all of whom were outstanding students in school. Roger did not excel in anything, with the possible exception of making up stories and daydreaming.

Unfortunately, nothing was known in school about Roger's early life and development other than that he had had several serious illnesses in infancy. The hypothesis of brain injury could not be confirmed since no medical reports were available. But his behavior and his responses on the psychological tests left little doubt that Roger suffered from some kind of cortical malfunctioning in addition to his emotional difficulties.

It was recommended therefore that he be treated in school *as if* he were a brain injured child with perceptual and emotional problems even though no official diagnosis was available. It was further suggested that Roger be given a neurological examination and an EEG.

Case 8: Susan, age ten

Susan had been known to the child guidance clinic for a number of years. When she was seven years old, she had been seen at the clinic for playtherapy on a regular basis. At that time, she had shown many signs of emotional disturbances as well as evidence of mild retardation. When Susan was eight years old, her behavior had markedly improved and she seemed to be doing fairly well in a class for slow learners. Treatment at the clinic was therefore discontinued. Now Susan had reached pre-adolescence and had shown marked moodiness and outbursts of aggressiveness and stubborn negativism. Both her mother and her teacher found her at times extremely difficult to cope with. When Susan was ten years and nine months old, her mother renewed the contact with the child guidance clinic and requested a reevaluation of her daughter.

Susan was literally dragged into the clinic by her mother. Once there, Susan was most reluctant to accompany the writer to her office. After some firm but gentle persuasion, Susan finally shuffled into the psychologist's office and plunked herself into a chair. She glared at the examiner, set her jaw defiantly and refused to say a word. Then Susan sullenly faced the blank wall and let it be known that she was not about to cooperate. Susan was completely negativistic and would have nothing to do with the writer until the latter asked her to make an HFD. Somewhat reluctantly, Susan complied with this request and produced the drawing shown on *Plate 110a*. When asked to comment on her drawing, Susan did not respond. The psychologist proceded to guess who the figure might represent, but Susan did not answer until she was asked: "Is it you?" Thereupon, Susan blurted out: "It's not me" and refused to utter another word. Under the circumstances, it seemed rather pointless to attempt any further testing of Susan. After explaining to the girl the purpose of her visit to the clinic and the function of the tests, the session was discontinued.

A week later, Susan was seen again at the clinic. This time she appeared to be in a much better mood; she was quite cooperative and talkative. Once again, Susan was asked to make an HFD. Her second drawing is shown on *Plate 110b*. The similarities and the contrast between the two drawings on *Plate 110* are striking. The following is an analysis of the two HFDs on *Plate 110*:

EXPECTED AND EXCEPTIONAL ITEMS (APPENDIX B). *Plate 110a* reveals no Exceptional Item and shows the absence of three Expected Items (mouth, neck, and arms pointing downward). The HFD score for this drawing is therefore $-3+0+5 = 2$ and indicates that Susan is probably of borderline intelligence with an IQ score somewhere between 60 and 80. *Plate 110b* is identical to *Plate 110a* except that the mouth is present on this drawing, so that the HFD score for this HFD is $-2+0+5 = 3$. This score implies that Susan is probably of low average intelligence and has an IQ score between 70 and 90. It follows therefore that both *Plate 110a* and *Plate 110b* suggest that Susan's IQ score is somewhere between 70 and 80 *(Appendix C)*.

When tested with the WISC, Susan actually obtained a Full Scale IQ score of 77, with a Verbal IQ score of 84 and a Performance IQ score of 74. The HFD scores of both of Susan's drawings placed her therefore in the correct range of mental ability, even though the score for *Plate 110a* was depressed by Susan's negative attitude. It appears that the basic and essential features of her drawings were not greatly altered by her temporary emotional state.

EMOTIONAL INDICATORS (APPENDIX F). *Plate 110a* exhibits three Emotional Indicators (no mouth, no neck, and long arms) and a strong tendency toward a fourth Emotional Indicator (big hands). Although the hands are not quite large enough to be scored as "big hands" (they would have to be as large as the face), they are unusually large and clearly reflect aggressive attitudes. *Plate 110b* reveals the same Emotional Indicators as *Plate 110a* with the exception of the omission of the mouth. From the number and kinds of Emotional Indicators on both drawings, it can be concluded that Susan has emotional problems and that she is an impulsive and overtly aggressive child who can be quite negativistic.

SCHOOL ACHIEVEMENT. The omission of the mouth had been found to be related to poor school achievement in the primary grades *(Table 17)*. This indicator seems to show that any young child who is so negativistic that he will not talk and will not cooperate is also apt to do poorly in school. The same seems to apply also to older children with strong negativistic tendencies who omit the mouth from their HFDs. It seemed certain that Susan's unwillingness to cooperate at times was bound to interfere also with her school progress. Beyond that, Susan revealed signs of emotional disturbances on her HFD (two or more Emotional Indicators) and showed every indication of modest mental endowment. Her performance on the Bender Gestalt Test was also exceedingly poor and it was suspected that her auditory perception was also impaired. All of these factors together suggest that Susan was well placed in a special class for slow learners and that she could not be expected to produce schoolwork in keeping with her age level (page 185).

ORGANIC SIGNS ON THE HFD (APPENDIX G). Susan exhibited four signs on *Plate 110* which had been found to occur significantly more often on the drawings of the ten year old brain injured children. These are: omission of neck, arms pointing upward, arms incorrectly attached, and lack of clothing detail. Because of the presence of these signs on the HFD, the possibility of neurological impairment cannot be ruled out and further investigations were indicated.

CLINICAL INTERPRETATION OF HFD. Susan designated her first drawing as representing "not me." Her second drawing was spontaneously labeled as "My sister Sally. She is six years old and has blond curly hair. She does not look like me." Through this drawing, Susan clearly revealed her intense sibling rivalry with her younger sister who was more attractive than Susan. By emphasizing that the curly-haired sister "does not look like me,"

Susan showed that she was painfully aware of her own plain appearance and of her mouse-colored, straight, stringy hair. Her self-concept was extremely poor. The huge hands and long arms of the figures on *Plate 110* reflect Susan's aggressiveness and hostile attitude, while the absence of the neck reveals her impulsivity and poor inner controls. The placement of the drawings on the paper further suggests that she was "up in the air" and lacked sound footing and emotional stability. The omission of the mouth is of course a sign of extreme negativism and a refusal to communicate with others. This in turn reflects her poor interpersonal relationships.

SUMMARY OF ANALYSIS OF HFD ON PLATE 110. From Susan's two HFDs on *Plate 110,* it was hypothesized that she was of borderline to low average intelligence. She seemed to be an aggressive, hostile, impulsive, and negativistic child with a poor self-concept. Susan appeared to be suffering from intense sibling rivalry with her younger sister. Her drawings are not incompatible with a diagnosis of brain injury. In view of her apparently limited mental ability, her emotional problems and poor perceptual functioning (as shown on the Bender Gestalt Test and the Wepman Test), it can be predicted that Susan will have considerable difficulty with her school achievement. She cannot be expected to hold her own with other ten year old girls of normal intelligence.

From the guidance clinic records, it was learned that Susan had been a normal, full term baby who had suffered from two bouts of pneumonia with high fever and convulsions in infancy which may have resulted in neurological impairment. Susan's development in all areas had been slow. At age seven, her EEG had been abnormal and she had been diagnosed as being a brain injured child. It was also discovered that Susan was constantly fighting with her more attractive and more capable younger sister who was the undisputed darling of the family. Thus, the impressions gained from the HFDs were confirmed by Susan's case history. It was concluded that Susan was well placed in the class for slow learners but that she could benefit at that time from a period of supportive therapy at the clinic.

Case 9: Cathy, age eleven

Cathy had always been a good student in school. She was usually a quiet but cheerful child who was well liked by her peers and teachers. But now that Cathy was in the sixth grade, she seemed to have changed. She suddenly withdrew from others, seemed preoccupied, and spent much of her time daydreaming. She neglected her schoolwork and her grades went down. The teachers were concerned about Cathy and referred her to the school psychologist, in order to find out what was troubling the girl.

When Cathy was seen by the writer, she was timid and a bit absent-minded but very cooperative. She readily complied with the request to make an HFD. Her drawing is shown on *Plate 111*. The following is an analysis of the HFD on *Plate 111*:

EXPECTED AND EXCEPTIONAL ITEMS (APPENDIX B). Cathy's drawing reveals none of the Exceptional Items and omits none of the Expected Items for eleven year old girls. Her HFD score was therefore 5 and indicates that she was probably of average to high average intelligence *(Appendix C)*.

 EMOTIONAL INDICATORS (APPENDIX F). The HFD on *Plate 111* shows only one Emotional Indicator, "slanting figure." One Emotional Indicator cannot be regarded necessarily as a sign of psychopathology or serious emotional disturbance (page 42). The slanting figure suggests that Cathy was somewhat off balance and was very unsure of herself, but it did not indicate, by itself, that Cathy was a girl with severe emotional problems.

ORGANIC SIGNS ON HFD (APPENDIX G). Cathy's drawing exhibited only one sign that had occurred significantly more often on the HFDs of the brain injured children. This item was slanting figure. From only one sign on an HFD, it is not possible to hypothesize either the presence or the absence of neurological impairment in a child.

CLINICAL INTERPRETATION OF HFD. The most outstanding features of Cathy's HFD are the position of the hands and the omission of pants. Cathy commented as she drew: "He is about six years old, he is going to the bathroom." The fact that Cathy drew a boy suggests that she was concerned with a boy or boys. Since Cathy did not have a little brother, it was hypothesized that Cathy was interested in boys as such rather than in a particular boy. The boy on *Plate 111* is six years old but looks older. The figure's age may reflect Cathy's own desire to return to an age when she was younger and did not have to worry about boys or a wish that boys would be only six years old, an age level at which they were neither threatening nor upsetting as males.

Cathy stated that the boy on *Plate 111* was "going to the bathroom," thus justifying the absence of pants and the position of the hands. The boy on the drawing is carefully shielding his penis, and by this very gesture, he is drawing attention to his genital region. This drawing strongly suggests that Cathy, a budding adolescent, was at the time greatly preoccupied with male sexuality. It can only be conjectured that she might have been exposed to some sexual activities or to sexual information which had upset her. At Cathy's age, it was only natural that she should become interested in sexual matters, but it appeared that she was overwhelmed by such thoughts to the exclusion of everything else.

SUMMARY OF ANALYSIS OF HFD ON PLATE 111. From the HFD, it is gathered that Cathy was probably of average to high average intelligence. There is no indication of serious psychopathology, but it appears that Cathy was at the time reacting to a specific sexual trauma and to her own awakening sexual impulses. She seemed to be preoccupied with thoughts about male sexuality to the exclusion of all else which may account for her failure to attend to her schoolwork. Her sexual concern and anxiety appeared to be so strong that it threw her off balance and interfered with her daily life.

Further testing and an interview with Cathy revealed that she was indeed of high average intelligence. Her WISC Full Scale IQ score was 114, with a Verbal IQ score of 115, and a Performance IQ score of 110. Cathy admitted being worried about sex and boys. It appeared that some older boys on the school bus had taken it upon themselves to enlighten the younger children about the facts of life in rather crude and graphic terms. Since Cathy was a very sensitive and somewhat timid child, she did not ask adults for further information or clarification; instead, she kept thinking about what she had heard and seen. Since Cathy had no brothers and had always lived a protected life, her knowledge of and experience with boys was limited. Cathy had become so obsessed with her thoughts and fears until she could no longer concentrate on her schoolwork. Cathy was clearly in need of some information and counselling in sexual matters.

Case 10: Gus, age eleven

Gus was a rather disorganized, schizoid youngster who had attended a special class for children with emotional problems for over three years. He was seen by the writer for routine reevaluation when he was eleven years and three months old. Gus was a social isolate among his peers who considered him a bit odd. But Gus related easily to adults; he was always eager for attention. Gus was most cooperative during the testing session—in his own fashion. He was extremely talkative and unusually distractible. Most of the time he distracted himself. Any chance word or phrase he might utter could start Gus off on a whole new trend of thought. Because of this, it was very difficult for him to follow through on any one idea or topic of conversation. As a result, Gus' verbalizations were often bizarre and incoherent despite his good intellectual potential. His performance on the HFD Test was equally disorganized and unusual.

Gus was very willing to draw a whole person and began by drawing the feet and legs, then he made the head and finally he added the body in between the legs and the head. He drew the figure in disconnected bits and pieces and tried to join them together afterwards. The result is shown on *Plate 112*. The following is the analysis of Gus' HFD on *Plate 112*:

EXPECTED AND EXCEPTIONAL ITEMS (APPENDIX B). Gus produced none of the Exceptional Items and omitted none of the Expected Items for eleven year old boys on his HFD. His HFD score is therefore —0+0+5 =5. This indicates that Gus is most likely of average to high average intelligence (*Appendix C*).

EMOTIONAL INDICATORS (APPENDIX F). The drawing on *Plate 112* reveals three Emotional Indicators: poor integration of parts, short arms, and clinging arms. The presence of three Emotional Indicators on a HFD is regarded as a sign of emotional disturbances. The specific Indicators depicted suggest that Gus is a poorly integrated, withdrawn boy who is unable to establish close social relationships with others.

SCHOOL ACHIEVEMENT. Gus was a special class pupil (page 187) and his test results were in keeping with what one might expect from such students. Gus revealed evidence of emotional disturbances on his HFD (three Emotional Indicators) while his performance on the Bender Gestalt Test showed serious malfunctioning in visual-motor perception. Because of emotional and perceptual problems, Gus' school achievement was apt to be poor despite average intelligence.

ORGANIC SIGNS ON THE HFD (APPENDIX G). The HFD on *Plate 112* shows three of the signs that occurred significantly more often on the drawings of the brain injured children at age eleven. These items are: arms incorrectly attached, incorrect number of fingers, and poor integration of parts. The presence of three such items on a HFD suggests the possibility of neurological impairment and indicates that further exploration in this area is necessary.

CLINICAL INTERPRETATION OF HFD. When asked about his drawing, Gus studied the HFD on *Plate 112* for some time and looked at it as if he had not really seen it before. Gus seemed aware of the poor integration of the different parts of the figure and tried to rationalize the odd angle of the head by saying: "A boy age eleven looking at a plane." It has been observed many times that brighter children are usually able to rationalize and to explain away any chance error or irregularity on their drawings. Gus was in effect implying that he had drawn the boy's head tilted so that he would look up at the planes overhead. Actually, the interpretation was an afterthought after the drawing had been completed.

The fact that Gus made an eleven year old boy suggests that the figure represents himself and that he was reasonably satisfied with his present age and condition. It also indicates that his main concerns and anxieties centered around himself. Even though Gus did not really intend to draw a boy looking at a plane, the image of a figure gazing up into the sky seems to symbolize and reflect Gus' own attitudes and preoccupations with re- mote ideas and fleeting thoughts and his remarkable lack of awareness of everyday life about him. His mind was usually off some place; Gus was rarely concerned with the real world he lived in.

The figure on *Plate 112* is just as poorly organized as Gus was. He drew a baseline under the boy as a means of support and boxed the figure in with vertical lines. Gus seemed to recognize the poor integration of the drawing and was trying to provide outer controls and support to counter- act the figure's lack of cohesiveness. In the writer's experience, only com- pulsive children who are basically very insecure and disorganized draw frames or boxes around their HFDs. This sign appears to be always clinically highly significant.

The sequence in which Gus drew his boy, starting with the feet, and the short, clinging arms reflect vividly Gus' poor interpersonal relation- ships. He was unable to communicate with others in a meaningful way since he was completely wrapped up in himself. The quality of the drawing reveals Gus' impulsivity and poor fine muscle coordination. Gus was ex- tremely careless about details. When he became aware of errors, he simply crossed them out or drew over them without bothering to erase or to re- draw portions of his figure. This sloppiness was bound to show up in his everyday behavior in school or at home.

SUMMARY OF ANALYSIS OF HFD ON PLATE 112. Gus' HFD suggests that he was a boy of average to high average intelligence with serious emotional problems and possible neurological impairment. From the HFD and from Gus' performance on the Bender Gestalt Test, it was predicted that Gus would have considerable difficulty with school achievement and that he was well placed in a special class. Gus appeared to be a highly disorganized, impulsive, withdrawn boy who had difficulty relating to others and who indulged in fantasies. Gus seemed to be aware of his own poor integration and was seeking outer controls and support since he lacked strong inner controls. He was careless and sloppy in his work and seemed to make some attempt at counteracting these tendencies through compulsive actions. Gus' chief anxieties and concerns seemed to be centered around himself; he had little involvement with the world about him.

When the WISC was administered, Gus obtained a Verbal IQ score of 100, a Performance IQ score of 113, and a Full Scale IQ score of 107, thus confirming the impression gained from the HFD that Gus was of average to high average intelligence. The other hypotheses derived from the HFD also found support in Gus' social history. Gus was indeed a poor student and his interpersonal relationships were extremely poor. He had no friends and was a complete social isolate. His development in speech and in walking had been quite slow and he had presented sleeping and feeding problems in early childhood. In addition, Gus' home situation was very unstable; his parents were divorced and Gus received little support from either parent. When Gus had been referred to the special classes, the child psychiatrist had diagnosed him as a brain injured child with serious emotional disturbances and schizoid behavior. Although Gus had matured over the years and had shown some slight improvement in his behavior, the basic problems had remained unchanged.

Plates

The drawings reproduced on the following 112 *Plates* were made by boys and girls ranging in age from not quite five through twelve years. With three exceptions, all of the drawings were executed with a number two pencil. The three exceptions *(Plates 23, 29, and 40)* were done with crayons. All the drawings were traced as faithfully as possible by the writer with India ink to assure a clear reproduction of the details which often blurr on photographs of pencil drawings. On the tracings, all identifying information, such as the child's name, date, etc., was eliminated. The drawings on eight of the *Plates (Plates 1, 13, 17, 21, 23, 24, 41 and 44)* were produced by well-adjusted children with above-average intelligence and good school achievement. The pictures on all of the other *Plates* were obtained from boys and girls who were seen for evaluation or treatment in a children's mental health center, a juvenile diagnostic center, or in any one of the numerous schools the writer has been associated with. To assure the children's privacy and the confidentiality of their clinical records, all the names of these youngsters and some of the details of their case histories were changed.

Below is a list of all the *Plates* together with the children's assigned names, their ages, the level of their IQ scores, their school achievement, the type of problems they presented, and the page numbers in this book on which each given *Plate* is discussed or referred to. The IQ levels reported here are based on the children's WISC or Stanford-Binet IQ scores. The IQ scores were divided into categories in accord with Wechsler's grouping of WISC IQ scores: Children are said to have an *Average* IQ if their IQ scores are between 90 and 109; a *High Average* level of intelligence encompasses IQ scores between 110 and 119; all children with IQ scores of 120 or higher are considered to have *Superior* intelligence; the *Low Average* IQ level includes IQ scores between 80 and 89; children with IQ scores between 70 and 79 are considered to be of *Borderline* ability; while all those with IQ scores of 69 or less are designated as *Mentally Retarded*.

The main problems presented by the children are grouped into four categories: BI, ep, bp, lp. Children checked as "BI" were medically diagnosed as *brain injured*. An absence of such a designation does *not* necessarily mean that the children were not neurologically impaired. In many instances, medical examinations had not been performed so that a medical diagnosis of brain injury could not be made. The marking "ep" refers to the presence of *emotional problems* which may manifest themselves in fears, anxieties, depression, crying spells, withdrawal, psychosomatic complaints, nervous mannerisms, etc.; "bp" means that the child has shown *behavior problems* including rebelliousness, overt aggression, enuresis or encopresis, stealing, firesetting, truancy, temper outbursts, etc.; "lp" signifies that the child has *learning problems*, i.e., that his school achievement is below what one could expect on the basis of his mental ability; these learning problems are usually due to malfunctioning in visual-motor and/or auditory perception, poor memory, distractability, short attention span, etc. Additional problems are specifically listed such as CP, aphasic, Petit Mal, undersized, sexual trauma, operation, etc.

List of Plates

Plates are here reduced photographically 35% from 8½″ × 11″ originals, except for Plates 37 and 82 which are reduced 65% from 8½″ × 22″ originals.

Plate Number	Child's Name	Child's Age	I.Q. Score Level	School Achievement	Problems	Page References
1a	Eugene	10–3	Superior	good	—	20, 30, 65, 73, 75
1b	Jean	11–8	Superior	good	—	20, 65, 76
1c	Andrew	7–2	Superior	good	—	20, 30, 65, 75, 124
2	Simon	7–0	Low Ave.	poor	BI, ep, lp	32, 45, 46, 172
3	Max	7–5	Average	fair	speech prob.	33, 57, 105
4	Jim	9–3	Superior	poor	BI, bp, lp	32, 58, 83
5	Ann	7–2	Low Ave.	poor	ep	44, 61, 70, 91
6	Eddy	9–0	Average	poor	bp	46, 113
7	Greg	5–11	Borderl.	poor	perseverat.	52
8	Ray	7–11	Low Ave.	poor	perseverat.	52
9	Connie	10–6	Average	fair	sexplay	60, 109, 110, 118
10	Nick	7–5	Low Ave.	poor	musc. dystr.	68
11	Jack	8–11	Average	poor	BI, ep, lp	83, 84
12	Jerome	8–5	Superior	fair	ep, lp	83, 84, 85
13a	Sidney	11–9	Superior	good	—	70, 73
13b	Pamela	10–9	Superior	good	—	61, 70
13c	Mark	6–6	Superior	good	—	61, 69, 70
14	Edith	7–0	Average	poor	BI, ep, bp	75, 77, 103, 107
15	Shirley	8–9	Low Ave.	poor	ep, lp, size	79, 80
16	Shirley	9–1	Low Ave.	poor	ep, lp, size	68, 79, 80, 97
17	Carl	11–5	Superior	good	—	81
18	Bill	10–11	Hi Ave.	fair	ep, lp	81, 82
19	David	11–11	Average	poor	BI, lp	82
20	Jerry	12–9	Hi Ave.	poor	bp, lp, ep	82, 83
21	Taneil	4–10	Superior	good	—	85, 86, 87, 129, 135
22	Richard	7–11	Average	fair	—	85, 86
23	Marjorie	6–0	Superior	good	—	85, 86, 87
24	Marjorie	5–5	Superior	good	operation	86, 87
25a	Frankie	7–2	Low Ave.	poor	BI, ep, lp	149, 159
25b	Frankie	8–0	Low Ave.	poor	BI, ep, lp	83, 127, 149, 159, 162
25c	Frankie	8–3	Low Ave.	poor	BI, ep, lp	57, 87, 149, 150, 159, 162, 173
25d	Frankie	8–6	Low Ave.	poor	BI, ep, lp	149, 150, 159, 162
26	Mickey	6–11	Retard.	poor	BI, ep	87, 135
27	John W.	10–6	Borderl.	poor	birth of sib	88, 103
28	Stephen	10–5	Average	poor	birth of sib	57, 88, 89
29	Stephen	10–6	Average	poor	ep	75, 89, 124
30	Dorothy	9–2	Average	poor	BI, ep, lp	88, 89, 90, 99, 109, 110, 141
31	Henry	9–2	Average	poor	BI, ep, bp, lp	88, 90, 136
32	Joel	11–8	Superior	poor	BI, ep, bp, lp	92, 113, 141
33	Timothy	8–1	Low Ave.	poor	ep, masturb.	65, 92, 93, 115, 124, 136, 137
34	Tommy	10–1	Average	poor	ep, lp, speech	95, 96
35	Eric	10–0	Average	poor	bp, lp	96, 160
36	Jonathan	7–9	Low Ave.	poor	lp	86, 96, 112
37	Peter	8–4	Average	fair	undersized	97
38	Laura	10–5	Low Ave.	fair	very tall	97, 98

Plate Number	Child's Name	Child's Age	I.Q. Score Level	School Achievement	Problems	Page References
39	Debrah	11–8	Average	fair	ep, bp	98
40	Odetta	10–8	Average	poor	ep, bp, hair	100, 101, 103, 119
41a	Lucille	12–4	Hi Ave.	good	—	100, 101, 103
41b	Marlene	8–5	Hi Ave.	good	—	100, 101, 103
41c	Diana	11–1	Hi Ave.	good	—	100, 101, 103
42	Benjie	9–0	Average	poor	obese, ep, lp	72, 101, 132
43	Keith	7–2	Average	poor	bp, skin col.	60, 102, 103, 109
44	Manuel	6–3	Superior	good	—	72, 103
45	Philip	8–3	Average	poor	ep, lp	103, 104, 115, 116
46	Sammy	7–7	Average	poor	lp, aphasic	105, 156, 157
47	Sammy	8–4	Average	poor	ep, lp, aphasic	64, 106, 126, 156, 157
48	Sammy	10–3	Average	poor	ep, lp, aphasic	75, 106, 120, 156, 157
49	Donald	7–9	Low Ave.	poor	BI, hearing	106
50	Mickey	6–5	Retard.	poor	BI, ep, vision	106, 172
51	Betty	8–2	Superior	good	CP	75, 107, 108, 109, 130
52a	Dennis	6–1	Borderl.	poor	CP, ep, lp	108
52b	Dennis	6–5	Borderl.	poor	CP, ep, lp	108, 109
53	Jennifer	11–9	Average	fair	colostomy	109, 110, 152
54	Jennifer	12–2	Average	good	colostomy	109, 110, 152
55	Kenneth	7–5	Average	poor	BI, ep, lp	111, 112
56	Carla	9–6	Average	poor	ep, bp, lp	103, 113
57	Jeff	10–3	Low Ave.	poor	BI, bp	113, 114
58	Mel	5–7	Hi Ave.	—	ep, bp	64, 114, 124, 125
59	Philip	8–7	Average	poor	ep, masturb.	115
60	Doris	5–6	Hi Ave.	fair	ep, masturb.	116
61	Burt	11–3	Average	poor	ep, masturb.	116, 117, 118, 146, 148
62	Burt	11–3	Average	poor	ep, masturb.	116, 117, 118, 124, 146, 148
63	Burt	11–7	Average	poor	ep, masturb.	116, 117, 118, 148
64	Burt	11–11	Average	poor	ep, masturb.	116, 117, 148, 149
65	Ernie	10–2	Low Ave.	poor	bp, sex play	64, 103, 118, 127
66	Julian	9–1	Average	poor	ep, bp, sex	103, 118, 119
67	Jay	11–2	Average	fair	bp	121
68	Joe	11–6	Average	poor	BI, ep, lp	64, 75, 121, 150, 151
69	Joe	12–0	Average	poor	BI, ep, lp	125, 126, 150, 151, 152
70	Joe	12–7	Average	poor	BI, ep, lp	150, 152, 160
71	Elliott	8–10	Hi Ave.	poor	BI, ep, bp, lp	64, 122, 125, 150, 151
72	Elliott	9–6	Hi Ave.	poor	BI, ep, bp, lp	64, 125, 150, 151
73	Elliott	10–4	Hi Ave.	fair	BI, ep, lp	150, 151
74	Kevin	10–1	Low Ave.	poor	bp, ep	75, 122, 123
75	Chuck	7–10	Superior	poor	BI, ep, np, lp	75, 123
76	Danny	11–9	Borderl.	poor	bp	102, 103, 123, 124
77	Michael	6–6	Average	poor	ep, lp	125, 144
78	Michael	7–3	Average	poor	ep, lp	143, 144
79	Michael	7–6	Average	poor	ep, lp	129, 144
80	Scotty	8–7	Average	poor	BI, ep, lp, bp	126, 127
81	Chris	10–5	Average	poor	ep, lp	130, 131
82	Matthew	8–3	Average	poor	BI, ep, lp	75, 131, 132
83a	Sheilah	12–6	Hi Ave.	good	ep, psychosom.	132, 133, 153
83b	Sheilah	12–11	Hi Ave.	good	ep, psychosom.	75, 77, 132, 133, 153
84	Alfred	9–0	Low Ave.	poor	BI, bp, lp	75, 77, 133, 134
85	Norman	6–3	Average	poor	BI, ep, bp, lp	135, 136
86	Shirley	9–11	Low Ave.	poor	ep, lp, size	134, 137, 138

Plate Number	Child's Name	Child's Age	I.Q. Score Level	School Achievement	Problems	Page References
87	Shirley	11–1	Low Ave.	fair	ep, lp, size	138
88	Bobby	6–4	Low Ave.	poor	BI, lp	138
89	Bobby	7–0	Low Ave.	poor	BI, ep, lp	134, 139
90	Duane	11–9	Average	poor	lp, lethargy	142
91	Butch	9–0	Borderl.	poor	BI, ep, sex	146, 147
92	Butch	9–0	Borderl.	poor	BI, ep, sex	146, 147
93	Butch	9–9	Borderl.	poor	BI, ep, sex	146, 147
94	George	9–10	Average	poor	ep, schizoid	153, 154
95	George	10–1	Average	poor	ep, schizoid	71, 153, 154, 155
96	George	10–2	Average	poor	ep, schizoid	57, 153, 155
97	George	10–3	Average	poor	ep, schizoid	153, 155
98a	Anthony	7–11	Average	poor	BI, ep, lp	159, 166, 173, 175
98b	Anthony	8–2	Average	poor	BI, ep, lp	127, 159, 166, 168, 173, 174, 175
98c	Anthony	8–7	Average	poor	BI, ep, lp	134, 159, 166, 168, 169, 173, 174, 175
99	Anthony	9–5	Average	fair	BI, ep, lp	83, 159, 166, 168, 173, 174, 175
100a	Leonard	7–2	Low Ave.	poor	BI, ep, lp	160, 162, 166, 168
100b	Leonard	7–10	Low Ave.	poor	BI, ep, lp	160, 166, 168
100c	Leonard	8–3	Low Ave.	poor	BI, ep, lp	160, 162, 166, 168
100d	Leonard	8–10	Low Ave.	fair	BI, ep, lp	160, 166, 168
100e	Leonard	9–3	Low Ave.	fair	BI, ep, lp	160, 162, 166, 168
100f	Leonard	9–8	Low Ave.	fair	BI, ep, lp	160, 166, 168
101a	Gordon	6–0	Low Ave.	poor	BI, ep, lp	160, 168, 172
101b	Gordon	7–10	Low Ave.	poor	BI, ep, lp	160, 168, 172
101c	Gordon	8–2	Low Ave.	poor	BI, ep, lp	160, 168, 172
102a	Patrick	11–8	Average	poor	BI, lp	160, 168, 169
102b	Patrick	12–6	Average	fair	BI, lp	160, 168, 169
102c	Patrick	12–10	Average	fair	BI, lp	160, 168, 169
102d	Patrick	13–4	Average	fair	BI, lp	160
103	JoAnn	6–2	Superior	fair	bp	71, 188, 189
104	Jake	7–4	Low Ave.	poor	BI, ep, lp	65, 67, 190, 191, 192
105	Craig	7–2	Retard.	poor	BI, ep	67, 192, 193, 194
106	Hubert	8–2	Low Ave.	poor	ep, lp	195, 196
107	Juan	9–6	Average	poor	ep, lp	197, 198
108	Mary	9–5	Borderl.	poor	ep, Petit Mal	72, 86, 199, 200
109	Roger	10–9	Average	fair	ep, bp, lp	201, 202
110a	Susan	10–9	Borderl.	poor	BI, ep, bp	203, 204, 205
110b	Susan	10–9	Borderl.	poor	BI, ep, bp	203, 204, 205
111	Cathy	11–3	Hi Ave.	fair	sex exp.	205, 206
112	Gus	11–3	Average	poor	BI, schizoid	207, 208

(a) "Beatle" (1965)

(b) "Elvis Presley" (1957)

(c) "Davy Crockett" (1955)

Plate 1:

(a) Eugene, C. A. 10-3
(b) Jean, C. A. 11-8
(c) Andrew, C. A. 7-2

Plate 2: Simon, C. A. 7–0

Emotional Indicators:
  —slanting figure
  —poor integration
  —tiny figure
  —no arms

Plate 3: Max, C. A. 7–5

Emotional Indicators:
  —shading face
  —slanting figure
  —cut off hands

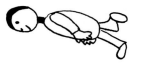

Plate 4: Jim, C. A. 9-3

Emotional Indicators:
—tiny figure
—shading of neck

Plate 5: Ann, C. A. 7–2

Emotional Indicators:
  —slanting figure
  —tiny figure
  —no mouth
  —no nose

Plate 6: Eddy, C. A. 9–0

Emotional Indicators:
—poor integration
—shading of body, limbs
—shading of neck
—slanting figure
—long arms
—big hands

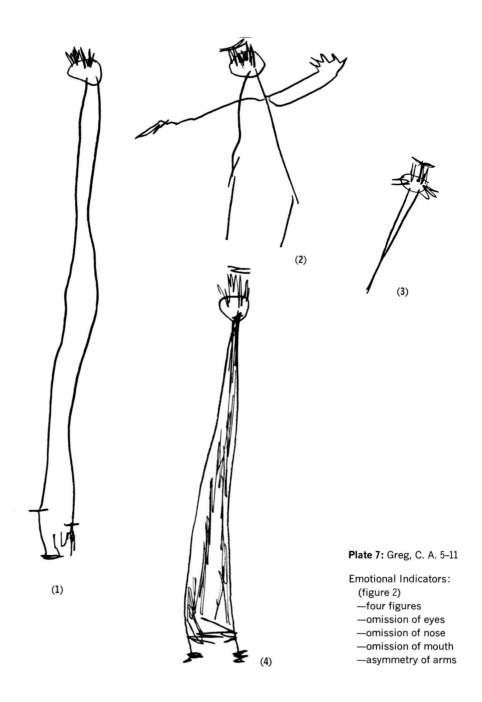

(1)

(2)

(3)

(4)

Plate 7: Greg, C. A. 5–11

Emotional Indicators:
(figure 2)
—four figures
—omission of eyes
—omission of nose
—omission of mouth
—asymmetry of arms

(1)

(2)

(3)

(4)

(5)

Plate 8: Ray, C. A. 7–11

6 figures
spontaneously
drawn

(6)

Plate 9: Connie, C. A. 10–6

Emotional indicators:
  —shading body and limbs
  —slanting figure
  —transparancies
  —no feet

Plate 10: Nick, C. A. 7–5

Emotional Indicators:
  —poor integration
  —no legs

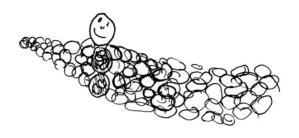

Plate 11: Jack, C. A. 8–11

Emotional Indicators:
  —tiny figure
  —poor integration
  —no arms
  —no legs

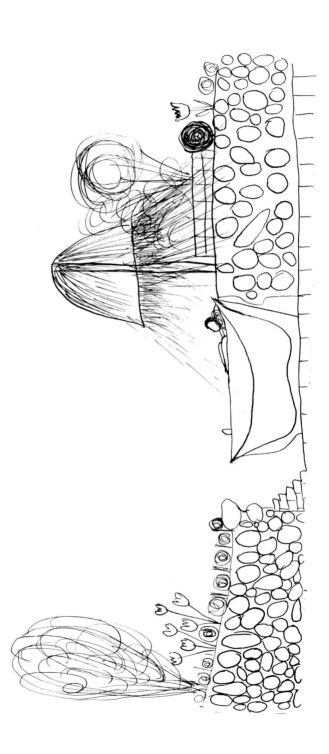

Plate 12: Jerome, C. A. 8-5

Emotional Indicators:

—no eyes
—no nose
—no mouth
—no hands
—no legs

Plate 13:

(a) Sidney, C. A. 11-9
(b) Pamela, C. A. 10-9
(c) Mark, C. A. 6-6

Plate 14: Edith, C. A. 7–0

Emotional Indicators:
  —poor integration
  —asymmetry
  —omission of foot

Plate 15: Shirley, 8–9

Emotional Indicators:
  —poor integration
  —shading body
  —short arms
  —no nose

Plate 16: Shirley, C. A. 9–1

Emotional Indicators:
  —big figure
  —crossed eyes
  —arms clinging
  —hands cut off
  —no legs

Plate 17: Carl, C. A. 11–5

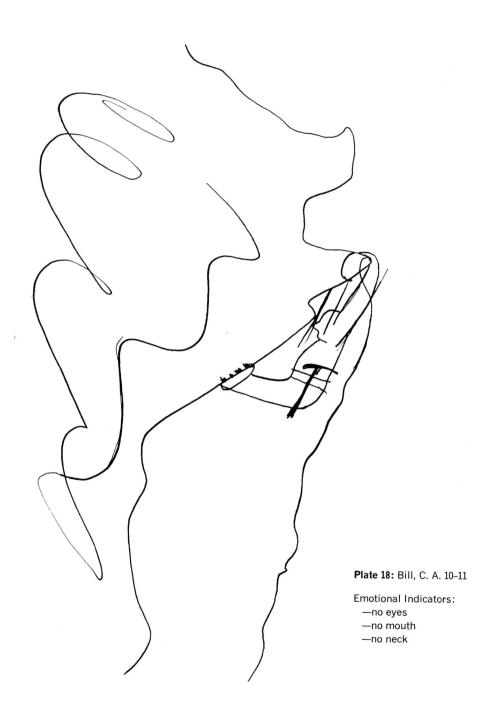

Plate 18: Bill, C. A. 10–11

Emotional Indicators:
  —no eyes
  —no mouth
  —no neck

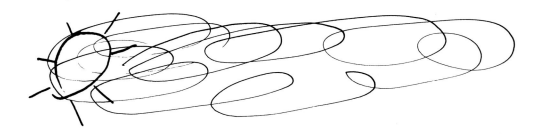

Plate 19: David, C. A. 11–11

Emotional Indicators:
  —tiny figure
  —clouds

Plate 20: Jerry, C. A. 12–9

Plate 21: Taneil, C. A. 4–10

Plate 22: Richard, C. A. 7-11

Plate 23: Marjorie, C. A. 6-0

Plate 24: Marjorie, C. A. 5–5

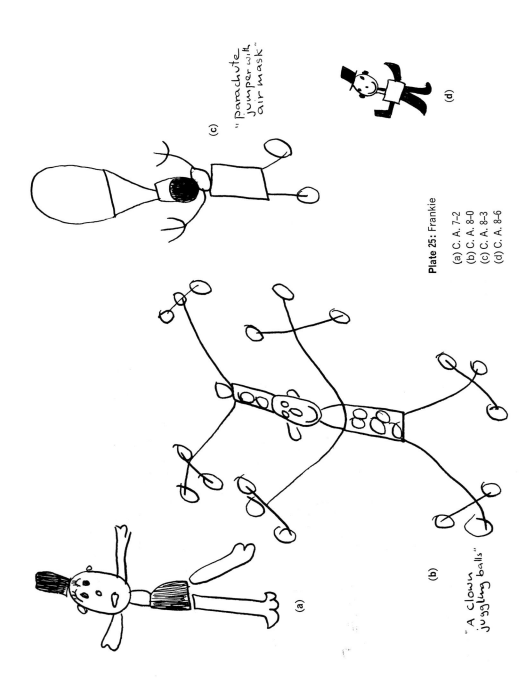

"Parachute jumper with air mask" (c)

(d)

"A clown juggling balls" (b)

(a)

Plate 25: Frankie

(a) C. A. 7-2
(b) C. A. 8-0
(c) C. A. 8-3
(d) C. A. 8-6

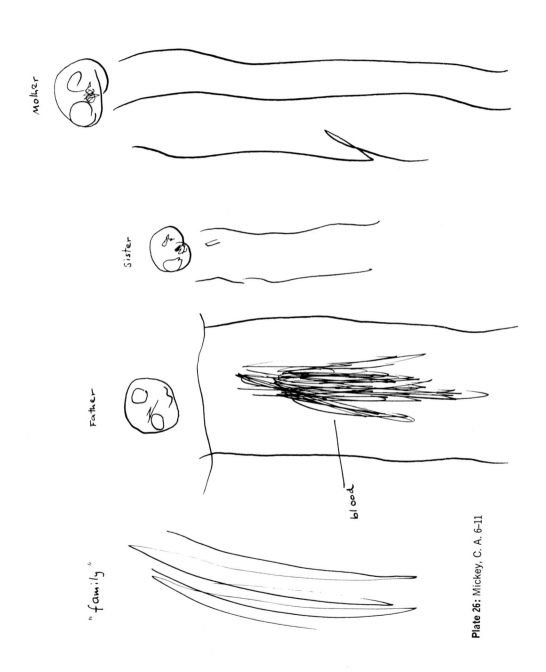

Plate 26: Mickey, C. A. 6-11

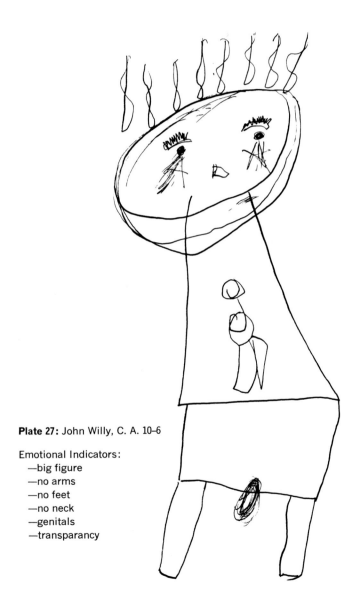

Plate 27: John Willy, C. A. 10–6

Emotional Indicators:
 —big figure
 —no arms
 —no feet
 —no neck
 —genitals
 —transparancy

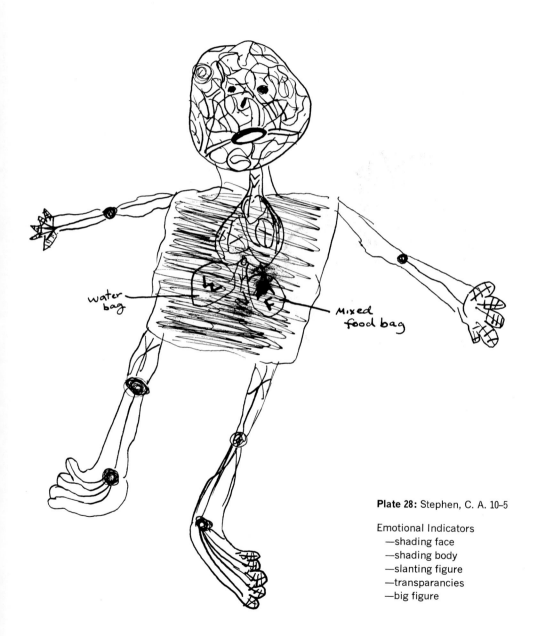

water
bag

Mixed
food bag

Plate 28: Stephen, C. A. 10–5

Emotional Indicators
—shading face
—shading body
—slanting figure
—transparancies
—big figure

Plate 29: Stephen, C. A. 10–6

Plate 30: Dorothy, C. A. 9-2

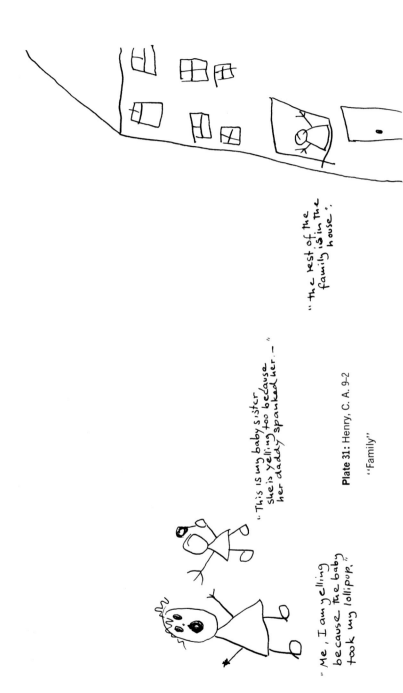

"the rest of the family is in the house".

"This is my baby sister she is yelling too because her daddy spanked her.—"

"Me, I am yelling because the baby took my lollipop."

Plate 31: Henry, C. A. 9-2

"Family"

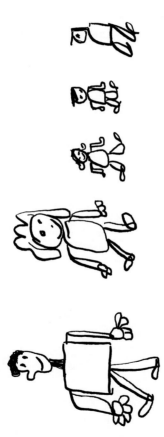

Plate 32: Joel, C. A. 11–8

"Family"

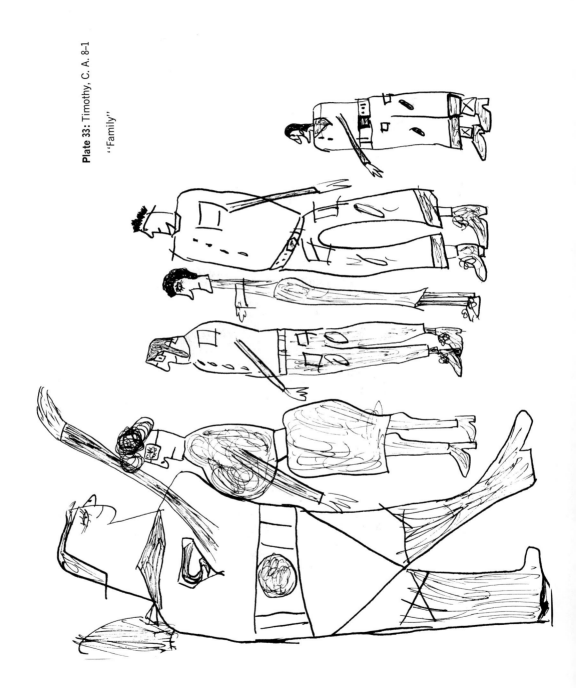

Plate 33: Timothy, C. A. 8-1

"Family"

Plate 34: Tommy, C. A. 10-1

Emotional Indicators:
—shading of body
—no nose
—short arms

Plate 35: Eric, C. A. 10–0

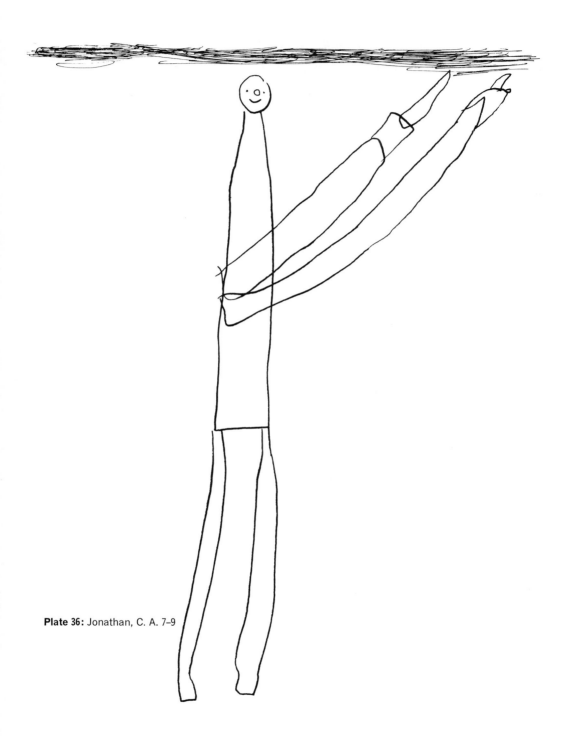

Plate 36: Jonathan, C. A. 7–9

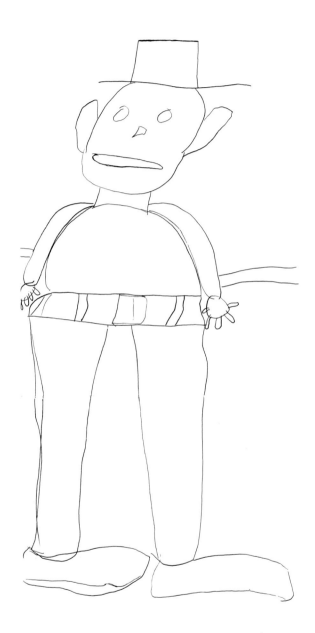

Plate 37: Peter, C. A. 8-4

Plate 38: Laura, C. A. 10–5

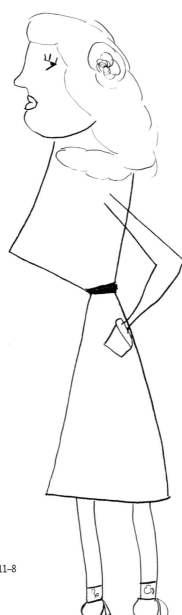

Plate 39: Debrah, C. A. 11–8

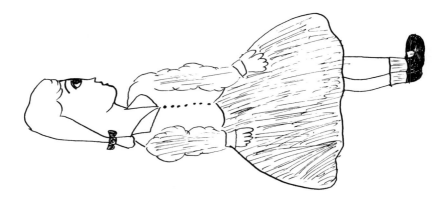

Plate 40: Odetta, C. A. 10–8

Plate 41:

(a) Lucille, C. A. 12-4
(b) Marlene, C. A. 8-5
(c) Diana, C. A. 11-1

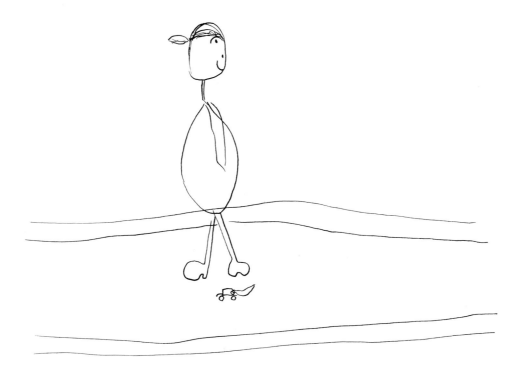

Plate 42: Benjie, C. A. 9–0

Emotional Indicators:
  —poor integration
  —hands cut off

Plate 43: Keith, C. A. 7–2

Emotional Indicators:
 —shading of face
 —transparancies

Plate 44: Manuel, C. A. 6–3

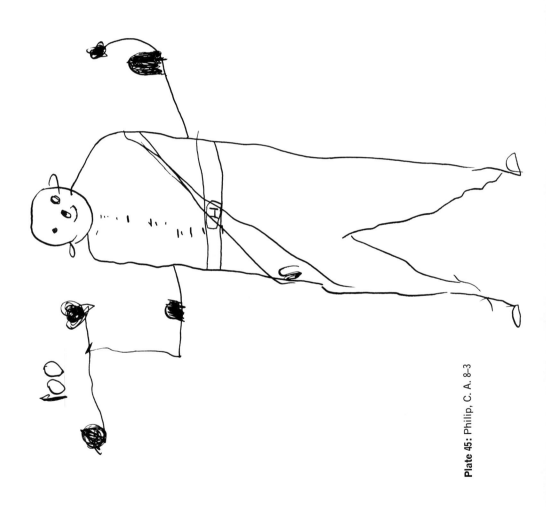

Plate 45: Philip, C. A. 8-3

Plate 46: Sammy, C. A. 7–7

— Indian corn

Plate 47: Sammy, C. A. 8–4

"Indian chief

Plate 48: Sammy, C. A. 10-3

Plate 49: Donald, C. A. 7–9

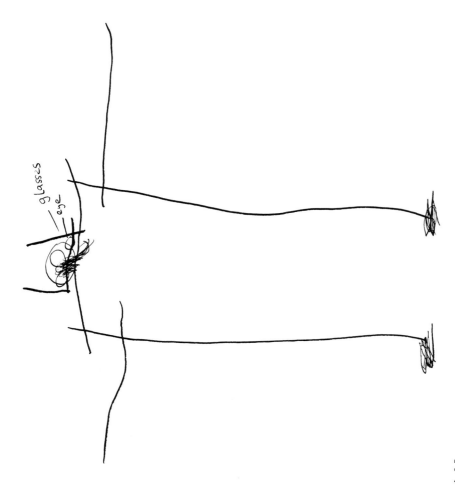

glasses

eye

Plate 50: Mickey, C. A. 6-5

Plate 51: Betty, C. A. 8-2

"Family going to church"

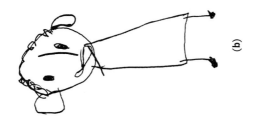

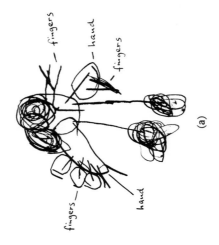

Plate 52: Dennis

(a) C. A. 6–1
(b) C. A. 6–5

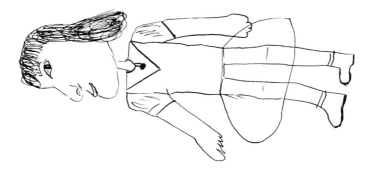

Plate 53: Jennifer, C. A. 11-9

Plate 54: Jennifer, C. A. 12–2

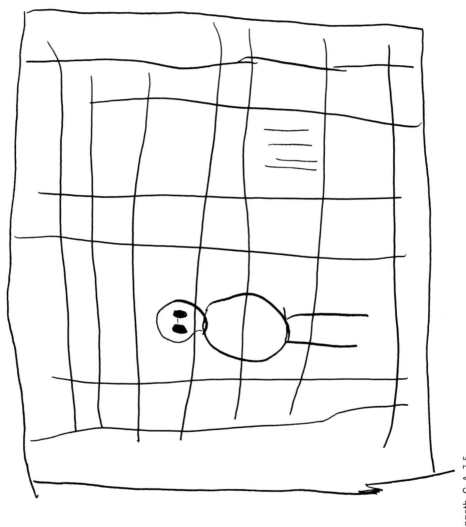

Plate 55: Kenneth, C. A. 7-5

Plate 56: Carla, C. A. 9–6

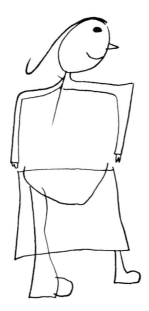

Plate 57: Jeff, C. A. 10–3

Plate 58: Melvin, C. A. 5–7

Plate 59: Philip, C. A. 8–7

Plate 60: Doris, C. A. 5–6

Plate 61: Burt, C. A. 11–3

Plate 62: Burt, C. A. 11–3

Plate 63: Burt, C. A. 11–7

Plate 64: Burt, C. A. 11–11

Plate 65: Ernie, C. A. 10–2

Plate 66: Julian, C. A. 9–1

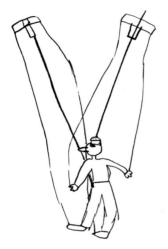

Plate 67: Jay, C. A. 11–2

Plate 68: Joe, C. A. 11–6

"Frenchman"

Plate 69: Joe, C. A. 12–0

Plate 70: Joe, C. A. 12–7

Plate 71: Elliott, C. A. 8-10

"Caveman"

Plate 72: Elliott, C. A. 9-6

Plate 73: Elliott, C. A. 10–4

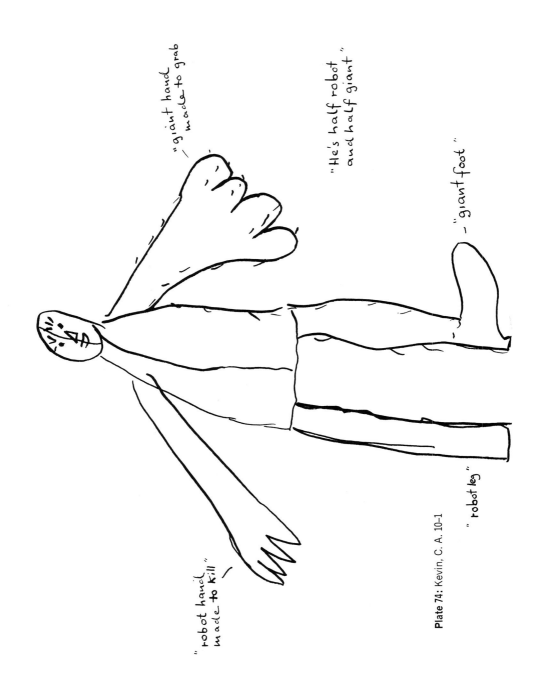

Plate 74: Kevin, C. A. 10-1

"giant hand made to grab"

"He's half robot and half giant"

"giant foot"

"robot hand made to kill"

"robot leg"

"Wolfman"

Plate 75: Chuck, C. A. 7–10

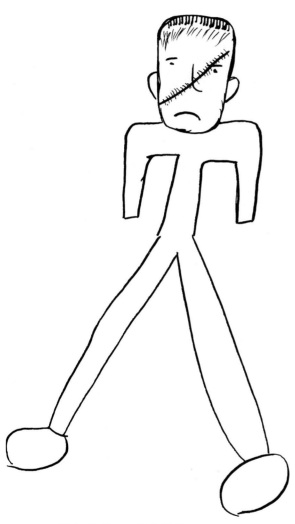

"Frankenstein"
and Apeman"

Plate 76: Danny, C. A. 11–9

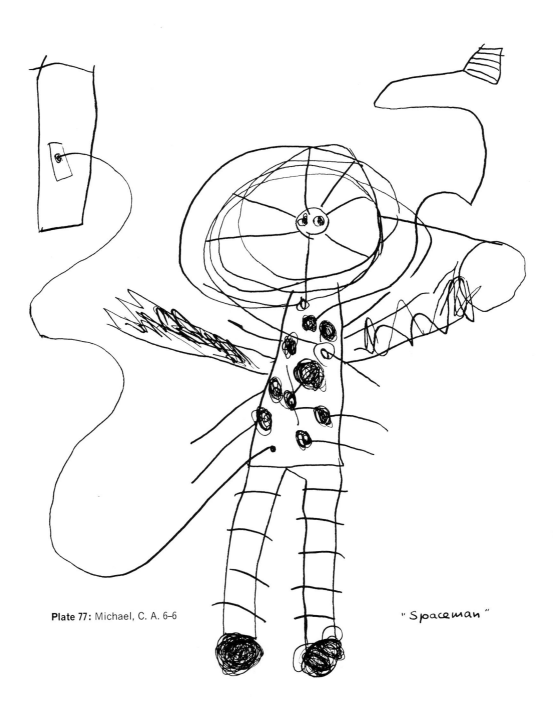

Plate 77: Michael, C. A. 6–6   "Spaceman"

Plate 78: Michael, C. A. 7–3

''Family''

Plate 79: Michael, C. A. 7-6

Plate 80: Scotty, C. A. 8–7

Plate 81: Christopher, C. A. 10-5

Plate 82: Matthew, C. A. 8-3

(b)

(a)

Plate 83: Sheilah

(a) C. A. 12-6
(b) C. A. 12-11

Plate 84: Alfred, C. A. 9–0

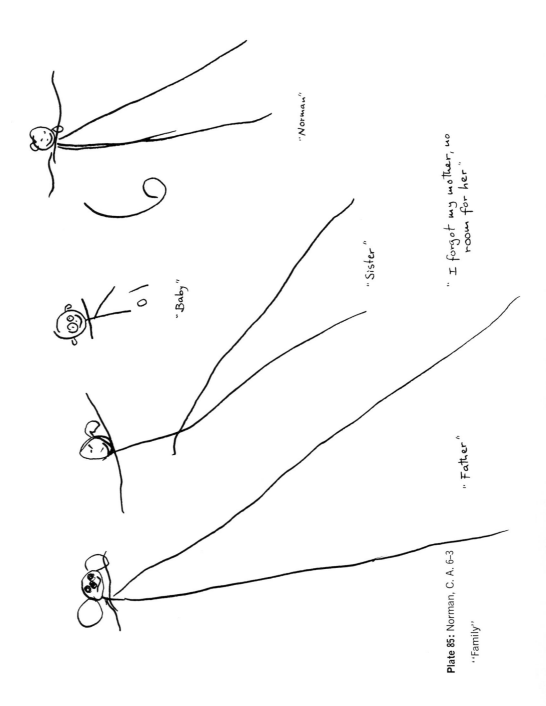

"Norman"

"Baby"

"Sister"

" I forgot my mother, no room for her"

"Father"

Plate 85: Norman, C. A. 6-3

"Family"

Plate 86: Shirley, C. A. 9-11

Plate 87: Shirley, C. A. 11-1

Plate 88: Bobby, C. A. 6-4

"Family"

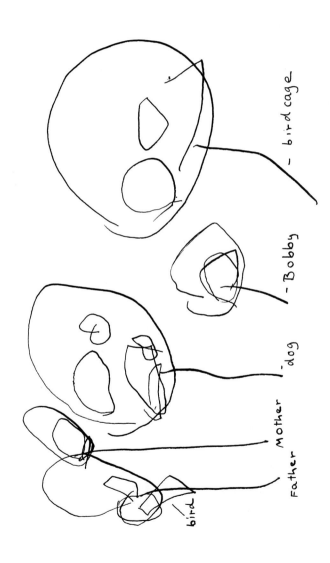

bird cage

Bobby

dog

Mother

Father

bird

" Spot , the beagle "

Plate 89: Bobby, C. A. 7–0

''Family''

Plate 90: Duane, C. A. 11-9

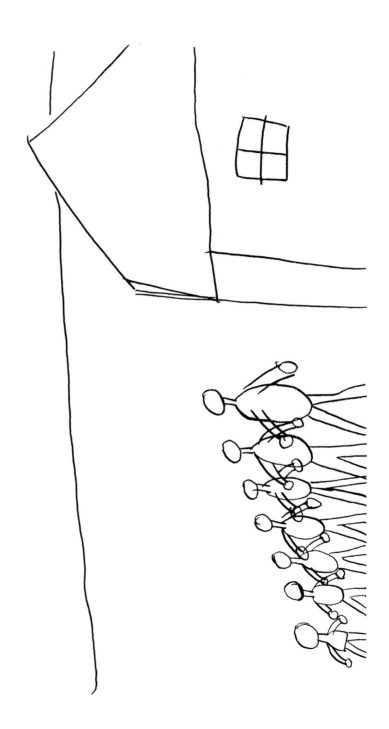

Plate 91: Butch, C. A. 9–0

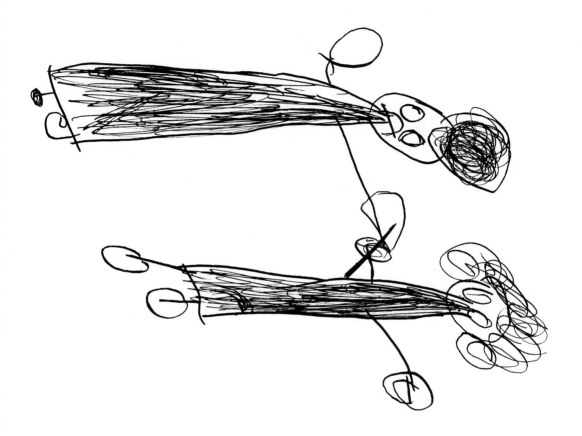

Plate 92: Butch, C. A. 9–0

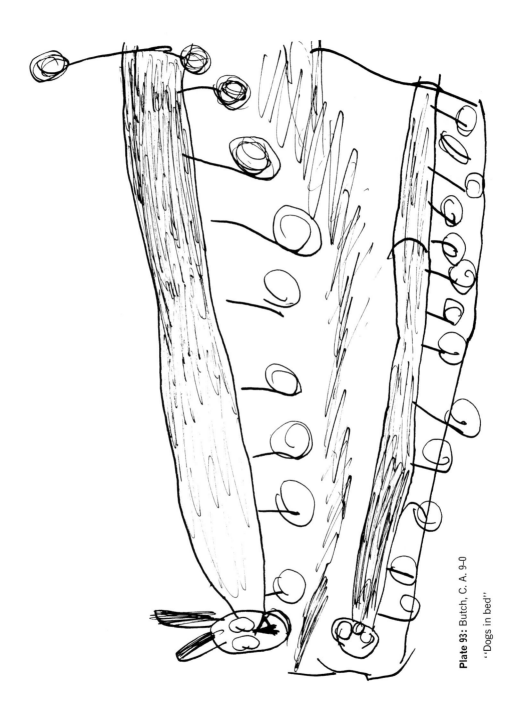

Plate 93: Butch, C. A. 9-0

"Dogs in bed"

Plate 94: George, C. A. 9–10

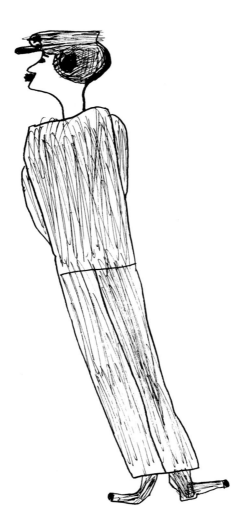

Plate 95: George, C. A. 10–1

Plate 96: George, C. A. 10–2

Plate 97: George, C. A. 10–3

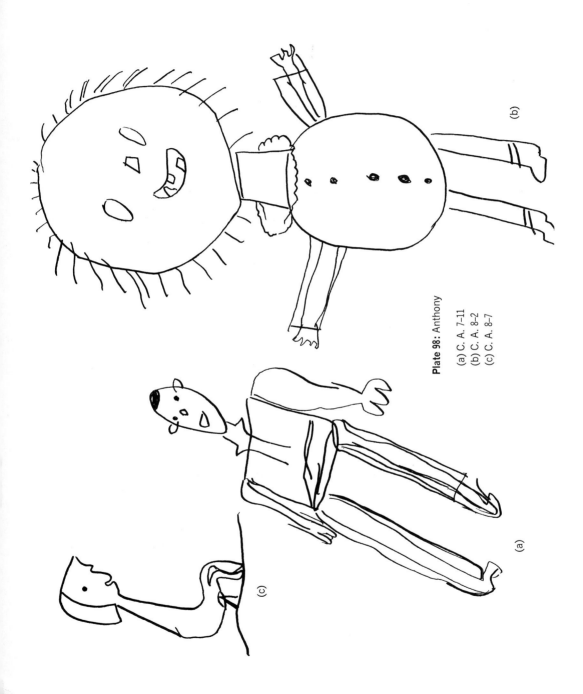

Plate 98: Anthony

(a) C. A. 7-11
(b) C. A. 8-2
(c) C. A. 8-7

Plate 99: Anthony, C. A. 9–5

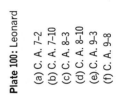

Plate 100: Leonard

(a) C. A. 7–2
(b) C. A. 7–10
(c) C. A. 8–3
(d) C. A. 8–10
(e) C. A. 9–3
(f) C. A. 9–8

(a)

Plate 101: Gordon

(a) C. A. 6–0
(b) C. A. 7–10
(c) C. A. 8–2

(b)

(c)

(a)

(b)

(c)

(d)

Plate 102: Patrick

(a) C. A. 11–8
(b) C. A. 12–6
(c) C. A. 12–10
(d) C. A. 13–4

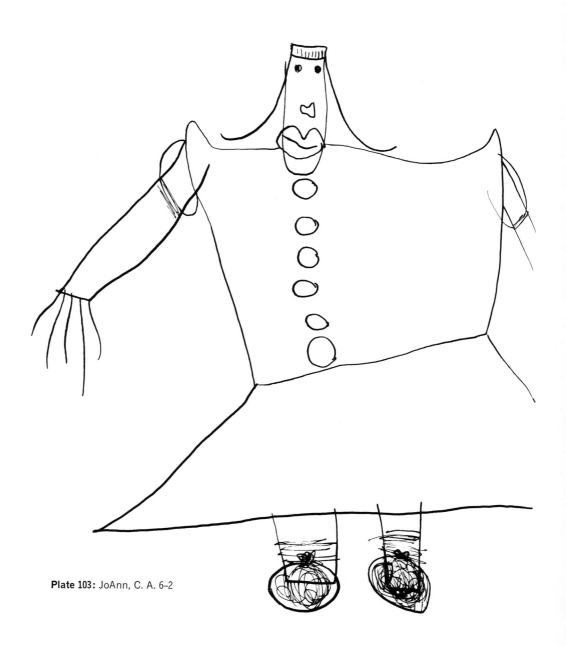

Plate 103: JoAnn, C. A. 6–2

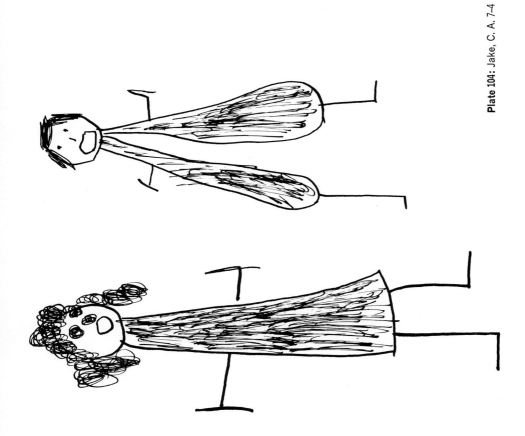

Plate 104: Jake, C. A. 7-4

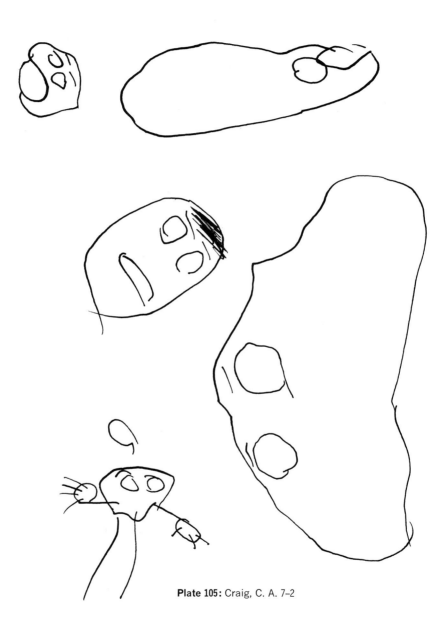

Plate 105: Craig, C. A. 7–2

Plate 106: Hubert, C. A. 8–2

Plate 107: Juan, C. A. 9–6

Plate 108: Mary, C. A. 9–5

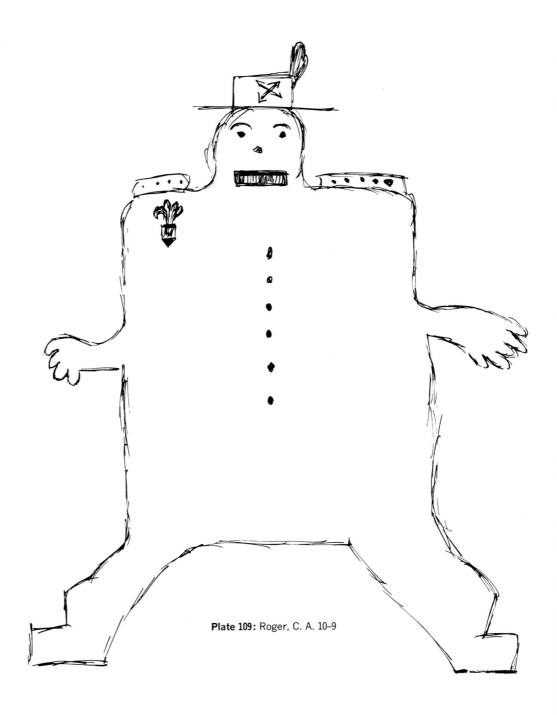

Plate 109: Roger, C. A. 10–9

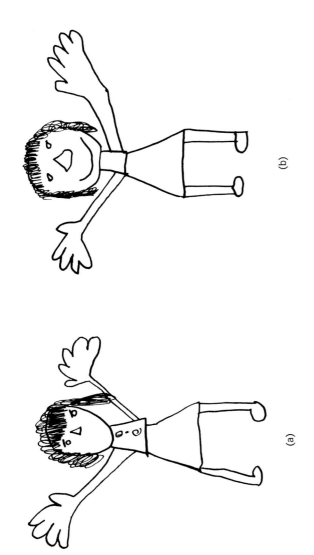

(b)

(a)

Plate 110: Susan, C. A. 10-9

Plate 111: Cathy, C. A. 11–3

Plate 112: Gus, C. A. 11–3

Appendices

Appendix A. Scoring Manual for 30 Developmental Items on HFDs of Children

(Some examples of the Development Items are shown on the *Plates* listed in parentheses.)

1. *Head:* Any representation, clear outline of head required.

2. *Eyes:* Any representation.

3. *Pupils:* Distinct circles or dots within outlines of eyes required. A dot with a line over it is scored as eyes and eyebrows. (*Plates 5, 8, 9, 13b, c, 14, 17, 34, 35*).

4. *Eyebrows or eyelashes:* Either brows or lashes or both (*Plates 8, 13a, b, 14, 19, 20, 25a, 27, 29, 34*).

5. *Nose:* Any representation (*Plates 2, 3, 4, 6, 8, 9, 13a, b, c, 14*).

6. *Nostrils:* Dots or nostrils shown in addition to presentation of nose (*Plates 13a, c, 17, 53, 54, 69, 86, 102a, 106, 107*).

7. *Mouth:* Any representation (*Plates 2, 3, 4, 6, 8, 13a, b, c, 14, 15*).

8. *Two lips:* Two lips outlined and separated by line from each other; two rows of teeth only are *not scored* (scored *Plates 13c, 14, 17, 39, 41a, c, 54, 56, 103, 111;* not scored *Plates 35, 62*).

9. *Ear:* Any representation (*Plates 5, 13a, c, 17, 19, 20, 25a, b, d, 35*).

10. *Hair:* Any presentation (*Plates 2, 4, 5, 9, 13a, b, 14, 15, 16, 17*) *or* hat or cap covering head and hiding hair (*Plates 8, 23, 37, 42, 47, 69, 77, 109*).

11. *Neck:* Definite separation of head and body necessary (*Plates 3, 4, 6, 8, 13a, b, c, 14, 16, 17, 19*).

12. *Body:* Any presentation, clear outline necessary.

13. *Arms:* Any representation.

14. *Arms in two dimensions:* Both arms presented by more than a single line (*Plates 3, 4, 6, 8, 9, 13a, b, c, 14, 15*).

15. *Arms pointing downward:* One or both arms pointing down at an angle of 30° or more from horizontal position (*Plates 3, 4, 6, 8, 9, 13a, b, c, 15, 16, 99*), *or* arms raised appropriately for activity figure is engaged in (*Plates 17, 18, 20*); arms extending horizontally from body and then turning down some distance from the body is *not scored* (*Plate 48*).

16. *Arms correctly attached at shoulder:* Indication of shoulder necessary for this item, arms must be firmly connected to body (*Plates 4, 13a, b, 15, 16, 20, 35, 40, 41a, b*).

17. *Elbow:* Distinct angle in arm required (*Plates 13a, 25d, 28, 39, 41b, 45, 47, 83, 111*); rounded curve in arm is *not scored* (*Plates 17, 29*).

18. *Hands:* Differentiation from arms and fingers necessary such as widening of arm or demarcation from arm by sleeve or bracelet (*Plates 4, 5, 9, 10, 13b, c, 14, 15, 17, 19*).

19. *Fingers:* Any representation distinct from hands or arms (*Plates 4, 6, 7, 8, 13c, 15, 17, 19, 25a, b, c*).

20. *Correct number of fingers:* Five fingers on each hand or arm unless position of hand hides some fingers (*Plates 13c, 19, 28, 35, 40, 41b, c, 54, 69, 70*).

21. *Legs:* Any representation; in case of female figures in long skirts this item *is* scored if distance between waist and feet is long enough to allow for legs to be present under the skirt.

22. *Legs in two dimensions:* Both legs presented by more than single lines (*Plates 3, 4, 6, 9, 13a, b, c, 14, 15, 17*).

23. *Knee:* Distinct angle in one or both legs (sideview) or kneecap (front view) (*Plates 4, 20, 28, 41b, 73, 98c, 109*); round curve in leg *not scored* (*Plates 17, 47*).

24. *Feet:* Any representation (*Plates 2, 5, 6, 13a, b, c, 15, 17, 18, 19*).

25. *Feet two dimensional:* Feet extending in one direction from heel (side view) and showing greater length than height, or feet drawn in perspective (front view) (*Plates 3, 4, 13a, b, c, 15, 17, 19, 37, 38*).

26. *Profile:* Head drawn in profile even if rest of figure is not entirely in profile (*Plates 4, 17, 18, 29, 39, 40, 41a, 42, 53, 57*).

27. *Clothing: One item or none:* No clothing indicated or only hat, buttons, or belt or outline of garment without details (*Plates 2, 4, 5, 13c, 14, 19, 28, 42, 43, 55*).

28. *Clothing: Two or three items:* The following items are scored for clothing: pants, skirt, shirt or blouse (upper part of dress separated by belt is scored as blouse), coat, hat, helmet, belt, tie, hair ribbon, barrette, necklace, watch, ring, bracelet, pipe, cigarette, umbrella, cane, gun, rake, shoes, socks, pocketbook, briefcase, bat, gloves, etc. (*Plates 3, 8, 9, 20, 25a, b, 29, 37, 41b, c*).

29. *Clothing: Four or more items:* Four or more of items listed above present (*Plates 13a, b, 15, 16, 34, 35, 39, 40, 41a, 45*).

30. *Good proportions:* Figure *looks right* even if not entirely correct from anatomical point of view (*Plates 13a, 18, 20, 40, 44, 54, 67, 70, 80, 81*).

Appendix B. Expected and Exceptional Items on Human Figure Drawings of Boys and Girls Age 5 to 12

	Age 5		Age 6		Age 7		Age 8		Age 9		Age 10		Age 11 & 12	
	Boys	Girls	Boys	Girls	Boys	Girls	Boys	Girls	Boys	Girls	Boys	Girls	Boys	Girls
N	128	128	131	133	134	125	138	130	134	134	109	108	157	167
Expected Items														
Head	X	X	X	X	X	X	X	X	X	X	X	X	X	X
Eyes	X	X	X	X	X	X	X	X	X	X	X	X	X	X
Nose	X	X	X	X	X	X	X	X	X	X	X	X	X	X
Mouth	X	X	X	X	X	X	X	X	X	X	X	X	X	X
Body	X	X	X	X	X	X	X	X	X	X	X	X	X	X
Legs	X	X	X	X	X	X	X	X	X	X	X	X	X	X
Arms	X	X	X	X	X	X	X	X	X	X	X	X	X	X
Feet			X	X	X	X	X	X	X	X	X	X	X	X
Arms 2 dimension					X		X	X	X	X	X	X	X	X
Legs 2 dimension							X		X		X	X	X	X
Hair				X		X		X			X	X	X	X
Neck						X	X	X	X	X	X	X	X	X
Arm down													X	X
Arms at shoulder														X
2 clothing items												X		X
Exceptional Items														
Knee	X	X	X	X	X	X	X	X	X	X	X	X	X	X
Profile	X	X	X	X	X	X	X	X	X	X	X	X		
Elbow	X	X	X	X	X	X	X	X	X					
Two lips	X	X	X	X	X	X	X		X		X			
Nostrils	X	X	X	X	X		X		X					
Proportions	X	X	X	X										
Arms at shoulder	X	X	X	X										
4 clothing items	X	X	X	X										
Feet 2 dimension	X	X												
Five fingers	X													
Pupils	X													

Appendix C.   Interpretation of Individual HFD Scores

HFD Score	Level of Mental Ability
8 or 7	High Average to Superior (IQ 110 upward)
6	Average to Superior (IQ 90–135)
5	Average to High Average (IQ 85–120)
4	Low Average to Average (IQ 80–110)
3	Low Average (IQ 70–90)
2	Borderline (IQ 60–80)
1 or 0	Mentally Retarded or functioning on a retarded level due to serious emotional problems (IQ less than 70)

Appendix D.   Quartiles, Means and Standard Deviations on HFDs of Children, Age 5 to 12, with Different Levels of Intelligence

WISC or Stanford-Binet IQ's	N	HFD Quartiles			HFD Means	Standard Deviations	plus/minus one S.D. (normal range)
		Q^1	Q^2	Q^3			
59 down	27	0	1	3	1.63	1.54	.09–3.17
60–69	43	1	3	3	2.51	1.33	1.18–3.84
70–79	98	2	3	4	3.31	1.18	2.13–4.49
80–89	185	3	4	5	3.72	1.17	2.55–4.89
90–99	142	3	4	5	4.20	1.28	2.92–5.48
100–109	135	4	5	5	4.82	1.00	3.82–5.82
110 up	105	4	5	5	5.00	1.43	3.57–6.43

Appendix E. Scoring Manual for 30 Emotional Indicators on HFDs of Children

(All Emotional Indicators are considered valid for boys and girls age 5 to 12 unless otherwise indicated. Some examples of the Emotional Indicators are shown on the *Plates* listed in parentheses.)

Quality Signs

1. *Poor integration of parts* (Boys 7, Girls 6): One or more parts not joined to rest of figure, part only connected by a single line, or barely touching (*Plates 2, 6, 10, 14, 15, 29, 36, 42, 52, 55, 96*).

2. *Shading of face:* Deliberate shading of whole face or part of it, including "freckles," "measles," etc.; an even, light shading of face and hands to represent skin color is *not scored* (*Plates 3, 25c, 28, 43, 50, 52a, 76, 96;* not scored *Plate 44*).

3. Shading of body and/or limbs (Boys 9, Girls 8): Shading of body and/or limbs (*Plates 6, 9, 15, 28, 29, 34, 56, 81, 95, 100e*).

4. *Shading of hands and/or neck* (Boys 8, Girls 7): (*Plates 4, 6, 45, 59*).

5. *Gross asymmetry of limbs:* One arm or leg differs markedly *in shape* from the other arm or leg. This item is *not scored* if arms or legs are similar in shape but just a bit uneven in size (*Plates 7, 14, 25a, 52a, 57, 58, 74, 75, 82, 98a;* not scored: *Plates 6, 28, 106*).

6. *Slanting figures:* Vertical axis of figure tilted by 15° or more from the perpendicular (*Plates 2, 3, 5, 6, 9, 28, 38, 61, 82, 95*).

7. *Tiny figure:* Figure two inches or less in height (*Plates 2, 4, 5, 19, 25d, 38, 49, 58, 60, 67*).

8. *Big figure* (Boys and Girls 8): Figure nine inches or more in height (*Plates 16, 27, 28, 29, 36, 37, 39, 65, 69, 96*).

9. *Transparencies:* Transparencies involving major portions of body or limbs (*Plates 9, 27, 28, 43, 53, 57, 82, 98a, b, 102a, b, c*) single line or lines of arms crossing body *not scored* (*Plates 4, 36, 39*).

Special Features

10. *Tiny head:* Height of head less than one-tenth of total figure (*Plates 36, 46, 50, 77*).

11. *Crossed eyes:* Both eyes turned in or turned out (*Plates 16, 107*); sideway glance of eyes *not scored* (*Plates 5, 13b, c*).

12. *Teeth:* Any representation of one or more teeth (*Plates 35, 60, 61, 62, 80, 96, 98b, 101a, 107, 109*).

13. *Short arms:* Short stubs for arms, arms not long enough to reach waistline (*Plates 15, 34, 56, 66, 76, 84, 97, 104, 109, 112*).

14. *Long arms:* Arms excessively long, arms long enough to reach below knee or where knee should be (*Plates 6, 25b, 29, 36, 58, 71, 74, 110*).

15. *Arms clinging to body:* No space between body and arms (*Plates 16, 40, 56, 57, 95, 107, 112*).

16. *Big hands:* Hands as big or bigger than face of figure (*Plates 6, 46, 52, 58, 71, 74*).

17. *Hands cut off:* Arms with neither hands nor fingers (*Plates 3, 16, 25d, 42, 49, 50, 56, 76, 96, 97*); hands hidden behind back of figure or in pocket *not scored* (*Plates 12, 13a, 39, 95*).

18. *Legs pressed together:* Both legs touch with no space in between, in profile drawings only one leg is shown (*Plates 40, 54, 66, 94, 95, 96, 108*).

19. *Genitals:* Realistic or unmistakably symbolic representation of genitals (*Plates 27, 59, 77*).

20. *Monster or grotesque figure:* Figure representing nonhuman, degraded or ridiculous person; the grotesqueness of figure must be deliberate on part of the child and not the result of his immaturity or lack of drawing skill (*Plates 26b, 47, 48, 61, 62, 65, 67, 68, 71, 74; not scored: Plates 27, 28, 50, 106, 109*).

21. *Three or more figures spontaneously drawn:* Several figures shown who are not interrelated or engaged in meaningful activity; repeated drawing of figures when only "a" figure was requested (*Plates 7, 8, 105*); drawing of a boy and a girl or the child's family is *not scored* (*Plates 51, 104*).

22. *Clouds:* Any presentation of clouds, rain, snow or flying birds (*Plates 19, 36, 108*).

Omissions

23. *No eyes:* Complete absence of eyes (*Plates 7, 12, 18, 25c, 52a, 73, 84*); closed eyes or vacant circles for eyes are *not scored* (*Plates 10, 13a, 25b*).

24. *No nose:* (Boys 6, Girls 5): (*Plates 5, 7, 12, 15, 25c, 34, 55, 60, 73, 75*).

25. *No mouth:* (*Plates 5, 7, 12, 18, 25c, 46, 55, 67, 73, 77*).

26. *No body:* (*Plates 50, 97, 101a, 104, 105*).

27. *No arms:* (Boys 6, Girls 5): (*Plates 2, 11, 27, 52b, 55, 65, 94, 98c, 108*).

28. *No legs:* (*Plates 10, 11, 16, 65*).

29. *No feet:* (Boys 9, Girls 7): (*Plates 9, 14, 27, 65, 68, 69, 74, 96*).

30. *No neck:* (Boys 10, Girls 9): (*Plates 18, 27, 38, 68, 70, 74, 76, 96, 109, 110*).

Appendix F. List of Emotional Indicators on HFDs of Children

(All of the Emotional Indicators are considered valid for boys and girls age 5 to 12 unless otherwise indicated.)

Quality Signs

Poor integration of parts of figure (Boys 7, Girls 6)

Shading of face

Shading of body and/or limbs (Boys 9, Girls 8)

Shading of hands and/or neck (Boys 8, Girls 7)

Gross asymmetry of limbs

Slanting figure, axis of figure tilted by 15° or more

Tiny figure, two inches high or less

Big figure, nine inches or more in height (Boys and Girls 8)

Transparencies

Special Features

Tiny head, head less than 1/10th of total figure in height

Crossed eyes, both eyes turned in or out

Teeth

Short arms, arms not long enough to reach waistline

Long arms, arms long enough to reach knee line

Arms clinging to side of body

Big hands, hands as large as face of figure

Hands cut off, arms without hands or fingers (hidden hands *not* scored)

Legs pressed together

Genitals

Monster or grotesque figure

Three or more figures spontaneously drawn

Clouds, rain, snow

Omissions

No eyes

No nose (Boys 6, Girls 5)

No mouth

No body

No arms (Boys 6, Girls 5)

No legs

No feet (Boys 9, Girls 7)

No neck (Boys 10, Girls 9)

Appendix G. Organic Signs on HFDs of Boys 6 to 12

(These signs occurred significantly more often but *not* exclusively on the HFDs of brain injured boys at different age levels.)

Sign on HFDs	Age of BI Boys					
	6	7	8	9	10	11 & 12
No body	X	—	—	—	—	—
No pupils	—	X	X	X	—	X
No neck	—	X	—	X	X	X
Stickarms	X	X	X	X	X	X
Arms horizontal	X	X	X	X	X	X
Arms incorrectly attached	—	X	X	X	X	X
No hands	X	X	X	—	X	—
Incorrect number of fingers	—	X	X	X	X	X
Sticklegs	X	X	X	X	X	X
0–1 clothing item	—	X	X	X	X	X
Less than 4 clothing items	—	X	X	X	X	X
Poor integration	—	X	X	X	X	X
Asymmetry of limbs	X	X	—	—	—	—
Transparencies	—	—	X	—	—	X
Tiny figure	X	X	X	—	—	X
Hands cut off	X	X	X	X	X	X
Slanting figure	—	X	—	—	X	X

References

BENDER, L.: A visual motor Gestalt test and its clinical use. *The American Orthopsychiatric Association Research Monograph*, No. 3, 1938.

———: The drawing of a man in chronic encephalitis in children. *J. ner. ment Dis.*, 41:277-286, 1940.

———: Bender Motor Gestalt Test: Cards and manual of instructions. *The American Orthopsychiatric Association, Inc.*, 1946.

BENNETT, V. D. C.: Does size of figure drawing reflect self-concept? *J. consult Psychol.*, 28:285-286, 1964.

BERRIEN, F. K.: A study of the drawings of abnormal children. *J. educ. Psychol.*, 26: 143-150, 1935.

BIELIAUSKAS, V. J. and KIRKHAM, S. L.: An evaluation of the "organic signs" in the H-T-P drawings. *J. clin. Psychol.*, 14:50-54, 1958.

BIELIAUSKAS, V. J.: Sexual identification in children's drawings of human figures. *J. clin. Psychol.*, 16:42-44, 1960.

BRADFIELD, R. H.: The predictive validity of children's drawings. *Calif. J. educ. Res.*, 15:166-174, 1964.

BROWN, D. G. and TOLOR, A.: Human figure drawings as indicators of sexual identification and inversion. *Percep. mot. Skills*, 7:199-211, 1957.

BRUCK, M. and BODWIN, R. F.: The relationship between self-concept and the presence and absence of scholastic achievement. *J. Clin. Psychol.*, 18:181-182, 1962.

BUCK, J. N.: The H-T-P technique: A qualitative and quantitative scoring manual. *J. clin. Psychol.*, 4:317-396, 1948.

BUTLER, R. I. and MARCUSE, F. L.: Sex identification at different ages using the Draw-A-Person test. *J. proj. Tech.*, 23:299-302, 1959.

CENTERS, L. and CENTERS R.: A comparison of body images of amputee and non-amputee children as revealed in figure drawings. *J. proj. Tech. pers. Ass.*, 27:158-165, 1963.

CRADDICK, R. A.: Self image in Draw-A-Person Test and self portrait drawings. *J. proj. Tech. pers. Ass.*, 27:288-291, 1963.

DENNIS, W.: *Group values through children's drawings.* New York: John Wiley and Sons, 1966.

ESTES, B. W., CURTIN, M. E., DE BURGER, R. A., and DENNY, C.: Relationships between 1960 Stanford-Binet, 1937 Stanford-Binet, WISC, Raven, and Draw-A-Man. *J. consult. Psychol.*, 25:388-391, 1961.

GOODENOUGH, F. L.: *Measurement of intelligence by drawings.* New York: Harcourt, Brace and World, Inc., 1926.

———: Studies in the psychology of children's drawings. *Psychol. Bull.*, 25:272-283, 1928.

GOODENOUGH, F. L. and HARRIS, D. B.: Studies in the psychology of children's drawings, II:1928-1949. *Psychol. Bull.*, 47:369-433, 1950.

GRANICK, S. and SMITH, L. J.: Sex sequence in the Draw-A-Person test and its relation to the MMPI Masculinity-Femininity scale. *J. Consult. Psychol.*, 17:71-73, 1953.

HAMMER, E. F.: *The clinical application of projective drawings.* Springfield, Ill.: Charles C Thomas, 1958.

HANVICK, L. J.: The Goodenough test as a measure of intelligence of child psychiatric patients. *J. clin. Psychol.*, 9:71-72, 1953.

HARRIS, D. B.: *Children's drawings as measures of intellectual maturity.* New York: Harcourt, Brace, and World, Inc., 1963.

HAWORTH, M. and NORMINGTON, C. J.: A sexual differentiation scale for the D-A-P Test (for use with children). *J. proj. Tech.*, 25: 1961.

HILDRETH, G.: *Metropolitan Achievement Test, Primary I Battery: Form R.* Yonkers-on-Hudson: World Book Co., 1946.

HULSE, W. C.: The emotionally disturbed child draws his family. *Quart. J. Child Behav.*, 3:152-174, 1951.

———: Childhood conflict expressed through family drawings. *J. proj. Tech.*, 16:66-79, 1952.

JOHNSON, S. R. and GLOYE, E. E.: A critical analysis of psychological treatment of children's drawings and paintings. *J. Aesthet. Art Crit.*, 17:242-250, 1958.

JOLLES, I.: *A catalogue for the qualitative interpretation of the H-T-P.* Beverly Hills, Calif.: Western Psychological Services, 1952.

———: A study of the validity of some hypotheses for the qualitative interpretation of the H-T-P for children of elementary school age: I. sexual identification. *J. clin. Psychol.*, 8:113-118, 1952.

JONES, L. W. and THOMAS, C. B.: Studies on figure drawings: A review of the literature (1949-1959). *The Psychiat. Quart. Supplem.*, 35:212-261, 1961.

KATES, S. L. and HARRINGTON, R. W.: Authority figure perspective and aggression in delinquents. *J. genet Psychol.*, 80:193-210, 1952.

KELLOGG, R.: *What children scribble and why.* Palo Alto, Calif.: National Press, 1959.

KEOGH, B. and SMITH, C.: Group techniques and proposed scoring system for the Bender Gestalt Test for children. *J. clin. Psychol.*, 17:172-175, 1961.

KOPPITZ, E. M., SULLIVAN, J., BLYTH, D. D., and SHELTON, J.: Prediction of first grade school achievement with the Bender Gestalt Test and Human Figure Drawings. *J. clin. Psychol.*, 15:164-168, 1959.

KOPPITZ, E. M.: Teacher's attitude and children's performance on the Bender Gestalt Test and Human Figure Drawings. *J. clin. Psychol.*, 16:204-208, 1960.

———: *The Bender Gestalt with the Human Figure Drawing Test for young school children.* Columbus, Ohio: Ohio Department of Education, 1962.

———: *The Bender Gestalt Test for young children.* New York, N.Y.: Grune and Stratton, Inc., 1964.

———: A comparison of pencil and crayon drawings of young children. *J. clin. Psychol.*, 21:191-194, 1965.

———: Emotional Indicators on Human Figure Drawings of children: A validation study. *J. clin. Psychol.*, 22:313-315, 1966.

———: Emotional Indicators on Human Figure Drawings of shy and aggressive children. *J. clin. Psychol.*, 22:466-469, 1966.

———: Emotional Indicators on Human Figure Drawings and school achievement of first and second graders. *J. clin. Psychol.*, 22:481-483, 1966.

———: Expected and Exceptional Items on Human Figure Drawings and IQ scores of children age 5—12. *J. clin. Psychol.*, 23:81-83, 1967.

KRAMER, E.: *Art therapy in a children's community.* Springfield, Ill.: Charles C Thomas, 1958.

LAWTON, M. J. and SEECHREST, L.: Figure drawings by young boys from father-present and father-absent homes. *J. clin. Psychol.*, 18:304-305, 1962.

LEVY, S.: *Projective figure drawing. In* Hammer: *The clinical application of projective drawings.* Springfield, Ill.: Charles C Thomas, 1958.

LEWINSON, P.M.: Relationship between height of figure drawings and depression in psychiatric patients. *J. consult. Psychol.*, 28:380-381, 1964.

LOWENFELD, V.: *The nature of creative activity.* London, England: Routledge and Kegan Paul Ltd., 1939.

MACHOVER, K.: *Personality projection in the drawing of the human figure.* Springfield, Ill.: Charles C Thomas, 1949.

———: Human figure drawings of children. *J. proj. Tech.*, 17:85-91, 1953.

———: *Sex differences in the developmental pattern of children as seen in Human Figure Drawings. In* Rabin and Haworth: *Projective Techniques with children.* New York, N.Y.: Grune and Stratton, 1960.

MARCUS, J.: Temporary vicissitudes in children's drawings: Their importance in diagnostic evaluations. *The Israel Annals of Psychiatry*, 1:217-224, 1963.

McHUGH, A.: Sexual identification, size and association in children's figure drawings. *J. clin. Psychol.*, 19:381-382, 1963.

————: Children's figure drawings and school achievement. *Psychology in Schools* 1:51-52, 1964.

————: Children's figure drawings in neurotic and conduct disturbances. *J. clin. Psychol.*, 22: 219-221, 1966.

MICHAL-SMITH, H.: The identification of pathological cerebral function through the H-T-P technique. *J. clin. Psychol.*, 9: 293-295, 1953.

NAUMBURG, M.: *Art Therapy: Its scope and function. In* Hammer: *The clinical application of projective drawings.* Springfield, Ill.: Charles C. Thomas, 1958.

PHELAN, H. M.: The incidence and possible significance of the drawing of female figures by sixth grade boys in response to the Draw-A-Person Test. *Psychiat. Quart.*, 38: 488-503, 1964.

PIKUNAS, J. and CARBERRY, H.: Standardization of the graphoscopic scale: the content of children's drawings. *J. clin. Psychol.*, 17:297-301, 1961.

REZNIKOFF, N. A. and REZNIKOFF, H. R.: The family drawing test: a comparative study of children's drawings. *J. clin. Psychol.*, 12:167-169, 1956.

REZNIKOFF, M. and TOMBLEM, D.: The use of Human Figure Drawings in the diagnosis of organic pathology. *J. consult. Psychol.*, 20:467-470, 1956.

RICHEY, M. H.: Qualitative superiority of the "self" figure in children's drawings. *J. clin. Psychol.*, 21:59-61, 1965.

RUCKHABER, C.: A technique of group administration of the Bender Gestalt Test. *Psychol. in Schools*, 1:53-56, 1964.

SILVERSTEIN, A. B. and ROBINSON, H. A.: The representation of orthopedic disability in children's figure drawings. *J. consult. Psychol.*, 20:333-341, 1956.

STONE, P. A. and ANSBACHER, H. L.: Social interest and performance on the Goodenough-Harris Draw-A-Man Test. *J. ind. Psychol.*, 21:178-186, 1965.

TERMAN, L. M. and MERRILL, M. A.: *Stanford-Binet Intelligence Scale.* Boston, Mass.: Houghton Mifflin, 1960.

THOMPSON, J. M. and FINLEY, C. J.: The relationship between the Goodenough Draw-A-Man Test and the Stanford-Binet Form L-M in children referred for school guidance services. *Calif. J. educ. Res.*, 14: 19-22, 1963.

VANE, J. R. and EISEN, V. W.: The Goodenough Draw-A-Man Test and signs of maladjustment in Kindergarten children. *J. clin. Psychol.*, 18:276-279, 1962.

VANE, J. R. and KESSLER, R. T.: The Goodenough Draw-A-Man Test: long term reliability and validity. *J. clin. Psychol.*, 20:487-488, 1964.

VERNIER, C. M.: *Projective test productions: projective drawings.* New York, N.Y.: Grune and Stratton, 1952.

WAWRZASZEK, F., JOHNSON, O. G., and SCIERA, J. L.: A comparison of H-T-P responses of handicapped and non-handicapped children. *J. clin. Psychol.*, 14:160-162, 1958.

WECHSLER, D.: *Wechsler Intelligence Scale for Children.* New York, N.Y.: The Psychological Corporation, 1949.

WEPMAN, J. M.: *Auditory Discrimination Test.* Chicago, Ill.: 1958.

WOODS, W. A. and COOK, W. E.: Proficiency in drawing and placement of hands in drawings of the human figure. *J. consult. Psychol.*, 18:119-211, 1954.

Index